STARS IN THE WATER

THE STORY OF THE ERIE CANAL

STARS IN
THE WATER

THE STORY OF
THE ERIE CANAL

___

GEORGE E. CONDON

DOUBLEDAY & COMPANY, INC.
GARDEN CITY, NEW YORK, 1974

ISBN: 0-385-06642-2
Library of Congress Catalog Card Number 72–84901
Copyright © 1974 by George E. Condon
All Rights Reserved
Printed in the United States of America
First Edition

This book is dedicated to my parents,

JOHN *and* MARY CONDON

CONTENTS

INTRODUCTION

A lot of people think they know where the West is, and some of them do. The answer is based on variables. It depends on where a person is standing at any given moment. Or in any given century.

The West is where we say it is. It is a changeable, elusive, inconstant reality; an accommodating, adaptable point whose location always must be determined by circumstance. Yet it always can be found in the same place, on the smart side of the setting sun, soaking up some of the last precious rays—as many as it can—and turning away others, reluctantly, to bring about a glinting that is the last glory of the departing day. We know that much as a sure, visible wonder, beyond question.

But there is another sure thing about the West that we tend to forget—that its origin always is in the East, and that is where it spends its earliest, brightest hours. The incontrovertible fact, the simple truth, is that the East always has to be the place where the West begins.

There was a long period in the dawning days of the United States when the western wilderness stood closed and unmoving. It stood still and tenacious, holding fast to its strategic position on the eastern shelf of the continent. The frontier then was no distant challenge but a back-yard reality to a gangling new nation that had only a handful of citizens to give it life and strength and will.

The people who lived in such outposts as Albany and Schenectady in the days after the Revolutionary War when the United States was taking its tentative first steps could tell you without hesitation where the West was. It was at their elbow, near their outstretched fingers, on their doorsteps. It was close enough for them to see, and the fragrant scent of its deep woods was in their nostrils. They could, if they wanted, reach out and feel the sweeping hem of its shadowy forests. The West was the silhouette they saw against the departing sun, a jagged line of tall treetops and uneven mountain peaks that raked the underside of the twilight sky.

The people who lived in those communities along the natural line of waters that flow from Canada down through New York State, past Manhattan Island and into the Atlantic Ocean, were at the gateway to the West, a portal just as forbidding as the reality beyond. That first West offered no splendid prospect of wide open spaces where a man could sight tomorrow's weather on its approach run and reconnoiter the distant reaches. Where civilization ended on the other side of the upper Hudson, it ended abruptly, and beyond it there was no tomorrow to be seen; only the wilderness. It loomed large and lonely, and beyond its front-line trunks of great girth there was a darkness and a mystery that offered no future at all.

Those congested forests were such a barrier to travel and expansion as to turn away all but the most adventurous and, it should be said, the most acquisitive. In congenial stands, the virgin trees, whose age ran into hundreds of years, reared high and in close cluster like a natural picket fence. There were a few trails that moccasins and hoofs and paws had pounded out through the years, but following them through the wilderness called for expert woodmanship and considerable courage. Such paths ran into mountain ridges lying athwart the route, or slumped into impassable swamps, or dwindled away at water's edge. No matter how the trails veered, or dipped, or rose, eventually they led the apprehensive travelers into territory where man was more the stranger and less the stronger; where the wild things maintained, in marvelous balance, their own special sovereignty—one that they shared in part only with the Indians and the frontiersmen, who were almost as much a part of the land as they were.

Here was the West, for a fact, but it was not enough. Beyond its vast expanse was more. Past its horizon was everything that restless, hungry men craved, as much as they dreamed and probably more than they hoped. The great land of the interior, on the other side of the mountains, was the subject of fables brought back by missionaries and solitary hunters. It was a country of glittering great lakes, of flatland that stretched as far as a man could ride on horseback for a week and that still stretched out some more; a country of black loam and rich muck, of inviolate forests with enough wood to build another world; a country of green meadows and gentle hills, of strange, beautiful new birds, different vegetation, and animals enough to fur all mankind and fill its belly full.

All of those intoxicating rewards were part of the golden vision which had yet to be realized as the first West stayed unconquered and blocked the way, its bulk wrapped around the spiny ridge of the Alleghenies. Even more important than the hope of fulfillment, however, was the singular fact that the thirteen colonies which had united against the British in 1776 now faced a larger battle in which the stakes were the same as they had been in the Revolutionary War. That is to say, the survival of the United States hinged on the conquest of the New York wilderness just as surely as it had on the defeat of the king's men by George Washington's forces.

The nation was in a precarious position. All that it controlled on this vast continent at the beginning of the nineteenth century was a beachhead along the Atlantic coastline. From a military standpoint, the situation was close to untenable, especially as unfriendly eyes were studying the struggling states with avid interest. Great Britain, still smarting from the ignominious defeat in the American War for Independence, continued to be a threat. Its power remained in being on the continent, directly to the north in Canada, while offshore the British navy and merchant fleet still ruled the waves. There was an English threat even within the struggling new nation, the nucleus of a powerful fifth column also in the thousands of loyalists who had stayed on in the United States after the surrender of the British and who remained loyal to the Crown. Spain still owned Florida, and France still owned the Louisiana Territory, through which it controlled the Mississippi River and the gulf ports.

In order to become strong enough to hold on to its independence, the United States had to solidify its mainland holdings and tap its inland resources. It had to establish communication and transportation between East and West, encourage the growth of a population that would subdue the wilderness and make it productive, and make markets accessible so that such settlements would be profitable to those willing to take the risks and hardships of pioneering.

The trouble was that this new political union ran counter to the established physical order. While the United States sought, for survival's sake, to establish the means of easy east-west movement, there was the inescapable fact that the land itself had been endowed with an irrevocable north-south axis; a natural physical tilt and contour that caused waterways to flow doggedly to the south and that found the Appalachians meandering toward the distant southwest, separating with their massive bulk the nation that called itself united.

There was much that had to be done still in the East. Even there the ties of union did not bind tightly. The federal government faced many problems in the member states and it had to move cautiously. Old jealousies lived on in the lingering provincialism, and there must have been an inclination among many statesmen to follow the path of least resistance by shrugging off the boundless country on the far side of the mountains as alien territory, too remote and indefensible. Better, they must have reasoned, to take what was available than to overreach and lose everything in the ensuing struggle.

But if the founding fathers of the United States had followed such a safe policy, it is easy to speculate on what would have happened on the other side of the mountains, in the Northwest Territory and in the Louisiana Territory. The people and the produce of the Ohio country, of the lush land to the south and west of the Great Lakes, would have continued to follow the natural, easy, economical routes of transportation and travel. They would have gone on shipping their cargoes across the lakes to Montreal and the Gulf of St. Lawrence or into the wide Mississippi and on down to New Orleans and the Gulf of Mexico. Their trade and their intercourse would have been, in the main, with the French, the English, and the Spanish; with the Floridians, the Cubans, the Texans, and the Mexicans.

Isolated long from the mother colonies on the eastern seaboard, the people to the west of the mountains perhaps would have formed their own nation. Or perhaps their commercial and cultural relationships with the European powers would have led to a wider sovereignty in Middle America for one or more of those foreign nations. Division in the land could have resulted in division in government, with a complex of small governments evolving across the continent.

That is how it could have been, and the evolution would have been so natural, so completely logical, that history might never have questioned the chain of events. But passion has a way of crowding out logic in the creation of political entities. There is a fire in men that causes them to see visions and to follow the drift of their hearts, submitting to the lure of their philosophy and shunting aside the easy compromise. They will ignore, however illogically, all interpositions and such material considerations as the pitch of the land, the height of the mountains, and the opposite flow of the rivers—all the odds against success—as they hasten to marry those parts in whose climate there grows a like idealism and where there prevails a common spirit.

So it was that when the thirteen colonies departed the British Empire and joined together in a new alliance, the ideological factors were paramount. The winning of the Revolutionary War was a brilliant opening victory, and in the immediate postwar years the spirit of all-for-one-and-one-for-all burned bright, but the long-range prospects for a prosperous, long-lived union remained poor. The new nation was underfinanced, underpopulated, and it lived in a house divided by nature.

The best hope for the future, the fabulous Northwest Territory, still was out of reach on the other side of the Appalachians—a fetching vision that filled the Western sky with its glowing promise, but one which would remain nothing more substantial than a distant dream unless the barrier could be breached, until it could be drawn into more intimate association with the struggling young nation.

Henry Adams summed it up: "Physical contact alone could make one country of these isolated empires."

The eyes of all the wise men searching for an answer inevitably came to rest on the map of New York State, caught by the intriguing possibilities for solution that were locked in its upstate wilderness.

New York State, from the first, was conspicuous for its wealth of waterways. Thanks to a northward-retreating ice cap which created a tremendous system of drainage as it melted, the area is lined with thousands of capillaries and hundreds of arteries to carry off water to the Atlantic

Ocean. The early Dutch colonists, who probably appreciated the potential of inland water navigation better than anybody, saw the possibilities in New York, but their grasp on that part of the New World was loosened before they could apply their special knowledge of waterways to interior America.

As a practical matter, there was general appreciation of the importance of rivers and lakes as travel routes. There was, after all, no better way to move about than by water. It was the fastest, safest, most comfortable, and most economical way to transport people and goods, even with the frequent interruptions. When one waterway veered off in the wrong direction or dwindled away, the passengers had to shoulder their boats and their cargo and follow the portage route overland to the next usable waterway.

More significant than the plenitude of water in New York was the insistent fact that the only open break in the entire bulky barrier of the Appalachian Mountains from Canada south into Georgia was the Mohawk River valley of New York. This magnificently scenic valley was unquestionably the strategic way to the future.

From meager, spidery beginnings north of what is now the city of Rome, New York (earlier known as Fort Stanwix), the Mohawk collects itself into a substantial river, bending into an eastward course that takes it some hundred miles, through the gap in the mountains, toward dramatic confluence with the Hudson River at Cohoes Falls, just above Albany. The Indian name for the Mohawk, "Te-non-an-at-che," had significant meaning: "the river flowing through mountains."

Just as important in the eyes of Americans seeking a way out of the eastern enclosure, there was a wealth of waterways west of the Mohawk on the route leading to Lake Erie. Among them were Wood Creek, the Seneca River, Oneida Lake, Lake Onondaga, the Finger Lakes, the Genesee River, Tonawanda Creek, Lake Ontario, and innumerable streams, creeks, and ponds.

Many minds visualized the kind of canal system in New York that had proven so effective in England in the latter part of the eighteenth century. But it took the press of history to force the canal concept into being, to make the nation pay serious heed to its dreamers and to undertake the building of one of the longest canals in the world.

Man has not ceased to marvel over the Erie Canal because it still stands out as a bold, even heroic, achievement whose epic dimensions have not been diminished by time. Beyond the physical wonder of the Erie Canal, there is the political wonder that it wrought in bringing together a nation, nurturing it and strengthening it until it reached full stature. It was the Erie Canal whose waters pushed back that first West beyond the mountains, all the way to the Mississippi and farther still. Its story is one of indomitable men, of wilderness, of newborn cities, of heroic immigrants, and—most of all—of a nation's pride.

ACKNOWLEDGMENT

Every author becomes obligated to others as he goes about the job of researching and writing a book. It is impossible to single out all the helping hands along the way because so many of them belonged to anonymous individuals, but among the known benefactors there are some whose generous assistance should be recognized. They would include Fritz S. Updyke, editor of the Rome *Daily Sentinel*, Rome, N.Y.; Earl Scothon, retired engineer of the New York State Canal System, Rome, N.Y.; Richard Tuttle, managing editor, Rochester *Democrat-Chronicle*, Rochester, N.Y.; Dr. Blake McKelvey, city historian, Rochester, N.Y.; Robert Atkinson, managing editor, Syracuse *Post-Standard*, Syracuse, N.Y.; Richard Wright, secretary, The Canal Association, Syracuse, N.Y.; Howard Hosmer, Station WHEC, Rochester, N.Y.; the late Clarence O. Lewis, Lockport, N.Y.; Lewis Brennan, Lockport, N.Y.; Charles J. Wellner, editor, the Lockport *Union-Sun Journal*, Lockport, N.Y.; Joseph A. Wadovick, Cleveland, O.; members of the staff of the Main Branch, Cleveland Public Library; Mrs. Ruth Morris, librarian, Fairview Park Branch, Cuyahoga County Public Library; Ronald Robbins and William Quirk of New York; De Witt Clinton of Buffalo, N.Y., and, most of all, Miss Sally Arteseros, my Doubleday editor, who patiently shaped and sanded the raw material and helped give it form.

To all of these kind people, I stand in debt.

GEORGE E. CONDON

Cleveland, Ohio

". . . I noticed one other idle man. He carried a rifle on his shoulder and a powder horn across his breast, and appeared to stare about him with confused wonder, as if, while he was listening to the wind among the forest boughs, the hum and bustle of an instantaneous city had surrounded him."

NATHANIEL HAWTHORNE,
*describing his visit
to Rochester, N.Y.,
in 1835.*

STARS IN THE WATER

THE STORY OF THE ERIE CANAL

CHAPTER I

THE SHORT CUT

There is a certain irony in the fact that when Henry Hudson turned his ship, the *Half Moon*, into what is now called the Hudson River in 1609, he was searching for a sea passage that would take him through the continent and provide a short cut to India and all its spices and riches.

The Hudson, with its wide channel and salty water, was a most promising lead to follow, and Hudson—an English explorer employed by the Dutch—determinedly sailed its beautiful length all the way to an anchoring place not far from the hillside site of today's Albany.

The water had lost both its saltiness and its depth by the time the exploration party had reached that inland point, and Hudson, after exchanging gifts with the Mohican Indians, wisely concluded that he was following the wrong course. He turned the green prow, with its figurehead of a red lion, back toward the Atlantic Ocean. He had found Indians, but not India.

The Mohicans called the river The-Water-That-Flows-Two-Ways, a name that told a factual story. As the tide rushes into the river channel twice each day, it overpowers the natural current toward the sea and gives the illusion that the Hudson is flowing north. When the tide has exhausted itself, the southward flow to the Atlantic is reasserted. The phenomenon did not escape the eyes of the observant Indians.

Hudson himself, after passing through such flanking scenery as the Palisades, the Highlands, and the Catskill Mountains, dubbed the waterway The River of Steep Hills. Some of those who followed him called it, in like descriptive vein, The River of the Mountains. Others knew it as the Mauritius River (in honor of Prince Maurice of the Netherlands), but it was most commonly known as Hudson's River, and his name stuck.

1

In the advantageous light of a later day, Hudson's probing of the great river to a place far inland in a quest for a sea passage to India may seem unreasonable, but it was precisely such systematic blundering by early explorers that improved the cartographic knowledge of following generations.

Furthermore, while India is just as far removed today as it was in Hudson's day, a determined traveler through the New York country can find such unlikely places as Greece (near Rochester), Mexico (near Oswego), Rome (near Utica), Liverpool (near Syracuse), Belgium (north of Syracuse), Batavia (northeast of Buffalo), and Warsaw (southeast of Buffalo). Pressing on through the state, he will come upon Cuba, Scotia, Ilion, Carthage, Dresden, Macedon, Dunkirk, Naples, Clyde, Lyons, Frankfort, Antwerp, Amsterdam, and—lo!—Delhi. Now Delhi, New York, does not resemble Delhi, India, in any way other than in name, yet it does stir a whisper of the Far East and it does mix in the faint scent of spices with the pine smell of the very country at whose gateway Henry Hudson paused—and then turned away.

A point to keep in mind is that if the *Half Moon* and its crew had been able to make a return cruise up the Hudson to the site of Albany a mere 216 years after that first probing expedition in September 1609, they would have been gratified to find what had not been there earlier—a water passage that flowed through the continental interior westward to the fresh water seas deep within! That improvement came about when the Erie Canal was completed in the year 1825. The man-made waterway connected the Atlantic Ocean with the Great Lakes and opened up a continent whose wealth, as it turned out, was far greater than that of India.

The official name of the waterway was the Erie Canal, but it had other names. It also was known as the Grand Canal, the Great Western Canal, the Grand Erie Canal, the Big Ditch, the Mother of Cities, the Lifeline of the Union, the Lifeline of the Empire State, Clinton's Ditch, Clinton's Folly, the Governor's Gutter, and the Governor's Gully. There were even some people who called it That Damfool Dig.

The Clinton whose name was used derisively in connection with the canal was, of course, De Witt Clinton, who served as either mayor of New York City or as governor of New York State during the critical years of the canal's gestation and birth early in the nineteenth century. He was a persistent, overbearing, determined man who unquestionably was the principal force in the creation of the waterway.

All the nicknames given the canal conveyed a certain appropriate meaning. The Erie deserved to be called the Grand Canal, for instance, because it was indubitably the grandest canal of them all—grand in concept, in execution, and in significance. On the other hand, there was no denying that it also stood out in the minds of many reasonable people as the supreme folly of the day. Among those who looked askance at the project were two Presidents of the United States, Thomas Jefferson and James Madison.

When New York State sent a delegation to Jefferson in 1809 and requested that the federal government underwrite the canal, the President was almost curt in rejecting the appeal, saying, "It is little short of madness to think of it at this time!"

While one of the world's most imaginative and progressive men himself, Jefferson took the position that such a canal was an impossibility at the moment; indeed, that it was a hundred years ahead of its time.

The nickname that seemed to find the widest circulation was Clinton's Ditch, first as an expression of scorn and later of intermingled affection and pride. Whatever the canal was, it was identified inextricably with Clinton. While he had not taken up the argument in favor of the canal as early as some of its other proponents, he became indisputably the most influential, the most famous, and the most eloquent of all of the Erie's advocates and promoters. Some called his support of the canal an obsession, but if there was an element of desperate determination in his campaign to bring the waterway into being, perhaps it was because an inner historical awareness was telling Clinton that the canal would be the crowning act of his lifetime of political achievement.

It could only have been a leader of Clinton's stature who could have persuaded the skeptical, frugal New Yorkers of his day to risk the construction of the canal and assume the tremendous financial obligation entailed—an expenditure so large as to cause even the federal government to shy away from the project. Preliminary estimates put the cost of building the Erie Canal, plus a sixty-six-mile canal connecting Lake Champlain with the Hudson River, in the vicinity of $6,000,000. (In order to win the support of the northern counties for the Erie project, it was necessary to promise construction of the Champlain canal.) The population of New York State in 1817 was only 1,300,000, which meant that the pro rata cost of the canal came almost to five dollars a person.

It was a lot of money to spend on a hole in the ground, even if it were a special kind of hole, with extraordinary dimensions. What Clinton and his fellow planners proposed to build was a super-ditch that would be 363 miles long, forty feet wide at the top, twenty-eight feet wide at the bottom, and only four feet deep! (The history of the Erie Canal records many drownings, but most of them have to be considered a tribute to the tenacity of individuals who are intent on suicide. People who hurled themselves into the murky waterway—and who did not fracture their skulls in the first dive—immediately discovered that drowning in the Erie was almost as much of a challenge as living on dry land.)

Many jokes were made about the canal's unimpressive, almost amusing, dimensions, but as it turned out, the four feet of water in the state-wide ditch served amazingly. If it was minimal depth for the floating of the heavy-laden boats, it was nevertheless the maximum depth that could

3

be financed. More important, it was enough to float a state, a nation, and a pioneer people into an unprecedented period of growth and prosperity.

The actual construction of the Erie Canal began in Rome, New York, on July 4, 1817. It was completed by the light of the harvest moon in the autumn of 1825, the final link being between Lockport and Buffalo.

Elapsed construction time for the entire project was eight years and four months—not too bad a performance, really, for the construction of the longest canal in the world; not too bad an achievement for an infant nation, for an underpopulated state, for amateur planners, for workers without power tools. Not bad at all.

Some European experts had guessed the Erie would take up to thirty years or more to build—if it were built at all. A suggestion of that pessimistic view is to be found in the condition attached by the Dutch-owned land-holding corporation, the Holland Land Company, to its gift of 100,632 acres of land for the benefit of the waterway. The company qualified its contribution with the conditional requirement that the canal be completed by the year 1842.

The people of New York actually did not have to wait until 1825 to begin using the canal or to realize some financial return from their gamble. The canal was built in sections and each section was put in use as soon as it was completed. Only two and a half years after the first shovel of dirt was turned at Rome, the middle section of the canal, reaching from Utica to the Seneca River on the west, was filled with water and given a successful test. That ninety-eight-mile section was opened to public use the following spring, in May 1820. Another section, which ran eastward to Little Falls, was completed and opened in 1821. By that time the construction crews were working in earnest, and in the following year, 1822, the canal reached to Schenectady on the east and Rochester on the west. By 1823 the waterway had completed its eastward run to Albany and the Hudson River, while its western length reached all the way to Brockport.

The last miles were among the most difficult to build, but the canal workers pushed through to Lockport in 1824 and through to the western terminal, Buffalo, in early autumn of 1825.

By that time the entire state was beside itself with excitement, and the attention of the small nation was fixed on upstate New York. The suspense and anticipation grew in geometrical progression, rather than in direct ratio, to the ground conquered each day by the diggers. When the Erie Canal crossed the finish line in October 1825, all of New York exploded with joy. It was the delirium of gratification that goes with great achievement. But the joy was not confined to New York State alone. Young America on all sides cheered and joined in celebrating the Union's greatest non-military accomplishment—a civil feat so dramatic in all its aspects as to give the whole nation reason for pride.

4

The celebration was properly spectacular. The official opening called for a flotilla to assemble in the canal basin at the western end of the canal, at the outpost village of Buffalo, and to take on as passengers the leading citizens of the state before embarking on the first cross-state trip by water from Lake Erie to the Hudson River. The flotilla then would make its way down the Hudson to the grand climactical celebration in New York City.

In after years, of course, Manhattan would become justly famous for its expertise in the celebration of historic events and in the welcoming of celebrities. It had shown much promise in this specialized department after the Revolutionary War in its spirited observance of victory and in its receptions for General Washington, the Marquis de Lafayette, and other heroes. But the city's approach to the Erie Canal opening, while unrestrained, carried an undertone of embarrassment because the metropolis had been the seat of opposition to the canal during the discouraging years when the promoters of the waterway were fighting for approval.

Shortsighted New York City politicians and conservative Wall Street financiers, jealous of their port's leading position in the state scheme of things, had refused to endorse a project that most of them thought would be of benefit mainly to the upstate New Yorkers and the people of the wilderness beyond Schenectady. Manhattan's leaders had fought De Witt Clinton and his companion visionaries almost all the way, yielding only as they had to. However, as sections of the canal that were opened early began to yield remarkable results that clearly promised great returns to the state's largest city, there was a massive shift of opinion and sentiment in favor of the Erie. The city's determination to outdo itself in the celebration of the canal's completion was as much an apology as anything else.

Governor Clinton, the canal commissioners, military notables, and politicians from all parts of the state gathered in Buffalo in the last week of October 1825 and made ready to board the boats that would take them on the historic inaugural voyage to New York City. Buffalo, while little more than a hamlet, greeted the distinguished guests with an extraordinary program of wining, dining, speeches, and songs, thereby conditioning the celebrities for the festivities they were to encounter in the next ten days as they rode the Erie waters to the Hudson River and Albany, then down the Hudson to Sandy Hook, and a final docking at Manhattan —a total journey of some 425 miles.

High on the *bon-voyage* program of entertainment in Buffalo was an original poem composed for the occasion by a "journeyman mechanic of the town." It may have been the first poem penned on the Erie Canal theme, but it was not the last lyrical tribute to the wondrous ditch, which overnight became a favorite subject of amateur and professional poets everywhere—few of them, by the way, with the talent of the Buffalo mechanic.

Creativity was rampant in Buffalo on that historic send-off day at the western terminus of the canal. After the boats bearing the celebrities had departed, the town whooped it up with street festivities and with a grand ball that lasted far into the night. The highlight of the ball was the singing of a "Celebration Ode" set to the tune of "Hail Columbia." Perhaps it was the very same poem written by the mechanic; historians are vague on the point, as they so often are on the really important details. Fortunately, the opening stanza of the inspired work was saved and passed along to posterity:

> Strike the Lyre! With joyous note,
> Let the sound through azure float;
> The task is o'er—the work complete,
> And Erie's waves, with ocean meet—
> Bearing afar their rich bequest,
> While Smiling Commerce greets the West.

The order of procession in the ceremonial flotilla called for the *Seneca Chief* of Buffalo to be first, and aboard this craft, which would be the first to make the through voyage from the lake to the ocean, would be Governor Clinton, United States Representative James Tallmadge, Jr., Stephen Van Rensselaer, Chancellor Livingston, Samuel Wilkeson, Thurlow Weed, Joshua Forman, and the official committee from New York. Immediately behind the *Seneca Chief* was to be a boat called *Noah's Ark*. Its home base, appropriately, was the community of Ararat on the Niagara River, and true to its name, its passenger list featured a rare assortment of birds, fish, and insects, including a pair of eagles, a pair of fawns, a fox, two young bears, and two Seneca Indian boys. Directly behind *Noah's Ark* was an elegant craft called the *Superior* which, perhaps inspired by the *Ark*, also carried two sleek fawns.

In addition to its distinguished passengers, the *Seneca Chief* had aboard two kegs of "the pure waters of Lake Erie," which were to be emptied into the Atlantic Ocean off Sandy Hook as a symbolic "wedding of the waters"; some logs of native red cedar and bird's-eye maple, whose wood later would be used to make boxes to hold the celebration medals; a canoe made by Indians on the shore of Lake Superior; some whitefish; and a quantity of potash. Symbolism was the order of the day.

The decor of the lead boat had been designed with this great opening trip in mind, of course, and the elegantly festooned cabin had as its most prominent feature a portrait of De Witt Clinton by George Catlin, the famous lithographer. It showed the governor dressed in Roman costume and in heroic pose, resting from his labors. Romans were very big in America of that day and togas were more or less *de rigueur* in art circles. It was almost unthinkable to portray great men on canvas or in statues wearing common dress. It simply didn't convey enough heroism or greatness. Not even George Washington was able to stand on his own

6

feet or cling to his regular habiliment when the famous sculptor Horatio Greenough put him on a marble pedestal. The finished work, portraying the Father of His Country in bare shanks and a simple but daring off-the-shoulder toga, caused loud furor and considerable embarrassment in the nation's capital when it was unveiled. As soon as the transfer could be arranged, it was moved discreetly to the Smithsonian Institution, where it still is. Clinton, like Washington, didn't seem quite like himself in Roman garb, but the hero-worshipers of that day were not as devoted to verisimilitude as they were to classical allusions. In such association they found exaltation.

Before any of the boats moved out of the Buffalo basin to begin the historic first trip, there was a program highlighted by a god-speed address by a man whose influence in the creation of the canal was of utmost importance. He was Jesse Hawley, a resident of Lockport and the author of essays that generally are credited with inspiring the cross-state canal. In his speech Hawley summed up what New York had done in building the Erie Canal with words that were extravagant, but indisputably true. He said the state had "made the longest canal, in the least time, with the least experience, for the least money, and of the greatest public utility, of any other in the world."

It was nearly ten o'clock in the morning when the speaking portion of the official inaugural program was concluded, but there was no sign of weariness in the large crowd. This was an event that most of the steadfast spectators had been looking forward to for more than eight years. On a frontier where entertainment was at a premium, they were of a mind to enjoy each minute of the formal happening to the fullest. Most of the people intently watched and listened, determinedly memorizing the scenes and sounds so that they could describe the event later to friends and relatives not so fortunate as to be among the eyewitnesses to history.

As the program moved toward its climax, though, there was a perceptible stir in the crowd because the last scheduled event promised to be the most spectacular of all. Americans from the very beginning have shown a rare talent for incorporating novelty features into their big premiere occasions. While other nationalities have been content at such times to have a band play and to snip a ribbon, Yankee ingenuity has had to make itself manifest in other, more unusual, ways. New Yorkers especially have shown such talent. When the 1939 World's Fair in New York was opened, for example, the officials didn't simply pull a switch to light the grounds. Instead, the splendid approach that was followed featured none other than the President of the United States, Franklin D. Roosevelt, a former governor of New York. While flash bulbs popped and movie cameras whirred, Mr. Roosevelt pushed a button that activated a photosensitive tube that, when exposed to the light of the distant star Arcturus, itself activated the electric illumination of the World's Fair buildings and grounds.

That, unquestionably, was a terribly complicated way to switch on the lights, but it met with general approval because it was somehow in keeping with the extraordinary importance of the occasion to give the big opening a cosmic boost.

Science had not progressed far enough in 1825 to permit any such magical system for opening the canal, but the officials met the challenge head-on and, with commendable originality, came up with a real crowd-pleaser. They decided that as soon as the first boat in the official flotilla should begin its eastward journey, the news should be flashed immediately to New York City. One awkward hitch was that the telegraph had not been invented as yet. Nor had the teletype, the telephone, the radio, or the television. But the officials were not about to let such details spoil their plan. They came up with a substitute that was more than adequate.

The telegraph, reduced to its simplest essential, is nothing more than the swift relay of a signal over a long distance. And there are ways other than electricity to achieve the same end. Jungle drums do the same thing very nicely; messages tapped out on stretched animal hide have been flying about the primitive countryside for centuries. But the canal committee went beyond drums. It set up what was unquestionably the world's most thunderous telegraph system, with old war cannon substituting for jungle drums along the entire 425 mile route between Buffalo and New York City. They weren't ordinary guns, either, but thirty-two-pounders that had armed the ships of Commodore Oliver Perry's fleet during his victorious battle with the British on Lake Erie in the War of 1812. Thurlow Weed of Rochester, a famous editor of the day and then a close political ally of Governor Clinton, saw to it that many of the historic guns were recovered from government arsenals to be used in the big Buffalo blast. The cannons were carefully spaced along the canal route and down the Hudson Valley so that each gunner was within earshot of another.

When, at ten o'clock on that morning of October 26, 1825, the four white horses whose tow lines were attached to the *Seneca Chief* stepped out onto the towpath that led on to the Hudson River and the Atlantic Ocean, the signal was flashed to the first gunner and he lighted the fuse. People clapped their hands against their ears and flinched as they waited for the roar of the cannon. It came quickly; not as loudly as some had feared, but fearsome enough to be heard by the next, unseen, gunner down the line because it seemed as if the echoing boom from the northeast came so quickly as to step on the lingering reverberations of the first roar. Some people swore that they heard the third shot, too, and even the fourth. Perhaps they did. Excitement sometimes heightens the senses.

All the people of New York State must have heard the cannons that day. But the message was not the same to all who heard it. There were grizzled frontiersmen still, men in buckskin and carrying long rifles, who must have lifted their heads and listened with heavy hearts to the noise. And there were Indian ears that would have heard it as a sound of foreboding as it rolled through the country of the Mohawks, the Senecas, the Onondagas, the Cayugas, the Oneidas, and the Tuscaroras. The entire Iroquois Confederation would have heard the measured cannonading as it moved east, through the Niagara Country, the Genesee Country, the Montezuma swampland, through the Mohawk Valley, past the Catskills, and down the Hudson. It was a relentless echoic sound. It was a sound to awaken Rip Van Winkle, but also a sound to make men dream; a sound to bring some men cheer and other men sorrow.

It took the cannon telegraph relay only one hour and twenty minutes to reach the island of Manhattan and deposit its historic word before turning about for the return relay to Buffalo, again stirring up the echoes in the fields and forests almost before they had settled from the first awakening. And somewhere on the final lap westward, the booming cannons brushed noisily past the toy flotilla moving slowly through the water-filled ditch, thrilling the people aboard the boats.

The reverberations haven't died away entirely. They are still there, still lingering in the air of upstate New York, and people who have an acute ear for history can hear them clearly. They telegraph a remarkable story.

CHAPTER II

GENESIS

Like so many of man's better ideas, the original concept of the canal, or artificial waterway, has been lost in the mists of time, and there, likely, it will remain hidden forever. But the conjecture of scholars is that the earliest canals evolved from irrigation ditches that were dug by ancient civilizations through the arid lands of Egypt, Assyria, and Babylonia.

The presence of a man-made gully carrying rushing water to some distant point where it was needed to irrigate the land must have stirred tantalizing thoughts of easy, water-borne passage in the minds of foot-weary and saddle-sore travelers. Under otherwise suitable conditions, a simple widening and deepening of the ditch would have been all that was necessary to make the ditch a canal capable of carrying craft filled with people and cargo.

Other natural circumstances may have stirred plans of canal cut-throughs, as when a navigable river abruptly became unnavigable because of a waterfall or a rapids; or when a narrow peninsula forced sailing vessels to travel many miles around its elongated point in order to reach a port that was fairly close in terms of actual lineal distance; or when two important, navigable bodies of water were separated by a relatively small wedge of land. In any one of these situations, the possibilities for improving on nature through some vigorous digging were obvious.

Egypt had canals in use as early as ten thousand years ago. Babylon had a canal system some sixteen or seventeen centuries before Christ, and one of the canals was said to have been more than seven hundred miles in length. The Mediterranean and the Red Sea were joined by an ancient forerunner of the Suez Canal more than thirteen hundred years before Christ, and it remained in use for about fifteen hundred years.

11

The Romans made extensive use of canals, as did the Spanish Moors, the Chinese, the Italians, the French, the Dutch, the Belgians, and the Swedes. Curiously, the usually quick-on-the-uptake English were relatively slow to adopt the idea of artificial inland waterways. They didn't begin to build canals until after the middle of the eighteenth century, even though engineers from Rome during the Occupation had shown Britons the way in ancient times by connecting the Lincoln with the River Trent through construction of the Foss Dyke, which in turn was an extension of the Caer Dyke, joining Lincoln and Peterborough.

The Chinese had a "Grand Canal" of their own some four hundred years or more before New York State did. The Grand Canal of China was built from the Yangtze-kiang to the Pei-ho, a distance of nearly a thousand miles, during the thirteenth and fourteenth centuries. An impressed Marco Polo reported that the Chinese engineers had devised a method for raising or lowering boats from one level to another as the canal encountered changes in the altitude of the land. He could have been talking about a system of locks, perhaps the most essential element in the success of canals, although credit for invention of the lock system usually is given to the Domenico brothers of Viterbo, Italy. They devised a canal lock in 1481. It was a thick-walled stone box closed at either end by heavy wooden gates. Water could be poured into the lock, or drained from it, through small openings in the wooden gates. A boat inside the enclosed lock therefore could be floated up to a desired level or brought down to a lower level. An "aquatic elevator" is what the canal lock sometimes is called, and that probably is the most descriptive name for it.

The Dutch also claim credit for the lock, saying the device was used in the canal system of Holland nearly a century before its appearance in Italy. That may be so, but the Italians still can claim to have originated the most artistic canals—which isn't surprising when you consider that one of the Italian canal engineers was a man named Leonardo da Vinci. He not only built six locks in the canals of Milan in 1487, he is credited also with being responsible for the earliest canal work undertaken in France.

White men hardly had touched foot in America when, characteristically, they began to mull over ideas for rearranging the continent. Among the obvious shortcomings of the New World was that it was a terribly difficult place for people to get around in, what with all those forests, high mountains, unnavigable rivers, narrow footpaths, and no roads at all. Some of the most obvious canal possibilities began to suggest themselves almost at once. In 1707, for example, the French commandant in Canada, Antoine de la Mothe Cadillac, recommended to Louis XIV an idea for connecting Lake Erie and Lake Ontario with a canal, thereby avoiding the portage made necessary by Niagara Falls. The plan made a lot of sense, but the king was not about to pay the cost of the project. The idea had to wait more than a century until the English built the Welland Canal.

As early as 1724 there was an allusion to the idea of a canal to ease travel across New York State. The surveyor general of New York, Cadwallader Colden, touched on the idea in a memorial on the fur trade which he addressed to the royal governor of the province.

Canals became a common subject of public interest and discussion in following decades, principally because the English at last were beginning to build a network of artificial waterways at home, and whatever happened in the motherland usually was imitated in the colonies. Benjamin Franklin was one whose fancy was caught by the concept of canals and he came out in favor of a complex canal system to be built in Pennsylvania.

"Rivers," he wrote to the mayor of Philadelphia in 1772, "are ungovernable things, especially in Hilly Countries. Canals are quiet and very manageable."

George Washington was another leader of the time who was fascinated by canals and their possibilities for good. As early as 1773 he was among those arguing the merits of a canal which would join the Potomac and the Ohio rivers. As soon as the Revolutionary War was ended—even before peace was declared—Washington toured the Mohawk Valley in New York, taking special note of the areas which might benefit from canals. At the end of his tour, on October 12, 1783, he wrote:

"Prompted by these actual observations, I could not help taking a more extensive view of the vast inland navigation of these United States and could not but be struck by the immense extent and importance of it, and with the goodness of that Providence, which has dealt its favors to us with so profuse a hand. Would to God we had wisdom enough to improve them. I shall not rest contented until I have explored the western country, and traversed those lines, or great part of them, which have given bounds to a new empire."

Washington fulfilled that promise the next year by making a 680-mile trip, mostly by horseback, through the "western country," and upon his return he was even more enthusiastic over the role that canals might play in bringing the sprawling young nation together. In a letter written on November 3, 1784 to Jacob Read of South Carolina, a delegate to the Continental Congress, Washington made the following recommendation:

"Extend the inland navigation of the eastern waters, communicate them as near as possible (by excellent roads) with those which run to the westward. Open these to the Ohio and such others as extend from Ohio towards Lake Erie, and we shall not only draw the produce of the western settlers, but the fur and peltry trades of the lakes also, to our ports (being the nearest and easiest of transportation) to the amazing increase of our exports, while we bind these people to a chain which can never be broken."

At the same time that Washington was urging his internal improvements program to facilitate travel between East and West, an Irish-born engineer named Christopher Colles was making a survey of the Mohawk Valley with a special eye to the obstructions in the Mohawk River as far west as Fort Stanwix. His findings, published in 1785, stressed the important possibilities of inland navigation on the Mohawk between Albany and Oswego. He proposed formation of a company to undertake construction of bypass canals around such obstructions as Cohoes Falls and Little Falls and at Fort Schuyler. He proposed seven miles of bypass canals in all, as well as the dredging of shallow parts of the river. It was a sound plan and would have eased river passage to a considerable degree, but the basic recommendations were not followed until many years later.

The Colles survey did serve to highlight the weaknesses in the old Iroquois Trail as a route for mass travel and transportation. It caused the people and their representatives to ponder the embarrassing inconsistencies of the principal waterways, especially the vital Mohawk River and its maddening manner of flowing smoothly for long stretches and then suddenly taking an unnavigable dive to a lower altitude. Cataracts are not at all compatible with canoeing or any other kind of serious boating. Land detours around such obstructions added considerably to the rigors of frontier travel. They discouraged settlement of the wilderness and slowed the commerce that was needed to subdue the frontier. Not only did portage points limit the quantities of goods that could be shipped by water, the repeated act of loading and unloading the cargoes at the carrying points added tremendously to the time and expense of shipments. In 1800, for example, it cost anywhere from seventy-five to one hundred dollars a ton for goods shipped from Albany as far west as Seneca Lake.

The closing years of the eighteenth century finally saw New York move to ease the difficult travel situation. George Clinton, the first governor of New York and uncle of De Witt Clinton, sent a message to the state legislature in 1791 urging improvement of the Hudson, the Mohawk, and Wood Creek. A year later, the legislators passed a bill ". . . for establishing and opening lock navigation within this state."

In effect, the legislature encouraged the formation and incorporation of two companies which it authorized to build canals and locks in two separate geographical areas. The Western Inland Lock Navigation Company was chartered to straighten out navigation on the Mohawk River from the Hudson west to Lakes Seneca and Ontario. The Northern Inland Lock Navigation Company was commissioned to build a navigable connection between the Hudson River and Lake Champlain to the north.

While these were private stock companies, each was assured of some state financial support—an unusual arrangement for the times. Another unusual arrangement was that General Philip Schuyler, a state senator, was elected president of both companies.

The Western Company began work on construction of a canal to bypass the Little Falls of the Mohawk in April 1793. Despite delays and work stoppages caused by financial difficulties and the problems of construction, the canal of nearly a mile in length—more than half of which was cut through solid rock—and its five locks was virtually completed by November 1795. Five hundred men were employed on the project at its peak, and before the job was finished, the state had to jump in to save the floundering company by buying $57,500 worth of its stock.

While the Little Falls detour canal was short in length, its effect on river traffic was important. It immediately made possible the use of larger boats with greater carrying capacity. There was an appreciable reduction in freight rates as a result. The river bateaux in common use, usually propelled by a crew of three men with poles, heretofore were no more than 1½ tons capacity because they had to be light enough to be carried around the falls. With the bypass canal in use, large flatboats, called "arks" or "Durham boats," of ten or eleven tons capacity could be floated around the falls. Expensive, time-consuming portage was eliminated. The cost of carrying a ton of freight from Utica (Fort Schuyler) to Schenectady was reduced from fourteen to five dollars. The volume of river traffic and tonnage leaped, bringing needed tolls to the Western Company at its Little Falls Canal facility.

With revenue coming in from this canal, the Western Company in 1796 turned its attention briefly to the idea of a direct connection between the Mohawk and Seneca rivers to the west. Meanwhile, at Rome, a canal was built to join the upper Mohawk with Wood Creek.

The possibility of a by-pass canal at Cohoes Falls was surveyed, but cost estimates indicated it to be far beyond the means of the struggling, underfinanced company which, in fact, was reaching unnavigable financial waters itself. It was able, in its final desperate months, to improve the Rome Canal, build a short cut with locks at German Flats in Herkimer County, and improve Wood Creek navigation from Rome to a tributary, Little Canada Creek, six miles to the west, before lapsing finally into inactivity in 1803. The state of New York purchased the ailing company in 1810 for slightly more than $150,000 and closed its books.

The sister enterprise, the Northern Inland Lock Company, meanwhile had compiled a record of unrelieved failure. It had surveyed the area between Lake Champlain and the upper Hudson River and had started on a canal between the two, but the waterway connection never was completed. Some $100,000—a fortune in that day—was wasted in the effort.

The general effect of the limited experiment in canal building in New York under a plan of state sponsorship and private enterprise was to dampen public and political enthusiasm for canals as a practical solution to the travel and transport problem. While navigation on the Mohawk River had been improved somewhat and the portage at Rome had been eliminated, movement of people and goods still was difficult. The trip across state from Albany to Buffalo still took about twenty days—painful, arduous days, at that. Shipping goods from Lake Erie to the Hudson River still was very expensive—an average cost of one hundred dollars a ton.

Much money had gone into the two lock companies and the minor results achieved were not deemed to be commensurate with the investment. Critics of canals rose in full voice to denounce any further wasteful attempts to substitute man-made waterways for the real thing. The need persisted, nevertheless, for some kind of improvement in transportation facilities. It became more urgent with each passing day as the pressures of nationhood continued to increase.

The traveler across New York State at the beginning of the nineteenth century had this typical itinerary to face as he struggled to go from New York City to Buffalo:

The first part of the trip was the easiest. He got passage aboard a sailing vessel that took him up the Hudson River to Albany. The trip, depending on weather conditions, took from two to five days. At Albany, after an indeterminate wait, he transferred to a coach that took him overland to Schenectady, a distance of some seventeen miles. There, after another wait, he took passage on a boat heading westward on the Mohawk River. Sometimes the boats were propelled by sails, sometimes by long oars and poles, but in no case were they speedy—and they had a long way to go. It was 104 miles from Schenectady to Utica. This stage of the journey took approximately a week.

At Utica the traveler would resort to a combination of land coach and boats to get to Oswego, another 114 miles to the west. He could count on that section of trip taking eight to ten days.

Once in Oswego, if he chose, he could take one of the boats into Lake Ontario and on to Lewiston, a few miles up the Niagara River. From there it was an easy overland ride to Buffalo.

A traveler in those days, clearly, did not shuffle off to Buffalo without giving the idea deep thought.

The alternative to the on-again-off-again water route was to travel on a road system of a sort that gradually was coming into being at the turn of the century, but it offered no relief to travelers who sought speed or ease of movement. The best of the primitive highways was the corduroy road whose base was logs. A ride on a corduroy highway was the kind of experience guaranteed to leave an impression on all who tried it. (In his *American Notes*, Charles Dickens writes poignantly and with painful recollection of his rides on America's corduroy highways.) Passengers on the stage coaches that jolted and jounced over the rough roadways probably looked forward eagerly to an attack by hostile Indians as a welcome interruption of the devastating ride.

A good many of the passable roads in 1800 were toll highways—an idea that caught on early in the New York scheme of things. They were as expensive to use as they were uncomfortable to ride, but they were better than the free roads. That is damning them with faint praise because the free roads usually were little more than muddy, rutted trails which were impossible to travel on in rainy or snowy weather and which, as far as most travelers were concerned, really didn't go anywhere, even if they were regarded highly by the settlers in the immediate vicinity.

Little wonder then that the eyes of the public and their troubled political leaders kept returning to the smooth, flowing water, to the profusion of rivers and streams and lakes in New York State, and to the dream of destiny on the wet highway called the canal—to a dream that had been incorporated, prophetically, by Joel Barstow in a poem published in 1787, entitled *The Vision of Columbus:*

> He saw, as widely spreads the unchannell'd plain
> Where inland realms for ages bloom'd in vain,
> Canals, long winding, ope a watery flight,
> And distant streams, and seas and lakes unite.
>
> From fair Albania, tow'rd the falling sun,
> Back through the midland lengthening channels run;
> Meet the far lakes, the beauteous towns that lave,
> And Hudson joined to broad Ohio's wave.

CHAPTER III

ENTER DE WITT CLINTON

In a manner of speaking, the idea for the Erie Canal came out of a jail cell.

Jesse Hawley, who is honored by many historians as the man who first came up with a clear-cut concept of a canal all the way across the state of New York, had been a flour merchant in Geneva, New York, until late in 1806. At that time the failure of his business partner impelled Hawley to flee New York and take up residence in Pittsburgh in order to escape the debts that suddenly had settled on his shoulders.

He may have done a lot of brooding about business and the injustices of the system while in Pittsburgh, but he also took time out to think deeply upon another subject—the difficulty and the expense of shipping goods to New York City from the western part of the state. His flour shipments, for example, had had to be loaded onto horse-drawn wagons at Geneva and taken overland to the Seneca River, where they were transferred to Durham boats for the long, expensive trip to the Mohawk, the Hudson, and finally New York City.

The high cost of such shipments undoubtedly was painful in the recollection, especially in light of Hawley's bankrupt condition. It may have been that the memory was the force that motivated him to write an essay that was printed in the Pittsburgh *Commonwealth* shortly after his arrival in the city in December 1806. In the piece, Hawley proposed as the best possible solution to New York State's transportation crisis the construction of a canal that would connect Lake Erie, the Mohawk River, and the Hudson River.

Pittsburgh would not be a likely place for an idea like that to germinate and blossom. Pennsylvanians, after all, were arch rivals of New Yorkers for supremacy in the young nation, and Pittsburghers had enough prob-

19

lems of their own without fretting over New York State's difficulties. But shortly after formulating and expressing his idea, Hawley, an honorable man, returned to New York and gave himself up to the authorities in Canandaigua because a friend of his had risked bail for him in a suit over Hawley's obligations.

Hawley shortly found himself in the county jail, confined "within the gaol limits" for twenty months for debt, and before he was released the state of New York was in *his* debt. This reversal came about because, with so much idle time on his hands, Hawley turned his analytical mind back to the idea that he had roughly outlined in his Pittsburgh essay.

"There I was!" he exclaimed later. "In a Debtor's Prison for the relief of my bail; betrayed and defrauded by my partner; broken down and almost destitute in despondency at the thought that hitherto I had lived to no useful purpose of my own; accompanied with many pensive reflections that I never want to recall.

"Recovering myself, I resolved to publish to the world my favorite, fanciful project of an overland canal, for the benefit of my country, and endure the temporary odium that it would incur."

Hawley had no more than a modest country school education, but he put together, "by laborious study," a series of fourteen essays that were published in the *Genesee Messenger* during 1807 and 1808 under the pen name of "Hercules." It was the fashion then in America, as it still is to some extent in England, for a contributor to a newspaper to maintain anonymity (and sometimes personal safety) by signing a nom de plume, preferably of classical origin. In this instance, "Hercules" came on very strong. His essays and their far-out concept of a continuous canal all the way from the Hudson River to Lake Erie caught the public imagination. In later years, when many individuals were vying for the credit of authorship of the plan, Hawley had to lift his voice and remind some of the politicians and editors that the most comprehensive description of the canal, as it later took form, was contained first in his Herculean work, written in a jail cell.

Governor De Witt Clinton was among those who, in later years, publicly gave Hawley major credit for his originality and for advancing the canal idea "in a tangible shape." In a letter to Hawley in 1822 the governor wrote: "I have no hesitation in stating that the first suggestion of a Canal from Lake Erie to the Hudson River which came to my knowledge was communicated in essays under the signature of 'Hercules,' on internal navigation . . ." Interestingly, the canal route suggested by Hawley was close to the one ultimately selected, even though he had never traversed the route or examined the center line that he recommended. Just as impressive is the fact that Hawley estimated, offhand, the cost of constructing the Erie Canal at about $6,000,000. The final tabulation on the project put the bill at slightly more than $7,000,000.

"Hercules" foresaw great advantages and rich benefits accruing to

New York State out of the canal—a general development of the land, a rise in property values, and a great increase in population. He predicted that New York City, as a result of the waterway, would cover its island with buildings and people, that Albany would "cut down her hills and fill her valleys," and that Buffalo would "exchange her forest trees for a thicket of marine spars."

". . . No situation on the globe offers such extensive and numerous advantages to inland navigation by a canal as this," he wrote. ". . . Nor do I conceive the idea to be vain, or even incorrect in saying that it appears as if the Author of nature . . . had in prospect a large and valuable canal . . . to be completed at some period in the history of man, by his ingenuity and industry."

Gouverneur Morris, the famous statesman-financier, was one who contested Hawley for the credit of being an originator of the canal idea. Morgan Lewis, who later became governor of New York, liked to recall that one night in 1777, during the Revolutionary War, Morris had related his dream of a canal to other American officers as they sat around a campfire. Morris, he recalled, "announced in language highly poetic and to which I cannot do justice, that at no very distant day the waters of the great western inland sea would by the aid of man break their barriers and mingle with those of the Hudson."

A visit to Scotland in 1795 renewed Morris' enthusiasm for the building of canals in America, especially in New York State. Scotland had benefited greatly from its system of waterways, and Morris saw no reason why the United States could not follow the example.

"When I see this," said Morris, "my mind opens to a view of wealth for the interior of America, which hitherto I had rather conjectured than seen."

In 1800, after having served as United States Minister to France, Morris, a speculator in Genesee Country acreage, toured the backwoods of central and western New York, the frontier land. He was visibly impressed by the improvements that had been brought about in river travel by the work of the Western Inland Lock Navigation Company, especially the elimination of the old portage practice at Little Falls and the connection of the Mohawk River with Wood Creek at Rome. When he reached Lake Erie, he was moved to strong prophecy by the sight of nine sailing vessels riding at anchor.

"Does it not seem like magic?" asked Morris in a letter to a friend in Europe. "Hundreds of large ships will in no distant period bound on the billows of those inland seas. At this point commences a navigation of more than a thousand miles. Shall I lead your astonishment to the verge of incredulity? I will: know then, that one-tenth of the expense borne by Britain in the last campaign, would enable ships to sail from London through Hudson's River into Lake Erie.

"As yet, my friend, we only crawl along the outer shell of our country.

21

The interior excels the part we inhabit in soil, in climate, in everything. The proudest empire in Europe is but a bauble compared to what America *will* be, *must* be, in the course of two centuries, perhaps of one."

Perhaps Morris's most notable contribution to the creation of a cross-state canal, however, rested neither in his visions nor in his optimism, but in the fact that it was he who was instrumental in winning De Witt Clinton to the company of canal enthusiasts. (Incidentally, Clinton himself, while liberal in his praise of Hawley's catalyst role, took the position that the honor of being the actual conceiver of the Erie Canal idea "unquestionably" belonged to Morris.)

Had Morris been content with the role of inspirational force, he would have been held in higher esteem by the practical men who sought a sensible, practical way to build the canal. But somewhere along the line, Morris had become infatuated with a plan of construction that seemed to overcome, with blinding simplicity, one of the major problems that any cross-state canal surely would encounter. The western terminus of the canal, on the shore of Lake Erie, would find itself 571 feet higher than the eastern terminus at the level of the Hudson River. The dropping altitude of the countryside as the canal moved eastward would have to be met, normally, through a series of locks. But Morris proposed a different solution. It was his thought that the canal should be built on an inclined plane of uniform slope over the entire 363-mile distance from lake to river!

There were others who held to this inclined plane theory, even though it was thoroughly impractical. It ignored the fact that the land from west to east did not drop in a smooth, gradual slope, which would have been necessary for the type of canal that was suggested. The terrain, instead, went down to the Hudson in a rough-and-tumble manner. It was wrinkled and glacier-scarred in places, gouged out and folded over by the natural pressures of the past; here there were deep river valleys and there high drumlins, and in between were placid, level meadows that could lead right into a marshland trap or directly into the wall of a virgin forest that stood so high that its shadow lay on distant fields. There was nothing consistent about the wilderness country of New York except its inconsistency. Because of this fact of nature, if the builders of the Erie Canal had followed the Morris plan and tried to build the waterway on an inclined plane, there would have been sections where the canal would have been as high as 150 feet above the surrounding countryside—a waterway high in the sky! That kind of canal, it goes without saying, would have been a lot more spectacular, a lot more interesting, than the conventional ground-level, lock-type canal that was built. A simple leak in the side embankment of a waterway 150 feet up, for example, would have had the same temporary effect as a minor cloudburst. More to the point, it would drain the canal of vitally needed water.

One thing that would have to be said in favor of the inclined plane canal was that it led to all sorts of interesting, entertaining speculation. There were imaginative if mistaken men, for instance, who feared that the canalboats would gain so much momentum going downstream they would find themselves pulling the tow mules, instead of vice versa. Some humorists thought that the downgrade trip to Albany would be similar to a ride on a water chute, the kind that delights the customers in modern amusement parks, but on a gigantic scale. A canalboat that had been steadily dropping a total of 571 feet over a distance of 363 miles, they reasoned, would have picked up a really impressive speed by the time it got to the last precipitate mile. If that theory had held, the old Dutch burghers in Albany likely would have bitten right through their long-stemmed pipes when the first boat came through on the inclined plane canal; just a roar, a blur, and a mighty splash! Even with its brakes on and all the passengers clutching at the bulrushes, it would have been a smashing finish.

Morris held to the inclined plane idea for a long time, but cooler heads prevailed and the idea was brushed discreetly away by men who knew that the only reasonable way to compensate for the changes in altitude from one end of the canal to the other was in the use of the tested device, the canal lock.

By 1808 the Erie Canal had moved out of the category of science fiction and was beginning to receive serious attention on the larger public level. In that year a resolution recommending consideration of the canal was introduced in the New York Assembly by Judge Joshua Forman. Some of the legislators scoffed at the idea as "a very wild or foolish project." Considering that any canal would have to be built through a vast wilderness of forest and swamp, through stone and mud, and that there were no excavating tools available except hand shovels and plows, no demolition device like dynamite and no professional engineers nor professional contractors available in America, the skeptical legislators seem to have had sound ground for their doubts.

But there also were thoughtful men in the legislature who knew that the need usually was the mother of the deed, and the need was real. It was one of national urgency. Despite the protests of the anti-canal bloc, the legislature authorized a tentative survey of the situation to try to determine which of the several canal routes proposed was the most feasible, if any. Six hundred dollars was appropriated to pay the cost of the survey. Judge James Geddes was appointed by Governor Clinton to make the survey.

Judge Geddes was a most remarkable man, a man of wide-ranging ability. American society in that early time did not allow itself to be hampered by the passion for specialization that asserted itself later. One man often represented many talents. Geddes, for example, was a lawyer, a judge, a former state legislator, an amateur surveyor, and a businessman. In Onondaga County, where he lived, near Syracuse, he had been one of the pioneers in the salt industry. The town of Geddes was named after him.

Geddes actually had used a level only once before he was commissioned to survey a suitable canal route across the state, but that lack of experience didn't deter him. Intellectuals frequently found themselves called on to perform in roles for which they were untrained. Furthermore, the state surveyor general, Simeon De Witt, who recommended Geddes, knew that in that year of 1808 there were no civil engineers to be found to fill the assignment.

In what has been described as one of the most remarkable walks in engineering history, Geddes spent most of 1808 examining first-hand the topography of upper New York State between the Hudson River and Lake Erie. His attention was centered on the feasibility of two possible routes for a canal.

One of the possibilities called for maximum use of Lake Ontario. Beginning at the Hudson River, this route went west past Oneida Lake, to the Oswego River valley, then northward to Lake Ontario. From there passengers and cargoes would sail the lake westward as far as the Niagara River, where, presumably, a connecting canal would bypass Niagara Falls and allow entrance into Lake Erie.

Less likely was the second route, which contemplated an overland canal, a direct cut-through between the Hudson River and Lake Erie through the wilderness land. Geddes had examined almost all of the route by December except a critical section between the Genesee River and Mud Creek, the area between today's Rochester and Palmyra.

Reports of travelers had described the section to be one "of great difficulty and uncertainty," and Geddes was prepared for high ground that would make any canal construction incredibly complicated. Instead, he found the deep Irondequoit Valley—and something that made him want to shout for joy: a series of high ridges within the valley which, according to his calculations, would allow the canal to be carried across "on a surface not surpassed perhaps in the world, for singularity." The series of ridges were, in general, "of just sufficient height and width for its [the canal's] support."

Geddes figured the project would require the filling-in of the spaces between the ridges to provide ultimately an artificial embankment sixty-eight feet in height and more than five hundred yards in length which would serve as a solid base for this skyway section of the canal. He was ecstatic over his finding. The discovery, in effect, removed the last barrier from the engineering path, at least, and made the overland canal a practical possibility, a dream that was achievable.

Geddes's "great joy and surprise" over what he found in the Irondequoit Valley was reflected in a letter he wrote later to a friend, William Darby, when the canal was actually under construction: "While traversing these snowy hills in December, 1808, I little thought of ever *seeing* the Genesee waters crossing this valley on the embankment now constructing over it. I had, to be sure, lively presentiments, that *time* would bring about all I was planning, that boats would one day pass along on the tops of these fantastic ridges, that posterity would see and enjoy the sublime spectacle, but that for myself, I had been born many, very many years too soon. There are those, sir, who can realize my feelings on such an occasion, and can forgive, if I felt disposed to exclaim *Eureka*, on making this discovery."

In his report to the surveyor general the following year, 1809, Geddes presented all the facts he had collected on the two routes under consideration, but as scientifically impartial as he tried to be, there was no doubt that the report favored, in tone at least, the long interior route. He undoubtedly had all the international implications of the situation in mind when he wrote that his field study had convinced him of "the complete feasibility and utter desirablity of leading an artificial waterway over the more equable and therefore less expensive levels to the southward, directly to Lake Erie."

Not all the factors in the determination of the canal's route were physical. Political and economic considerations were profound in their influence on the ultimate decision. The Revolutionary War had not settled the question of sovereignty on the American mainland. The British still commanded Canada to the north, and Lake Ontario was very much within the British sphere of influence and power. In light of this fact of international life, any routing of traffic and commerce into Lake Ontario would be risky. In peacetime, eastbound ships would be tempted to stay on Lake Ontario and take their cargo from the American inland to the market offered by Montreal or continue down the St. Lawrence River into the ocean lanes and foreign markets. That course would be much easier and much swifter than turning from Lake Ontario into the narrow confines of a canal leading from Oswego to the Mohawk River, on to the Hudson River, and down to New York City. The ponderous, exasperating pace of horses and mules and the time-consuming passage through locks could not be expected to compete with the relatively swift travel to Montreal on the open waters of Lake Ontario.

The advantage clearly would be on the side of the British if the ship-borne commerce from America's rich lands on the other side of the mountains were diverted into Lake Ontario, around the falls of the Niagara. More important, perhaps, was the inescapable probability that in event of war with the British again, the supply lifeline of the United States between East and West would be snipped immediately by the British warships dominating the waters of Lake Ontario.

After absorbing Geddes's scholarly conclusions, Judge Forman and another state legislator, William Kirkpatrick, went to Washington early in 1809 and laid the idea of an overland canal before President Thomas Jefferson. They had reason to believe the moment was propitious for New

York to request federal help in the project. Fresh in mind was the 1808 report by Secretary of the Treasury Albert Gallatin on the subject of internal improvements. It had included a specific recommendation for better communication between the Atlantic Ocean, the Great Lakes, and the St. Lawrence River through a system of canals.

The advocates of the Erie Canal also were encouraged by the fact that this was a most remarkable moment in American history—the United States Treasury not only was solvent, it was acquiring surplus funds at the rate of $5,000,000 a year. The young nation's riches were about to become an embarrassment unless some part of the surplus were put to productive use. The most compelling need in all the states was for internal improvements to facilitate travel and transportation. The Gallatin plan proposed a national expenditure of $2,000,000 a year on such works, and the Erie Canal appeared to qualify ideally as the kind of improvement that would merit such federal subsidization.

President Jefferson listened to the argument of the two New York legislators that an Erie Canal would benefit the entire nation, but rejected their appeal for financial help in words that left no doubt of their finality:

"It is a splendid project and may be executed a century hence," Jefferson was quoted as saying. "Why, sir, here is a canal of a few miles projected by General Washington, which, if completed, would render this a fine commercial city, which has languished for many years because the small sum of $200,000 necessary to complete it cannot be obtained from the general government or from individuals. And you talk of making a canal three hundred and fifty miles long through a wilderness!"

Forman and Kirkpatrick returned to New York disappointed but not discouraged. Jefferson's words had not dampened their ardor for the canal cause as much as might have been expected. The President had not yet mounted the pedestal to take his place among the American immortals and his contemporaries still saw in him human weaknesses that history would gloss over. The New Yorkers had every right to suspect that the Jefferson pessimism on the Erie Canal project, and his unwillingness to help it to completion through government financing, was more the stand of a Virginian than the unbiased judgment of the President of all the people.

Sectionalism still was very strong in the young nation, and nowhere did it evidence itself more strongly than in the continuing rivalry between New York and Virginia. At the same time that Jefferson was scoffing at the idea of the Erie Canal, he was urging construction of canals in his native state and had given strong backing to the plan for a canal that would join the Potomac River and the Ohio River within the vast Virginia empire that he loved so much.

There was, in fact, a general disinclination among all the advocates of the New York canal to be disheartened by the President's unco-operative stand. Few, actually, had expected Jefferson to extend any help. But the

Gallatin report itself, by pointing to the need for some kind of improvement in travel facilities between the Hudson River and the West, nevertheless had strengthened the hand of the canal promoters. When Forman and Kirkpatrick returned home, it was to find the Erie Canal more of a subject of popular debate and discussion than ever before.

The canal had moved out of the crackpot classification at last. Now it was being viewed as an attainable goal, however controversial. The many legislators, editors, preachers, and other civic leaders who had avoided taking any position on the issue heretofore were beginning to express themselves in response to the mood of public inquiry that had arisen.

Interestingly enough, among those who had not shown previously more than a detached interest in the idea of the Erie Canal was De Witt Clinton. Clinton, a man whose own spirit of inquiry was intense, had been caught up in the maneuverings of an incredible complex of state rivalries, and he had had more than enough to occupy his mind dealing with the day-to-day intrigues of high-level politics.

Although he was still a relatively young man of forty-one in 1810, Clinton already had served with distinction as a United States Senator from New York, as a member of the State Assembly, and two terms as mayor of New York City. A political setback only recently had terminated Clinton's second term as mayor, but he still held a seat in the state legislature. In that time, it was not unusual for politicians to hold more than one public office at the same time.

Clinton, fortunately, was between major political engagements when, in late 1810, he was sought out by erstwhile political enemies belonging to the Federalist party, who paid him the high compliment of asking for his support of the canal cause. The appeal was made by a state senator, Jonas Platt, leader of the Federalists in New York, and Thomas Eddy, also a state senator. While the possibility of high-mindedness could not, in all fairness, be ruled out entirely, the political and business motives behind the move to enlist Clinton's help showed through the earnest solicitation. Senator Eddy was treasurer of the old, faltering Western Inland Lock Navigation Company, and he originally had approached Senator Platt, a candidate for governor, for help in getting the company back on its feet—perhaps through state subsidization of construction by the company of a canal from Oneida Lake to the Seneca River. Platt, a resident of western New York, had countered with the suggestion that the company think in larger terms—perhaps consider a canal all the way across the state to Lake Erie.

Getting legislative approval of any such ambitious undertaking was unlikely except through a bipartisan approach. Republican co-operation was essential, and it could come only through somebody who was influential enough to control votes and command attention—a strong man. There was no stronger man in New York State at the time than De Witt Clinton, not even his leading antagonist, Martin Van Buren.

With Clinton as spokesman and guiding genius of the campaign to bring the canal into being, and with political support cutting across party lines, Platt saw a winning combination taking shape. It was his plan, should Clinton agree to back the canal, to request the legislature to create a bipartisan canal commission which would undertake its own route survey and make recommendations directly to the Assembly.

Perhaps the fact that the fiercest opponents of the canal were the political and business leaders of New York City made the wooing of Clinton more determined. The former mayor's personal following in the city was large and influential and trusting in his judgment.

"Mr. Clinton listened with intense interest and deep agitation of mind," wrote Platt of the fateful meeting in which Clinton was drawn irrevocably to the side of the canal cause. "He . . . said that he was in a great measure a stranger to the Western interior of our State; that he had given but little attention to the subject of canal navigation, but that the exposition of our plan struck his mind with great force; that he was then prepared to say that it was an object worthy of thorough examination . . ."

The jubilant Platt almost immediately—on March 13, 1810—presented to the state legislature a resolution calling for creation of a canal commission to examine the subject, to make surveys of possible routes, and to report its findings to the legislators. The commission would have seven members, and it would be bipartisan in makeup.

Clinton seconded the Platt Resolution, and it passed both houses by unanimous vote. Named to the commission were Gouverneur Morris, Stephen Van Rensselaer, Simeon De Witt (first cousin of De Witt Clinton), William North, Thomas Eddy, Peter B. Porter, and Clinton. Judge Geddes was hired as an expert-consultant and agreed to accompany the new commission on its tour of the routes he had studied so thoroughly only two years before.

All of the commission members were notables, men of distinction not only in the state, but also nationally. Yet, from the time the group came into being, it was plain that De Witt Clinton was its leading member, just as it swiftly became clear that the Erie Canal had found its most eloquent spokesman, its most ardent champion, its most influential friend.

The cause and the man finally had come together. From 1810 on, they were one.

CHAPTER IV

A FAMILY OF DESTINY

De Witt Clinton was an outstanding politician at a time when the woods seemed to be alive with immortals, all impatiently waiting to take their places in the history books. He commanded attention and respect from the voters, the scholars, and from his peers in politics. His name held its own in a time when almost all the great founding fathers of the nation were alive, many of them in their prime; in a time when it took the stature of a giant not to get lost in the crowd.

The same Thomas Jefferson who opposed federal support for "Clinton's Ditch" was one of Clinton's admirers. He had an appreciation of Clinton that approached Clinton's appreciation of him. Their differences never seemed to diminish their respect for one another.

Once, asked by his neighbors who should be the President of the United States, Jefferson gave an answer that could not easily be disputed. The President, he said, ought to be the greatest man in America.

Some of Jefferson's neighbors, not content with his reply, pressed for a more specific answer. They wanted from him, they said, a name, not an aphorism. Who would the grestest man in America be?

"De Witt Clinton," said Jefferson.

The honor of the presidency was denied Clinton, even though it still appeared to be within his grasp at the time of his death, in 1828. He was then fifty-nine and a formidable political figure. There was no more famous man in America nor any better qualified for the White House.

Perhaps the presidency would have been something of an anticlimax for Clinton, improbable as that may seem. He had enjoyed a career choked with achievement and accolades. He had known high responsibility and high honor. Victory had not been a stranger to him, not in politics, anyway. He had been a three-time mayor of New York City, four-term governor of New York State, one-term United States Senator from New York, former lieutenant-governor of the state (at the same time he was serving a term as mayor), a state senator, and, in 1812, when he was only 43 years old, he had been the presidential nominee of both the Federalists and the Republicans of New York State.

Clinton's success probably was as predictable as the cycle of the seasons. He came onto the New York political scene with a great name, out of a winning family background, scrupulously groomed for a public career in the English tradition. He was a well-educated man at a time when only few men had even a minimum education. He was slim and erect and tall—six foot three—in a day when short stature was normal. His face was handsome and he had brown, curly hair. In every conceivable way he was a strikingly impressive representative of the colonial aristocracy upon whom the young United States would depend so much in striving for a democratic utopia.

Among the minor distinctions of Clinton's younger days was the fact that he was the first man to be graduated from Columbia University. There is an asterisk and a footnote attached to this distinction. Before the War of Independence, Columbia was named King's College. It was given the name of Columbia after the war, in 1784, and in 1786 Clinton received the first diploma awarded to members of the first postwar graduating class. Later he received a master's degree from Columbia, and among those present at the ceremony was President George Washington, in his first outing as the nation's Chief Executive.

Clinton's quick rise in politics was due not so much to his intellect, education, or physical attractiveness as it was to his name. Genealogy was on Clinton's side. The Clintons were of English origin, members of the nobility as a matter of fact, and they had been well-placed among the landed gentry, but their loyalty to the ill-fated King Charles I resulted in the loss of the family estates and banishment from England. The exiled Clintons wandered to France, Spain, and Scotland before settling, at last, in Northern Ireland. There, in County Longford, Charles Clinton was born in 1690.

In 1729 Charles Clinton was leader of a group that, for religious and political reasons, decided to start life anew in America. A ninety-ton frigate named *George and Anne* was chartered for the voyage. The intended destination of the ship was Philadelphia. Included in the seventy passengers who went aboard the ship were Charles Clinton, his wife and three children, two of his sisters and their families, and many of Clinton's old friends and neighbors.

A trip across the Atlantic Ocean from Ireland to America usually took about six weeks, depending on the vagaries of the weather, but there was nothing usual about this particular voyage. The captain of the charter ship, a man named Rymer, would have been more at home sailing under the Jolly Roger. He had the kind of personality that would have made

Captain Bligh of the *Bounty* look like a kindly, garrulous old salt who liked to laugh it up with the hired hands.

The first intimation that Captain Rymer was less than the perfect ship's master came shortly after the voyage got underway, before Ireland had faded from view. One of the ship's crew members somehow crossed the captain by asking the wrong question, and the captain, obviously a testy sort, beat the sailor to death with a pipe stave. The passengers and crew alike, impressed, immediately and understandably became wary in their dealings with the captain.

Thus it was that after six weeks at sea had passed and still no land in sight, the Clintons and their friends maintained a discreet silence. But the ship rolled on and the weeks passed without sign of America—not officially, anyway. One day some of the people on deck thought they spotted a distant smudge on the horizon that could have been land. The boatswain even identified it as Virginia, and that made Captain Rymer very angry. He not only denied that Virginia was in sight, he denounced the boatswain for a "lying, skulking dog." The *George and Anne* then, by captain's orders, immediately took a fresh tack in the opposite direction and the weary voyage continued.

The second month at sea passed, and then the third, but the ship continued to lurch about in the open, boundless waters of the Atlantic. Supplies of food and drink dwindled to dangerous levels. The food ration was reduced to a half biscuit a day and drink was restricted to a half pint of water apiece. Illness began to take its toll of the passengers, especially the very young and the very old. Death became an everyday occurrence. Among the many who succumbed were two of the three Clinton children.

At last it became apparent to Charles Clinton and his friends that theirs was a journey to nowhere, that Captain Rymer was merely criss-crossing about in the open sea as part of a campaign of attrition which eventually would end in the deaths of all the passengers, allowing him to sequester all the worldly wealth and possessions of the well-to-do victims. Clinton, acting as spokesman for those who still survived, pointed out to the villainous captain that he needn't go to such extremes simply to acquire the holdings of the passengers. He proposed that Rymer simply land his passengers safely ashore somewhere on the American continent and scoot off with the possessions that the immigrants gladly would yield to him in exchange for their lives. The captain, perhaps being weary of the marathon voyage himself, agreed to the terms. He landed the emaciated survivors somewhere near Cape Cod on October 4, 1729—approximately five months after the ship had left Ireland!

The English refugees stayed in Massachusetts for two years, until their strength and their spirits were renewed. Then, led by Charles Clinton, they made their way to New York, sailed up the Hudson to remote Ulster County, about sixty miles north of New York City, and there, close to the river, they established their own colony. They gave it the name of Little Britain.

The only one of the Clinton children to live through the ghastly ocean trip was a daughter, Catherine. Once the family was settled in America, however, four more children—all sons—were born to Charles Clinton and his Irish wife. They were Alexander, Charles, James, and George.

The elder Clinton, a well-educated man with a reverence for books, quickly was acknowledged as leader of the community by the other settlers. He eventually was named judge of the Court of Common Pleas.

Clinton did not allow the wilderness environment to interfere with the family tradition of advanced education and military service. The second youngest of the Clinton sons, James, became a lieutenant colonel in the Ulster County militia, and his older brother, Charles, was an officer-surgeon in the king's army. The youngest, George, became an officer in the colonial army. Alexander, the oldest, a poet, musician, and a doctor, died a young man.

James married a girl named Mary De Witt in 1765 and of their union De Witt Clinton was born, in 1769.

If the child needed any genealogical strengthening, the maternal side of the family surely provided it. One of the De Witts, a seaman, had sailed a ship called the *Little Fox* into the waters of Long Island Sound in 1613, only four years after Henry Hudson had been there. The first De Witt to establish residence in America was Tjerck Classen De Witt, who settled in Kingston, New York, on the Hudson in the early 1630s.

While the Clintons were not on the New York scene until a century later, once they arrived they made their presence felt quickly. At a time when all the colonists were going through the painful process of alignment, taking up positions for or against His Majesty's Government in America, the Clinton influence was evident on both sides.

There was, in fact, a confusion of Clintons. King George in 1741 had appointed as governor of the Province of New York a member of the nobility named George Clinton. George, the youngest son of the sixth Earl of Lincoln, was a distant cousin of the Charles Clinton who had fled to America. Instead of finding the refugee-backwoods Clinton an embarrassment, Governor Clinton apparently was delighted to find a blood relative in the primitive land. The two became good friends, as did their sons. But while the American Clinton gave the English Clinton his friendship, it was with political reservations. Blood may be thicker than water, but it was not as viscid as provincial patriotism.

When the Revolutionary War broke out, the Clintons did their patriotic best on both sides. Major General Sir Henry Clinton, son of the former royal governor, succeeded Sir William Howe as commander of the British forces in the colonies in 1778. On the other side, in colonial uniforms, were two sons of Charles Clinton—Brigadier General George Clinton and Brigadier General James Clinton.

32

The British General Clinton helped lead the forces that captured New York City early in the war. The following year he turned his Redcoats northward, up the Hudson River, to capture, first, an American stronghold named, ironically, Fort Clinton. It was commanded by General James Clinton. Then, tossing aside all family sentiment, the British General Clinton pushed on to capture Fort Montgomery, which was under the command of General George Clinton.

In neither victory, though, was the British General Clinton able to capture either of the American Clintons. Each time, as soon as the stockades had yielded, the British general had gone dashing about, grabbing trapped colonials and demanding to know if they had seen either of his cousins lately. All he got in reply was a lot of shrugging of shoulders. The closest he came to a civil reply was when he questioned Irish-born Colonel McLaughry, widower-husband of Catherine Clinton (who had died in 1762).

"Where is my good friend George?" asked the British commander in chief.

"Safe," answered Colonel McLaughry, adding tartly: "Thank God, beyond the reach of your friendship!"

It was a harsh rejoinder to a cousinly inquiry, but war often has a way of blunting the amenities.

Among the mysteries of the Revolutionary War in the minds of some military analysts was the British Clinton's failure to pursue his advantage once he had gained control of the upper Hudson. It was expected he would push north to relieve General Burgoyne's hard-pressed forces coming down from Canada via the Lake Champlain-Lake George route. Instead, he held fast to his position while Burgoyne went down to defeat. Another British force under the command of General Barry St. Leger which had moved down into central New York from Lake Ontario, heading for junction with Burgoyne, had been stopped in the Mohawk Valley. That was in the bloody Battle of Oriskany on August 6 in which colonial troops under Brigadier General Nicholas Herkimer performed a military miracle, suffering heavy losses but gaining time for Major General Benedict Arnold's men to lift the British siege of Fort Stanwix. It was a turning-point battle.

A kindlier fortune, meanwhile, had settled on the American generals named Clinton. James distinguished himself as second-in-command to Brigadier General John Sullivan in one of the most famous campaigns of the war—an assignment by an aroused General Washington to seek out and destroy the Iroquois Indians. The confederation of tribes, allies of the British, had horrified the colonies with its savage raids, burnings, and massacres, especially in the Wyoming Valley of Pennsylvania and in the Mohawk Valley and Cherry Valley in New York.

In early summer of 1779, after fresh outrages by the Senecas, Washington called in General Sullivan and ordered him to take his 4,000 troops against the Indians and deal with them in no uncertain way. He demanded "the total destruction of their settlements and the capture of as many prisoners of every age and sex as possible." He directed Sullivan to see to it that the country of the Iroquois was not only overrun "but destroyed."

What followed was an application of the "scorched earth" policy without precedent on the American side. Generals Sullivan and Clinton led the colonial troops in a wide swathe through Seneca and Cayuga territory in the fiercest American punitive action ever. Some forty Iroquois villages were burned—one village had more than 130 buildings in it—and 160,000 bushels of corn vital to the Indians were seized. The reprisal action left thousands of the Iroquois in desperate straits with winter coming on and virtually eliminated them as a military factor. Thousands of Senecas fled their home territory in the Genesee Valley area to seek refuge in British forts to the north.

General James Clinton won a lasting reputation among the Indians for his role in the Sullivan campaign. They called him a "ruthless and merciless fighting man," which was more complimentary than critical because the Senecas understood that kind of warrior-leader. That was their style of fighting, too.

When General Cornwallis surrendered his colors at Yorktown, it was to the brigade commanded by General James Clinton.

General George Clinton, his brother, was one of the delegates from New York to the Second Continental Congress in 1775 and took part in the deliberations that drafted and passed the Declaration of Independence. After voting affirmatively on the issue of independence on July 2, 1776, George hurried home to take on his duties as a brigadier general in George Washington's hastily assembled army. He became one of Washington's closest aides.

It was after the war, however, that George Clinton's star rose to full ascendancy. In 1777 he was elected first governor of New York State, filling the seat of power held in provincial days by the British George Clinton. Nepotism was firmly in the saddle in that first Clinton administration after the war. General James Clinton, the governor's brother, was named colonel in the New York Militia at first and later, brigadier general. James Clinton's son Alexander was appointed secretary to Uncle George, but died of drowning shortly after the appointment. Governor Clinton in early 1790 named in the youth's place his brother, De Witt Clinton.

It was a timely development for De Witt, then twenty-one years old and anxious to broaden his own career. He had hung out his shingle and begun the practice of law, but he needed more excitement and challenge than an attorney's life offered. His new position at the side of the governor during the fervid years that followed, years of yeasty development in the political order, offered him the opportunity to become personally acquainted with the great men of the nation and to be a part, even if only in a minor sense, of history itself. There is no question that the years he spent as his uncle's secretary whetted De Witt's appetite for politics and turned his course irrevocably into the political mainstream for life.

There was another significant happening during that period with long-range results on De Witt Clinton's life. He met and fell in love with Maria Franklin, a nineteen-year-old girl who was not only beautiful but who also came from a wealthy, influential family. The presidential mansion occupied by George Washington at the corner of Cherry and Pearl streets in New York was, in fact, the former Franklin home. In 1795, the year that Governor Clinton declined to run for re-election, Maria Franklin became Mrs. De Witt Clinton.

Now a married man and on his own, no longer in the shadow of his great uncle, De Witt Clinton was ready to begin his own political career in earnest. He resumed the practice of law while he studied the New York scene and prepared himself for the first move. It came shortly, in 1797, when he ran for a place in the State Assembly from New York City and won. (Another bright young man to win election—his third—to the Assembly at the same time was Aaron Burr.)

Four years later, then a state senator, Clinton gained a seat in the New York Council of Appointment, probably the most important single political agency in the state because of its extraordinary patronage power. Although he was only thirty-two years old, his place on the council made De Witt the acknowledged leader of the Republican party in the state.

That year, 1801, was a very good year for the Clintons. While De Witt was winning a seat on the Council of Appointment, Uncle George Clinton was again being elected governor of the state.

De Witt Clinton's tenure on the council, according to some political experts, was of special significance because of the way he opened the door wide to admit the spoils system. There was nothing subtle in his approach to the division of political jobs of importance which were within the appointive power of the council. Clinton took the position, simply, that all major offices were to be filled by Republicans. All minor offices were to be divided equally between the party in power and the party out of power.

The raw power philosophy exemplified by the "to-the-victor-belongs-the-spoils" practice may seem at odds with the idealism of a De Witt Clinton—dreamer, scientist, nature lover, humanist, and philosopher. But there also was De Witt Clinton, politician. The rival Federalists had been in power in New York without break since 1795, and the new Council of Appointment under the leadership of Republican Clinton saw it as their duty to "bring about a more equitable array of office-holders."

Those formative days in American state and national politics were strictly rough-and-tumble, no-holds-barred, and it took a lot of toughness to survive. The spoils system was a natural, perhaps ineluctable policy of survival, and it added an element of high reward that increased the competitiveness of politics in the young nation.

But Clinton did not linger in the Council of Appointment. Less than a year later, on January 29, 1802, he was elected to the United States Senate by the New York State legislature to succeed General John Armstrong. He joined New York's senior senator, Gouverneur Morris, in Washington.

It was during those opening years of the nineteenth century that Aaron Burr, also a Republican, drew a lot of attention to himself. Some of his machinations, especially in the attempt to snatch the presidency away from Thomas Jefferson and in the organization of a Republican-oriented Manhattan Bank through some devious state legislation, simply were too much to stomach, even by members of his own party.

Among those who disapproved of Burr and his penchant for subterfuge were the two Clintons, uncle and nephew, and the powerful Livingston family. A combination of their forces was enough to turn Burr and his close friend, John Swartwout, out of their positions as directors of the municipal holding company that controlled the bank.

There was nothing even faintly subtle about the ouster. De Witt Clinton, in an exchange with Swartwout, called him "a liar, a scoundrel, and a villain." Those fighting words led to a duel between the two men in an open field on the New Jersey shore in late afternoon of July 31, 1802. Colonel William Stephens Smith, son-in-law of John Adams, acted as Swartwout's second. Richard Riker, acting attorney general of New York, was Clinton's second.

Swartwout insisted on the dramatic back-to-back technique, with a set distance between the duelists, who would whirl and fire upon the proper signal. The first time the signal was given, each man fired and each man missed. Clinton was willing to end the matter at that point if Swartwout were satisfied, but Swartwout was not. There was a second exchange of bullets and, again, both bullets missed.

On the third firing of pistols, Swartwout put a bullet through Clinton's coat. Some onlookers claimed he had whirled ahead of time. But Swartwout still was not satisfied. He shook off another Clinton offer to end the duel and shake hands. De Witt's lips tightened and he went to work.

In the fourth exchange of bullets, Clinton hit Swartwout in the leg. A physician, Dr. Douglass, took the bullet from Swartwout's leg, but the wounded man refused to allow the duel to end. He insisted on another firing. Clinton, reluctant to continue, turned to the people in attendance and made a statement:

"I beg you all to bear witness," he said. "I have no enmity to Mr. Swartwout, and I am compelled to shoot at a man whom I do not wish to hurt; but I will sign no paper. I will not dishonor myself."

In the fifth exchange, a bullet from Clinton's gun struck Swartwout's leg once again. Lying on the grass with blood spurting from his leg, he loudly demanded a continuation of the duel, but Clinton's second, Riker, ordered a halt.

"Mr. Clinton shall not fire again," he announced.

The Burr-Swartwout forces in the next few days loudly claimed victory because of Clinton's refusal to continue the duel. Clinton only expressed regret over the fact that his opponent had not been the "principal" in the political controversy—meaning Aaron Burr.

After nearly two years as a United States senator, Clinton was appointed mayor of New York City in October 1803. In the political order of priorities that prevailed in those days, federal positions often were rated below state and local power bases. Washington in 1803 was far from being the center of influence that it later would become.

The mayoral position in New York City still demands much from men of the present day, but not the degree of versatility that it demanded in De Witt Clinton's time. As mayor, he also was (a) presiding justice of the Mayor's Court; as such he had to hear all cases from misdemeanors to felonies; (b) head of the Common Council; (c) chief of police; (d) clerk of the markets. The last-named responsibility was not, as it would seem, an anticlimax. For most mayors it represented the best part of being chief executive of the city because it allowed the mayor to collect, and keep, all fees paid by merchants for licenses. Clinton apparently felt that was going too far with a good thing. He decided to divide the market fees—half for the city, half for himself.

It was during Clinton's first term in City Hall that the most shocking political tragedy in early American history occurred. Aaron Burr, frustrated in his ambitions to become governor of New York, as he earlier had been frustrated in his effort to wrest the presidency from Thomas Jefferson, picked a fight with one of his Federalist foes, Alexander Hamilton, and shot him to death in a duel in Weehawken, New Jersey, in July 1804.

President Jefferson, meanwhile, had chosen De Witt's uncle, George Clinton, to be his running mate on the national ticket and the pair won handily. Now there was a Clinton as mayor of New York and a Clinton as Vice-President of the United States.

De Witt Clinton's later achievement in bringing the Erie Canal into being was such a dazzling piece of politicking and statesmanship that it has tended to overshadow some of his other accomplishments, especially his part in the creation of the free public school system. Mayor Clinton went to Albany in April 1805 and won a state charter for what was called the Common Public School Society—a charter, but no money. Then he and another education enthusiast, Frederick De Peyster, went from house to house in New York City begging for voluntary contributions to the society. They raised $5,000, enough money to begin classes the following May in a house on Bancker (Madison) Street. Out of that modest beginning grew the American system of free public education, and it is fair to say there is something of De Witt Clinton in every public school classroom in the nation today.

Clinton was ousted as mayor in 1807 after a coalition of his political enemies captured the state Council of Appointment, but his retirement from public life was short-lived. The new governor of New York, Daniel D. Tompkins, was friendly to Clinton and restored him to the office of mayor of the state's largest city at the beginning of 1808. During this new term he coaxed money out of the state legislature and built gun emplacements and fortifications in the Narrows. British and French warships, which had been notably contemptuous of American authority in New York Harbor, thereafter showed new respect, and Mayor Clinton's popularity rose considerably higher among the intensely nationalistic New Yorkers.

No doubt the mayor received a lot of unsolicited advice on how to deal with the French and British commanders who had been misbehaving in the harbor. Clinton had many friends among the seafarers and shipping tycoons of the city. One of the men who was close to him was a testy mariner with a standout name—Captain Preserved Fish.

To be absolutely accurate, the old salt's full name was Captain Preserved Fish, Jr. His father had enjoyed the same name, if that is not overstating the fact, and thoughtfully had passed it along to his son when the young'un appeared on the scene in the family's home port of Portsmouth, Rhode Island.

Captain Fish, junior, was a highly successful seaman who, in time, became New York's harbor master and a senior partner in the firm of Fish & Grinnell, shipping merchants. Briefly he also had been in partnership with a man named Saul Alley. The way in which the fledgling firm of Fish & Alley foundered provides an insight to the personality of the sea captain.

Alley entered the firm's office one morning and cheerily greeted his partner, who already was at work at his desk.

"Hope you are well this morning, Captain Fish," said Alley cordially, preparing to take off his greatcoat.

The captain turned a fishy eye on Alley.

"This," he said heavily, "is the place for business, sir, not for compliments!"

From that point on the conversation deteriorated and the firm went out of business.

The probability is that Mayor Clinton, like most New Yorkers, savored to the fullest another popular Fish story. This tale alleged that one time, upon his return from a long voyage, Captain Fish's ship was hailed by a revenue cutter in New York Harbor. The official aboard the cutter called out to the ship, demanding identification.

"What's the name of that brig?" he yelled.

"*Flying Fish*, sir!" yelled back one of the ship's officers.

"What's your cargo?"

"Pickled fish, sir!"

"Who's your captain?"

"Preserved Fish, sir!"

At that point, it was said, the revenue officer became quite upset over the japery of the ship's officer and boarded the brig with the angry intent of flattening the smart aleck. It took a number of men to convince him that all the replies were straightforward, factual and honest.

No doubt there were frequent intervals of lightheartedness and laughter, even in the serious times through which De Witt Clinton lived, but history was moving the nation relentlessly toward a new, critical confrontation with England, just as it was moving Clinton toward the unique role which would enable him to make his own special contribution to the preservation of the American Union.

In 1810 Clinton was again ousted as mayor of New York by the Council of Appointment, thanks to some political skulduggery. At almost the same time, one of his children, a son named Walter, suddenly died. It was at that bleak, cheerless moment in De Witt Clinton's life that his old political foe Jonas Platt approached him and asked him to take up the reins of leadership in the campaign for a canal that would cross the roof of the state and open up the West.

Instead of Clinton's career being at an end, it was just beginning.

CHAPTER V

SURVEY AND STRUGGLE

The way it was in 1810 in New York State was largely, still, the wilderness way. There was, to be sure, the teeming city on Manhattan Island at the mouth of the Hudson River with its 80,000 people—a fantastic place with its bustling, cobblestoned streets, and always a thick cluster of masts of sailing ships at anchor. And there were the old settlements northward, hugging the banks of the Hudson, pockets of civilization that poked abruptly out of the green forest bush that trimmed the water.

But beyond the quaint Dutch rooftops of Albany and past the storied streets of tiny Schenectady, those outposts of the New Netherlands of another day, the land belonged mainly to itself and not to man. Travelers could cross it at their own risk, just as they could cross the boundless, swelling ocean, but they could not claim either as conquests. A footprint left no more mark in the forests of the West than it did in the Atlantic.

There were a few determined men who rode the Mohawk and followed the Indian trails, now trade routes, to Oswego on Lake Ontario. And there were other men who moved across the Genesee Country on foot to the tiny settlements of Lewiston on the Niagara River and Black Rock, just north of Lake Erie, and Buffalo, at the edge of the great lake, but the travelers were few and the trees were many. The branches gave way when the frontiersmen pushed their way through in passage, but they quickly sprang back into place, barring the path again, and except for a final quiver it was just as if they had not been disturbed.

It seemed as if the wilderness wall still held as it had through all the yesterdays of time, yet the future already had arrived and some were wise enough and sensitive enough to know it. The Indians, confused and uncertain, knew. So did the animals and the birds and the serpents. It was

41

a time of incongruities as the front runners of civilization mixed with the primal pattern of nature. A classic anomaly available for all to see was the steamboat that pushed its way up the Hudson in the first week of July in 1810, carrying De Witt Clinton and Thomas Eddy, members of the newly named Canal Commission on the first leg of their journey to survey the suggested routes for the cross-state canal.

The steamboat had been built by Robert Fulton and had been put into passenger and cargo service between Albany and New York City. While it was more of a novelty than a challenge to the sailing ships that plied the Hudson, it stood out, unquestionably, as a forerunner of the future. The boat carried Clinton and Eddy from New York City to Albany in thirty hours. Its white plume of smoke as it moved gracefully between the forested bluffs was the panache worn by a new kind of invader confidently challenging the age-old fastness.

There were prophetic overtones in the combination that had De Witt Clinton riding a steamship into combat and there was a quixotic tilt to the sight. Between the two of them, the steamboat and the statesman would change a part of the New World that had stood unchanged for so long.

In Albany, Clinton and Eddy met with other members of the state commission on July 2 in the office of Surveyor General Simeon De Witt to make arrangements for the commission's trip into the West to study proposed canal routes. Only one member of the commission was missing— General Peter B. Porter had elected to await the arrival of the commission at his home in Black Rock, close to Lake Erie's shore.

It was a distinguished group that came together in Simeon De Witt's office. There was De Witt himself. This cousin of De Witt Clinton still stands out as one of the most remarkable public servants in the history of New York State. He spent his adult lifetime, fifty years (1784–1834) altogether, as the state's surveyor general, and during that incredibly long term of service, he in effect presided over the opening of New York State and its colonization.

Gouverneur Morris was also an outstanding man of his time, a rare combination of financier, statesman, soldier, scholar, diplomat, dilettante, and dreamer. He was the senior member of the commission and he arrived fully prepared to withstand the rigors of the surveying mission in style by traveling in his own elegant chaise "with a case or two of claret underfoot."

Stephen Van Rensselaer bore with impressive dignity a great name and a great tradition. He was, in some respects, the last of the Dutch patroons—those venturesome aristocrats who held dominion over the Hudson Valley during the days of New Netherland and later. Unlike most of his ancestors, however, he was a public-spirited man, deeply interested in the canal project.

Thomas Eddy, another notable of the time, knew more about canals, their advantages and their problems, than most men. He had been treasurer of the old Western Inland Lock Navigation Company for a long time. His previous involvement in canal building promised to be invaluable.

General William North, a veteran of the Revolutionary War, stood high in the esteem of his fellows for his integrity and for his political and social acumen.

Judge James Geddes, the commission's consultant, was the most knowledgeable of all, of course, on the subject of canal routes, having filled the role of trail blazer.

The first leg of the survey journey, from Albany to Utica, gave the commission members an immediate insight into the terrible conditions of travel that blocked westward expansion of trade and population. This experience gave added meaning to their mission. Five members of the group—Clinton, Eddy, De Witt, North, and Geddes—traveled by stage coach to Schenectady, where they boarded river boats for the rest of the journey to Utica. Morris and Van Rensselaer, the two aristocrats, chose to ride overland the entire hundred miles from Albany to Utica, presumably polishing off the flagons of claret along the way to speed the dragging, uncomfortable hours.

The trip altogether took five days, with the water-borne travelers arriving a few hours later than their colleagues. Reunited in Utica, the commissioners took to river boats to travel to their next destination, Rome. The only land transport westward from Utica was a stage that ran three times a week to Geneva; there was no stage service westward from Geneva.

Rome was a place of deliberation and decision by the survey party, a place to confer on future procedure and movement because it represented a kind of crossroads. It would be appropriate even to call the conference there a "summit meeting" because Rome was the summit point in any likely canal route. There the waters flowing down from the north diverged, either turning to the west, like Wood Creek, or veering to the east, like the Mohawk River.

In Rome, on July 12, the commission members made their decision to study with open minds both of the major canal propositions that had been set forth through the years—one that would connect the Hudson with Lake Ontario and the other that would connect the Hudson with Lake Erie. The rival canal routes separated and headed their individual ways a short distance to the west of Rome, and so did the commissioners. Morris and Van Rensselaer pushed off together by coach toward Lake Erie, while the other members of the party inspected the route that a canal to Lake Ontario could be expected to take, all the way to the port settlement of Oswego.

Clinton and his colleagues then returned inland and took up a westward trek along the suggested route of a canal directly connected to Lake

43

Erie. This final leg of their long journey was by horse-drawn coaches over the roughest of roads, and under the crude circumstances that attended this part of their trip, it is reasonable to surmise that the commission gained its most poignant appreciation of the need for a canal. When they finally reached the Niagara River, they clambered out of their coaches with the flushed faces and the tentative walk of men who had endured much in the name of public service.

As uncomfortable as the trip was, however, Clinton found it a totally absorbing experience. His curiosity as a natural scientist was excited by the unspoiled wilderness through which the party rode, and he made careful notes on the interesting, uncatalogued flora and fauna which he observed along the way. One of his most notable wayside observations involved a broad-leafed herb plant with yellow flowers which subsequently was named in his honor "clintonia." Another of his discoveries, near Utica, was a species of wheat which was growing wild, a find that drew wide attention from European scientists.

Awaiting the arrival of the commission to the Niagara country were Morris, Van Rensselaer, and General Porter, who played the role of host. But before the weary travelers would sit down to discuss their findings, they gave their attention to a matter of higher priority. They were not so preoccupied with their fact-finding mission that they were beyond the lure of Niagara Falls. Like any group of normal American tourists, they took a side trip to gape at the colossal cataract before they knuckled down to business in a conference held in the settlement of Chippewa on August 3.

The commissioners had spent a month bumping and battling their way across the state, but the trip had been worthwhile. They knew the problem and the need as never before, and they no longer had reason to wonder why it cost a hundred dollars to ship just one ton of freight across the 360 miles from Albany to Lake Erie. Now they understood why westward migration was being held to a virtual standstill.

There is clear indication that it was in this meeting at Chippewa that De Witt Clinton asserted his leadership of the Erie Canal movement. Until then, no doubt aware that other members of the commission possessed greater knowledge of the problem and the proposed solutions, he had held back and played a listening, studying role. His commitment as a proponent of the canal, whichever route it might take, had been made on an abstract intellectual basis. But the long journey added a new, personal, emotional element, the kind of understanding and feeling that could only grow out of weeks of struggling through the wilderness.

Now that Clinton understood the problem more fully and had viewed both of the suggested routes, there no longer remained in his mind any question about which path the proposed canal should follow. He took an unequivocal stand in favor of the long, overland canal—the direct connection between the Hudson River and Lake Erie.

When General Porter argued for a canal that would go, instead, to Lake Ontario, Clinton reminded the other commissioners of the obvious objections to that route, of the danger that eastbound trade might be diverted to Canadian ports once it reached Lake Ontario, of the awkward necessity of transferring cargo and passengers from lake boats to canal-boats and back again at the junction ports.

Clinton's principal argument was the most convincing: that a canal which continued overland all the way to Lake Erie would open up the entire western territory and nourish that great expanse of country with people and trade, while a canal that veered off to Lake Ontario would isolate western New York even further.

The report of the survey commission was made to the state legislature the following spring, on March 2, 1811. It presented the diverse viewpoints within the commission, took a positive attitude toward the practicability of a canal to Lake Erie, and recommended that the construction project be undertaken directly by the state, not by private individuals or through corporate ownership of any canal that might be built.

Even as the report stirred widespread discussion all over New York, the legislature empowered the commissioners to continue their investigation and specifically appointed Clinton and Morris to solicit financial aid for the canal from the federal government.

Beyond this high point, however, the campaign in behalf of the Erie Canal was to slump and be buried in the rush of more overwhelming events. Relations between the United States and England had deteriorated to such an alarming extent that the oncoming War of 1812 had become an inevitability. It was no time to speak of domestic spending, even on an internal improvement that conceivably could be of considerable military value.

The champion of the canal, Clinton, also had other matters demanding his time and attention. The Republican party had returned to state power the previous autumn and Clinton was restored to his old position as mayor of New York City by the Council of Appointment. It was his third term of service in that position. With each term, however, the city had grown and the job had become more complex. Now, with war in the offing, the mayor also had to worry about defense problems faced by the vital port placed under his stewardship.

There apparently was some feeling, however, that De Witt Clinton was capable of extending himself further. The next thing the mayor knew, he also was lieutenant governor of New York State. The office had come open upon the death of the incumbent, and a party caucus in March 1811 nominated Clinton as his successor. He did not have to resign as mayor when elected to the state post.

What lifted the nomination of Clinton to the lieutenant-governorship out of the ordinary was that Tammany Hall preferred a man named Marinus Willett. Two of the Tammany spokesmen who denounced the choice of Clinton were Teunis Wortman and Mangle Minthorne. The Federalist candidate for the job was Nicholas Fish. (It has been a long time since New York political circles could boast names like those.) It is testimony to Clinton's power that he was able to down Marinus Willett, Teunis Wortman, Mangle Minthorne, and Nicholas Fish, all at once. A fell swoop if ever there was one.

Summertime 1811 brought no lull to Clinton's life. It started out peaceably enough with the June commencement exercises of Columbia College, which were held in Trinity Church. The last notes of the entrance march hardly had faded away before there was a free-for-all in the church. Columbia was way ahead of its time when it came to student riots. This one arose because one of the student speakers on the program had been asked to alter his prepared remarks. When he refused, the college officials decided to withhold the youth's diploma. Somehow, though, the obdurate senior managed to gain command of the platform for a few minutes during the formal graduation ceremonies, and what he had to say was of such fiery nature that the student body in attendance was incited to physical action and a general melee resulted.

The miscreants were brought before Clinton, holder of Diploma No. 1 from the college, and he dealt heavily with them in his Mayor's Court—more severely, indeed, than modern courts generally have dealt with student rioters. Clinton insisted on the families of the students being on hand as he denounced the troublemakers for their violent misconduct. He then fined them large amounts of money, at the same time making it clear that only their tender years saved them from jail. His words must have seared the 1811 activists because one of the ringleaders of the group, Gulian C. Verplanck, no less, thereafter could be counted among Clinton's enemies.

What would have been the peak of the public careers of most men was hardly more than a painful passing incident to Clinton when, in 1812, he was a candidate for the presidency of the United States. The incumbent, James Madison, was a Republican like Clinton, but whereas Madison spoke on the issue of Anglo-American relations from a platform of "righteous belligerency," Clinton spoke out for peaceful settlement of differences with Great Britain.

The war with England got under way during the election campaign, and Clinton, who had been nominated by New York Republicans, found himself in the hopeless position of preaching peace when the nation already was at war. He suffered a resounding defeat in the national election.

The dream of the Erie Canal persisted despite the war. Clinton and his fellow canal commissioners met regularly and talked of the great project, biding their time for a renewal of the effort, refusing to let go of their vision. When the war ended in 1815, they were ready. They called a mass meeting for December 30 in the City Hotel to rally support for the canal, and to this meeting came men from all walks, old friends and old enemies, political allies and political rivals—all drawn together by the persuasive power of Clinton and the compelling magnetism of the canal dream and what it promised for the future.

William Bayard, a prominent merchant, presided over the meeting. Jonas Platt was the principal speaker. At his urging, a committee was appointed and charged with the important task of preparing a memorial to be presented to the state legislature, one that would be a convincing argument for immediate construction of the canal. The four-man committee named to draw up the memorial was itself a reflection of the issue's power to pull men together, including, as it did, De Witt Clinton as chairman; John Swartwout, his old dueling adversary; Thomas Eddy; and Cadwallader D. Colden, grandson of the famous man who had served as surveyor general of the colonial province of New York in 1724 and who, in that position, had written imaginatively of the inland water travel possibilities offered by the Great Lakes and the Hudson River. Colden the elder had marveled in his remarkable report that New York Province was "such a Scene of inland Navigation as cannot be parallel'd in any other Part of the World."

Now, nearly a century later, it was time for another memorial on the same subject—one that had to be so powerful in its exposition of inland water travel possibilities and so compelling in its presentation of the great promise that the New York legislature would be moved to build a canal that seemed almost to be beyond the reach of its technology and means.

Clinton wrote that memorial with an inspired pen. It was a powerful affirmation of faith in the concept of the canal as a feasible, practicable, necessary means toward a great end; a canal that, in reaching out to the Great Lakes, would pass "through the most fertile country in the universe" and "would perhaps convey more riches on its waters than any other canal in the world."

To document his position, Clinton gave the legislators more specific information than they ever had received on the subject. His memorial informed them, for example, that the waterway would have sixty-two locks to compensate for changes in the altitude of the country through which it passed. It calculated the cost of building the canal at about $6,000,000, or about $20,000 a mile. It estimated construction time of the canal would be from ten to fifteen years.

"It remains," Clinton concluded, "for a free state to create a new era in history, and to erect a work more stupendous, more magnificent, and more beneficial than has hitherto been achieved by the human race."

A thousand copies of his memorial were distributed to leading citizens, politicians, newspaper editors, teachers, and other influential people in the state. Suddenly there was no livelier or more controversial subject of conversation than the "crazy" canal that no longer seemed quite so crazy. People long ago had gotten used to calling it "Clinton's Ditch,"

47

but the early scorn had gone out of the nickname, to be replaced by a note of respect and even admiration.

Canal partisans, especially those who lived near the line of the proposed route and who stood to benefit personally from the immediate prosperity promised by the Ditch, whooped it up at public rallies, and more than 100,000 citizens signed petitions of support to accompany the memorial to Albany. Opponents of the canal were not silent in the face of the renewed drive for action. Spokesmen of the southern tier of counties, especially, joined leading citizens of New York City in denouncing the whole scheme. They were joined by vested interests in Long Island and in the prosperous counties of the old patroon country along the Hudson.

Curiously enough, the War of 1812, which had been responsible for the collapse of the canal movement earlier, now gave strength and impetus to the project. The war had illustrated dramatically the need for a canal connection between the East and the West. It was a painful matter of record that the American military effort against the British had been seriously hampered and diminished by the difficulties encountered in moving war material and the national necessities between the eastern and western halves of the nation. There was no question but that the inadequate supply line between Washington and Buffalo contributed in considerable degree to the failure of the military invasion of Canada by the United States. It had cost the government $2,000 to ship a cannon worth only $400 across New York State to the Niagara frontier. The time it took to move men and war supplies through the same territory was even costlier. Had the conquest of Canada succeeded and American dominion over the St. Lawrence River been established, of course, the landlocked canal would not have been so essential.

The canal issue virtually dominated the deliberations of the state legislature through 1816 and into the spring of 1817. Victory seemed to be at hand, fleetingly, when the Assembly on April 12, 1816, approved a trimmed-down bill that sanctioned immediate construction of part of the canal at least—the middle section, from the Seneca River to Rome. It stipulated that the cost of the undertaking was not to exceed $2,000,000 and that the lands bordering on either side of the canal, to the distance of twenty-five miles, should be taxed to provide funds for the project. This measure was something less than the Clinton forces were seeking, but it was better than nothing. It represented a beginning.

But when the bill reached the State Senate, Martin Van Buren's probing interrogation brought to light the fact that the Canal Commission had not performed the physical prerequisite of staking out the precise line of canal route anywhere between the points to be connected. Van Buren's amendment to the legislation changed it from one that authorized construction of part of the canal to a mere authorization for further surveying and the establishment of the precise center line. It was, unmistakably, a setback.

The bill also established a new Canal Commission whose members were named by the Assembly. They were De Witt Clinton; Myron Holley, a state representative from Ontario County; Stephen Van Rensselaer; Joseph Ellicott of Batavia, agent of the Holland Land Company; and Samuel Young.

The new commission immediately instituted surveys of the canal route which, for the purpose, was divided into three sections. James Geddes surveyed the western section, from Lake Erie east to the Seneca River; Benjamin Wright was given the middle section, from the Seneca River to Rome; and Charles C. Brodhead was assigned to the eastern section, from Rome to Schoharie Creek.

The achievements of those three men and their assistants represented a masterful performance. Their report, completed early in 1817, was a document filled with infinite detail relating to every foot of the 360-odd miles over which the waterway would flow. Their study was as basic to the canal's construction as the raw materials to build it. Perhaps Martin Van Buren had been the villain of the canal piece for the moment, but his questioning opposition had led to the accumulation of knowledge that presently would be essential to success.

It was during that year of 1816 that Clinton, not one to overlook any medium that might further the cause, took his goose quill in hand again and, under the nom de plume of "Atticus" which he had used since 1811, he began writing letters on his favorite subject to newspapers of the state. He called the canal the "child of the people . . . an object of such magnitude that the blind may see it." One day, he said, when the canal was finished, New York City would stand "unrivalled by any city on the face of the earth." He urged the New Yorkers, in effect, to cease their opposition to the canal and raise their line of vision to the western frontier and beyond.

"Is it with you a subject of no consideration," he demanded to know, "whether the millions of people, who are settled or may settle upon the waters of the great lakes, shall be a virtuous or vicious generation, whether they be civilized or savage?"

A major obstacle in the way of the canal certainly was the $6,000,000 estimated cost, but the United States Congress appeared fortuitously to have reduced the size of that obstacle in its session of 1816-17 when it voted favorably on a "bonus bill" which would have been of major benefit to the proposed New York waterway.

Senator John C. Calhoun was the author of the bill, which proposed to set aside for internal improvements the accumulated dividends of the stock in the Bank of the United States held by the federal government. The bill specifically included the Erie Canal project as a beneficiary of the funds to be distributed to the amount of some $90,000 a year for twenty years. The bill was vetoed by President James Madison, a Virginian, and many, including the New York *Evening Post*, saw in the veto

49

further evidence of sectional rivalry between New York and Virginia at work again.

Undaunted by the setback, the canal promoters introduced a bill authorizing the beginning construction phase of the canal in the state Assembly on March 18, 1817, and after a month of spirited debate the Canal Law of 1817 was passed.

Curiously, the hero of the parliamentary struggle that resulted in victory was the same Martin Van Buren who had reduced a similar piece of legislation the previous year into another obstacle. Van Buren, who was Clinton's strongest political adversary, was not known for nothing as "the Fox of Kinderhook." His acutely developed nose for public opinion, his educated eye for public enthusiasm, had told him that the Day of the Canal at last had arrived. He was enough of a statesman and politically prudent enough to shift his stand this time to support of the new legislation.

"Now the scene is entirely changed," he declared in announcing his vote in favor of the Canal Law. By the time he had finished his historic speech to the clamorous upper house, Clinton had arrived at his side and was pressing the hand of his old opponent in gratitude.

There still remained, however, one formidable obstacle in the way of the canal construction. Before state legislation in New York could take effect in those days, it had to be passed on by a Council of Revision which had the power of veto. Its membership at the time included the acting governor of the state, John Taylor, who had taken over as chief executive when Governor Daniel Tompkins earlier in the year had become Vice-President of the United States. Other members of the council were Chancellor James Kent, Chief Justice Smith Thompson, of the New York State Supreme Court, and two associate justices, Joseph C. Yates and Jonas Platt.

The chances of the Canal Act winning approval of the Council of Revision were poor. Two members of the council were known to be firmly opposed to the project. They were Acting Governor Taylor and Chief Justice Thompson. Justices Yates and Platt were in favor of the canal. Chancellor Kent, the man who held the deciding vote, admittedly was impressed by the possibilities of a canal, but he had made it clear that he felt the ambitious project was premature.

In all likelihood, the legislative permission to build the canal would have been canceled by the Council of Revision if it had not been for the interference of the former governor, Vice-President Tompkins.

The Vice-President dropped in on the council meeting as it began to discuss the canal legislation, but he couldn't restrict himself to the role of onlooker. He insisted on contributing his unfavorable opinion of the canal project, even though his remarks were out of order.

"This peace with Great Britain, gentlemen," he declared, "is a mere truce. There is no doubt whatever that we shall soon be again at war with that country. Instead of wasting the credit and resources of this State in this chimerical project, we ought to employ all our revenue and all our credit in preparation for war."

"Do you really think so, sir?" asked Chancellor Kent, who was much more strongly opposed to war than he was to the Erie Canal.

"I do," replied the Vice-President. "Depend upon it. England will never forgive us our victories. Take my word for it, we shall have another war within two years."

Chancellor Kent rose to his feet, a determined set to his jaw.

"Gentlemen," he said, "if we must choose between the canal and war, I am in favor of the canal!"

So it happened that on April 15, 1817, after decades of dreaming and years of planning, the building of the Erie Canal at last was approved.

CHAPTER VI

ROME: THE BEGINNING

On July 4, 1817, in the bright early morning sunlight, a group of quietly jubilant men in formal frock coats and silk hats gathered in a level meadow on the outskirts of Rome, New York, and opened a new era in American history.

Perhaps not everyone who participated in the brief ceremony that took place there at the western end of the Mohawk Valley that morning was fully aware of the significance of it all, but some of them knew it instinctively. Standing there among the yellow buttercups and the purple clover and the sweet-smelling grass, still moist with morning, the perceptive ones must have looked about them at the lovely pastoral setting and known that this was the time and the place of commitment.

The remarks of the spokesman of the New York State Canal Commission, Colonel Samuel Young, were spoken in a low voice that conveyed, nevertheless, a sense of excitement. He spoke only briefly. Somebody later counted the words and passed the total along to be entered in the records: 163 words. Of these, the most thrilling and the most important were the last ones:

"Let us then proceed with the work," concluded Colonel Young, handing a spade to the contractor.

It was not by accident that the beginning of the canal construction took place on the Fourth of July. De Witt Clinton and his friends had a fierce awareness of history, and the young nation had no date more hallowed in the historic sense than the anniversary of the Declaration of Independence. If the Erie Canal proved to be all that its sponsors hoped it would be, it too would further American independence.

The foe facing the canal builders was an alliance of natural adversaries —land and distance, hills and valleys, rain and sunshine, heat and cold, forests and swamps. To win over all these would take a mighty effort, but it had to be.

An event almost as essential to the success of the Erie Canal as the actual groundbreaking took place just a few days before the Rome ceremony, and it made the first week in July, altogether, the happiest week that any of the canal partisans could have hoped for. It was the elevation of De Witt Clinton to the governorship of New York, filling the seat left vacant by the election the previous November of Daniel Tompkins to the vice-presidency.

Some political strategists, led by Van Buren, had contended that Tompkins was entitled to serve as Vice-President of the United States and governor of New York concurrently—at least, until his term as governor expired in 1819. Dual service in public office was common; Van Buren himself was both a state senator and the attorney general of the state. Tompkins might have gotten away with this bold extension of the dual-office tradition if he had allowed Van Buren, the toughest of political infighters, to carry the battle to a conclusion. But Tompkins either had no heart for the fray or no wish for the dual role itself. He resigned as governor. Clinton was named governor in a nominating convention, defeating General Porter, and assumed the office on July 1.

One of the many embarrassments that would confront the builders of the Erie Canal during its period of construction came to light at the very beginning. It was the inability to find trained civil engineers to mastermind the project. The awkward truth was that there weren't any American colleges offering civil engineering degrees. As it turned out, the first real school of civil engineering in America would be the Erie Canal itself.

"Many of the distinctive characteristics of American engineering originated with those Erie Canal engineers," said President Ashbel Welsh of the American Society of Civil Engineers in 1882. "We practice their methods today . . . As a class they wrote little. There were then no engineering papers prepared, and no engineering societies to perpetuate them, if they had been prepared. They were not scientific men, but knew by intuition what other men knew by calculation. What science they had they knew well how to apply to the best advantage. Few men have ever accomplished so much with so little means."

So much knowledge came out of the struggle to build the canal that trained engineers from abroad were drawn to New York State to view the waterway with wonder and admiration, to listen to the ingenious men who were building it against overwhelming odds, and to absorb the lessons that were being taught daily as the project progressed.

Rensselaer Polytechnic Institute in Troy, on the canal route, grew directly out of the great undertaking. So did the civil engineering department of Union College in Schenectady. But in the beginning the field belonged to the non-professionals, notably such extraordinary men as Benjamin Wright, James Geddes, Canvass White, Charles Brodhead, Nathan Roberts, David Bates, and others who rose to the challenge.

The commission, in choosing to begin the canal by building the middle section first, using Rome as the starting point and digging east and west simultaneously, was neither casual nor capricious. It had sound reasons for its decision. Test borings of the ground in the Rome area had come up with soft, workable earth and there were some ninety-four miles of flat terrain between the Seneca River and the Mohawk River at Utica which posed no major problems and offered the possibility of quick progress. This was important, both physically and psychologically. An important consideration for the canal was, of course, an adequate water supply, and the Mohawk offered that. Furthermore, this particular section of canal would be so strategically important in itself when completed that even if the remainder of the canal to the east and to the west were never built, for whatever reason, the middle section would stand as a vital improvement and justification enough in itself for all the work and money expended.

One of the lesser considerations that led to the choice of the middle section for the canal beginning was that Benjamin Wright was a resident of Rome and the adjacent countryside was an area he knew well. Wright's family had moved from Connecticut to Rome when he was a youth of nineteen, and here he had begun his career as a surveyor at a time when the wilderness around Fort Stanwix was being subdivided for sale to venturesome easterners. In a period from 1792 to 1796, Wright had laid out into farms about 500,000 acres of land in Oneida and Oswego counties. Later, when the Western Inland Lock Navigation Company undertook to connect the Mohawk River and Wood Creek by canal near Fort Stanwix, it was Wright who had done the surveying. He also, of course, had surveyed the eastern half of the entire Erie Canal route. Nobody knew this part of America better than Benjamin Wright.

The residents of the region had passed through a very strange and difficult period when the big groundbreaking ceremony was held. They were just beginning to thaw out after one of the most trying years that anybody could remember. For some strange meteorological reason, the year of 1816 had been one of unrelieved cold weather. Winter had lasted all summer long.

One Storrs Barrows, an amateur meteorologist who was on hand to observe that phenomenal year, kept a careful, chilling diary of what had happened. The year had begun naturally enough. April, in its early weeks, had been positively balmy. But then the weather had turned cold and had gotten steadily worse as the weeks wore on. Barrows recorded the grim facts in his diary:

"May—Oh! How chilly. Buds and fruit were frozen. The 18th day Col. Hicks planted his corn the second time with an overcoat and mittens on. Corn was planted and replanted until anticipations of a crop were no more.

"June—Our latitude is N. 33 degrees 10 minutes. This was the coldest June ever known in this latitude. The 28th day Charles Gouge and John Younglove were chopping a hemlock tree some three feet in diameter; at the heart of that tree they found ice. There was a sprinkling of snow on the 25th.

"Snow fell to the depth of six inches in Maine on the 22d day of July. There was frost and ice on the 4th. Indian corn was nearly all destroyed. There was not one sound ear in Oneida County. We had to depend on seed corn raised in 1815 for the spring of 1817. It was worth six dollars a bushel.

"August, if possible, was more disagreeable and cheerless than the summer months already gone. The 16th ice was formed as thick as window glass. Almost every green vegetable was destroyed.

"September—From the 5th to the 19th was the mildest weather of the season. After that to the 30th was very cold. The mercury was down to 28 degrees. For a number of nights it fell below the freezing point."

Altogether, summarized Barrows, "it was a cold year. Frost in every month. Old Sol refused to give his accustomed warmth during the summer. The price of grain was very high—wheat flour $16 per hundred. Many a person went to bed supperless. I know whereof I affirm."

But now it was 1817, a fresh summer and a fresh start for everything. The weather had returned to its normal pattern. The springtime had been mild and the summertime, thus far, had been warm and favorable to growing things. The fields gave great promise of future harvest and the woods had never smelled more fragrant than they did on the morning that the canal was begun.

No roll of drums said so, but it was the end of the wilderness in New York State that morning. Civilization would ride the canal. All through that summer of 1817 man set about the job of changing the natural environment to suit his ends. Hundreds of men tore at the shrubs and the trees, hacking and slashing, clearing the way. Stakes first went into the torn-up ground along the path of canal—outer rows of stakes that were sixty feet apart to set off the land that was to be grubbed, or cleared of brush, and then an inner row of stakes forty feet apart to mark the precise width of the canal itself.

Behind the stake-setting crews and the soil-boring teams, who bored to a depth of twelve feet to ascertain the nature of soil, came the heavy workers, the real shock troops, who faced the job of clearing the sixty-foot-wide path of its giant trees, pulling out the root systems, topping the hillocks, filling the depressions and digging the ditch, building embankments.

Problems cropped up immediately, the first being the tall trees. Until a fairly quick, efficient way to topple them could be devised, there was little hope of meeting the tight canal construction schedule. Yankee ingenuity, fortunately, was neither a myth nor a folk legend. It was a genuine talent for improvisation, and it revealed itself brilliantly in this situation. The machine that was devised to remove trees from the path was relatively small and simple. It consisted of an endless screw connected with a roller, cable, and crank, and it applied the principles of both screw and lever. The cable would be secured to the treetop. As the crank was turned, the cable wound itself around the roller until such pressure was exerted that the tree was pulled down.

Removing the root system of the tree was more of a problem, but this too was met and solved with dispatch. A machine was invented that yanked the stump and most of its root system out so neatly that the grandfather of Samuel Hopkins Adams, who operated one of the stump-pullers, recalled once that, with his work gang of seven laborers and four horses, he could extract forty large tree stumps from the ground each day. It was a giant machine with wheels sixteen feet in diameter and with an axle twenty inches in diameter and thirty feet long. Mounted on the axle, midway, was a drum fourteen feet in diameter. A cable was fastened on to the stump. A team of horses or oxen was hitched to a rope that encircled the central drum, and as they turned the drum, the cable was drawn in and the stump was pulled easily from the ground.

Grubbing out the underbrush was not so difficult, but it was time consuming until somebody attached cutting blades to a cast-iron plow, which sheared its way through the roots of shrubs and bushes in half the time. Even as simple and as efficient an instrument as the wheelbarrow was redesigned to fit the needs of the canal construction workers. Jeremiah Brainard of Rome invented a wheelbarrow in which bottom and sides were made of a single board bent to semicircular shape. The advantage of the Brainard design was that the wheelbarrow was lighter, more durable, and much easier to unload.

Each new day seemed to bring with it a new crisis as the inexperienced workers and contractors grappled with one problem after another. Somehow they managed to muddle through, but now and then there arose a crisis that promised to bring the entire project to an ignominious end. Meeting the demand for a cement that would harden underwater—hydraulic cement—was such a problem.

The canal locks had to be built of stone blocks because wooden locks would deteriorate too quickly underwater. This meant that hydraulic cement would have to be employed, but the only source of hydraulic cement was Europe, and as it would be needed in huge quantities, the logistical problem of hauling the special cement across the ocean and into the frontier country was staggering. Even more to the point, the expense would be unbearable.

That was the dark, perplexing situation when Canvass White, an assistant engineer on the canal, returned from a remarkable field trip to Europe. White, a native New Yorker, born in Oneida County, was a protégé of Benjamin Wright. In autumn 1817 Wright sent him to Europe with specific instructions to inspect the canal systems, get some modern surveying instruments, and otherwise absorb such knowledge as would prove helpful in the building of the Erie.

With a zeal that few men would be capable of summoning, White not only inspected the canals of Great Britain first hand, he walked 2,000 miles on the towpaths of the system that laced England and Scotland, making sketches and detailed drawings of locks and construction methods all along the way. He came back with a portfolio bulging with invaluable data and sketches. But the joy over his return was diluted by the air of gloom that had been generated by the hydraulic cement crisis.

White, buoyed by the optimism of youth and confidence in his own ability, refused to be depressed and set about, instead, on a search for the solution. He found the answer right in the path of the canal, at a place near Chittenango in Madison County. There a lime rock deposit with unusual properties intrigued White. With the help of a Dr. Barto, "a scientific gentleman from Herkimer County," and a memorable experiment in Elisha Carey's barroom, White, using the local limestone, was able to make a hydraulic cement that was judged to be as good as any produced in Europe, perhaps better. And it was right at hand.

There is a rather unhappy footnote to this particular development, the sort of footnote that has won history a reputation for repeating itself. While Canvass White's discovery of a good waterproof cement was a rare piece of good luck for New York State and the builders of the Grand Canal, it didn't net White himself much more than a public commendation and a pat on the back from his superiors. He generously permitted contractors to use his discovery generally for all masonry work on the canal on the strength of a promise by the canal commissioners that he would receive just compensation for his wonderful product.

That promise never was redeemed. Although some half-million bushels of the special cement were said to have been used in the Erie work, White received no extra compensation. A measure supported by the governor and the canal commission would have paid him $10,000 some years later, but the bill was defeated by the legislature. Even the private manufacturers failed to pay White the royalties due him.

The Canal Commission followed an unusual plan in letting out contracts for the work. Individuals were invited to make sealed bids for the construction of sections of the canal as short as one fourth of a mile. Each of these bidders had to agree to furnish their own tools and hire their own labor. Funds were advanced to successful bidders under bond to enable them to buy teams of horses and such equipment and supplies as might be needed.

What the commission had in mind was providing an extra source of work and income for farmers and their hired hands along the route of construction. Labor was not plentiful in that frontier country, which still was so remote that there was not even a stage service connecting Buffalo to Albany, a country that was particularly low in population and the creature comforts west of Utica. The farmer-contractor system, it was thought, would have the doubly beneficial effect of dipping into the farm labor supply and of plowing some of the canal money back into the counties through which it passed.

More than fifty contractors were involved in work on the first fifty-eight miles of work authorized by the commission. Their laborers were paid anywhere from 37½ cents to 50 cents a day. Even that minimal pay scale left many of the contractors with only a marginal profit, and where the contractor-farmer himself was inefficient or his help not satisfactorily productive, there was no profit at all.

While the system was used, it did have the fringe benefit of inspiring some more interesting mechanical aids and more efficient methods of construction. The conventional approach to excavation used in the beginning, for example, called for men to dig up the earth with spades and for wheelbarrows to carry away the dirt. Some of the farmers decided that a better system would be to use a horse-drawn plow to break the ground and then have a scraper pull the broken earth off to the side. Using that method, it was found that three men, aided by horses or oxen, could excavate a mile of canal in a season. As a kind of bonus, the hoofs of the horses pulling the plows and scrapers back and forth helped to solidify the side embankments, which was much to be desired.

The Canal Commission's luck in finding a solution to the hydraulic limestone crisis was duplicated in its discovery near the canal route of a muck called the "blue mud of the meadows," which proved highly effective in preventing water seepage when applied to the lining of the canal.

That first summer of work on the Erie Canal was, in the main, one of testing of methods and tools, of improvisation and invention, of grappling with problems that could not have been foreseen, and generally shaping the construction machinery. It was a trying time in every sense of the word. The effort sputtered, lurched, and stalled occasionally, but the commissioners and engineers who nervously hovered over the project probably exulted privately that the beginning was not more disastrous.

By the end of the first year, 1817, which represented only about six months of actual work, some fifty-eight miles of the waterway were under contract. Approximately fifteen miles had been completed and it could be said that the canal, after years of talking and planning, really was underway.

CHAPTER VII

THE MEN WHO DUG THE DREAM

Even though there was something wonderfully democratic in the idea of having the canal built by farmer-contractors and their field hands, with neighbor competing against neighbor in the best tradition of rugged American individualism, there were flaws inherent in the scheme and they stood out rather clearly before the end of the first construction season.

First, there was a terrible inconsistency to the work pattern that nettled the engineers and planners no end. With different contractors and different laboring crews at work every mile or so, each following his own tempo and technique, with some progressing efficiently and some moving at a painfully slow pace, the over-all construction pattern necessarily featured a good deal of confusion. It was recognized in a short time that what was needed in the fight to build the canal was what any successful army has to have when it is marching—a uniformity of attack procedure, a common rhythm, a matching cadence, the ability to act and to move as a unit.

Even if the farmers and their field hands had had the necessary disciplines, there still would have been the awkward fact that the canal job was only a sideline to them, a choice bit of moonlighting, and that their fields, their crops, and their animals enjoyed the priority of their time and attention. When the harvest moon was on the rise and the crops had to be gathered in, nearly all work on the canal had to cease. The construction season, of necessity, had to be a limited one.

Finally, there was the unfortunate fact that no matter how long the work on the Erie continued, the troops in the front line of construction—the trench that had to be dug 363 miles across the state—would always be inexperienced rookies. As the canal moved along, new farmer-contractors and new laborers would continually be moving into the ranks, replacing the ones who had completed their brief tours of duty. Without any continuity of work force, there never would be any accumulation of the experience so vitally necessary to real efficiency and accomplishment.

The system, in brief, was terribly wasteful of human resources. While it might be all right to supplement an army of regular, professional workers with a number of farmer-reserves, there simply had to be a standing force of shock troops to lead the battle. But where were they to be recruited? The canal was being built through a country that had no more than a token population—a few frontier farmers, some fur trappers, some loggers, some hunters. It was an understatement to say that laborers were in short supply—especially for the types of jobs the canal offered. About the best that could be said for the work was that it was backbreaking, and as backbreaking employment goes, it was not even unusually remunerative. The prospect of working from sunup to sundown, wielding a shovel or pick or trundling a heavy wheelbarrow, for fifty cents a day or less, somehow failed to bring a lot of ambitious young Americans on the run to the hiring shanty.

An attempt was made to recruit some of the former slaves who had gained their freedom and moved North, but there weren't enough of them and few found the work to their liking.

Fortune made the appearance of the Irish in the canal drama inevitable. The cast of characters desperately needed hungry laborers to do the hard work. That the response was a bravura, tour de force performance was entirely in keeping with all the other extraordinary aspects of the show.

The mass migration of the Irish to America had begun early. While it did not reach peak volume until shortly after the terrible potato famine in Ireland of the 1840s, it was significant in its size long before that period. The first official government census of 1790 counted among its citizenry some 44,000 persons of Irish birth, more than half of whom lived south of Pennsylvania. (America's population was approximately four million at this time.) As far back as 1654 cries for a curb to Irish immigration were heard when the ship *Goodfellow* arrived in Boston with 400 passengers from Ireland.

It is estimated that by the early 1800s approximately 10,000 persons every year were leaving Ireland for a new life in the New World. That average jumped to 20,000 a year between 1825 and 1830 and kept increasing in the years that followed until the peak mark was reached in 1851. A record total of 216,000 Irish fled to the United States in that mid-century year.

What made the Irish uniquely eligible for jobs as laborers on the Erie Canal was that their low social estate in America made them grateful for any kind of work at all. It is said that they were the first people in this country to be tagged as "foreigners"—even at that early date when hardly a family could trace residence in the United States back more than one or two generations, and when, in fact, almost every other person was a foreigner.

The Irish, nevertheless, were looked upon as an inferior breed and they quickly became familiar with segregation and discrimination. It was an especially virulent form of discrimination, one that extended to employment as well as to the usual social exclusion. Advertisements in newspapers frequently specified "Irish Need Not Apply."

The Irish colonies in Boston, New York, and Philadelphia were large and worrisome to the authorities and to the white, Anglo-Saxon, Protestant establishment of the day. The arriving ships, meanwhile, were bringing thousands more of the rough-cut, bewildered Irish immigrants each year to complicate further the growing problem. The cold, unwelcoming attitude of the native population and the natural magnetic pull of like nationality and like culture in a strange land drew the newcomers into the already crowded Irish neighborhoods, giving America its first introduction to European-type ghettos. They were slum areas, in the main, natural breeding grounds for crime and violence, which further turned the communities against the Irish newcomers. Only a part of the problem was the Irish talent for putting away the poteen and brawling, but it was a conspicuously offensive part of the over-all picture. The drunk tanks in all the city jails resounded with the rich overtones of the brogue.

In that Irish population, made up of people desperate for work, social acceptance, and a chance to prove themselves in the New World, there was a labor pool of great depth and talent waiting to be tapped. The English, in building their canal system, had turned to Irish laborers to get the job done as economically as possible, and the Irish still were employed in canal maintenance work in England. Even the Erie Canal had felt the Irish influence already at a high level. Robert Fulton, son of poor Irish parents, had been an outspoken proponent of the Grand Canal. Christopher Colles, one of the early advocates and planners of the Erie, had been director of navigation on the River Shannon in Ireland before migrating to America in 1766. De Witt Clinton himself, of course, had an Irish grandmother.

It was Canvass White who led the campaign to recruit Irish laborers as part of a permanent work force on the canal, although in this idea he had the support of others, including Governor Clinton. White, while in England on his canal inspection tour in late 1817 and early 1818, had become acquainted with an experienced canal construction engineer named J. J. McShane, an Irishman from Tipperary, who was engaged in maintenance of the Trent-Mersey, Ellesmere, and Bridgewater canals. White persuaded McShane and his crew of experienced canal maintenance men to come to America and take up jobs on the Erie construction project. Then he set about the task of recruiting a force of Irish laborers to work under McShane's direction.

A treasury of idle manpower already resided in New York jails, unproductive, non-paying guests of the state, victims of their own alcoholic appetites and the social milieu that scorned them and kept them on the outer fringe of society. Governor Clinton, in a gesture that was a mixture of compassion and good sense, agreed to pardon those Irish prisoners convicted on minor charges who would agree to work on the Erie for the duration of their unexpired sentences. The terms were that the erstwhile prisoners would receive standard, prevailing wage rates for the jobs to which they were assigned. Any who might renege on the agreement by attempting to escape would be returned to prison upon recapture and would have to serve their original terms of imprisonment from the beginning.

The principal source of Irish labor was in the cities, and when the call went out, hundreds of brawny, strapping young men responded willingly and were hustled into the front line in 1818—a time when that part of the canal which had been under construction since the previous July looked, in the words of one historian, "like a dotted line of poorly dug, unfinished ditches." In Albany, meanwhile, Martin Van Buren's political machine, known as "The Regency," was eyeing the unhappy canal state of affairs with a speculative eye, considering it as an issue that very well could redound to Van Buren's advantage.

The rivalry between Van Buren and Clinton for political supremacy in New York State was very keen, and every skirmish on home ground was but the buildup for the eventual battle—a future fight for the presidency of the United States. Everything pointed toward 1825 as the presidential target year for the two leading candidates from New York State. James Monroe had been elected President in 1816, and it seemed certain he would win a second term, holding the nation's highest office until 1825.

It was essential to Clinton's candidacy that the Erie Canal be completed and in successful operation by 1825 if he were to capitalize on the most publicized single undertaking in the country in his bid for the White House. Van Buren definitely was running second to Clinton in the popularity sweepstakes, but the Fox of Kinderhook was shrewd enough not to fight Clinton's Ditch—not at the moment, anyway, because he was well aware how extensively it had captured the public imagination. Van Buren, like all good politicians, knew the importance of timing.

The Van Buren strategy in the first full year of canal construction, 1818, was one of watchful waiting, of stalking Clinton while holding on to office as attorney general of the state, even though Clinton was governor. Not until 1819 was Van Buren removed from his high position in the state government.

But if the political opponents of Clinton, led by Van Buren and Tammany Hall, were holding back and waiting for the strategic moment to strike at the governor, not all of the electorate were content to follow such subtle, restrained tactics. The Erie Canal and Clinton both were subjects of controversy, and one of the popular chants of the day among members of the anti-Clinton faction was

> Clinton, the federal son-of-a-bitch,
> Taxes our dollars to build him a ditch!

That lilting refrain, incidentally, was terribly unfair to the governor. His system of canal financing was very easy on the general taxpaying public. Clinton had fought off all plans to invite private financing and control of the canal, insisting that it must be a state project completely. Van Buren joined him in insisting that the general credit of the state must be pledged for the redemption of loans and that a special fund, reserved for this use only, should be set up and vested in the control of a canal board.

Clinton proposed a tax of 12½ cents on each bushel of salt manufactured in the western part of the state to be earmarked for the canal fund, and to this was added income from duties upon all auction sales in the state, a tax on steamship passengers and certain lotteries, plus the money realized from the sale of the property of the old canal navigation companies which had been taken over by the state.

Those revenue provisions were more than adequate to take care of the obligations assumed. The salt duties alone added up to very large sums of money, and to the treasury soon would be added tolls from the canal itself. The income derived from the several sources by the canal board proved to be more than enough to pay off the interest, and ultimately the principal, of the loans subscribed to finance the Erie by individuals, banks, and investment houses at home and abroad.

One of the beneficial side results of the Erie Canal undertaking was that it improved the international standing of the United States as a reliable, profitable place for foreign investors to put their money. At the same time, of course, it heightened the prominence of De Witt Clinton's name in Europe—a fact that did not escape the attention of the highest political councils in New York and Washington.

From this point on, high political stakes depended on the success or failure of the canal construction effort. If the preliminary estimates of cost or the preliminary judgments of construction time proved to be in error, Clinton and his confreres would pay heavily through their public careers.

The self-made engineers in charge of the Erie construction, their independent farmer-contractors, and the unskilled Irish immigrant laborers unwittingly held the power to influence the political future. They were the ones who had to take the job handed to them out of the conjectural stage and bring it to reality, staying all the while within the framework of time and money laid down by the theoreticians and dreamers.

The turning point in the faltering campaign came early with the beginning of mass employment of the Irish. A canal expert, Lionel D. Wyld of the University of Buffalo, put it this way in his book *Low Bridge!*:

"The Irish have come in for perhaps more than their share of the ribbing of foofoos (non-native workers on the canal), on the canal as well as off it, but they were, by and large, well respected as the backbone of canal construction. Imported largely to serve as laborers, the Irish proved to be the greatest of boons to the digging of the Ditch. They turned 'Clinton's Folly' into the Grand Western Canal. Few people could stand the conditions which the Irish laborers tolerated. Local inhabitants, Pennsylvania Dutch, and Negroes from the South were all tried, but the Irish bogtrotters proved always the best of the lot. They had stamina and they had grit. Some of the Irish, like Paddy Ryan of prizefighting fame, made names for themselves after they left the canal behind; but the bulk of the Irish made their contribution as diggers and construction help. And, among their other qualities, they had a sense of humor . . ."

Hiring agents for the contractors were at the ship docks in New York in the spring of 1818 and many of the incoming Irish hardly had put foot on American soil before they found themselves on their way up the Hudson by sloop toward the interior and their jobs on the canal.

"The country at the end of the voyage was rougher than anything the men had known in Ireland," wrote Samuel Hopkins Adams. "Owl and wildcat music in the woods kept them awake and scared at night. The first time a snake came into camp, the whole lot nearly deserted. There are no snakes in Ireland. They thought this one was the devil.

" 'Wild Irish,' the upstate folk called them. They looked it, and the language they spoke was strange to American ears. Frightened farmers got out their 'scatterguns' and stood nightly guard over their homes.

" 'Mohawks and Senecas we have survived,' an Oneida County housewife wrote my grandmother, 'but these strange folk look fitter for crime than for honest work. I misdoubt that we shall find ourselves murdered in our beds one fine morning.'

"Grandma's correspondent was wrong. The Irish proved to be a law-abiding lot so far as their neighbors were concerned. If they fought among themselves of a Saturday night, that was their business. When it came to digging, they set a pace that made the Americans blink."

The truth was that the Irish diggers were mostly trying to make the best of things in the new land. The role of laborer actually was a strange one to most of them. The Irish at home had been farmers and field workers. Their roots were in agriculture as they still are to this day on their home island. But in the New World, fighting for a survival that no longer was possible at home, they had to adapt to the new role. They were glad to get the work and the wages offered. The pay of 37½ cents to 50 cents a day was not overly generous for the work demanded, perhaps, but the Irish laborers knew that a day's wages back home averaged about a dime. Besides, really industrious men could make even more money than the set daily wage. They could, if they wished, elect to be paid not by the day, but by the amount of dirt they were able to excavate each day.

Working teams, which numbered three men, would be paid 12½ cents per cubic yard of dirt. One team of Irishmen dug out three rods of canal in 5½ days, a total of 250 cubic yards of dirt! The Canal Commission, noting the achievement in its report, marveled that the pay earned by the men in that particular team came to "the very liberal wage of $1.88 per day."

Once the sluice gates were lifted and the green tide began to rush into Clinton's Ditch, there was no stopping the surge of Irish workers. Before the construction season of 1818 ended, some 3,000 sons of Erin were at work on the canal, and their work was producing gratifying results. Simply having permanent work crews, experienced and knowledgeable, would account for much of the headway and the stepped-up pace of construction that was apparent. But there also was a spirit to these workmen that couldn't be overlooked as a morale-lifting factor. Whether it was simply in their burning desire to make good and climb a rung or two in the social ladder of the New World, or just a basic craving for the kind of subsistence that the canal job could give them, or a conscientious determination to return honest effort for honest pay, there is no telling. No doubt many motives were intermingled, but it is a fact that once the Irish work crews took over, the canal began to take form at an accelerated pace.

"When the Irish began to pick up the pickaxes and shovels most of the Americans were glad to put down, the singing started," wrote Codman Hislop in *The Mohawk*. "Before the towpath songs there were the diggers' songs, full of nostalgia for an Ireland few of the singers ever saw again. Paddy's song came early, a Paddy who arrived in Philadelphia but couldn't stand the place and moved on to New York:

> When I came to this wonderful empire,
> It filled me with the greatest surprise
> To see such a great undertaking,
> On the like I ne'r opened my eyes.
>
> To see a full thousand brave fellows
> At work among mountains so tall
> To dig through the valleys so level,
> Through rocks for to cut a canal.
>
> So fare you well, father and mother,
> Likewise to old Ireland, too,
> So fare you well, sister and brother,
> So kindly I'll bid you adieu.

One of the important fringe benefits of the canal laboring job was an institution called "grog time." It was as much a part of the working day as the coffee break is today in the offices and factories of modern America. In every canal section under construction there was a boy whose inspiring title was "jigger boss." It was his job to carry a ration of whiskey up and down the line at set intervals. The amount given to each worker varied from section to section, job to job. Sometimes it came to as much as a half gill of the spirits to each workman sixteen times a day. If that maximum dosage seems like a lot of whiskey, it is—one quart of whiskey per man per day, enough alcohol, ordinarily, to keep a man moderately fried, if not boiled. But it wasn't that way. Either the alcohol evaporated as it was ingested by the steaming hot diggers or it was carried off quickly in the torrents of sweat that poured from their bodies. The usual ration was much smaller, anyway, and the jiggers were spaced over a long period from sunup to sundown—a twelve- to fourteen-hour day—and the whiskey served more to revive the men than to intoxicate them. The canal contractors apparently went on the enlightened theory that whiskey does have medicinal properties and, in proper dosages, remarkable restorative powers. The medicinal effect on the Erie workers was most gratifying, at any rate, so much so that some onlookers claimed it was the marginal influence that kept the men going—the stuff of survival, so to speak, especially to men who had been bogged down all day in the swamplands or who had been digging the baked ground under a burning summer sun for long hours at a time. Perhaps it was.

CHAPTER VIII

DEATH AND THE DITCH

By late 1818 work on the canal had progressed to the edge of the forbidding Montezuma swampland, west of Syracuse, acknowledged to be the most difficult part of the middle section. Travelers on the New York Thruway today pass the edge of the marsh, a wildlife refuge, and even at the blurring effect of eighty miles per hour, the desolate nature of the area presents itself in the gray, lifeless look, in the profile of dead trees, and occasionally in the smell of stagnant water.

Montezuma is grim country still, but much more then than now. It was a place avoided by Indians and white men alike, a dank and fetid wasteland so saturated with water that the laborers who undertook to build the canal often had to work in water up to their chests. It bore the name also of the Cayuga Marsh because it is the watery tapering off of Cayuga Lake, neither land nor water but, as Canvass White described the area, "a streaky and unpleasant mixture of both."

There was more than discomfort awaiting the workmen who sloughed their way into the muck and mire of Montezuma. There also was death. It was carried on the wings of the female Anopheles mosquito whose bite could cause malaria.

The Cayuga Indians, noting the reckless path of the canal forces, predicted that "great sickness" would come to the men working in the swamp and they proved to be tragically accurate. Malaria and pneumonia took their toll. Men of all nationalities and backgrounds were counted among the victims, impartially, even though some historians since have taken the untenable stand that the Irish laborers somehow were better able to endure the rigors of the swamp than their fellow workers—as if they enjoyed a special kind of immunity to the swamp sicknesses.

It is an unreasonable belief, unsupported by fact. A more likely possibility is that the Irish laborers, products of a poor potato diet and decades of general malnutrition, were hit harder by the swamp conditions than the others. Neither their regular rations of whiskey nor their own determination were protection enough for the Irish against the generally debilitating effects of the swampland. They toppled over like all the other men, of all nationalities, who were exposed to the mosquitoes and the dampness; how many is not known.

"Men died like flies when the canal line approached the swampy valley of the Seneca," wrote Robert Payne in *The Canal Builders*. But the Canal Commission did not issue a casualty toll. If it had, the Montezuma Swamp probably would have been enough of a disaster area to horrify the country.

Alvin F. Harlow wrote in *Old Towpaths:* "In the summer of 1819 a thousand men were incapacitated in that district [the swamp] between July and October by malaria, ague and bilious and typhus fevers, and many of them died."

In midsummer, according to an account by Samuel Hopkins Adams, the mosquitoes "fell upon the diggers in hordes. The men came in with eyes swollen almost shut and hands so poisoned that they could hardly wield their tools." Not much of a defense was a device called the "Montezuma necklace"—a smudge-bucket packed with twigs and damp leaves which, when lighted, gave off a heavy, smoldering smoke. This was supposed to drive off the mosquitoes, and perhaps it did to an extent, but it also choked the man who hung it around his neck.

Adams recalled the scenes of sickness and death that had greeted his grandfather on his visits to camps in the marsh during the canal construction period.

"The first bunkhouse that he visited on his horse was silent except for the chattering teeth of those whose chills were upon them, and the muttering of the delirious. Grandfather said to a man who was sitting on the edge of his bunk with his head between his hands:

"'Where's your boss?'

"'Outside,' the man replied.

"'There's no one outside but a dead man,' said Grandfather.

"'That's him.'

"'Aren't you going to bury him?' Grandfather asked, shocked.

"'Ain't a man here could lift him. All the able ones ran away.'"

At another camp the men were suffering not only from malaria but food poisoning as well. There the camp doctor told Adams's grandfather: "Most of 'em have this Montezuma Fever, too, and three of 'em are likely to die. The Irish have no resistance to the shakes."

The doctor's usual treatment of the malaria-infected men was to bleed them, after which he administered feverwort, snakeroot, green pigweed, and "Seneca oil"—the last being plain kerosene—and something called "Jesuit's bark" from Peru, which was producing good results. This, as it turned out, was a crude form of quinine.

70

So many men died in the swamp that a lot of the workers panicked and fled. Hiring manpower to complete the section became a serious problem, especially as word of the dread conditions spread. There was even a rumor current that fumes released by the digging, given the name of "effluvia miasmatica," was spreading poison through the land and inevitably would claim a large toll among the innocent bystanders. Detractors of Clinton began to call the project "Clinton's Folly," and the canal fever was called "De Witt's Disease." Nevertheless, the work went on and the work force grew in spite of the casualties. It has been estimated that between 2,000 and 3,000 men and 700 horses were employed in the construction of this first section of the canal in the summers of 1818 and 1819.

As bad as it was, the casualty toll in this troubled section probably was less than that which was counted later in the construction of the Chesapeake and Ohio Canal, a waterway built in the 1830s from the Potomac River to the Maryland coal mines. In 1833 cholera struck the crews digging the canal—again mostly Irish and including a lot of men who had worked on the Erie Canal—and hundreds of them died. Their companions panicked at the sight of so many falling by the canalside, dying in the fields, and lying stricken in the rude shanties, and there was a wave of desertions. For many of those who tried to escape the dread disease, though, it was too late to flee. Men collapsed and died miles away from the canal path. Disposal of the bodies of the victims became such a critical problem that the board of directors of the canal construction company authorized its engineers "to use any waste ground owned by the company for the interment of persons dying upon the works of the company."

Those who were struck down and who died on the construction line of the Erie were buried in the anonymous graves that so often are reserved for heroes. They were buried in the open meadows and in the quiet glens, for there were few cemeteries, as such, on the frontier. The formalities and refinements of civilization hardly existed, either in life or in death, and perhaps it was more appropriate that the men whose lives became forfeit during the building of the Grand Canal should have taken their place, in a quiet matter-of-fact way, with the other rugged men of the wilderness who already had gone to the ground, their work finished. No vertical slabs of stone marked their resting places, either; no chiseled inscriptions memorialized their deeds or gave their bones a name. In time there were not even any about who could remember where the heroes were at rest. Indians and explorers, trappers and hunters, scouts and soldiers, pioneer settlers and venturesome surveyors—and now the canal builders. So many; yet so few.

It took considerable doing, but the difficulties of the swamp eventually were overcome. Cold weather proved to be the greatest factor. It not only eliminated the mosquito problem, but the half-frozen earth was easier to work in than the quicksand and muck of summer. By late 1819 it was apparent that victory was within grasp. It was a turning-point victory that answered scores of questions, resolved doubts, reassured those who had supported the canal concept, and virtually assured authorization for construction of the remaining two sections of the waterway. The middle section was not only the beginning, but the testing ground for all the talk and theory. Its completion, now near, already stood as a vindication of the dreamers who had campaigned for the canal.

Almost two and a half years had passed, and there was a general anxiety to see some part of the canal in operation. The entire ninety-four-mile distance of the canal from Utica on the east to the Seneca River on the west would not be finished until the following summer, but that fact could not be allowed to stand in the way of a proper celebration. The Canal Commission, just as impatient as everyone else, hit on the brilliant plan of opening the canal from Utica to Rome, no great distance but a very important segment in itself and one that would ease the transportation problem more than its short length would indicate.

The inaugural use of the Erie Canal—a happy preview of things to come and the first of many celebrations—took place on October 23, 1819. For the excited spectators who came from miles around to witness the doings, it was one thrilling sight after another. First, of course, there was the important first step of letting the water into the dry canal bed linking the two communities. It had to be proven that the Ditch was capable of the very basic function of being able to hold water. The first gush had an electrifying effect on the spectators.

One of the eye-witnesses that day, an anonymous gentleman who was identified simply as a "Gentleman from Utica," wrote feelingly of the event and of his own sensation as water flowed into the canal bed for the first time. "I consider it," he wrote, "one of the privileges of my life to have been present to witness it.

"On Friday afternoon," he continued, "I walked to the head of the Grand Canal . . . and from one of the slight and airy bridges which crossed it, I had a sight that could not but exhilarate and elevate the mind. The waters were rushing in from the westward and coming down their untried channel toward the sea . . .

"You might see people running across the fields, climbing on trees and fences and crowding the banks of the canal to gaze upon the welcome sight. A boat had prepared at Rome, and as the waters came down the canal, you might mark their progress by that of this new Argo, which floated triumphantly along the Hellespont of the West, accompanied by the shouts of the peasantry, and having on her deck a military band . . . The scene was extremely interesting and highly grateful . . . truly sublime."

The "Argo" was, in fact, a boat named *Chief Engineer of Rome,* and aboard it were Governor De Witt Clinton, his fellow members of the

Canal Commission, the executive engineers, members of the state legislature, and leading citizens of the Rome-Utica area. In all, there were
some fifty notables aboard that first craft to float on the waters of the
Erie Canal, which, incidentally, was towed by a single, anonymous horse.
The name of the boat was struck in honor of Benjamin Wright, who
richly deserved such signal recognition for having masterminded successfully the keystone piece of canal construction.

In the spring of the following year, 1820, the first passenger packet boat,
a giant craft seventy-six feet long and fourteen feet wide, made its way
through the canal westward from Rome all the way to the port of
Syracuse, completing its historic trip on April twenty-first. But the formal
opening of the full middle section of the canal, from Utica to the Seneca
River, was reserved for the third anniversary of the great undertaking—
July fourth. On that date, a procession numbering seventy-three boats,
each carrying a full complement of celebrities including De Witt Clinton
himself, made its way over the shallow waters.

It would be a while before another such opening day celebration would
be staged, but nevertheless the Erie Canal, in part, was in business at
last, and there was money coming in from the toll collections for the first
time. That was the bright side of the picture.

There was another, darker side ahead, however, and it was beginning
to show itself already. It told of trouble in wait—trouble with the next
two sections to the east and to the west, each of which promised major
difficulties, trouble in keeping the canal project from falling victim to the
political expediencies of the time. There was plenty of reason to worry.

CHAPTER IX

SHADOWS AND SUNLIGHT

The personal and political fortunes of De Witt Clinton, like those of his beloved canal, followed a highly uneven course. Together they seemed to move in tandem, through strangely shifting patterns of sunlight and shadow, under inconstant skies. Even when the peaks were bright, the valleys were dark. It was that way to the very end.

Three days before the first shovelful of dirt had been ceremoniously scooped up in the Rome meadow, in 1817, Clinton had been sworn in as governor of New York. That same year the Clintons welcomed their tenth child, a girl, whom they named Julia Catherine. It was a good year, the beginning of good things. The sun shone brightly.

The shadows crowded in the following year. They clouded the future of the canal as inexperienced work crews struggled to master the techniques of the job and fought to level the frontier way. There were problems that seemed beyond solution, and there was pessimism in high places. But Clinton had other problems to harry him—all the questions that a governor has to answer, and more. Most of all, there was the personal question about his wife's well-being. She had been in delicate health, especially after the birth of their latest child, and in the summer of 1818 Clinton took her and the children to green and lovely Staten Island, to vacation where the salt breezes usually blew free and fragrant and where the prospect was one of almost unbroken beauty.

But Staten Island that summer was under attack by swarms of vicious mosquitoes. The offshore breezes ordinarily would have driven them toward the mainland, but it was a strangely listless summer and the air that hung over the island was stagnant. Mrs. Clinton grew sicker and the alarmed governor moved her and the rest of the family to a resort hotel at Mount Vernon, New York. It made no difference. His wife was in her last illness. She died on July 30, 1818, leaving Clinton with seven surviving children, all minors.

Shortly after that tragic happening, the governor, an ardent horseman, fell and injured one of his legs so severely that he never again was able to ride nor to take the long walks that he loved. He could, in time, discard the crutches, but thereafter this tall, statuesque man walked with a pronounced limp—no longer quite so tall and certainly not nearly as statuesque as he had been. A common criticism of Governor Clinton had been that he was too haughty and too aristocratic. Perhaps the limp softened the hard lines of his appearance and brought him closer to the people. It certainly didn't lessen him noticeably in the sight of the eligible women of the day. He married again, less than a year after his first wife died, this time to a socialite named Catharine Jones, member of a prominent New York family.

In the midst of all this personal turmoil De Witt Clinton still had to be alert to the day-to-day maneuverings of the political opposition. If he was to see the Erie Canal successfully through to its completion, holding fast to his power base as governor was important.

Fittingly enough, Clinton's opponent in the gubernatorial election of 1820 was a familiar foe of Clinton and the canal alike—Daniel D. Tompkins, former governor and still, at the time, Vice-President of the United States. He was a formidable opponent, and with him in the lists there was no doubt what the main issues would be. The campaign that followed was a bitter one. All the old factional and sectional hates were raked up, including side allusions impugning Clinton's patriotism. Most of all, the canal was the issue.

The political opposition bore heavily on the fear of things to come, brushing aside the fact that the first stage of the canal had been constructed and already was in successful operation. It wasn't enough that the waterway already had provided great relief to the transportation problem that had existed in the middle miles of upper New York, they went to great pains to point out what the Clinton canal forces had to concede—that the Rome section had been the easiest to build, that the big job was still ahead, and that much trouble was ahead for the builders on either side of the completed section. The Tompkins forces were graphic in their description of forthcoming physical and financial disaster. All the pent-up problems and expenses of the canal project, they promised, were about to burst through and turn the enterprise into a debacle.

The election was a squeaker. Clinton won by fewer than 1,500 votes out of some 180,000 cast. It was a victory, but hardly one that could be interpreted as a heartwarming vote of confidence. And there remained still another campaign that had to be fought and won—the push for legislative authorization for construction of the two other sections of canal. There was a struggle, but the approval finally was won. The full project was assured; or so it seemed.

Tammany Hall, representing a large number of New York City merchants who still were not convinced that an Erie Canal would be anything but a deleterious influence on the city's position of strength, refused to concede defeat even after the work had been started on both the eastward and westward sections. They came up with the proposal that the westward progress of the canal be halted at Rochester and that canal traffic at the point be connected, via the Genesee River or Canal, to Lake Ontario to the north. It was virtually the same argument that had been advanced in former years to turn the canal into Lake Ontario at Oswego, and it was quickly brushed aside for the same sound reason, that any such routing simply would divert commerce from the American West to Montreal and the St. Lawrence River passage to the ocean. Eastbound cargo ships would not likely take the inland canal route, by way of Rochester, when they could go to Montreal or down the St. Lawrence to the Atlantic more easily.

The canal opposition forces then came up with yet another delaying action. It was a proposal that work be stopped on the western branch of the canal, from the Seneca River on, until the eastern section, from Utica to the Hudson River, was finished, and until the northern canal, connecting Lake Champlain with the Hudson, also was completed. The proposals were defeated, probably more through passionate eloquence than rational argument because, in all truth, it did seem as if the canal builders were biting off more than they reasonably could be expected to chew in attempting to build both east and west sections of the canal at the same time.

Perhaps the political furor had a salutary effect simply by acting as a reminder to the construction crews that enemies still stood in the background, ready to attack anytime the canal project should falter.

But the men who were building the Erie had more than enough to worry about without the addition of the political element. Pushing the Erie westward through the Montezuma Swamp had been difficult, but the physical obstacles that stood in the path further west and to the east were even more formidable.

On the eastward route, the canal would have to squeeze through the narrow, mountainous confines of the Mohawk Valley, contending all the while with the vagaries of the undisciplined Mohawk River, respecting its rapids and waterfalls as it coursed through the breached Appalachian barrier and dropped steadily toward tidewater at the Hudson—a fall of more than 400 feet in altitude in approximately 100 miles. The most challenging area in this distance was the narrow, precipitous stretch from Schenectady to Albany, a high-walled gorge that had been cut through the Catskills by the ancient progenitor of the Mohawk, a glacial age drainage river called the Iromohawk. In building the canal through this steep canyon, the strategy, dictated by Canvass White, the engineer in charge, was to shift the canal to the north side of the river by means of an aqueduct and to groove the canal into shelves cut into the towering stone walls. At a place called Crescent, some four miles from the Hudson, the canal would shift back to the south shore by another aqueduct, itself a masterful work measuring 1,188 feet in length. The final connection with the Hudson would not come easily. The Erie, in its spectacular climax, would have to bypass the high Cohoes Falls and take its final steps down to Hudson River level—some 184 feet below. There it would turn south and, with the great river to the left, it would continue another five miles to the big boat basin in Albany.

A profile view of the Erie in its eastern phase, from the summit level at Rome to its terminus at Troy and Albany, shows up like a flight of steps built by a crew of drunken carpenters. But if ever there was a stairway to glory for the rugged builders of early America, this was it.

At the opposite end of the canal, from the Seneca River westward, the engineers were painfully aware of a number of extraordinary problems that had to be solved and of some unusual obstacles that had to be overcome before the canal could be linked successfully with its western terminus. One of the problems, in fact, was determining the location and identity of the ultimate western terminus itself. Even though the canal was headed determinedly toward Lake Erie, nobody knew precisely where it would end. There were two contenders for the honor and profit that presumably would be claimed by the port selected as the westernmost end of the canal. One was Buffalo, a tiny village on Big Buffalo Creek, close to Lake Erie. The other contender was the small community of Black Rock, a few miles to the north, on the Niagara River.

The fierce competition between the two villages was not resolved in Buffalo's favor until 1823, and repercussions from the political infighting were felt long beyond that date.

Among the most challenging of the physical problems that presented themselves to the engineers planning construction to the west of the Seneca River was the deep, wide Irondequoit Valley just east of Rochester. From rim to rim, the valley measured more than 4,950 feet. The original plan to build a high wooden trestle using the ridges as supports was abandoned as impractical. Instead, the engineers joined three natural ridges within the valley with two stone-and-earth embankments—the first 1,320 feet long and 50 feet high; the second, 231 feet in length. The amount of fill required to build the connecting embankments was enormous. The final effect was to carry the canal on a kind of skyway, 76 feet above the valley floor and the Irondequoit brook, which was allowed to follow its normal course, thanks to a stone culvert.

Having leapfrogged successfully over the Irondequoit Valley, the engineers turned to the next challenge, the turbulent Genesee River at Rochester, with a confidence that almost had a suggestion of insouciance. It turned out that the men who designed the Erie Canal were very good at building aqueducts, and in Rochester they sailed the canal over the river on an aqueduct that stood out as one of their most impressive efforts, one which won world-wide attention and admiration.

The Rochester aqueduct was an 802-foot-long structure which was bolted and bound into a single unit and placed on top of eleven stone arches. Each of the arches was 50 feet across. Supporting the arches and the superstructure were heavy, elephantine piers that had to be sunk into the solid bedrock of the temperamental, rough, rapid-flowing river. The end result was something more than an efficient aqueduct, something more than a high-legged platform that would carry the canal across the river. It was a thing of beauty, a sky-borne river, a masterpiece of its genre in which all could share a feeling of pride. When it was completed, in 1823, Rochester became—for a while—the westernmost port on the Grand Canal. And for many of the travelers on the canal, the aqueduct on which their boat floated high over the Genesee River in the final minutes of the trip was the most satisfying sight to be seen on the entire voyage from Schenectady.

By the time the canal reached Rochester, there no longer was any question about the state carrying the project through to its planned completion, no further question about the canal's brilliant future. The aqueduct at Rochester became a symbol. The canal was riding high.

Not as much could be said about the man who was the father of the canal.

The air suddenly had become filled with questions about De Witt Clinton. Even as his famous ditch steadily moved toward successful completion, Clinton's career seemed to lose most of its momentum. As the canal turned into its final triumphant phase, Clinton's political enemies were predicting his downfall. The governor's political power had declined alarmingly following his narrow victory over Vice-President Tompkins in 1820. It was a predictable development. The governor was much too busy attending to his dual duties as chief of state and president of the Canal Commission to keep his political fences mended or to devote the time necessary to fend off the opposition. His chief adversary, Van Buren, was the kind who demanded the full attention and total powers of anybody engaging his steel, and Tammany Hall was a relentless foe, especially effective in the kind of political infighting that had occurred in the early months of Clinton's new term as governor.

It wasn't long before the anti-Clintonians had won control of the powerful state Council of Appointment, thereby reducing considerably Clinton's influence. In addition to the humiliation of seeing his choices removed from appointive office, the governor presently found his executive powers curtailed sharply by a constitutional amendment conceived and passed by his enemies.

When Clinton dispiritedly announced his decision not to run for reelection in the 1822 state campaign, it did not come as any particular surprise. Some of his friends appealed to him to stay in the race, but his party generally accepted his decision without undue protestation. Politics is seldom a sentimental business. De Witt Clinton, for all his glamour as the bearer of the most famous name in the state, and for all the prestige he had won through his years of service, was close to being a political burden in autumn of 1822. Even if he had chosen to run for governor at the time, he probably would have lost.

His successor was Joseph C. Yates, who took office in January 1823. But De Witt Clinton was not allowed automatically to step down to a life of quiet retirement. He still was head of the Canal Commission, no empty ceremonial job, and while the Big Ditch was making commendable progress toward completion, there still were problems to be solved, decisions to be made.

If New York needed further proof that Clinton's involvement in the promotion and construction of the canal was activated by unselfish motives, it came in 1823 as the former governor threw himself full time into the job of guiding the great undertaking in its final stages—a job, incidentally, for which he had refused to accept any remuneration from the very beginning. During many weeks of 1823 he traveled the canal route with other members of the commission, inspecting the work that had been done, conferring with engineers about future projects, discussing problems, and settling minor disputes.

The main issue demanding the attention of the commissioners that year was the official selection of the western terminus of the canal. The rivalry between Buffalo and Black Rock had taken on comic overtones with the shifting back and forth between the rival ports of the engineering experts since 1819, and now even the commission was divided on the issue. Behind the scenes there was fierce lobbying and political maneuvering, with General Peter B. Porter the leader of the Black Rock forces and De Witt Clinton as a champion of the Buffalo group.

A meeting of the Canal Commission was held in Buffalo in June to argue the issue again. The result was a compromise. Buffalo was chosen as the westernmost terminus, but Black Rock was selected as the harbor in which the cargoes and passengers would be transferred between lake ships and canalboats, making it the more important port. The result had to be interpreted as a victory for Clinton's old political foe General Porter. Some observers, coupling the setback with the earlier election loss, were convinced that Clinton's political powers had been so seriously weakened that he was ready for the kill.

What followed, in the early part of 1824, may have been intended as the *coup de grace*. If so, the timing was bad and the aim was poor.

Even as Clinton was pondering new strategy to assert Buffalo as the western terminus in fact as well as name, the shocking news came out of Albany: De Witt Clinton had been ousted from his position as president and member of the Canal Commission by the New York State Legislature!

New York State stood still, in shock, as it tried to assimilate the news and understand it. The equation by that time was too well established and accepted. Clinton equals Canal. Canal equals Clinton. The two were indivisible in their union, coalesced by time and trial into a single entity. And yet the reality of the news was there: The legislature had cut Clinton loose!

New Yorkers were not alone in being stunned or in feeling a mounting sense of outrage over the news. The Erie Canal was no local, provincial undertaking. It had become a national vision—the instrument that promised national unity and growth—and De Witt Clinton stood as a national hero, the giant who towered astride the great project and personified it as nobody else would.

Behind Clinton's dismissal, of course, there had been intrigue, devious maneuvering, and involved political give and take. It was a state assemblyman by the name of Victory Birdseye who began the push that toppled the Colossus of the Canal. It is a puzzle how his name could have become lost in the pages of history, but the facts were these: Birdseye, a representative from Onondaga County, had been given the floor in caucus and suddenly had demanded that Clinton be removed from the Canal Commission. Most of his colleagues apparently were coiled in expectation of the motion, judging from the way they all sprang to approve it. The caucus turned into an anti-Clinton rally, and when its members sent their motion to the floor, it was approved by the overwhelming vote of both houses of the legislature. Only three senators voted against the resolution. Approval of Clinton's dismissal was given by a majority of some thirty votes in the Assembly, and among the "aye" votes, surprisingly, were several from men who ostensibly were political friends of the former governor. But not all of his friends turned their backs on him; one, at least, Senator Cunningham of Montgomery County, spoke passionately in behalf of Clinton and tried to sway the body from its course, but the ouster movement had too much strength to be stopped.

The main parties to the anti-Clinton movement were the long-time Clinton adversaries—the Tammanyites in New York City and the Albany Regency, the anti-Clinton faction in the State Senate led by Van Buren, and the friends and allies of General Porter. In addition there were the New York City representatives and assemblymen from the southern tier counties who had long been opposed to the canal project. All of these, in combine, were able to upset the man who so long had commanded the greatest political power and prestige in the state. But all of them were so intent on their scheme to get Clinton out of the way that they forgot to reckon with the boomerang effect of outraged public sentiment.

The people of New York, once recovered from the initial shock of the legislature's action, immediately rallied to the side of the man who had served them so long and so well. One of Clinton's long-time critics, the editor of the New York *American,* wrote of the ouster: ". . . A more pitiful and contemptible exhibition of impotent malice was never recorded in any legislative annal."

The Rochester *Telegraph*, edited by the political genius Thurlow Weed, denounced the action against Clinton as "a deed which will ever blacken the annals of the State.

"Every contemptible effort to rob Mr. Clinton of his well-earned fame, serves only to identify him still more indissolubly with these great national works. Clinton does 'swim' triumphantly upon his 'big ditch,' where he will continue to 'swim' long after the memory and offenses of his enemies are forgotten and forgiven."

The failure of the New York public to return Clinton to the governorship two years previous clearly had misled most of his enemies. They had mistaken this seeming indifference to his continuation in the office of governor for personal disaffection. The balance of political power simply had swung the other way at the time.

The ouster of Clinton from the Canal Commission was something else again. The state could continue to operate without Clinton at its head, but it was inconceivable that the canal could be built without the great man at the helm. In this non-partisan role he was not viewed as a politician but as a public-spirited, selfless statesman, a quixotic crusader who had tilted against man and nature to lead the state toward the greatest internal improvement in America's history.

The crudity of the legislature in dismissing him from a post of public service out of base political motives angered the people of the state. As fast as the news spread, rallies and demonstrations of protest sprang up, especially in the communities along the line of the canal. The state capital, Albany, was the scene of a huge meeting—"the largest meeting ever held in this city," reported the editor of the Albany *Gazette*, who estimated that "nineteen-twentieths" of the state were aligned on the side of the former governor.

There was irony in the Albany rally. Only a few months before, on September 10, Clinton had ridden as a guest of honor in the first passage of sloops through the lock and dam of the canal at Troy, and on October 8, proudly standing on the deck of the decorated packet bearing his name, he had joined in the celebration attending the opening of the last eastern link of the canal to the Hudson River. He had been guest of honor at a great civic banquet in the state capitol and, as "the hero of the hour," he had led his wife out to dance a cotillion at the great Albany Canal Ball on October 9.

The angry crowd that gathered in Albany's City Hall Park to register its indignation over the shelving of Clinton was said to number more than 10,000 persons. Most of them, no doubt, were painfully aware how recently he had been honored as a hero in their midst. The chairman of the meeting, Colonel William Few, had been a political enemy of Clinton. He now renounced his past position of opposition and publicly proclaimed himself a Clinton supporter because of the legislature's iniquitous behavior.

Even in New York City, where the canal and Clinton alike had been maligned for more than a decade, there were mass rallies in his behalf, and scores of resolutions praising him were sent to the legislature from the state's largest city.

Nothing could have endeared Clinton more to the people of the state and the country than to be attacked by petty politicians. It set him apart from the crowd more than ever, this time in the position of a martyr.

When, a few months later, Clinton received word that his twenty-two-year-old son, James, a sailor, had died at sea of yellow fever, the nation grieved with this big, bent man whose ill fortune seemed to have no end.

There no longer was doubt that De Witt Clinton would be returned to power. His name again was heard in all councils of government as a likely candidate for President, and there was insistent demand for his immediate return to the governorship, even though the Van Buren majority still controlled the state Senate.

Clinton was nominated for governor at Utica in September 1824. He won the election in November by a vote of landslide proportions.

And off in the political wings, keeping track of the mounting Clinton victory that night, was the wise, understanding Martin Van Buren, whose followers, under the leadership of Judge Skinner, had been responsible for ousting Clinton from the Canal Commission in the spring of the year.

"I hope, judge," finally said Van Buren, in a voice filled with asperity, when the results of the election were conclusive, "you are now satisfied that there is such a thing in politics as killing a man too dead!"

It was an astute observation. Clinton's political enemies had been guilty of overkill. Now, thanks to their brutish behavior, he never was more completely alive than he was at the end of that year. The shadows had been dispelled and there was sunshine again.

CHAPTER X

THE MIRACLE OF LOCKPORT

In modern Lockport, in Niagara County, which, fortunately, still looks a lot like ancient Lockport, it is possible to stand in the heart of the downtown district and see the dramatic evidence that tells better than anything else what the Erie Canal was all about.

Lockport, in a real sense, symbolizes the canal.

The canal gave the town its being, its name, its prosperity, its look, and its lore.

The celebrated Big Bridge in the heart of the city is there because the old canal, while changed by time, still passes underneath. It is a most unusual bridge in several respects. It comes by its name deservedly. It has the appearance not of a bridge, but of a very wide thoroughfare, and it is rated almost as much of a civic attraction as the canal itself because it is one of the widest bridges in the world—just a few inches shy of 400 feet. It represented a tremendous achievement when it was built in 1914.

From the Big Bridge you can see such landmarks as the old building of Fire Headquarters House No. 23, Slattery's Restaurant, Jake Stoll's Restaurant, and an eating place simply called The Lox. It would be too much to imagine that the specialty of the house might be bagels, but no matter; the important point is that the name of the restaurant suggests how thoroughly the Erie Canal and its complex lock installation at this site are interwoven in every fiber of this picturesque city.

Before the canal there was nothing on the scene to hint at civilization or to offer hope of future prospects. It was, by all descriptions, a dark, forbidding area, covered mostly with hardwood forests of oak and black walnut trees which were interrupted frequently by sharp stone outcroppings and massive ledges of gray rock. The closest settlers were at a place nearby called Cold Springs. Apart from the wild animals that roamed

85

the woods freely, the principal living inhabitants of the area were, in fact, the rattlesnakes that abounded here, as they did in many areas of northwestern New York. Frontiersmen and Indians alike had such respect for the reptiles that they avoided the area as much as possible.

The chief characteristic of the Lockport site was not its universally gloomy appearance nor its large colony of snakes, but its location atop the Niagara Escarpment, a mighty upthrust of solid rock that had been shoved high above the surrounding terrain by some natural caprice of prehistoric time. It is the same escarpment that was responsible, with the assistance of the Niagara River, for the creation of Niagara Falls, some seventeen miles west of Lockport.

The challenge of the escarpment was the immediate problem that confronted the builders of the Erie Canal at the western end of the waterway. Eastbound boats somehow would have to be lowered from the stony heights down to the level of the countryside almost 70 feet below before they could move on. Conversely, westbound canal craft would have to ascend the heights.

A single lock to take boats up and down was out of the question; even so, the final solution was breathtakingly dramatic. It required the construction of twin flights of locks to accommodate the two-way traffic of the canal, and each flight included a series of five consecutive locks to take the boats up and down the high-rising stone mountain—not precipitously, but gently and gracefully, like a grand dame mincing down the stairway of a great mansion.

The locks, built between 1823 and 1825, were enlarged in 1854 and continued to serve the canal into the early years of the twentieth century. When the Erie was modernized and incorporated into the present New York Barge Canal system between 1909 and 1918, two huge power-operated locks, formally identified as Locks Nos. 34 and 35—were installed at Lockport. One set of the original locks had to be razed to make way for the new facilities, but the other set of historic locks survived and still stands, continuing to serve in a modest way by acting as a spillway for excess water and, more importantly, by providing a splendid reminder of an early American miracle.

The section of the canal that was to run through Niagara County was contracted for by the state early in 1821. Shortly afterwards contractors placed advertisements in New York City newspapers and journals in other cities of the state announcing that a total of 1,200 laborers would be hired to build the Lockport section and that the remuneration would be "Twelve Dollars a month and found." From such reports as are available, it would appear that virtually all of the 1,200 men hired were Irish. A historian of the area, Clarence O. Lewis, estimated that about half of those laborers made Lockport their permanent residence when the job was finished, giving the city an Irish cast that is still discernible.

Lockport was a place to test the mettle of any canal worker, of any nationality:

"The most difficult and expensive section of the canal to be constructed was southwest of the locks, where rock excavation became necessary," wrote Lewis. "And as work progressed southwestward, the necessary rock cut became deeper and deeper, and for about three miles an average depth of the rock cut was from twenty-five to thirty feet. This three miles was the most difficult and costly section of the canal to be excavated . . ."

It was in this area that another shining example of the canal builders' genius for improvisation presented itself. In their initial attempts to drill holes in the rock escarpment, the workers quickly discovered that the five-foot-thick stone simply was too hard for available drills to penetrate. Emergency appeals were sent to New York and Philadelphia, but nowhere could adequate drills be found. The work was approaching a standstill until somebody on the job recalled that there was in Niagara, close by, a man named Botsford who had a high reputation for solving such problems. A call went out to Mr. Botsford and he responded. After examining the stone barrier, he asked for the use of the blacksmith shop and went to work. When he emerged, after some hours, he carried a highly tempered, hardened drill which he handed to one of the Irish laborers.

"Try this," he said.

The historian who raked up this legend then unabashedly quoted the Irish laborer as saying, after close inspection of the new drill: "Be jabers, it won't last a minit!"

Well, be jabers, he was wrong. The drill not only lasted a minute, it worked very well. It penetrated the rock and provided a hole in which coarse black gunpowder could be packed, ignited, and exploded.

There is disagreement on what explosives were available to the canal builders. Some historians say that the rock cut was made only with the help of manpower and gunpowder. Some say that ice power also was used, that is, holes were drilled in midwinter and filled with water that promptly froze and cracked the rock as it expanded, making it easier for the men wielding sledge hammers to make progress. But there also are casual references to the use of "newly-invented Du Pont blasting powder," and there is no question that it was used at Lockport. Gunpowder couldn't have caused the explosions that occurred there.

Whatever it was that the contractors used to blast their way through the stone wall that stood in their path, it not only was effective in clearing the way, but it also helped to make the colony that had sprung up at the Lockport site a more interesting place to live.

The Niagara County Historical Society has an interesting volume of personal recollections of canal construction days dictated just before her death by an eyewitness known to the townspeople as "Aunt Edna" Smith.

She was the wife of Lockport's first physician, Dr. Isaac Smith, the man who gave the new town its name in 1821.

According to Aunt Edna, the force of the blasting was such that "stones several inches in diameter were daily thrown over into Main Street.

"When the warning cry of 'Look out!' was sounded for a blast," she wrote, "everyone within range flew to a place of shelter. The small stones would rattle down like hail, and were anything but pleasant, particularly when one was caught with uncovered head. One stone weighing 18 pounds was thrown over our front yard. Judge Ransom [Elias Ransom], then a young lawyer, had a narrow escape. He had a small office on the south side of Main Street, about halfway between Pine and Cottage streets. He was one day sitting in the front room, his chair tilted back, and his feet resting on the table, when, crash, came a stone weighing 20 pounds, just within the door, rolled in, hit the legs of the chair and down came the young counselor, in a very undignified manner, and a surprised state of mind, at his unexpected fall.

"Many accidents occurred from the carelessness of the men in the use of powder, such as staying too near the blast at the time of explosion, etc. If the fuses went out or burned slowly, they would rush back recklessly to see what was the matter, often blowing them to revive the dying fire. Many a poor fellow was blown into fragments in this way. On some days the list of killed and wounded would be almost like that of a battlefield."

The townspeople, under daily siege from the blasting, hit on the idea of taking cover under the trees. That is, they cut down small trees, removed the branches, and propped the trees together against the sides of their houses, "putting the lower part eight or ten feet from the house and leaning them against the roof, letting the tops extend above it."

The tree cover provided some measure of protection and also helped to solve the nagging problem of living quarters for the Irish laborers. Aunt Edna praised the trees as "a great safeguard . . . and the space underneath was utilized by our Irish brethren by being converted into a pig sty or cow house—no cholera in those days or impertinent health officers prying into people's domestic arrangements and interfering to prevent their being as dirty as they chose."

The construction work at Lockport was still underway when the Marquis de Lafayette paid a visit to the site during his triumphant tour of the United States in June of 1825. The French hero of the American Revolution had returned in August 1824 to the scenes of his youthful glory on a 5,000-mile tour of the nation at the invitation of President Monroe.

When the French nobleman arrived in Buffalo from Dunkirk, New York, via Lake Erie steamboat, on June 4, he quickly became the prize in a tug of war between the rival Buffalo and Black Rock civic delegations. He managed to bed down in the Eagle Tavern in Buffalo (every town in the state had an Eagle Tavern or an Eagle Hotel) following the welcoming rituals there, but at six the next morning he found himself being whisked to Black Rock for breakfast—and more welcoming speeches. His host there was the ubiquitous General Porter.

Lafayette was a man who knew his own mind, and what he had in mind was seeing Niagara Falls. He finally managed to get to the Eagle Hotel in Niagara Falls, admired the cataract, visited Fort Niagara on Lake Ontario to receive military honors, and then made his way back toward Lewiston. On the road his party passed the Tuscarora Indian Reservation, and members of the tribe lined the road in tribute to the great general about whom legend already had grown thick. One of the Indians, Chief Cusick, an old leader of the tribe, once had fought at the side of Lafayette and was credited with having saved the French general's life. The feeble chief was "affectionately greeted and invited to ride with the general." He also was given "a handsome belt" as a sign of Lafayette's friendship.

Lafayette's overland trip to Lockport, where he planned to take a canalboat eastward, was not without its highlights. At Howell's Tavern on Howell's Creek he drank lemonade with ten-year-old Harriett Howell— "an event which she remembered to her dying day." Lemonade obviously was very unusual stuff in the forest.

Farther east, at Gould's Red Tavern, the marquis was greeted by a Lockport committee on horseback. Among the welcomers were several old friends and comrades-in-arms, including Colonel Asher B. Saxton and Stephen Van Rensselaer, at the time president of the Canal Commission. After an exchange of greetings, the ceremonial procession made its way through the forest and emerged at the site of Lockport at Prospect Street, where it was greeted by "a tremendous blast of what sounded like artillery fire."

In their anxiety to impress Lafayette, the canal crews had planted gunpowder charges every few feet in the rock wall along the way, from the head of the locks to Gilbert's (now Hitchen's) Bridge.

"These were connected by trains of powder and the resulting explosions sounded like hundreds of cannon fired at intervals of a few seconds," one account relates, adding that the marquis was "much pleased" by the reception.

"The very rocks rend to welcome me," said Lafayette, after the barrage had died away and he had had a chance to dust off his tricorner hat and pick the stones out of his powdered wig. He had a real knack for saying the right thing at the right time.

In response to all the hearty words of welcome extended to him at the big banquet held in the Washington House (on the site of the Park Hotel of a later day), Lafayette, alluding to the twin sights of the locks and nearby Niagara Falls, asserted that "Lockport and the County of Niagara

89

contain the greatest natural and artificial wonders, second only to the wonders of freedom and equal rights."

During the brief visit, Lafayette's secretary wrote in his diary: "I have nowhere seen the activity and industry of man brought into operation against natural difficulties as in this young village . . . The sound of the axe and hammer are everywhere heard. On one side trees fall, which are fashioned by the hands of carpenters on the same spot in the form of houses; on another, in a public square, which is only marked out, a large inn already opens its doors to the new citizens, who have as yet no other shelter.

"There are hardly to be found in the village the means of satisfying the first wants of life; and yet, beside a schoolhouse where the children can be instructed while their fathers are building houses to shelter them, is erected a press which issues a newspaper that informs the workmen during their hours of repose, how the magistrates of the people perform the task with which they have been honored.

"In the streets marked out in the forest, and still embarrassed with the trunks of trees and thick branches, luxury already presents herself in light carriages drawn by fine horses, and finally in the midst of these encroachments of civilization on savage nature, that great canal is proceeding with a rapidity which seems to mark the hand of union, will at the same time diffuse life and abundance in the deserts through which it passes."

It was an accurate observation. The work was proceeding at a pace faster than anybody had thought possible, but now the construction crews were fighting a deadline. Plans had been made to complete the canal by the end of summer and to have the grand opening in October. The sense of urgency made the rocks fly even faster as the workers redoubled their efforts, presumably driving the townspeople under cover around the clock.

One of the problems at first that had tended to slow the work of blasting through the rock mountain was the steady accumulation of rock rubble. The hundreds of laborers pushing wheelbarrow loads of the broken rock found it most difficult to keep up with the growing mountain of the debris, especially as they had to trundle it uphill from the bottom of the cut to the spoil bank above.

The situation clearly clamored for more of that timely improvisation that had rescued the canal builders in the past. This time it was a man with the interesting name of Orange H. Dibble who came forward with the solution. Dibble's contribution was a horse-operated boom, or crane device, that stood high above the cut in which the stone blasting was being done. The boom lowered a wooden bucket to the bottom of the cut, where it was filled with broken rock and raised to the spoil bank above; a quick, effortless operation that eliminated a lot of hard labor and hastened the rubble removal work considerably. Cranes were set up approximately every seventy feet along the stone ridge overlooking the deep section of the canal southwest of Lockport and were credited with advancing the completion of the cut by an appreciable margin of time.

(Even in recent years, the City of Lockport has had to deal with the problem of removing the rubble deposits left over from the canal excavation and blasting. Millions of cubic yards of the earth and rock were piled high and left in unsightly mounds in the wake of the canal construction. On old Canal Street, now Richmond Avenue, for example, the piled-up debris was said to be "as high as a house," and the mound along the south side of the canal in places reached seventy feet in height.)

Though their handiwork alone gave Lockport its reason for existence, the Irish canal builders were not popular members of the growing community; even to describe them as members of the community may be stretching words. Segregation was the order of the day, with the Irish aliens shunted off to whatever hovel refuges they could put together for their wives and children, with primitive dormitories to house the single men. The Irish Road was one of the streets on which many of the workers and their families lived in log shanties.

The townspeople made it a point to avoid unnecessary association with the crude, strange-sounding foreigners, not necessarily from a sense of snobbery, either. Fear, decidedly, was an element that shaped the attitude of the community. The Irish simply didn't fit the usual pattern. Whatever possibilities may have existed for a melding of the diverse groups were just about eliminated by an incident that occurred on Christmas Eve 1822. On that night, a group of canal workers identified as young Irishmen gathered in front of the J. P. Lawes Tavern on Canal Street and behaved in unruly manner, shouting and fighting and finally hurling stones through the window of the tavern.

In a modern day of full-scale riots that destroy whole city blocks, the kind of uprising that occurred in old Lockport probably would go without notice, but this one brought the townspeople out on a dead run and in fear of their lives. A general muster of men of the village was sounded and the disorder turned into a general battle. One of the canal workers, John Jennings, was killed in the melee and other men, on both sides, were injured before the riot was brought under control. Twelve of the Irish workers were arrested and jailed, but another twenty were said to have escaped across the border to Canada.

It wasn't until the following autumn that the arrested workmen were brought to trial, the first ever held in Lockport. The temporary courtroom was in the Mansion House, then at the southeast corner of Transit and West Main streets. (The building is still standing, but now is second from the corner.) Judge William B. Rochester, who presided at the trial, was the son of Nathaniel Rochester, founder of the neighboring city to the east. He found one of the defendants guilty of second-degree manslaughter and sent twelve other defendants to prison for their part in the riot. To guard against any interruption of the trial by angry canal workers in the area, armed villagers maintained a guard around the Mansion House during the proceedings. There was no further outbreak of violence, however, and the canal work went on.

With the decision in mid-1823 that Buffalo should be the western terminus of the canal, at De Witt Clinton's insistence, the work began in August to connect Buffalo with the canal. The construction crews pushing westward now knew at least where they were headed, and the tempo of the work picked up with the end in view.

It was decided that the full length of canal from Albany to Buffalo, 363 miles, should be opened to traffic for the first time in October 1825 and that the celebrations which had been building up from the river to the lake for so long would be uncorked at that time. Everything now depended on the Irish construction gangs digging their way through the last miles and last days of eight years of hard labor on time. If they faltered or if they encountered unexpected problems, the cold winds would be sweeping out of the lakes and winter would settle down on Upper New York, freezing the canal waters and postponing the grand opening until springtime of the following year.

But the weather stayed bland through the summer and early autumn, and the work progressed according to schedule. It may be that one of the positive factors in the marked rise in the productivity of the workmen as they moved closer to Buffalo was a stratagem employed by the contractors. In this they improved on the old incentive system of whiskey breaks. A barrel of whiskey was placed directly in the path of the oncoming workers, a reasonable distance away but not so far that the men couldn't see it—or, as some claimed, smell it. Beyond the first barrel, in the distance, was a second barrel. Still farther on, a third barrel, and so on down to the finish line.

Whenever construction advanced to one of the barrels, the men were permitted to take time out to drink down the contents. It was a glorious reward, and as the canal got closer to a barrel there were smiles and shouts of joyful determination up and down the long trench, with everybody bending to his shovel or barrow. And heaven help the man who failed to do his share at a crucial time like that, as those twin prizes —the whiskey barrels and the completion of the canal, each in its own way an intoxicating prize—were within grasp.

It was a splendid, swaggering, staggering finish, with songs and smiles and laughter coming up out of Clinton's Ditch, just as if the men with the grimy faces and the red faces and the clay pipes tilted at crazy angles were aware that what they were about to finish was something more, really, than just an outsized gully. It is not unreasonable to give them credit for knowing better.

CHAPTER XI

THE WEDDING OF THE WATERS

The formal opening of the Erie Canal was made memorable by many things, but none more than the devastating torrent of words which it unloosed throughout the state. Speechmakers sprang to platforms, soap boxes, balconies, low-hanging tree branches, the backs of buggies—any elevation that would give them prominence and permit them to command an audience—and pulled out all the oratorical stops in praise of the great waterway.

The speechmaking began even before the *Seneca Chief* and its distinguished passengers—including Governor Clinton and Jesse Hawley, the visionary whose letters to editors had helped promote the Erie—started to move down the canal from Buffalo about nine o'clock on that memorable morning of Wednesday, October 26, 1825. And when the cannons along the route began firing in telegraphic relay, it seemed as though each of the big guns was serving as an outsized starter's pistol for thousands of orators. Every town on the route had dignitaries ready to rise to the challenge of the big celebration; determined to outdo each other in florid, ponderous salutations and tributes, many of which reached the outer edges of grotesquery with their unbridled figures of speech and classical allusions.

The likelihood is, nevertheless, that Governor Clinton, his wife, and all the other members of the official party enjoyed the heavy schedule of speechmaking as they proceeded on their historic inaugural trip. Even the most outrageous cliches and unmanageable metaphors must have sounded like music in their ears after the long, troublesome years of endeavor. More marvelous than their ability to endure the oratory, perhaps, was the magnificent performance of the dignitaries at the banquet tables that lined the way.

The flotilla, which started out with the *Seneca Chief*, *Noah's Ark*, *Superior*, *Commodore Perry*, and *Buffalo*, grew as it went along. Waiting at Lockport, for instance, was the *Niagara* from Black Rock, with General Porter aboard. Once the polite formalities were over, though, Porter's boat pushed on ahead of the main party and reached Albany three days before the arrival of the grand flotilla. Such haste did not represent sheer impetuosity. It had been bad enough for the old soldier to lose the war between Black Rock and Buffalo for the prize of being selected as western terminus of the canal without having to listen to all the gushy praise, in town after town, of the man—Clinton—who had been the principal adversary.

The welcoming ceremony at Lockport was especially elaborate. Just in case any of the villagers might have had the bad form to plan on sleeping past sunrise, the town officials began the day with a thirteen-gun salvo at sunrise. By nine that morning the principal citizens were assembled in front of the Washington House on West Main Street. Under the direction of General Parkhurst Whitney of Niagara Falls, the grand marshal, they moved in formal procession to the great locks, where a huge crowd was waiting to see history made.

The Lockport plan of participation in the grand celebration called for a number of boats carrying dignitaries to move west on the canal and meet the oncoming flotilla between Buffalo and Lockport, then to escort the official fleet back to Lockport for formal ceremonies. And to make the beginning more exciting, it was decided that the boats carrying the welcoming delegation first would convene at the foot of the mighty flight of five locks, then *ascend* to the top before heading west, thus putting the locks into official use for the first time.

The passenger list of those aboard the welcoming boats was a distinguished one. In Lockport, waiting to join the official procession to New York City, were members of the Canal Commission and the most prominent of the engineers who had built the canal. They went aboard a packet, the *William C. Bouck*, while a select group of women went aboard another boat, the *Albany*. Segregation of the sexes was the style of the times and was honored, celebration or not. Lesser lights in the social order of the countryside crowded onto several other boats moored in the lower basin.

When the report of a cannon five miles to the west was heard, a thirty-two-pounder in Lockport, part of the cannon relay network, was fired and the band began to play. No pains were spared to make each of these contributions as significant as possible. The cannon, for example, was one that had been used by a ship in Commodore Oliver Hazard Perry's fleet in the Battle of Lake Erie. It was fired that morning in Lockport by a former French lieutenant who had fought under Napoleon, a fact which presumably added something to the occasion. The band music, too, was given an extra dimension by the fact that the leader was a man who had been captured and held prisoner once upon a time by the Barbary Coast pirates.

Following the firing of the Perry cannon, there was round after round of mass artillery fire. A contrapuntal effect, meanwhile, was set up by a deliberate series of powder blasts in the rocky walls of the canal canyon. In the midst of this thunderous racket, the canalboats loaded with dignitaries began to move up to the top level of the stone mountain by way of the five locks while the crowd of spectators looked on and marveled.

Once the boats had achieved this historic height, a man named John Birdsall stepped forward on the deck of the *William C. Bouck* and made an address which included this declaration: "The last barrier is passed. We now have risen to the level of Lake Erie and have before us navigation open to its waters!"

The welcoming delegation rode westward to Pendleton and there intercepted Governor Clinton's flotilla. After the ceremonial greeting, the full contingent of boats made its way to Lockport and tied up along the towpath above the locks. The most thrilling moment for the crowd that had gathered there came when the tall, dignified Governor Clinton made his appearance. He stepped off the *Seneca Chief*, looked about in grave interest, lifted his silk hat in acknowledgment of the cheers, and then held out a helping hand to his wife. All the celebrities and the local dignitaries then went to the elegant Washington House, threading their way through the stumps of trees still left from the forest that so recently had covered the site. By seven that night, sated with food, drink, and talk, the Clinton party was back on the canalboats and the flotilla resumed its eastward journey.

That first stop set the pattern. Much the same sort of reception was awaiting the official inaugural delegation at every town along the canal. There were variations, even signs of raw originality at places, but there was a general sameness in the garlanded arches over the waterway, the flags and bunting, the banners with congratulatory messages, the bands and the banquets, the gun salutes, and the ribbon snipping. All blended together in the consciousness of the traveling celebrities to form one large, welcoming celebration. There was the fact, too, that the flotilla grew larger and longer as the bigger communities added their boats to the official fleet.

When the canal-borne dignitaries arrived on Thursday afternoon in Rochester, which already had been harvesting the rich commercial fruits of the Erie for three years, the ritual was according to the book: cannonading, rifle volleys, band music, and, finally, the banquet and speechfest in the Mansion House. (The site of that pioneer inn today is partly occupied by the modern Flagship Rochester Motel operated by American Airlines.)

Rochester's contribution to the fleet was a boat with a toplofty name, *The Young Lion of the West*. Rochester was a boom town and was feeling its oats, or, more accurately, its wheat, being well on the way toward becoming the country's most important flour milling center. It already was being called the "Flour City." The canal had been largely responsible for this development by providing an economical form of transportation. The other factor was the city's waterfalls, which provided the power to turn the wheels of the flour mills.

The Young Lion of the West, not to be outdone by the curious assortment of animals carried aboard other boats in the flotilla, had on board a pair of eagles, a pair of wolves, a fox, a fawn, and four raccoons. The welcoming committee at the pier in New York City was in for a real surprise when the gangplank was dropped.

At times during that exciting first trip across state by canal the greetings took on the sound of a lodge ritual. The following colloquy, for example, was overheard by a history-minded passenger at one of the towns:

"Who goes there?"

"Your brothers from the West, on the waters of the Great Lakes."

"By what means have they been diverted so far from their natural course?"

"By the channel of the Grand Erie."

"By whose authority, and by whom, was the work of such magnitude accomplished?"

"By the authority and by the enterprise of the patriotic people of the State of New York."

That apparently exhausted the subject and the flotilla moved on its way.

Not all was joy and jollity and good will on the long trip, however.

The arrival at Weedsport, just east of the Montezuma Swamp, was given tragic overtones when two gunners were blown to bits in the misfiring and explosion of a cannon they were trying to shoot in salutation. The accident, coming as it did after the boats had moved through the dismal swampland, cast a pall on the whole flotilla.

The flotilla arrived in Syracuse on the afternoon of Saturday, October 29, and the local committee in that salt center rose to the occasion with a big affair at Williston's Mansion House. Governor Clinton, not one to overlook the obvious, gave the following toast among the thirteen offered that night:

"The citizens of Syracuse and the adjoining villages—may they prove the salt of the earth and enjoy the fullness of prosperity!"

The somber spirit that suddenly prevailed after Weedsport was appropriate for what was ahead—a show of resentment by some of the citizens of Rome who felt that their community had been dealt a hand off the bottom of the deck in the routing of the canal a half mile to the south. To show their displeasure, a number of people filed down to the canal landing in solemn procession, marching to the sound of muffled drums, as the ceremonial procession came into view. Several of the marchers carried a black barrel full of tar, which they poured into the canal in a gesture that could not be mistaken for one of good will. But once their anger had been vented, the demonstrators made their way back to town, where, at Starr's Hotel, "they put aside their ill-humor, and joined with heart and hand in celebrating the event."

The fleet of boats paused in Utica on Sunday morning so that all could debark and attend church services. A civic program observing the canal opening followed and then the boats continued eastward. It was nighttime when Little Falls came into view. There the governor and his party received one of their most spectacular welcomes. Barrels of tar, placed along the edge of the cliffs high above the locks, were ignited and their flames lighted the night sky and threw a flickering illumination over the canal waters below, adding the element of beauty to the reception.

Fort Plain, the stop beyond Little Falls, went beyond its neighbor in the competition for spectacular welcomes. There the ingenious locals had hoisted barrels of burning pitch to the tops of high poles erected atop Prospect Hill. The fiercely blazing barrels, which seemed to be suspended in space, caused Governor Clinton to exclaim: "My God! What is *that?*"

The members of the welcoming committee were greatly pleased to hear that they had startled the governor. It made all their work worthwhile. The same committee apparently had whiled away the hours awaiting the arrival of the flotilla by dipping into barrels that contained something other than pitch, although probably just as flammable. But the committeemen were feeling unusually mellow by eventide.

The meal that had been arranged in Wagner's Hotel in Fort Plain that Monday night was one of the most impressive yet encountered by the travelers. The tables had been set up to cover the entire length of the great ballroom, and the "sumptuous dinner" was preceded by and peppered throughout with the most impressive collection of alcoholic toasts in the history of the young nation. Thirteen toasts had been planned in advance, and the organizers of the dinner thought they had covered every conceivable subject worthy of salute, from the loaf of bread that Ben Franklin had purchased on his arrival in Philadelphia to Washington's oarsmen on the trip across the Delaware. There were creative men in the dining hall that night, and by the time all of them had been given the floor and had been appeased by a general hoisting of glasses, a total of thirty-two toasts was racked up—a record for the day, without question.

One of the hints that Fort Plain would be different came at the outset, when one of the members of the welcoming delegation, a schoolteacher named John Taylor, was pushed forward and suddenly found himself facing the famous De Witt Clinton. Drawing on his inner reserves and struggling to suppress his hiccoughs, the teacher swept his hand gracefully in front of him in the approved style of the day and, bowing low, very low, he toppled over and fell into the canal.

Word of that spectacular greeting got around quickly, adding much to the hilarity of the occasion. It even may have stirred a bit of envy. At any rate, it is a matter of record that after the thirty-two toasts had been observed during the banquet, the local schoolmaster, perhaps anxious to top the teacher, exuberantly leaped onto the old groaning board and caused it to collapse. The guests, spattered with gravy and littered with half-gnawed chicken bones, undoubtedly were relieved when their boats resumed their eastward journey. But they talked about that stop at Fort Plain for a long time. It was what would be called today a fun stop.

Things have a way of balancing themselves, even on such a generally gala trip as this one was. Memories of the big binge at Fort Plain, for instance, were chased by the somber, funereal reception tendered to the flotilla and its guests upon their arrival in Schenectady on Tuesday afternoon.

The old Dutch city was in a melancholy state of mind over the canal. Schenectadians felt that it was bound to destroy the comfortable, prosperous position the town had enjoyed as a port of transfer. All westbound traffic wanting to ride the Mohawk River previously had to make its way from the Hudson River overland to Schenectady before it could take to the water again because of the rapids on the Mohawk and the falls at Cohoes. For the same reason, passengers and cargo headed eastward also had to disembark at Schenectady and take the land detour to the Hudson River. A prosperous warehousing business had come into being at this important transfer point and a substantial boat-building industry had developed there. Concomitantly, the town had profited further through the growth of commercial supply houses, warehouses, inns, taverns, and other services catering to travelers.

In Schenectady, in 1825, in the words of one historian, "there was gloom, for everyone knew that the town, once the port of entry for goods going west, was at the mercy of the canal." However, while no attempt was made to celebrate the opening, the townspeople covered their chagrin in a proper, sportsmanlike manner. A newspaper suggestion that the Clinton party be greeted with a funeral-type procession was rejected out of hand. The natural hospitality of the Dutch residents asserted itself in a polite, respectful reception and a quiet dinner—"eaten in a sober manner," according to one account.

The only outward demonstration in Schenectady was provided by a group of cadets from the town's Union College. The students marched in their smartest military cadence to the bank of the canal and there, under the eyes of the celebrities aboard the canalboats, they fired a rifle salute, marching away then almost as quickly and as precisely as they had come.

A mere thirty miles separated the flotilla from the Hudson River when it left Schenectady on the last leg of its long journey, but they were among the most difficult miles of all. In that short distance, the land dropped 218 feet—some seven feet to the mile—as the Mohawk ran its final precipitant course.

The canal zigzagged its way through the steep stone gorge, being carried to the north bank by an aqueduct at a place called Alexander's Mills, then back to the south bank by another aqueduct at Fonda's Ferry, some four miles above the river's mouth. Meanwhile, it received a considerable assist from the locks, twenty-six of them in that thirty-mile run gently lowering the boats, taking them around the thundering falls of the Cohoes, and eventually depositing them safely at the Hudson level, where the canal turned southward along the west bank of the river.

There still was one lock left, but its use was optional. Boat captains who wanted to dock in the basin at West Troy could use the lock to leave the canal at that point. Otherwise they followed a straight course to the south, and the final five miles of the Erie took them into the great terminal basin in Albany.

The state capital's welcome was as enthusiastic as it was elaborate. The canal, after all, was as much a political creation as a physical achievement, and Albany before all things was the seat of New York politics. De Witt Clinton was the first man of the city as he was the first man of the state, and while he had suffered in Albany, there he also had been highly honored. None knew better than the man in the state capital how hard Clinton had fought to bring the canal into being. It was a sincere welcome that the city tendered him. It included a twenty-four-gun salute, speeches at the capitol building, and the unveiling in the Assembly chamber of oil portraits of De Witt Clinton, George Clinton, and George Washington.

State officials, employees of the government departments, units of the militia, veterans of the Revolutionary War and the War of 1812, school children, uniformed Masons, and people dressed in the quaint costumes of the early Dutch settlers, all marched in the big parade, with band music to give their steps an extra lift. Tables were set up on the Columbia Street Bridge, which had been wrapped in colored bunting and festooned with flags, to accommodate some 600 outdoor diners.

There had been nothing quite like this anywhere, and it was a fitting preliminary to the welcoming celebration that awaited the first boats to ride the canal when they would arrive in New York Harbor a few days hence, on November 4. An advance delegation from New York City, headed by Mayor Philip Hone, met the Clinton party at Albany and rode with the flotilla as it was towed down the Hudson to Sandy Hook and the Atlantic Ocean.

There was no mistaking the change in attitude toward the canal that had taken place in the big city. Nothing now was too good for De Witt Clinton. In the short time that trade benefits from the partially completed canal had begun to pour into the state's largest city, there had come about an awakening to its significance, a realization that the canal promised to be a golden sluice that would float the wealth of interior America to the port of New York, depositing a considerable part of that wealth on the island of Manhattan as it moved on, the way a fast-moving river, suddenly slowed when it reaches the sea, builds a delta of rich soil.

Eight steamboats towed the Clinton flotilla toward the culminating ceremony that awaited at the mouth of the Hudson. Scores of small craft sailed alongside the official fleet, vying for the honor of accompanying the historic procession even for a small distance. From the shore, also, there came expressions of the excitement and enthusiasm that gripped the entire state by then. Cannons boomed and bonfires blazed all along the high Hudson way.

New York City's long-standing tradition of being the world's most expressive and appreciative city in the reception of heroes may have begun with its welcome to its former mayor Clinton in that autumn month of November 1825. What gave an extra glow to the city's celebration of the canal opening was that it represented an about-face, an act of contrition, and an attempt at reparation. Most of all, it was an expression of apology to Clinton, the hero come home again, vindicated and victorious after dark days out in the field. What he had wrought would give New York City primacy among all the cities of the new nation, and that dawning realization had Clinton's old city in its grip as the flotilla arrived.

With Sandy Hook almost in sight, the boats were met by the steamship *Washington*, which had a committee of the Common Council of the city aboard.

"Whence come you, and where are you bound?" boomed a voice from the *Washington*.

"From Lake Erie—and bound for Sandy Hook!" replied a voice from the *Seneca Chief*.

The historians are at odds over the order of marine events in New York and how the dramatis personnae played their respective roles. One account holds that Clinton and other dignitaries went aboard the *Chancellor Livingston* for the formal ceremonies at sea, while Mrs. Clinton and her ladies in waiting went aboard the barge named *Lady Clinton*. Sergregation again seemed to have been the order of the day, but the barge had the distinction, at least, of not only being graced with flowery garlands, but of having in prominent position, perhaps on the bowsprit, a sculptured head of Governor Clinton wearing a laurel wreath on his brow!

Never had the waters around New York witnessed such an invasion of boats and ships of all sizes, types, and nationalities as occurred on the morning of Friday, November 4. As the canalboats moved into the East River at seven o'clock that morning—eleven days after their departure from Buffalo, some five hundred miles distant—a heavy barrage of welcome was fired from the Brooklyn Navy Yard. Following that salute, the flotilla went to the Battery to participate in the "Grand Aquatic Display," which saw some forty-six vessels, including twenty-nine steamboats, surround the tiny canal craft and execute a series of intricate maneuvers.

Following another gun salute at nine o'clock, this time from the Battery, the great fleet of vessels moved out toward the ocean and a rendezvous with the United States schooner *Porpoise,* anchored at Sandy Hook since the night before. The role of the *Porpoise* was to have aboard a "deputation from Neptune" to participate in the solemn ceremony that would be enacted in the symbolic marriage of Lake Erie and the Atlantic Ocean —the "wedding of waters" that would be brought about by the pouring of Lake Erie water, from casks carried from Buffalo, into the waters of the Atlantic.

As Governor Clinton spilled the lake water into the sea, harbor guns boomed and hundreds of people aboard the many boats cheered. Some of the women brushed their eyes. It was just like a real wedding.

Then the governor spoke:

"The solemnity, at this place on the first arrival of vessels from Lake Erie, is intended to indicate and commemorate the navigable communication, which has been accomplished between our Mediterranean seas and the Atlantic Ocean, in about eight years, to the extent of more than four hundred and twenty-five miles, by the wisdom, public spirit, and energy of the people of the state of New York; and may the God of the Heavens and the Earth smile most propitiously on this work, and render it subservient to the best interests of the human race."

The governor had another keg of Lake Erie water at his side, but it was given to the Marquis de Lafayette, a spectator aboard the *Seneca Chief,* as a memento of the great event. What the marquis did with his keg of *eau d'Erie* is not known. The Atlantic Ocean, it goes without saying, was never quite the same after that ceremony off Sandy Hook. Marriage does something to oceans just as it does to people.

Committee members, enthralled by the ritualistic mystique of the Clinton ceremony, then came up with vials filled with water from the Rhine, Ganges, Nile, Mississippi, Columbia, Thames, Seine, Danube, Amazon, La Plata, Orinoco, Indus, and Gambia rivers. Dr. Samuel Latham Mitchill presided over the pouring of water from those great rivers of the world with great dignity and finesse while onlookers gaped, some almost fearfully, as if the mixture might turn out to be chemically explosive. The New York *Evening Post,* commenting on the symbolic ceremony, termed it "a piece of ridicule and absurdity."

Many splendid orations were delivered on that red-letter day off Sandy Hook, to be sure, but none topped the remarks made by Dr. Mitchill in the concluding speech of the ceremonies at sea. Dr. Mitchill obviously had given his subject a lot of thought. He spoke with great fervor and nobility of expression, ignoring the pitching of the deck even to the extent, occasionally, of letting loose of the ship's railing to raise his hands to the sky whenever he found it necessary to draw some thunderous phrases out of the clouds.

"Sir!" roared Dr. Mitchill, easily drowning out the sound of the sea. "He who now accosts you has no contrivance to conjure up new associations of ideas nor to utter them in phrases novel or unheard before; yet if he did possess that power he would tell you how recently imparted influence of republicanization would henceforward co-operate with the sea's phosphorescence to render it luminous, and with its salinity to continue it wholesome; he would portray freedom pervading the billows and rolling with every wave to the shores, and trace its workings upon the compacted continents and scattered islands comprehended within its embrace.

"Had he the ability he would observe that this renovating and regenerating would rise, exhalation into the atmosphere, and impart some of its qualities; that it would impregnate the clouds and descend in rains and dews; that it would enter the vegetables and animals which constitute the food of the human race; and that finally, the frame of man himself would be gradually so modified and mended by it, that at length even the sable and savage tribes dwelling in the tracts bordering on Senegal, the Gambia, and the Congo, shall lay aside their ferocity and enjoy, as we ourselves do, Liberty, under the guidance of the Law."

Some of the listeners thought Dr. Mitchill had gone overboard. Others doubtless wished he had. But everybody agreed it was a very classy speech, which, of course, is what the occasion demanded.

Cadwallader Colden, the descendant and namesake of the man who had foreseen the possibility and utility of a canal in New York a century before, was among those who participated in the Sandy Hook ceremony. He was given the responsibility of preparing the official memoir of the occasion and in it he enthusiastically wrote:

"The Aquatic display transcended all anticipations, twenty-nine steamboats, gorgeously dressed, with barges, ships, pilot-boats, canal-boats, and the boats of the Whitehall firemen, conveying thousands of ladies and gentlemen, presented a scene which cannot be described. Add to this the reflections which arise from the extent and beauty of our Bay—the unusual calmness and mildness of the day—the splendid manner in which all the shipping in the harbour were dressed, and the movement of the whole flotilla. Regulated by previously-arranged signals, the fleet were thrown at pleasure, into squadron or line, into curves or circles. The whole appeared to move by magic."

When the ceremonies were concluded and the ships, in special formations, were making their way back to dock in the East River, sailors on two British ships standing outside the harbor, the sloops-of-war *Kingfisher* and *Swallow*, serenaded them with "Yankee Doodle." It was a notable show of sportsmanship, considering that the War of 1812 still was very fresh in memory. Not to be outdone, though, musicians from West Point who were aboard the *Porpoise,* returned the compliment by striking up "God Save the King."

A breakfast and reception for some of the distinguished Americans was held aboard the *Swallow* later, and the commander of the English sloop, one Lieutenant Baldock, was the hit of the party. In his anxiety to express forcefully the prevailing sentiments of Anglo-American friendship, he had painted in water colors a scene that depicted the symbols of the two nations, the lion and the eagle, in affectionate embrace; no easy mating, really.

The friendliness of the English on the heels of an elaborate program at sea which had been remarkably free of untoward happenings, like dignitaries falling into the drink, heightened the mood of the occasion and sharpened the anticipation of the all-day celebration that was to follow on Manhattan Island.

"The Grand Procession" was the name of the parade that was programmed to begin on Manhattan Island at the Battery as soon as all the ceremonial boats had docked at Pier One on the East River, and principals had hustled to the points of assembly designated for them. Bugles called all the marchers to order, and precisely at 11 A.M. four mounted trumpeters rode out in front with a fanfare. The hush that followed was broken after a few seconds by a band that began marching at brisk cadence, playing a martial number composed for the big occasion. Behind the musicians, striding in solitary splendor, came the grand marshal of the parade. Aides of the grand marshal trailed him at close range, rather grand themselves in their white satin collars with colored rosettes and their short white batons tipped with gold.

It was the most wonderful demonstration by far that New York ever had seen—indeed, that any American city ever had seen. Every organization, every profession, trade, school, church, and commercial enterprise was represented in the parade that day. Somebody counted more than 200 different banners and standards as the pageant made its colorful way down Greenwich Street, Canal Street and Broadway.

Many of the floats were sensational in their symbolism and the crowds that lined the street showed their appreciation by cheering and waving. Among the standouts were floats that showed live butchers "mounted and wearing aprons," caged wild animals, uniformed firemen in striking tableaux, and similarly dramatic postures by tanners, cordwainers, hatters, bakers, cobblers, and other tradespeople. The float that drew the most attention and praise, however, was the one sponsored by the Typographical Society. On a platform wagon drawn by four horses in fancy harness the printers had mounted two presses, gilded for extra effect. Seated between the presses, on Benjamin Franklin's old armchair no less, was the city's oldest printer, one James Cram. The most marvelous touch of all was that both presses were in operation as the float moved along. They were busily striking off copies of an ode written in honor of the great day by Samuel Woodworth. Helping Mr. Cram fold the printed matter and toss it to the outstretched arms of the spectators were two men dressed as heralds and two dressed as Mercury. Symbolism simply knew no limits that day. As far as that goes, Poet Woodworth hadn't exactly shown himself to be a master of restraint when he composed his ode, the closing stanzas of which sang racily:

> 'Tis Done! The monarch of the briny tide
> Whose giant arm encircles earth
> To virgin Erie is allied
> A bright-eyed nymph of mountain birth.
>
> Today the *Sire of Ocean* takes
> A sylvan maiden to his arms
> The goddess of the crystal lakes
> In all her native charms.
>
> She comes attended by a sparkling train;
> The Naiads of the West her nuptials grace
> She meets the sceptred father of the main
> And in his heaving bosom hides her virgin face.

The fact that broadsides were being printed on the run and simultaneously being distributed to readers was hailed by the wonder-struck celebrators as a most appropriate illustration of the new era that was being ushered into being by the Grand Canal—an era of speed and progress and mechanization that promised a fuller, more satisfying life—certainly, a different life.

From time to time, as the procession moved toward City Hall, spectators took up the sing-song chant from Woodworth's epic:

> 'Tis done! 'Tis done! The mighty chain
> Which joins bright Erie to the Main,
> For ages shall perpetuate
> The glory of our native state!

There was another float that drew special attention and commendation. The entry of the journeymen coopers featured a group of coopers at work on the platform wagon as it moved along. They were busily putting together two large wooden casks, one of sixty-gallon capacity and the other of forty-gallon capacity, and they finished their projects before the parade had ended.

More philosophical was the presentation of the tailors. Inspired, no doubt, by the wedding-of-the-waters theme, they carried two large banners, the first of which showed Adam and Eve standing under a tree in the Garden of Eden. Underneath was the triumphant wording: "United

We Are!" The other banner hit closer to the tailoring scheme of things. It read, "I was naked and ye clothed me!" The crowd liked that.

It seemed that the celebration picked up vigor as the day wore on. The parade, the speeches at City Hall, the street decorations, the universal air of excitement, and the anticipation of fresh delights ahead kept the milling crowds in high humor. At all times, the magic name everywhere in the city was "Clinton." There was no question about him being the man of the hour; more than that, the man of the young century. Hawkers everywhere peddled badges with the governor's face profiled against an appropriate state background, and there were such memorial items as Clinton kerchiefs, Clinton hats, and even Clinton glassware. A popular souvenir was a cane with a green-and-white pennant on which was emblazoned the name, "De Witt Clinton." The pennant was attached to the cane just below the crook of the handle. At times, during the more emotionally pitched speechmaking, thousands of canes would be thrust high into the air and the pennants waved in a furious show of approbation. As for Clinton himself, it was said that he spoke so often and listened, in turn, to so many speeches, that he finally fell asleep.

The middle hours of the great day saw only minimum activity. Most of the families, with foresight, had brought basket lunches, and at lunchtime New York became a large picnic ground as the celebrators spread out their tablecloths and food in the grassy fields that abounded everywhere off Broadway. Some played games after they ate, with horseshoes the most popular pastime, but the wise ones dozed under the mellow autumn sun, gathering new strength for the festivities still ahead.

More affluent families crowded the restaurants, all of which had entered into the spirit of the day with special dishes appropriately named. All of the restaurants featured as their *pièce de resistance* a dish called "Canal Beef." It was nothing short of an expression of patriotism to order that meal because, as the name hinted, it was beef which had been transported to New York City by way of the Grand Canal. And if that fact weren't enough, it was advertised as beef from "the largest cow ever raised in this country!"—an irresistible combination, altogether, for people determined to honor the Erie Canal in every possible way, even by eating.

Among the most popular attractions of the day was the exhibition of one of the canalboats, the *Noah's Ark*, at Castle Garden. The boat itself was of intrinsic interest, of course, but the real crowd-pleaser was its cargo—the Seneca Indians, birds, insects, fish, fawns, and two brown bears, all of which had ridden the boat from Buffalo on the inaugural voyage. In all the glorious confusion of the day, however, the fate of the eagles, wolves, fawns, foxes, whitefish, raccoons, and other assorted livestock carried in other canalboats, was lost sight of. There is the outside possibility, to be sure, that the widely advertised Canal Beef was not exclusively beef, but there is no way of knowing for sure.

The historians of the day had more important things to hold their at-

tention, not the least of which was a small riot that occurred in the Vauxhall Garden.

(New York, while never claiming to be a garden city, from its very
beginning has been partial to the old English use of "garden" as a place
of public amusement. The Winter Garden and Madison Square Garden,
among others, carried that tradition into modern times.)

What brought about the uprising in Vauxhall Garden was the failure
of some promoters to come through with an event as advertised. It was
supposed to be a free balloon ascent with a Mme. Johnson in the bag.
As it turned out, Mme. Johnson dutifully fulfilled her end of the contract.
She was in the bag all afternoon. But there were technical difficulties.
The ground crew found it impossible to inflate the balloon enough for
it to take off, and thousands of spectators who had paid fifty cents to
see the ascension got increasingly surly as the afternoon wore on. When
it became clear that the event was not about to take place, the crowd
tore the Garden apart.

Darkness brought out the frolickers in force as nothing else could have,
and the pitch of the civic celebration rose to a new high level. New York
that night was nothing less than a fairyland in the eyes of those who
milled its streets. Even without electricity, the effect that was achieved
on that memorable night of Friday, November 4, 1825, deserved description as brilliant. Torches lighted most public buildings, business
places, and streets, but, appropriately enough, it was on Broadway that
the brightest lights burned.

City Hall, in particular, was a dazzling sight. It was aglow with 2,302
"brilliant lights"—by actual count of some dedicated statistician on the
scene. Among the lights used were "1,542 wax candles, 450 lamps, and
310 variegated lamps." The light that was beamed out from City Hall,
impressed onlookers swore, went so high into the dark night that the
glow could be seen from remote parts of Manhattan Island and even
across the rivers in such distant places as Brooklyn and Hoboken.

People on foot, on horseback, and in slow-moving carriages clogged
the streets around the City Hall. It was the center of things, and, furthermore, it was the position of best vantage from which to watch the formal
program of entertainment. The tour de force of the nighttime program
was a display of fireworks that was shot from the City Hall lawn. It
turned out to be everything the sponsors had hoped for, and probably
more than they had expected. In this show, an early American pyrotechnic
genius named Richard Wilcox reached the peak of his highly specialized
career. At one time during his fireworks exhibition he had in the air,
against a ground background of dazzling lights, as many as 1,500 large
fireballs busily crossing and recrossing "in intersecting arcs of concentric
circles."

Another of Wilcox's pyrotechnic productions was described in these
rapt words: "A gleaming willow tree, decorated with yellow stars, hung

106

for a moment in the night sky, and then a poplar lifted boughs of flame. A shower of golden rain descended, and suddenly the rain was silver. Three hundred and twenty rockets of four pounds each, thirty of nine pounds, twenty-four of twenty pounds, hurtled upward from both wings of the composition, and, as their arcs crossed, burst into fiery serpents, scrolls of light, the delicate tracery of snails. The largest rockets, fired at a 40-degree angle so as to fall into the Hudson, left behind them wide peacock spreads of colored lights that drifted slowly down to meet the water."

On a smaller, less exuberant, more artistic level, what was described as "a large transparency . . . representing the introduction of Neptune to the Lady of the Lake by the Genius of America" was exhibited at City Hall and won a gratifying share of respectful attention.

Some 3,000 fun seekers that night paid their way into the Lafayette Amphitheater where the Grand Canal Ball was held. The price of admission was high, five dollars a person, but the amphitheater, said to be the largest room in the country, was filled nevertheless and the ball was a great success. The striking centerpiece decoration alone was worth the price of admission to those who attended. It was a large pond of genuine Lake Erie water in which there grandly floated a miniature canalboat made of maple sugar!

One of the many interesting side-sights of the ball was a special souvenir headgear called the "Grand Canal Turban." It was worn by many of the women that night and it gave the ball a sort of Arabian Nights coloration, a touch of the exotic East, which, in a sense, New York really was so far as the canal travelers from western outposts like Buffalo and Rochester were concerned. The turban got a big boost that night, but somehow it failed to catch on as a popular American headgear.

That was how the Erie Canal joined the American scene, anyway—with solemn ceremony and joyous clamor, with dignity and with garish display; a splendid mixture in which every ingredient added something spicy to the flavor of the long day and the long night. Behind the gaiety, though, there was a touch of uneasiness, too—a nervous awareness that an epochal period of American life had ended and that a new, unknown, different world was ahead, thanks to a long, long ditch that was only forty feet wide and four feet deep.

Exit the old world of pioneer America. Laughing.

CHAPTER XII

THE WAY FOR DREAMERS TO GO

It was late in 1825 when they gloriously opened the Erie Canal from one end to the other, so late that the first trip was the final trip of the season. The wind blows free across the waters of the Great Lakes and winter comes early to the western and northern parts of New York State. The ponds and rivers often freeze in early November, and the snow sifts in hard pellets across the frozen fields even while apples still hang from brittle branches.

The canal men already knew a lot about the winters that usually visited Upper New York, experience being a quick, arbitrary teacher. The canal was shallow. It did not take four feet of water long to freeze. First there was a congealing on the surface, with the brownish water turning into a film that looked like smoky celluloid, and then the ice reached down acquisitively until in a few days there was no water left in the ditch at all—only a stubborn block of ice, prism-shaped, that couldn't be cracked by the dull-nosed boats no matter how hard the mules and the horses strained and dug their hoofs into the towpath.

The tricky thing, from the very beginning, was trying to anticipate what was ahead, to outguess the elements. A capricious nature might choose to usher in the winter freeze early. Or it might hold back the chill and lavish the land with sunshine and temperate breezes until the last possible minute. The canal captain whose boat was heavy with cargo or whose packet was jammed with passengers had to worry about the weather as much as an aircraft captain does today, but with special concern when it was late in the season. He had to notice such signs as the thickening morning frost and the steamy vapor that snorted out of the nostrils of the plodding tow animals. He noticed the fragile shards of ice laying on the undisturbed water where it met the side banks and he smelled the advancing season in the shifting winds that carried the sharp smell of the north country. He got so he knew the pure scent of snow itself. All the way across the state, he kept his eyes open and his senses alive; he counted the signs and studied all the fresh evidence as it presented itself. He learned to move warily when it was late in the year, carefully estimating time and distance between one port and the next lest the boat one day find itself caught between basins, unable to move because of a sudden freeze. It happened often. A boat would over-reach itself in challenging the elements and find itself locked in ice for the winter or beached for the winter on somebody's farm—a strange, embarrassing fate for any boat; one to be avoided, certainly.

There were no such embarrassments recorded at the end of the 1825 shipping season on the Erie Canal. The big inaugural trip on October 26 was just for show and it was barely completed before the winter closed in. The ice soon choked the Ditch and the heavy snows covered the freshly made scars and the rubble of recent excavation. There was nothing left to do that first historic autumn but dream of what might be ahead.

Not even the most optimistic men among the dreamers could have dared to hope for the things that came to pass in the years that followed.

As soon as they thought the ice had become thin enough in the early spring of 1826, impatient canal men hitched extra horses and mules to their boats and rammed open a channel through the waterway. It was then that the new era of travel and movement in America began in earnest.

The nation was caught up in what was called "canal fever," and it was, for a fact, a kind of delirium. At the beginning of 1826 there had been a count of 160 freight boats and a small number of packets for passengers. Within a decade, by 1836, there were 3,000 boats of all types on the canal, and it was said that if you stood on one of the bridges and looked either toward the east or the west, you would see unbroken lines of boats moving in either direction. It seemed as if the number of boats available would never be able to meet the demand. Shortly after the Civil War years, there were close to 7,000 boats choking the Grand Canal, not to mention the log rafts that represented a special kind of traffic and a special kind of problem.

Money flowed into the coffers of the Canal Commission from the beginning in amounts exceeding all expectations. Cost of construction had been a staggering $7,770,000, but in the first full year of operation, 1826, total canal income from all sources was more than $1,000,000. By 1836 the surplus was large enough to pay off the remaining debt of approximately $3,500,000, even though the schedule of tolls had been reduced one third since 1833 because financial returns had been so embarrassingly large. The reductions in rates, however, did not seriously diminish profits. As traffic on the canal grew, the income poured into the state treasury in an ever-increasing flow. It was a pleasant problem to contemplate, and the eyes of the politicians glowed with the incandescence that is generated only by a surplus of funds.

One popular school of political and economic thought in the state went so far as to advance the possibility of a tax-free future, one in which the revenue from the canal would be sufficient to serve as the sole financial support of the state. Utopia itself seemed almost within grasp. Meanwhile, there was need for some of the money to be diverted back to the canal from whence it came. Even before the Erie had been put to full use, it grew increasingly apparent that it could not support the full burden of traffic seeking to use it. Those early murmurings that suggested hesitantly that perhaps the canal be enlarged turned into loud demands for action as traffic volume rapidly rose to crisis stage. There were boat jams even between ports and almost always bad tie-ups at the locks. A part of the general clamor was an outcry for enlargement of the canal to receive larger boats, able to carry heavier loads of cargo and people.

The original dimensions of the canal had been set at minimum measurements in order to keep the initial cost down. When put to the test of heavy use, they were pitifully inadequate. Only ten years after the waterway opened for business, in 1835, authorization was given for the widening and deepening of the canal. The reconstruction plans called for an expansion of the width from 40 feet to 70 feet and for its deepening from 4 feet to 7 feet. The shallow draft of the original canal permitted load limits up to only 150 tons. The reconstruction plan also provided that there be built double locks, measuring 110 feet by 18 feet.

The program of enlargement necessarily had to be carrried out without interrupting the heavy daily use of the waterway, and that made the job, in some ways, a more difficult undertaking than the original construction project. Political squabbling, economic depressions, and engineering problems caused repeated delays in the work. It was not until 1862 that the work was finished—twenty-seven years altogether, but in time to allow the canal to make an important contribution to the Union cause in the Civil War.

Even as the state studied the need for rebuilding the Erie, there were loud voices calling for action on proposals to build feeder canals that would tie into Clinton's Ditch. Communities and areas far from the regions served directly by the Erie saw their future to be dependent on some kind of connection with the canal. With it, they could tap the prosperity it was carrying wherever it went. Within a period of a few years a whole system of side cuts—lateral canals reaching into remote areas— was authorized.

Almost as soon as the Erie itself had been completed in 1825, the state had begun this system of feeder canals by starting construction of the twenty-four-mile Oswego Canal, a link between the Erie and Lake Ontario at Oswego. It was opened in 1828. Among other auxiliary canals authorized was the Cayuga and Seneca Canal, which joined the largest of the Finger Lakes and brought them within the Erie's system; it also was finished in 1828. The Chemung Canal in 1833 extended the system farther south, to Elmira, near the Pennsylvania border. Oneida Lake was connected through a five-mile canal in 1835, and two years later the Chenango Canal joined the Susquehanna River with the Erie Canal at Utica. The Genesee Canal, from Rochester south to Olean, New York, and ultimately to the Allegheny River, was started in 1837.

No part of the sensational success of the Grand Canal in New York escaped the attention of people in other states. Canal construction became a form of madness in the young nation, a madness called, in fact, canal fever. New York State had proven to the nation that the canal was the answer to the condition of restricted movement that had kept the great new land from realizing its destiny. With the recklessness of men bursting their bonds, many other states followed New York's lead with ambitious canal projects of their own. Pennsylvania, Maine, Massachusetts, New Jersey, Virginia, Connecticut, Ohio, Delaware, and Maryland were among the states that became involved in the building of artificial waterways. The competition for Irish ditchdiggers was fierce.

Some 800 miles of canals altogether were opened and put in use between 1820 and 1830 in New York, Pennsylvania, Delaware, and Maryland. Another 1,300 miles were started and under construction during that decade. In the words of one observer, "the whole land was aflame with the fever of progress."

As it turned out, none of the many canals that were built in the wake of the Erie enjoyed anywhere near the success, impact, or significance of the New York masterpiece. Many of them, reckoned in terms of cost and operating losses, were outright failures. Yet, from the standpoint of the over-all effect of these canals on the nation, it would have to be said that most of them represented a worthwhile investment.

It is a certainty that the nation would have been a lot poorer without the experience of having lived through the canal age, no matter how few in number the years. No time in American history stands out in such romantic light as the time when the mule-drawn boats moved in leisurely procession through the peaceful countryside that so recently had been the wilderness frontier. No mode of transportation quite so tranquil in its basic form ever has been known to man. That is not to say that all canal rides were tranquil. According to reports passed down, there were times when the canal ride was both suspenseful and exciting. But if matters followed their usual course, a trip by canalboat was a dreamy, languid experience, deliberate and unhurried. No hissing of steam; no clanging or roaring of engines; only the muffled, steady, clop-clop of the hoofs on the towpath, the rippling sound of the boat moving through water, perhaps the screech of a hawk soaring overhead or the lowing of a cow in the meadow or the croaking of some puffed-up frogs along the muddy banks.

The canal was the way for dreamers who wanted nothing more than a slow-moving panorama as a backdrop for their thoughts, who preferred to laze along and lose themselves in the fresh beauty of the country. For these, the scenery never got tiresome. What they couldn't find on the bankside or in the sky above, they saw in the canal itself—in the reflections of the high trees and overhanging bushes and the dappling pattern of the sunlight in the quiet daytime hours, or in the night that blotted out the side banks with its dark shadows but thoughtfully sprinkled stars in the water.

There never was a better form of transportation than this for the man who wanted to see the new country as he traveled, for the person who felt that getting there really was half the fun of a trip. But if the canal was the way for patient, relaxed travelers, it, paradoxically, also was the way to travel for people who were in a hurry. The alternative, after all, was the horse-drawn wagon or coach over rutted roads and rough terrain or going by foot. The canal was the frontier's equivalent of the limited-access highway of the twentieth century—smooth, level, graded, and set aside for the exclusive use of the traffic willing to pay the toll. Canal travel was the fastest and most comfortable way to travel through the type of country represented by Upper New York State, and when compared with the arduous overland journeys over the mountains it stood out as nothing less than a rapturous experience, even though the top legal speed on the canal was only four miles per hour. There was a good reason for such a modest speed limit; any speed above that maximum caused waves that were most damaging to the earthen banks of the canal. The average speed of travel, while closer to two miles per hour, nevertheless represented a considerable improvement over precanal days, when people could expect to take three weeks or more to travel from Buffalo to Albany. Travel time over the same distance by canal was from eight to eleven days.

Not everybody was elated by the sudden acceleration in travel tempo and the prospect of rocketing across the state at close to four mph. One Rochester resident, faced with his first ride on a canalboat, described his apprehension:

"Commending my soul to God, and asking his defense from danger, I stepped on board the canalboat, and was soon flying towards Utica."

Many kinds of boats rode the Grand Canal. The variety was especially rich in the beginning days before multiple-ownership and operation of fleets of canal craft by companies became the order of things. Before sophisticated designs took over, it was every man for himself, and many farmers took it on themselves to build their own boats for transporting crops to market via the waterway. There were no bothersome government regulations to interfere with this expression of free enterprise. The canal was open to any traffic willing to pay the tolls and for that reason it sometimes was known as "Everyman's Highway."

In the opening years a strange and wonderful assortment of homemade boats came floating out of the farms of New York State, perhaps the most bizarre fleet of boats ever to sail anywhere, and with crews to match. There simply isn't any part of the normal agricultural routine around the farm that prepares a person for a life before the mast.

Part of the lore that lives on from the pioneering days on the canal system is the story of the farmer who, using homemade plans, built a boat that he proposed to use for general hauling. With two of his farm hands serving as the crew, he launched the boat and started out on his first voyage on the canal. On the first night, wisely, the farmer moored the boat in the basin of one of the towns along the line and he and his crew took to their bunks. While they were sleeping, some of the young bloods in town, knowing of the farmer's inexperience as a sailor, turned the boat around and pointed it in the opposite direction. The farmer and crew failed to notice the switch-around the next morning and blithely sailed out of port, headed in the wrong direction. It occurred to the amateur sailors after a while that much of the scenery looked vaguely familiar, but the men shrugged off their feeling of unease and sailed on. It wasn't until they came to a town they had passed the previous day that it became clear to them that they were doubling back on their trail.

In comparison with other farmer-sailors, the wrong-way victim looked like a real marine expert, though, because his boat at least floated. There were any number of do-it-yourself products that foundered on launching. Others had a habit of sinking at their moorings in the basins overnight. The four-foot depth of the canal proved to be a blessing at such times.

The most common type of boat on the Erie at first was the long, graceless Durham boat. It had been used for many years on the Mohawk River, especially, and it had acquitted itself well as a carrier of people and goods. Its propulsive power had been the long poles of strong-muscled boatmen, but it was easily adapted to canal use and served well. It was many years before the Durhams vanished from the active canal scene.

Prominent in the family of boats that evolved purely out of the needs of canal transportation were the packets, named after the swift oceanic passenger ships. The canal packet was not appreciably faster than any other type of boat, although it held an edge; but it was designed strictly as a carrier of people and that fact alone made it distinctive. Passengers also were carried on the so-called "line" boats, given that name because they usually were operated by lines rather than individual owners. The packet, by comparison, was a deluxe carrier. Where passengers on the line boats had to compete with cargo and less comfortable accommodations, the packet passenger went first class.

People had priority in those days, curiously enough, and packets, for that reason, enjoyed preferential treatment in the rules of the canal. A packet, for instance, always was passed through a lock ahead of other boats, even if the others had gotten there first and may have been waiting in line for a long time. This sort of special advantage, perhaps more than the actual speed of the packet, enabled it to travel the canal in much better time than boats that carried freight. Passengers, in return, paid a premium fare to ride the packets.

Although the packet was the greyhound of the canal and something of an aristocrat among boats, it didn't have many friends. The crews of other boats resented its favored position in the rules of passage, its passengers usually grumbled about its cramped quarters, and even the Canal Commission had reason to dislike the packet. Because of its speed, the packet did a lot of damage to the banks of the canal, but worse, the revenue paid into the canal coffers by the packet operators was no more than one twentieth of the amount contributed by the freighter traffic. Nevertheless, packets continued to enjoy a position of primacy until the railroads relieved them of their human cargo and put them out of business in the 1850s.

In their prime days, the patronage of the packets usually was confined to the well-to-do. Immigrants and frugal Yankee travelers almost always settled for the canal version of steerage travel, the line boats, which featured minimum fare and maximum discomfort. Line boats carried both freight and people and it was a tossup which got better treatment. Horace Greeley made direct allusion to the painful realities of this type of canal facility when he wrote: "I say nothing about the good old times, but if anyone would recall the good old line boats—I object!"

If the packet cabins were small and confining—and they were—the line boat's accommodations were even more restrictive and generally less hygienic. After riding a line boat from Weed's Basin (later Weedsport) to Lyons, a short ride, an irascible passenger named Colonel Stone wrote that "the cabins were too small to turn around in, the beds dirty, fleas and bedbugs numerous, and the passengers . . . all Jackson men, as the color of their shirt collars abundantly attested."

The people who rode the line boats had to pay extra for their meals, buy their food at stores along the canal, or forage. The latter, incidentally, was a very real way of subsistence. The line boat was so slow that its passengers could hop off and pick berries in the fields, hunt rabbits, and otherwise live off the land in the measured course of their journey. The horses and mules that pulled the heavy craft were called on to deliver maximum service, and they showed it in their plodding pace. Where a packet might be given fresh tow animals every ten miles or so, the line boat team would stay on the towpath at work for fifteen or twenty miles, or even more. That was one of the reasons why a line boat usually traveled only about forty miles a day, against the eighty or ninety miles covered by the packet. Several factors determined a boat's speed, but the most important one was the number of animals pulling the towline. Freighters usually were towed by a team of horses or mules. Packets, as a rule, were pulled by three mules trotting in tandem. Horsepower was a variable, however. Boats would be towed by a single mule in some instances, or there might be as many as six animals in harness. The weight of the cargo was a determining factor, as was the need for speed.

The line boat was so uncomfortable that even customers who didn't have to forage for food as they traveled chose to spend a lot of time on foot, ambling alongside the boat that was supposed to be carrying them. When the weather was inclement, of course, the confinement in the small cabin was a stern test of everybody's powers of survival and all-around ability to endure close quarters.

Even though the line boat was uncomfortable, at least the passengers did not have the fear of foundering and drowning that usually besets people who travel on the water. No matter how wildly the wind blew, lashed the waters and sent streams of spray across the bow; no matter how the driving rain splattered against the cabin full of huddled, pinch-nostriled humanity, there still was the heartening awareness that it is not easy to sink in four feet of water. The real fear was not drowning, but suffocation.

Most numerous by far of all the boats that rode the Erie were the ones that carried freight exclusively. Because they generally were of a design characterized by a rounded bow, the boats most commonly used as freighters were called "ball heads," but in the course of time, probably through mispronunciation, the common name became "bullheads." Most of the bullheads, not having to set aside room for human passengers, boasted their own water-going stables. While two mules (or horses) were at work on the towpath, their replacements would be on board, resting or munching feed. There were operators, however, who preferred to use all available space aboard for freight, and they would rent fresh tow animals at stations found at regular intervals on the canal.

It would be unfair to consider the Grand Canal only in the light of its utilitarian value as a mover of freight and people. The Ditch also brought into the lives of otherwise isolated communities a variety of advantages that they never had known before. To be a backwoodsman, as western New Yorkers had been before the canal, was to be in exile so far as the arts and the social frivolities were concerned. The canal changed that situation. Among the many floating wonders were traveling general stores that took groceries, dry goods, and utensils into the heart of what had been Indian country only a few years before. The Indians, in fact, were among the most enthusiastic patrons of the marine merchants, although they were not nearly as fervid in their feeling for the floating grocery store as they were for the floating saloons that drifted up and down the canal, meeting the customers, you might say, more than half way.

There also were the show boats that took the legitimate theater into areas that never had known such culture and sophistication in entertainment. The small size of the average canalboat made it impractical for use as a theater and the traveling show company usually performed in a local hall. At least one of the itinerant showmen, however, overrode the problem of boat size by using a fleet of three boats. Each of the boats was so constructed that the sides were removable, and when all three were lashed together at dock in the basin of a town, they created one fairly large stage on water.

There could have been no more dramatic setting than this for high drama, with the canalboats as the stage and the woods of the receding wilderness as the backdrop. Little wonder that the show boat was such an important part of the canal scene.

CHAPTER XIII

NO HEIGHTS LEFT

De Witt Clinton and his family in Albany had a box seat, nothing less, from which they could observe the great stirring of humanity that followed the opening of the West by New York's canal system. The effect it wrought immediately on the picturesque, slow-moving old capital was profound.

Albany was the vital junction point that received the traffic from the Champlain Canal from the north and the Erie Canal from the west. Everything and everyone came together here, sooner or later.

The governor and his family lived in one of Albany's most imposing mansions, looking out upon the corner of North Pearl and Steuben streets, among the busiest of the city's intersections. There must have been many nights when, too captivated by the scene to sleep, Clinton looked out upon the bustle from the dark of his bedroom and marveled over the change his own energy and suasion had wrought in the state's capital city.

New boats were being built and launched every day in every port on the canal, and it was impossible, even for the authorities, to keep accurate count of the number of craft plying Erie's waters. Any tabulation became obsolete by nightfall. But the people of Albany didn't need any statistician to tell them that the last lingering traces of the tranquil Dutch dorp at the head of the tidal Hudson were being routed by progress. In 1824, shortly after partial canal service had connected the city with much of the western interior of the state, the population of Albany was put at slightly more than 12,000 persons. Within twenty-six years, by 1850, the population had grown fourfold, to 50,000.

It was this great human tide sweeping inland that was part of the bustling scene that the Clintons could watch from their windows and their wide portico, not merely players in the scene of awakening America, but part of a living pageant that was only beginning and which would grow still more. At every hour of the day and the night the rumble of freight-laden wagons and of sturdy coaches filled with travelers could be heard, and over the rumble the ringing sound of iron rims rolling over cobblestones.

There were those who were leaving and those who were arriving, some going south and some going north and some going west. The direction didn't matter. The country was on the go, and Albany, like Schenectady only fifteen miles away, suddenly had taken on fresh importance as a point of transfer and distribution. The Erie Canal, it was true, opened the water connection between the two cities, but anybody who was in a hurry to get along took the quicker land route. The short stretch of canal between the Hudson and Schenectady was scenic to the point of being spectacular as the Mohawk tumbled down between canyon walls to the level of the Hudson, but the many locks made it trying passage to anybody in a hurry.

Freighters stayed on the canal all the way, of course, but the passengers eastbound found it expedient to leave their packets at Schenectady and proceed to Albany by land coaches drawn by teams of fast horses rather than ride the locks. The last stage of their journey to New York City, if they so elected, could be on a comparatively luxurious, fast steamer. In the reversal of this travel chain, westbound passengers waited until they arrived overland in Schenectady before they resigned themselves to the slow pace and cramped quarters of the canalboats.

What the Erie had set in motion, assuredly, was more than Clinton had foreseen as a consequence of his plan to improve internal travel in New York State. A small part of the movement by canal would have been a rich return on the investment and more than enough justification for its construction. But instead of being merely a sensible improvement that allowed freer, cheaper movement of people and goods, the canal was proving to be an instrument of revolutionary change in many areas of living. From the very beginning it began shifting some basic factors in the national life on which the political, economic, and social institutions of the day were delicately balanced.

Clinton was an astute man. The realization of change beyond expectation did not escape him as he looked from his mansion out on streets clogged with carts and coaches or as he contemplated the huge Albany canal basin and its great pier, capable of handling some 2,000 canalboats at a time but already taxed to the limit by business. Beyond the Mohawk gap, he knew, his Ditch was carrying civilization and population to the western part of the state and beyond.

Widespread settlement in the newly opened territories of New York meant significant things to a working politician: new political alignments, changing issues, shifting geographical emphasis, different techniques of campaigning, and fresh personalities. There was coming into being, in sum, a new power base on which future political successes would have to rest, a different constituency that would have to be satisfied.

More to the point, it did not escape Clinton that the swelling population of New York assured a stronger hand for the state in the national political scene. It was in this direction that Clinton's ambition was turned. Once before he had run as a candidate for President of the United States, in 1812, and he had made a fairly creditable showing under the unfavorable circumstances that found him running as a peace candidate when to be for peace was almost to be unpatriotic. That candidacy had been somewhat premature. However, as far as Clinton was concerned, the defeat was not at all conclusive. He had held patiently to his presidential ambition through the years, biding his time until the White House would be within reach again.

Conditions for Clinton's political advancement should have been in their most propitious quarter at this time. His fame was at its peak. Thanks to the canal, he was acclaimed everywhere in the nation as a miracle-worker, but his attractiveness as a presidential possibility was compounded of more substantial ingredients: he was a man of proven probity, scholarship, vision, courage, and determination.

The Clinton touch was felt in all parts, for his canal was uniting a separated nation, nourishing its economy, pushing back the frontiers, replenishing the population, and strengthening the country's military position.

Even if his credentials as an extraordinary individual and statesman were put aside, there still remained in Clinton's favor the formidable fact that he was governor of New York. Anybody in that office dealt nationally from a position of great strength. Beginning the quest for the presidency with the support of the most populous state in the nation was no small advantage.

Despite these positive points, Clinton knew as well as anybody else that he was, at best, a dark horse in the race for the White House in the national election coming up in 1828. John Quincy Adams, also a Republican, was President, but it was a foregone conclusion that he would be a one-term President. The popular choice to unseat Adams was Democrat Andrew Jackson, whom Clinton admired and supported.

The power of the Jackson personality and his tremendous appeal to the people overshadowed all other political considerations. He was a determined man and he would not be denied his bid for the presidency as he had been in 1824, when, even though he had led the field over the three other candidates in popular votes and in electoral votes, he had not polled the required majority and the House of Representatives awarded the election to Adams.

The Clinton victory in the New York gubernatorial election of 1826 kept his candidacy alive in the unlikely event that Jackson's campaign should falter, and there was a minor ground swell in other states in Clinton's behalf—public rallies in Virginia and in Ohio, as well as in New York State, which called on him to make himself available as a candidate. Clinton felt compelled to announce through the newspapers that he did not desire the presidency. He reiterated that position in letters to friends and political associates.

The rumors persisted. Politicians who disclaim any desire for the White House are never taken at their word. Clinton meanwhile continued to act like a candidate. He traveled a good deal outside of his home state and he made a great many speeches. They were easily arranged. He was in great demand, a glamorous figure, especially in states anxious to begin canal projects of their own. Clinton could claim much of the credit, in fact, for the two great north–south canals built in Ohio in the years immediately following the construction of the Erie. Ohio had been the only state to step forward and offer financial assistance to New York in the building of the Grand Canal, and while the offer had been declined, Clinton remembered Ohio's generosity and took a personal interest in promoting the two canals which had been proposed there— one, the Ohio and Erie Canal to connect Lake Erie and the Ohio River, following a line from Cleveland to Portsmouth; the second to connect the lake and the river in the western part of the state, between Toledo and Cincinnati. It was Governor Clinton who induced John Jacob Astor to lend $1 million to the Ohio and Erie Canal project. The governor also lent Ohio the services of James Geddes as chief engineer of the project. In 1825, when the first shovelful of dirt was turned on the project, it was Governor Clinton who did the honors.

Instead of resenting Clinton's widespread traveling and his ceremonial appearances in out-of-the-way places, most New Yorkers took a vicarious pleasure in the national recognition being lavished on their governor. Even Martin Van Buren had worked tirelessly in behalf of Clinton's bid for re-election as governor in 1826. At the same time, he promoted the candidacies of his own supporters seeking election to the legislature, minor state posts, and local offices throughout the state. In the end, Clinton had won the governorship again, but it was the Van Buren forces who won control of the state. When Clinton moved on to whatever honors awaited him in the national capital, as he was expected to, Van Buren presumably would make his move toward the governorship.

Strangely, the state election of 1826, while resulting in victory for Clinton, was anything but a pleasant experience for him. His opponent, William B. Rochester, was not a powerful one—no competition, really, for the incumbent governor. Yet the election was unexpectedly close. A lot of Clinton's old friends and supporters deserted him at the polls—an estimated 30,000 of them—not by voting for Rochester, but simply by not voting for either candidate.

The main issue of the campaign, which has been described as one "shot through with excitement, hatred and malice," was not political in nature. Clinton could have coped with it easily if it had been. For all his idealism and intellectualism, he was as well versed in the ins and outs of practical politics as any man could be. The thing that hurt his candidacy most, however, was his high standing as a member and officer of the Masonic order.

The election campaign came at a time when a wave of resentment, even revulsion, toward Freemasonry because of the notorious William Morgan case was sweeping the United States. The only thing that prevented Clinton from being defeated by the issue was the fact that his opponent, Rochester, also was a Mason. The only way in which the anti-Masonic voters could show their feeling was by not voting for either man, by not voting at all.

The election and all its unpleasantness over, Clinton was happy to return to the subject of his favorite project, the Erie Canal, in his opening message to the state legislature in January 1827. The returns from the first full year of operation were incomplete, but they still were impressive enough to dazzle all onlookers, even the most skeptical. Income from all authorized canal sources in 1826, he reported, exceeded $1,000,000. It was a most remarkable initial return for one year on an investment of $7,700,000.

"This state," said Governor Clinton, "has derived great reputation from its enterprise in undertaking, and its perseverance in executing, a work of immense benefit, and it ought to set another example of the extinguishment of a great public debt. This precedent will be more beneficial in itself, and more animating in all its aspects and consequences, than any fugitive or even permanent advantages that can emanate from another course."

After being returned as governor, Clinton went to special pains to disavow any presidential ambitions. He became so outspoken in support of his friend Jackson that political experts, including Van Buren, began to favor the idea that Governor Clinton would be Jackson's running mate— if not the vice-presidential candidate, that he would be Jackson's Secretary of State.

The reasoning was fairly sound. Jackson looked to be unstoppable in his run for the presidency, and there was a nice rapport between these opposites, Clinton the aristocrat from New York and Jackson the backwoods fighter from Tennessee. Each, in his own way, was a rugged individualist. Each was a big man with respect for the other. And joining the two was the bond of Freemasonry. They were united in this fellowship, as in other parts of their philosophy, against Adams, who was known to be anti-Masonic.

The one sure thing was that change of some kind was in the offing. Clinton's job in New York was finished. He had no heights left to climb in his home state, no challenge there to meet. The Erie Canal was built and it was an assured success—all that he had promised it would be, and more. The governorship had lapsed into a routine political post, and with Clinton in his fourth term it had begun to pall. It stood to reason that a Jackson triumph in the national election of 1828 would provide the vehicle that would take Clinton to Washington in some high capacity.

But none of this was to be. In December of 1827, Governor Clinton suffered a severe attack of influenza from which he was not to recover. His health had not been the best since the accident that had injured his leg in 1818, and he had spent his energies recklessly during the critical years of the canal construction, riding the route by horseback in all kinds of weather and pushing his endurance to the limit. When illness struck, he was in no condition to resist.

In February 1828 when a physician friend of Clinton's, Dr. Hosack by name, paid a call on the governor before leaving Albany on a journey, he found him in such poor condition that he wrote to a friend: "I shall never see Clinton again."

Not long afterward, on February 11, the governor appeared before the state Senate and delivered his annual message. He looked like a man who had been through a severe illness. His face had an unhealthy pallor and he walked across the chamber with an uncertain gait and with a noticeable stoop to his large shoulders. But his voice was strong, and he spoke with the authority that was so much a part of the public man. After he had finished speaking, he stayed in the chamber long enough to exchange greetings with old friends and to acknowledge the comments of well-wishers.

He spent the early part of that afternoon at his desk, writing letters, talking to his assistants, discussing matters with state officials. After an early supper, he conferred with his son Charles, who served as his secretary. They sat for a while in the library of the executive mansion and discussed the pressing problems of the moment and the schedule of appointments immediately ahead.

Suddenly the governor sat back in his chair and complained of a pain in his chest. His face turned ashen gray as he clutched at his shirtwaist.

Charles Clinton bolted to his feet and ran for assistance. When he returned a few minutes later, a glass of water in his hand, his father was dead.

Knowledge of the governor's poor health had been widespread, but his death was a shock. The governor, while only fifty-eight, had been so long a fixture in the political life of New York State that few people could remember when he had not been a factor in their government. During the administration of President George Washington, Clinton had been secretary to his uncle, Governor George Clinton. Beginning in 1797, when he was elected to the state Assembly, he had served in public office almost without break, up to the time of his death, a period of some thirty-one years.

124

Just as his canal came to cross the state and join the separated parts of America, Clinton's political career spanned time itself and connected the founding days of the nation with the beginning of its rise to a position of international strength.

All government offices closed in Albany the day after the governor's death, and the state went into a period of official mourning. Newspapers carried long columns of florid editorial praise and somber recollections of the highlights in Clinton's long political career. All the members of New York's congressional delegation met in Washington to honor the departed governor, and they heard Martin Van Buren eulogize his former adversary.

A tribute in the New York *American,* written by the editor, Charles King, son of the governor's old foe Rufus King, said:

"In the great work of internal improvement, he persevered through good report and through evil report, with a steadiness of purpose that no obstacle could divert, and when all the elements were in commotion around him, and even his chosen associates were appalled, he alone, like Columbus on the wide waste of waters in his frail bark with a disheartened and unbelieving crew, remained firm, self-poised, and unshaken."

The funeral services for Clinton were held on February 15, and thousands of mourners stood in the streets, heads bared. In its representation, the cortege was impressive enough to be the ceremonial procession for a dead President. Among the marchers were units of the Army and the Navy, high-ranking officials from all levels of government, representatives of every branch of civil life as well as of many of the communities of the state that had benefited so much from Clinton's Ditch.

It was an impressive farewell that New York gave De Witt Clinton—but the political realities asserted themselves quickly as the legislature set about the painful job of determining what amount of financial payment should be settled on the family of the late governor as severance allotment. The words of eulogy, all the rich encomiums, had come cheaply, but the legislators grew tight around the purse strings when it came to the death payment.

The sorry part of the wrangling was that it mattered a good deal to Clinton's widow and family how much money should be allotted them. The great De Witt Clinton, after a lifetime of public service, had left his family in distressing financial condition. He had not made important money as a politician, but apparently it wouldn't have made much difference in the final auditing if he had, because, while a fine administrator in government, Clinton had handled his own affairs loosely. He had been an easy touch for friends pressed for money, and, besides lending out of his own meager treasury, he also had been quick to give his name as a guarantor of notes. In a number of instances, the borrowers had welshed on their debts and Clinton had had to take up the payments.

The Clinton family not only found itself without means of support after the governor's death, it was badly in debt. One creditor alone put in a claim for $6,000. Fearful that he might not get his money, he obtained a judgment that resulted in a public sale of most of the family possessions. Among the personal items of the late governor that went under the liquidator's hammer, was a magnificent set of silver which had been presented to Clinton by a group of "grateful" merchants of New York City after the canal they had opposed, and which had proven so beneficial to their business, had been formally opened.

Enough was realized from the sale to satisfy the judgment, but nothing was left to see the Clinton family, the widow and four minor children, through the difficult years ahead. Several measures of state aid were introduced. One, recognizing that Clinton had refused payment for his services as a canal commissioner for more than a decade, proposed to pay his widow the full salary he had been entitled to in all those years. The governor's old adversary, General Porter of Black Rock, objected, however, with the pious argument that as Clinton had not been willing to accept such compensation in life, he probably would be opposed to it in death.

Among the several who spoke out feelingly against giving any financial aid whatsoever to the Clinton family was the famous Erastus Root. General Porter, however grudgingly, at least was willing to introduce a bill which would provide the governor's surviving children a grant of $10,000, plus the remainder of the salary due the governor for the current year, 1828. That arrangement, as it turned out, was as far as the state of New York cared to go in extending financial help.

The most poignant part of the final scene in the De Witt Clinton drama was that while the dead governor received the grandest of state funerals, when it was all over the family had no place in which to bury him. His widow was without funds with which to purchase a suitable gravesite.

Pending the day when that embarrassing situation could be righted, Governor Clinton's remains were given into the care of an old family friend in Albany, a Dr. Stringer, who had volunteered to keep the body in his own family vault. Some old friends, including two former secretaries of the governor, General Peter Gansevoort and Simeon De Witt Bloodgood, offered to purchase a vault in which the governor's remains could rest, but the proud family decided instead that it would be more appropriate to allow a general subscription of contributions to such a fund.

Eventually enough money was collected to provide a suitable burial—some sixteen years later. On June 21, 1844, a newspaper in Albany printed this small announcement:

"The remains of De Witt Clinton, which had been deposited in the cemetery in Swan Street, were removed to New York for interment under a monument created by the family."

Governor De Witt Clinton at long last was laid to rest in Greenwood Cemetery in Brooklyn. In later years a great bronze statue of him was placed at the gravesite. But Clinton was one of the few men who really needed no formal monument. The great canal system that he built and the public school system that he helped bring into being were reminders enough of this exceptional statesman.

CHAPTER XIV

LIFE ON THE CANAL

Life on the Erie Canal constituted a culture all its own—a way of existence that included its own vocabulary, its own laws, its own dangers, and its own beauty.

In the view of some, it was a hard, demanding life—and no doubt it was for many of the 50,000 or more human beings whose livelihood depended on it during its peak years. Yet it offered special rewards that those same people found irresistible. The world of the canal was an escape from boredom; it had its own special excitement and its people breathed the exhilarating air of freedom.

The canallers had colorful vocabularies and were themselves among the most creative word-coiners in American history. Many of their expressions found a permanent place in America's speech, but most of them disappeared at the end of the canal era.

A "hoodledasher," for example, was a hookup of two or more empty cargo boats to a full cargo boat so that one span of mules could pull all three at the same time. To "hit the logs" had the same meaning as today's "hit the road"—the roads then were mostly of the so-called "corduroy" type with a log base. "Long-eared robins" referred to mules; so did "hayburners." A "hoggee" was the term for a boy driver, apparently an outgrowth of an English word, "hogler," which meant a field laborer of the lowest class in early England.

Child labor was an accepted part of the national scene in America of the nineteenth century, and young boys found ready employment on the Grand Canal. The glamour of canal life naturally had a great attraction for youth—as much, say, as going to sea or joining the circus—even for a future President of the United States. Among the children of the canal era was James A. Garfield, who at the age of sixteen became a boat driver on the Ohio and Erie Canal. His father had been one of the workers in the construction of that canal and of him it was said "he could take a barrel of whisky by the chime and drink out of the bung-hole, and no man dared call him a coward."

A Captain Parkhurst of the boat *Blue Bird* had a story that he relished telling, of the time he witnessed a fight "at Lock No. 1, Akron, between a boatman and a heavy-set, muscular boy, the driver of the canal boat, *Evening Star*, on the side-cut canal.

"The former's boat reached the lock first and a taunting remark by a member of the crew caused the boy driver to take the black-snake whip from around his neck and pitch it at the fellow, knocking him down, with the result that the boy's boat entered the lock first. This boy was afterwards President Garfield!"

A missionary report in 1848 claimed that some 10,000 boys were employed on the canals of New York. Nearly all of them worked as drivers; that is, they walked the towpath with the mules and horses, keeping them in line and moving at the necessary speed. It was not an easy job, nor were the employers generous in the scale of remuneration they provided the youngsters. Boy drivers made from $8 to $10 a month—the bottom of the financial scale in the canal table of organization. Many of the boys never even received that pitiful pittance due them—the boys customarily were paid their wages in full at the end of each navigation season, but it was not uncommon for unscrupulous captains to cheat the youngsters out of part or all of their earnings.

Some of the boys eventually found a good deal more on the canal than employment, encountering every form of vice and corruption. The exposure of youth in large numbers to such adult depravity eventually became something of a national scandal.

Evil travels a two-way street, of course. It seeks out some and by others is sought out. There is plenty of evidence to suggest that many of the boys who worked on the canal came to overtake their elders in the matter of immorality—no easy accomplishment if we can believe the allegations contained in some of the eyewitness reports of the time. The Rochester *Observer*, for instance, once made the wry editorial observation that, in light of the "prostitution, gambling, and all species of vice practiced on our canals" the Erie Canal should be called "Big Ditch of Iniquity."

In 1845 a proposal was brought forward which would have established a "House of Refuge" in Syracuse, where an effort could be made to reform "vicious drivers." At the same time, other dormitories—not reformatories—were proposed so that homeless canal boys would have a place to live during the winter months.

Winter was the unhappy, often desperate, time of the year for canal people, boys and adults alike. The curse of the canal was that it was seasonal. Widespread public disapproval of the manners and morals of the canallers could be shrugged off, perhaps, when the boats were in operation and everybody was busy, but during the four or five months when the bleak upstate New York winter held the canal in its grip, the canallers had to scramble for a means of subsistence.

There is little doubt that the least of their lot, the boy drivers, suffered the most in the wintertime layoff period. The mortality rate was horrendously high among the homeless, friendless youngsters, most of whom were victims of malnutrition, disease, overwork, and the harsh indifference of a harsh time. Yet a surprising number of the boys lived to become men, and out of their ranks came some of the storied characters of the canal—the steersmen, locktenders, and even captains, with brass-buttoned uniforms and high black silk hats.

One of the success stories was that of Michael Moran, the child of a large Irish family that settled in the town of Frankfort on the canal in 1850. He hired out as a driver at fifty cents a day to help in the support of his family. The job called for him to walk with the mules on the towpath on the eighty-mile stretch to Albany—six hours of steady walking and six hours off. Unlike most of the canal workers, the young, ambitious Moran made his job pay off. He saved his money and became a steersman, saved more money and bought his own boat and became a captain. In only ten years, by 1860, he owned a fleet of canalboats and was becoming involved in the business of towing canalboats on the Hudson River between Albany and New York. Out of his enterprise emerged the large and successful Moran Towing and Transportation Company which today is so prominent in the New York Harbor scheme of things.

During young Moran's time, the Hudson became probably the busiest river in America. After the odd-looking canalboats had been towed downriver to New York City, they were given space at the foot of Broad and South streets, at piers numbered 5 and 6. To either side of them were the tall-masted sailing clippers from the exotic ports of the world, the great barks and schooners that were awash with all the mystery and romance of the seven seas. In contrast to them were the small, squat boats from places like Rochester, Syracuse, and Weedsport, boats built to ride in four feet of water and which never were more than jumping distance from land during a voyage. It was a curious mixture.

To say that there was friction between the salt sailors of the ocean-going ships and the crews of the canalboats is to toy with understatement. The way in which that friction generally was dispelled was so ferocious that the term "a Pier Six Brawl" found its way into American speech as the ultimate in personal combat.

The same kind of exciting recreation ashore was waiting for the canal men at the other end of the Erie Canal, in Buffalo, where the sailors of the Great Lakes ships were just as eager as the ocean-going sailors to back up their low opinion of canal men with their fists, clubs, and knives.

Fighting was no novelty on the canal itself; on the contrary, it was almost a way of life among the rugged men who kept the boats moving. The hours were long, the pace of travel was maddeningly slow, living space on the boats was cramped and uncomfortable, the work of loading and unloading the boats was hard, wages were low, and every canal trip was beset with exasperating delays that frayed the nerves. Small wonder that when the crews got shore leave at the end of a trip, they were in a fighting mood! Nor was brawling confined to the terminal cities at either end; it was a commonplace occurrence the entire length of the waterway.

Natural rivalries developed between individual boats, between competing lines, and, of course, between individuals on the boats. Fighting was as much a recreation as it was an expression of anger, and men who excelled at fighting were held in high estate. Captains vied for the services of leading muscle men, commonly known as "bullies," so as to have their boats properly represented on the field of honor.

Among the most famous of the bullies was a giant Negro whose full name has been lost to history. He was known simply as "Sleepy Frank." Besides his great reputation for fighting, he was famed for his ability to jump great distances. It was said that, when aroused, he was capable of leaping across a fifteen-foot lock to get at a taunting foe. More interesting, though, than his leaping prowess was what he was able to do with his fists. He left a lot of battered men in his wake.

Another famous bully was a man named Ben Streeter, known as "The Rochester Bully." Streeter worked on the Genesee Canal most of his life, but he left his mark on the Erie, too, because so many of his foes were from the Grand Canal's boats. Rochester was the natural battleground because it was where the Genesee and the Erie canals met. A dispute at that junction led to an impromptu battle between Streeter and a bully from a Buffalo-based boat that is still recalled with relish by local historians who treasure such memorabilia. The fight took place in the old Rochester Arcade and aroused such high feeling in the city—among townspeople as well as canallers—that it was said the police "dared not interfere." Streeter won the fight, but only after many hours of shattering give and take.

Another fight in Rochester, one that took place on the Exchange Street Bridge in 1829, drew such a large crowd that the bridge collapsed and spilled fifty persons into the water.

More serious in its results was the collapse of a bridge in the town of Albion in 1859. A daredevil from Brockport had advertised that he would walk a tightrope across the canal as a feature of the county fair being held in Albion. The bridge was an ideal vantage point for the great spectacle, but so many persons jammed onto the span that it gave way under their weight. About 250 persons fell into the water. The bodies of fifteen youngsters later were found tangled in the wreckage.

The same weaknesses in human nature that make motorists angry with one another and cause them occasionally to stop and slug it out were at work among the canallers. When the crew of one boat violated the rules of the waterway, the crew of another boat would take offense and spoil for a fight.

Canalboats traveling downstream, or eastward, always had the right of way. It was an important distinction because the teams of horses and mules pulling the boats in either direction used the same towpath and it was just as narrow, in its own way, as the canal itself. When the captain of a downstream boat spotted an upstream boat ahead, he ordered his team of horses to the outside of the towpath and halted. The towline to his boat, gone limp, sank into the water. His boat, meanwhile, was steered to the opposite side of the canal, the side away from the towpath, leaving room for the upstream boat and team to pass between the downstream boat and its team.

When two boats were moving in the same direction, the attempt of one boat to pass another sometimes resulted in an argument or even a pitched battle, unless the passing boat was a packet, in which case the line boat or freighter had to yield the right of way, however grudgingly. The rule that compelled them to yield to packets at locks and in passing situations galled the crews of the freighters and line boats. The packet passed on the portside, and as it moved abreast, the crew of the boat that was yielding even had to help the passenger boat by carrying its towline over their own craft until it was clear. The operation always had lively potential for an occasional skirmish and almost always evoked crude comments that drove genteel female passengers aboard the packet into the cabin, flapping their skirts in horror.

There was one boat that had priority over all others on the canal, over even the packets, in the same way that a fire engine had priority on land. It was a craft called the "hurry-up boat," and it was just that—an emergency boat that was dispatched to the scene of any break in the canal wall to make emergency repairs that would stem the flow of water out of the ditch.

One of the most difficult phases of canal construction was the building of channels that would hold water. Where the soil was porous, it might leak for three years or more after it was built, even though a thick layer of stuff clay, called "puddle," was applied to its side walls. After that period of seasoning, it could be expected to harden enough to contain the water successfully. A continuous lookout to guard against breaks in the walls had to be maintained along the entire length of the canal by watchmen, called "towpath walkers." Whenever they spotted a break or leak, if it were serious enough a call would go out for the hurry-up boat.

The rush of a hurry-up boat to the scene of a break was a grand sight to canal-watchers. The horses towing the boat were allowed to gallop full speed to the spot, and the boat itself stirred up such fierce waves that all other boats on the canal had to lay to for a quarter of an hour before they could resume their journeys. The men on the emergency boat were expert in patching leaks, but time often was an important factor in preventing a major disaster, one that might lower the water level of a canal section to the extent that boats would be unable to travel or, worse, might even be "mudlarked"—stuck in the mud of the canal bottom.

The walls of the canal were terribly damage-prone. Erosion of the sides was a natural, weakening process that had to be fought all the time. Waves caused by speeding boats were another major contributor to the deterioration of the channel. But perhaps the most persistent enemy was the happy little muskrat. A single industrious muskrat could bring boat traffic on the canal to a complete halt simply by digging a hole in the side wall in a critical place. Rewards for the capture of muskrats, dead or alive, were offered by the Canal Commission. If that sounds cruel, consider that in 1872 it was estimated that muskrats were doing $50,000 damage to the canal annually. Sometimes, to be sure, the muskrat was not the guilty party—eels, moles, mink, and even crawfish were considered enemies of the canal.

A recurrent test of tempers always was to be found at the locks as scores of boats awaited their turn to be passed through. The locks were the bottlenecks, even though generally they were very efficient operations. Conditions and factors considered, in fact, their performance was nothing short of remarkable. It was said that under normal conditions a boat could expect to pass a lock in as little as three minutes, once it reached its turn—that, of course, being the catch. In the busiest months of the navigating season, an average of 250 boats a day would go through a lock, and that often meant long lines of waiting boats.

The fact that so many boats could be accommodated was a tribute to the amateurs who built the locks and the men who operated them. An idea of the complex arrangement can be found in the following description by a canaller named Richard G. Garrity, whose *Recollections of the Erie Canal* were published by the Historical Society of the Tonawandas:*

"Most of the old Erie Canal locks had two swinging gates on each end of the lock which closed against a miter sill at the bottom of the lock," wrote Garrity. "The gate edges were also mitered to resist the pressure of the water when the lock was full.

"Each gate had two valves in it to empty and fill the lock. The valves were just flat boards, about 12 by 24 inches, pivoted in the middle and hand-operated by a 4-foot lever attached by bell cranks and linkage to the valves in the gates.

"When boats were lowered in the lock, the lower gates were opened

---

* Excerpt from *Recollections of the Erie Canal* by Richard G. Garrity. Reprinted by permission of the Historical Society of the Tonawandas, Inc.

along with the valves in the closed upper gates. This flushed the boat out of the lock because the water could not get around the boat in the lock. The early lock builders designated this type of valve built into the gate as a 'paddle valve.' Locktenders and canal men called the valves 'paddles.'

"Each gate on a lock had a long balance beam attached to it to balance the weight of the gate which hung on a sort of hinge. Many times as a boy, I put my back against the gates and balance beam and pushed with the locktender to open or close the gate. I was never allowed to touch the paddles because of the danger of being injured when the lock was filled or emptied.

"When the paddles, pivoted on center, reached a certain position, the water rushed through the opening with a force strong enough to tear the lever out of one's hands. No harm was done if this happened when one stood on the proper side. If the operator, however, stood on the wrong side of the lever, it usually knocked him into the canal. There were quite a number of injuries and drownings due to the improper operation of these lock paddles. This type of valve was built into the wooden lock gate and had to be operated from a foot plank about 12 inches wide which crossed each gate. The paddles were usually operated with one hand on the lever and one hand on the railing attached to the gate. This type of gate and valves for filling and emptying the locks was the most common in use on the 72 locks in the Erie Canal."

Another system, used in a few of the locks, featured drop gates and a different valve arrangement.

"After this type lock was filled or emptied to allow a boat to enter or leave," Garrity wrote, "the gate was lowered and lay flat on the bottom. The boat then passed over it. The gate was raised or lowered by means of a chain attached to each corner of the gate and was motivated by a hand-cranked windlass on each side of the lock.

"The valves to empty or fill the lock were located ahead of each gate at the side of the lock and tunneled around the gate. Water entered the lock from the side instead of the end. These valves were also operated by a chain and hand-cranked windlass with the water entering from the side. This arrangement was not as efficient in swelling a boat out of the lock and it also required a man on each side to operate the windlass which raised and lowered the gate. In contrast, the swing gate locks could be operated by one man. At most locks, the canal men helped the locktender as it shortened the time required to get through the lock."

"Swelling" was a tricky technique that could be invoked to hasten a boat out of a lock. An expert locktender used it to good effect in expediting the movement of traffic.

"The swells," explained Garrity, "were caused by the opening of the paddle valves in the gates while the locks were being emptied, or by opening the paddle valves in the upper gates of the lock. The resulting

135

rush of water 'swelled' the loaded boats out of the lock after the boats were lowered.

"The average canal boat after 1862 was 16 feet wide, and as the width of a lock was 18 feet at the top and only 17 feet, 2 inches, at the bottom, this narrow clearance often caused the loaded boats to bind in the lock when lowered. Ordinarily, as soon as the lower gates were opened, the tow lines from the team was made fast to the head boat. The team then pulled both boats from the lock and were on their way. If the boats were hard to start, however, or would not start at all, the locktender opened a paddle or two and started the boats moving.

"A slight swell always got the boats started faster and shortened the time going through the locks. If the locktender happened to be a good fellow, he gave the boats a swell when needed without being asked . . . Many of these fellows, however, would not give the boats a swell unless they were first given the price of a couple of beers, which in those days cost a nickel. For a dime, you were really speeded on your way."

There were locktenders, Garrity wrote ruefully, who "held out for a quarter and then it was pay or be stuck."

"If the boats were hung up in the lock too hard, the boatman then had to run out all six mules to get the boats started out of the lock. If the boat captain refused to pay off, there was little else he could do as the practice of swelling the boats out of the locks was frowned upon by the canal authorities. Swelling used too much water and lowered the water on the level above the lock which, at times, caused loaded boats to run aground.

"Swelling also raised the water on the level below the lock, causing cabins on light, or empty boats to strike the low bridges, thus causing considerable damage to the cabins.

"I recall occasions when loaded boats were passing or meeting each other and one of them would run aground. If the team could not start them going, they usually waited for a swell from the locks to start them moving. Occasionally, word was sent back to the last lock requesting an extra heavy swell which was made by opening all four paddle valves on the gates at the same time. This created a swell that travelled the whole length of the shorter levels. It was usually necessary to swell loaded lumber boats from the locks as they always had some list to them because of the high deck load . . ."

The tempers of the canal men often snapped when the waiting was prolonged beyond what they considered reasonable limits. The passage through the lock of a Johnny-come-lately packet was reason enough for rage, but log rafts also infuriated the men on the line boats and the freighters. The log raft likely was the least popular of all the assorted floating objects on the canal waters.

As the tall trees of New York's forests were felled, many of them were floated by stream and river to a canal port, where they were bound together in sections. No section was longer or wider than the size of a lock.

A single log raft would be made up of six to ten detachable sections of logs linked together and towed as a unit by two or three horses in tandem or by a team of oxen. Each raft had a crew of four or five men, who helped keep the raft in line by the expert use of long poles. The crew ate and slept in a rough shanty set up on one of the sections.

Boats had priority over log rafts, but passing a raft with many sections always was a tedious business that invariably slowed the stream of traffic. The crew of the raft was obliged to carry a passing boat's towlines over the log sections as their contribution to the operation. The temptation at such time to utter disparaging remarks couldn't always be repressed, and frequently the remarks bore physical fruit when the men came together later in a lock traffic jam. From all accounts, though, the battles between the canal crewmen at those places was all that kept the waiting periods from being unendurable.

Log rafts had to be passed through the locks in piecemeal style, one section at a time. When a lineup of boats was waiting to go through, however, the locktender would alternate each section of the raft with a boat. After all the sections had been passed through, the raft had to be reassembled on the other side before it could resume its journey.

No matter how efficiently this cumbersome operation was handled, the log rafts slowed the pace of the canal traffic and were viewed with the same distaste that is reserved today by motorists for slow-moving, broad-beamed trucks on narrow highways. They caused the worst tieups on the canal. One of the classic traffic jams they brought about was recorded at the Macedon Locks, where at one time 131 boats were brought to a stop as the harassed locktenders tried to pass through an especially long log raft with many sections. It finally occurred to the frantic tenders, as they sighted an unbroken line of boats in either direction and after they had listened thoughtfully to the cacophony of whistles, shouts, and insults, that the situation was beyond solution.

At that critical point, the tenders did what many traffic policemen caught up in hopeless automobile jams since have wanted to do. They walked out on the mess. They simply left the scene and went home, leaving the confusion behind them and abandoning everybody to his own devices. Three days and nights passed before the impasse at Macedon Lock was overcome and waterway traffic was able to resume. Locktenders the length of the canal, and those on other canals, always savored that walkout and thought of it as a victory for their side—which it undoubtedly was.

Rain or shine, boatmen and passengers alike looked forward to those parts of the canal known as the "long levels." The designation was reserved for several extraordinary sections that were free of locks and where the canal ran uninterrupted through nice, flat, no-nonsense country in which the crews could relax and the boats had the kind of clear sailing that enabled them to make up lost time.

The long levels provided the most restful phases of any canal journey —no stops, except to change horses, and no vexations—just the steady, reassuring sound of the hoofs thudding on the towpath, splendid scenery to look at, the sibilant sound of the water shearing away from the prow, and always somewhere the lowing of cattle.

The most famous of the long levels was in the middle section of the canal. The Rome Level (also known as the Utica Level) extended from Frankfort to Syracuse, a record distance of 69½ miles without a lock. Just west of this admirable section was the Rochester Level, sixty-five miles of uninterrupted waterway between Rochester and Lockport. When the Erie was reconstructed in later years, the Rome Level was shortened to some fifty-six miles by an alteration of route, thus allowing the Rochester Level to take top honors as the longest of the clear runs.

The tranquil hours on the long levels probably gave the immigrant travelers their best opportunity to begin appreciating the immensity of America and the natural wonders it contained, to observe, without distraction, the vast sweep of field and sky, forests and swamps, and all the strange flora and fauna that were as unfamiliar to the eye as the land itself.

The panorama of the newly opened western lands of New York was one of infinite variety, fresh and clean and fragrant in all its aspects and indescribably appealing. The minds of people who so recently had known the squalor of crowded European cities must have been benumbed when their canalboat slid silently into the high-walled forests that reduced the lateral width of the world to a mere sixty feet, and the tall trees on either side made a majestic canyon that was a proper setting for the still water below and the unbroken sky above, with nothing of the meanness of man in between.

This was the promised land that all the immigrants had heard about, and its beauty and its bounty exceeded all hope and expectation. There was much more beyond, but for many of the newcomers this was land enough, and, for that matter, travel enough. What they had seen was such that they were content to cast their lot with the present reality rather than whatever future fantasy lay ahead, and so they settled in such strange-sounding places as Syracuse, Rochester and Lockport. The truth is they were anxious to begin living, eager to get at the joys that were clearly within reach in America. They got off the canalboats fearfully and shyly, aware of their own alien look and foreign sound, but the light in their eyes said that they were home at last.

CHAPTER XV

THE WAY OF THE IMMIGRANT

No minor achievement, either from the logistical or the human stand-point, was the Erie Canal's performance as the vehicle that carried thousands of European immigrants each year into the heartland of America. It served as a lifeline in the fullest sense as it pumped new blood into the frontier and gave it strength.

Every port along the canal received the newcomers in large numbers, and while there was some social discrimination and snobbery shown to-ward the people from another world—the wearers of babushkas and the speakers of broken English—they still were received gladly because their talents were needed. It was a time of building, of growth and develop-ment, that begged for artisans and mechanics of all kinds to help in the basic jobs that had to be done.

Many of the Yankees who had been numbered in the first surge of population into western New York had made their stay only temporary. Once they had wrenched themselves loose of their old homesteads to the east of the Hudson, it was easy to pick up again and follow the trails that were spreading out farther west, beyond Buffalo. Their replacements were the immigrant families.

The turbulence and restlessness of the time is suggested in an eye-witness description of the Buffalo waterfront that appeared in a publica-tion called the *Genesee Farmer* on June 9, 1832:

"Canal boats filled with emigrants, and covered with goods and furni-ture, are almost hourly arriving . . . Several steamboats and vessels daily depart for the far west, literally crammed with masses of living beings to people those regions. Some days, near a thousand thus depart. Hundreds and hundreds of horse wagons arrive every spring and fall with emigrants from our own state."

The same publication added to this observation, a year later:

"Never before has there been such a crowd of emigration to 'the great west' as during this spring. It seems as though the whole eastern country was pouring out its millions for Ohio and Michigan . . . I have this spring seen great numbers of good substantial people from Ontario, Seneca, Livingston, and the central counties of Western New-York, who are emigrating to the west with their families—more than I have ever known before. They say that they find no difficulty in selling their farms, and at good prices, too."

The extent of the population upheaval is illustrated in the experience of Rochester, which stood out at the time as the most striking example of boom town growth in the country, outside of New York City. While Rochester's population leaped upward every year, it was a restless, transient population. A study of the village's directories of 1827 and in 1834 shows that there was a turnover in that brief time period of approximately 70 per cent of the population!

The same sort of incredible coming and going was occurring in all the other sprouting towns of the canal country. Just as fast as the Yankee settlers, seized anew by the recurrent fever of fortune-hunting and adventure, had pulled up stakes for a plunge further inland, their successors, the newly arrived immigrants, were streaming off the canalboats to fill the vacuum created by the departure of the old American stock. The effect was a significant one—a transfusion of hardy, industrious, ambitious European peoples into a land that was waiting to be used. By 1855, 44 per cent of Rochester's population was foreign-born—a representative statistic.

The one feature of the inland-bound canal trip that probably appealed most to the immigrants was the relative lack of danger. It was a tremendous relief, following the long journey across the stormy Atlantic in some old wooden tub, to be on a boat that was so close to land that a passenger could reach out and almost grab the branches of overhanging trees. There was further assurance in the knowledge that the craft rode on only four feet of water. No matter how wildly the wind blew, lashing the waters and sending streams of spray across the deck, no matter how the driving rain splattered against the cabin filled with human beings, it was still difficult to sink.

Some of the poets of the robust canal days gave a lot of creative thought to the somewhat incongruous drama of a canalboat fighting its way to port through a storm—a drama in a ditch obviously caught their fancy, as it probably did all people with a sense of humor. One of the most quoted tongue-in-cheek songs of the time was titled "The Raging Canal," which spoke in lugubrious language of the ordeal of a canalboat caught in a fierce storm.

Mark Twain appreciated the old song to the extent of writing some sardonic doggerel of his own dealing with such a stormy crisis. He called it, *The Aged Pilot Man:*

On the Erie Canal, it was,
　　All on a summer's day,
I sailed forth with my parents
　　Far away to Albany.

From out the clouds at noon that day
　　There came a dreadful storm,
That piled the billows high about,
　　And filled us with alarm.

A man came rushing from a house,
　　Saying, "Snub up your boat I pray,
Snub up your boat, snub up, alas,
　　Snub up while yet you may."

Our captain cast one glance astern,
　　Then forward glancèd he,
And said, "My wife and little ones
　　I never more shall see."

Said Dollinger the pilot man,
　　In noble words, but few—
"Fear not, but lean on Dollinger,
　　And he will fetch you through."

The boat drove on, the frightened mules
　　Tore through the rain and wind,
And bravely still, in danger's post,
　　The whip-boy strode behind.

"Come 'board, come 'board," the captain cried,
　　"Nor tempt so wild a storm;"
But still the raging mules advanced,
　　And still the boy strode on.

Then said the captain to us all,
　　"Alas, 'tis plain to me,
The greater danger is not there,
　　But here upon the sea.

"So let us strive, while life remains,
　　To save all souls on board,
And then if die at last we must,
　　Let . . . I *cannot* speak the word!"

Said Dollinger the pilot man,
  Tow'ring above the crew,
"Fear not, but trust in Dollinger,
  And he will fetch you through."

"Low Bridge! low bridge!" all heads went down,
  The laboring bark sped on;
A mill we passed, we passed a church,
Hamlets and fields of corn;
And all the world came out to see,
  And chased along the shore

Crying, "Alas, alas, the sheeted rain,
  The wind, the tempest's roar!
Alas, the gallant ship and crew,
  Can *nothing* help them more?"

And from our deck sad eyes looked out
  Across the stormy scene:
The tossing wake of billows aft,
  The bending forests green,

The chickens sheltered under carts
  In lee of barn the cows,
The skurrying swine with straw in mouth,
  The wild spray from our bows!

    "She balances!
    She wavers!
Now let her go about!
  If she misses stays and broaches to,
We're all"—[then with a shout]
      "Huray! huray!
      Avast! belay!
      Take in more sail!
      Lord, what a gale!
Ho, boy, haul taut on the hind mule's tail!"

"Ho! lighten ship! ho! man the pump!
  Ho, hostler, heave the lead!
And count ye all, both great and small,
  As numbered with the dead!
For mariner for forty year
  On Erie, boy and man,
I never yet saw such a storm,
  Or one 't with it began!"

So overboard a keg of nails
    And anvils three we threw,
Likewise four bales of gunny-sacks,
    Two hundred pounds of glue,

Two sacks of corn, four ditto wheat,
    A box of books, a cow,
A violin, Lord Byron's works,
    A rip-saw and a sow.

A curve! a curve! the dangers grow!
    "Labbord!—stabbord!—s-t-e-a-d-y!—so!—
Hard-a-port, Dol!—hellum-a-lee!
    Haw the head mule!—the aft one gee!
Luff!—bring her to the wind!"

"A quarter-three!—'tis shoaling fast!
    Three feet large!—t-h-r-e-e feet!
Three feet scant!" I cried in fright.
    "Oh, is there *no* retreat?"

Said Dollinger the pilot man,
    As on the vessel flew,
"Fear not, but trust in Dollinger,
    And he will fetch you through."

A panic struck the bravest hearts,
    The boldest cheek turned pale;
For plain to all, this shoaling said,
A leak had burst the ditch's bed!
And, straight as bolt from crossbow sped,
Our ship swept on with shoaling lead,
    Before the fearful gale!

"Sever the tow-line! Cripple the mules!"
    Too late! . . . There comes a shock!

      *   *   *   *   *

Another length, and the fated craft
    Would have swum in the saving lock!

Then gathered together the shipwrecked crew
    And took one last embrace,
While sorrowful tears from despairing eyes
    Ran down each hopeless face;
And some did think of their little ones
    Whom they never more might see,
And others of waiting wives at home,
    And mothers that grieved would be.

But of all the children of misery there
  On that poor sinking frame,
But one spake words of hope and faith,
  And I worshipped as they came:
Said Dollinger the pilot man—
  (O brave heart, strong and true!)
"Fear not, but trust in Dollinger,
  For he will fetch you through."

Lo! scarce the words have passed his lips
  The dauntless prophet say'th,
When every soul about him seeth
  A wonder crown his faith!

For straight a farmer brought a plank—
  (Mysteriously inspired)—
And laying it unto the ship,
  In silent awe retired.

Then every sufferer stood amazed
  That pilot man before;
A moment stood. Then wondering turned,
  And speechless walked ashore.

Stormy perils or not, there were people who liked the canal waters enough to live on them during the months of the year when the waterway was open to navigation. There were houseboats, better known as "shanty boats," that carried tinkers and other tradesmen and their families across the span of the state and up and down the side cuts to the most remote places. These were the gypsies, the nomads of the canal, who preferred the free way of life on the water to the routine existence of the conventional life on land.

Not as carefree, but far more numerous, were the families of freighter captains who lived on the boats the year round. The space left over for living quarters was terribly limited, during the sailing season especially, but the families of the canallers adjusted to the cramped life in the small cabins and few of them would have exchanged their way of life for any other.

The children of those water-borne families especially loved the bohemian existence. It was a life made to order for the curious, adventure-seeking minds of the very young, a life in which a boy could fish at any time, go swimming when he wished, wander the towpath when only the buzzing of insects broke the silence of the summer day, go berry picking in the fields, and otherwise consort with nature to his heart's content.

To such as these, the canal was everything.

CHAPTER XVI

PEOPLE FOR THE EMPIRE

The corduroy roads, the gravel turnpikes, the broken river routes, and the portage paths—all had done their best to ease people into the frontier land, but their best allowed no more than a thin stream of humanity to move into western New York in the four decades that followed the Revolutionary War.

There were enough people to create crossroads settlements and river-edge towns, to bring about millstream colonies and to dot the deep forests with farm clearings. Over-all, though, the presence of people was so slight they hardly made any real impression on the immense spread of greenery. Even in their full number, the settlers to the west of Schenectady as late as 1817 represented little more than a token population, a kind of advance party.

It was with the construction of the Erie Canal that the main body of settlers came. Where the old routes had done no more than pry open the wilderness and let slip through the opening a few hardy souls, the canal boldly carried whole cities and enough people to fill the countryside almost overnight. The canal carried civilization, with all its virtues and with all its evils.

The great empire at last began to take shape, springing into being so suddenly that the men who so long had lived and hunted in the forests, who had walked leisurely with nature and known the solitude of the wild, at once were out of place, bewildered by the pace of change.

Nathaniel Hawthorne was among those who saw the wonder of it all, and he felt the regret that goes with sudden realization of loss. He noted that something precious had slipped away forever when, in 1835, he described the Rochester that had materialized out of the wilderness:

"Its edifices are of dusky brick, and of stone that will not be grayer in a hundred years than now; its churches are Gothic; it is impossible to look at its worn pavements and conceive how lately the forest leaves have been swept away . . . The whole street, sidewalks and centre, was crowded with pedestrians, horsemen, stage-coaches, gigs, light wagons, and heavy ox-teams, all hurrying, trotting, rattling, and rumbling, in a throng that passed continually, but never passed away . . .

"I noticed one other idle man. He carried a rifle on his shoulder and a powder horn across his breast, and appeared to stare about him with confused wonder, as if, while he was listening to the wind among the forest boughs, the hum and bustle of an instantaneous city had surrounded him."

But the past left echoes that some men were given to hear.

A mere forty-six years before Hawthorne's observation was published, the first white man had taken up residence on the site of Rochester. The settler was Ebenezer "Indian" Allan, who built a grist mill on the west riverbank at the falls of the Genesee in 1789. When the mill was completed, he gave a party to celebrate the achievement. All the frontiersmen for miles around showed up to help Allan consume a canoe-load of rum, but the party remained on a rather intimate basis because the most men the countryside could yield was fourteen.

As late as 1812 there were encampments of Seneca Indians on the outskirts of the settlement, and it was not until 1817 that the town was formally incorporated under the name of Rochesterville in honor of Colonel Nathaniel Rochester. The canal made the difference shortly thereafter. Its effect on the new town was magical. In 1816, Rochester had 331 people; in 1820, 1,502; in 1822, 2,700. By 1825, with the canal in operation, the total population of the town had grown to 4,274; by 1828, 11,000, and in the census of 1850, Rochester counted 36,403 residents.

The phenomenon of exploding population was similarly felt in other communities in that thirty-year period between 1820 and 1850 as Clinton's Ditch began force-feeding the state with newcomers. Buffalo shot from 2,095 population to 42,261, Albany from 10,000 to 50,000.

The canal not only added people to existing settlements, but also created villages, towns, and cities where none had been before. The prime examples were Lockport, Syracuse, Rochester and Buffalo. In the case of Syracuse, the canal had bypassed the principal salt-producing center of Salina, near Onondaga Lake, but a mile-long side cut southward from the canal to Onondaga Creek connected the salt works to the new waterway. There, at the junction of the canal and the side cut, grew the new town of Syracuse, which eventually absorbed Salina and its salt works. Syracuse in 1820 had a population of only 250 persons. Thirty years later, there were 22,000 living in the booming city. Lockport, similarly, had about 2,500 population at the time the canal opened in 1825. It grew to more than 12,000 by 1850.

Out of the canal sprang an entire family of communities whose

1. Governor De Witt Clinton of New York stands proudly in the prow of the *Seneca Chief,* with his wife and other guests, as the boat leads the flotilla that opened the Erie Canal in November 1825. *Painting by Charles Yardley Turner.*

(Art Commission, City of New York)

CANAL BOATS ON THE NORTH RIVER, NEW YORK.

2. The colorful New York waterfront took on a new look when the small, stubby canalboats were docked alongside the tall, graceful ocean-sailing vessels of the middle nineteenth century.

(Prints Division, New York Public Library; Astor, Lenox and Tilden Foundations)

3. The waters of the Hudson River at Albany were busy with sailing ships and the newfangled steamboats even before the boats from the Erie and Champlain canals added new clutter to the maritime traffic. This view of the Albany river front is from an illustrated copy of *Memoir*, prepared at the request of a Committee of the Common Council of the City of New York. It was presented to the mayor of the city by Cadwallader D. Colden during the program marking the completion of the New York canals.

(Prints Division, New York Public Library; Astor, Lenox and Tilden Foundations)

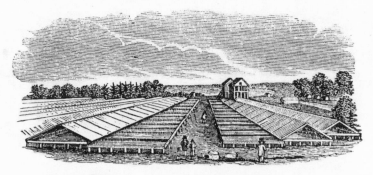

View of a field of salt-vats, Salina.

4. Salina village, out of which grew the city of Syracuse, was one large salt works, as this early sketch shows. The opening of the Erie Canal unlocked the inland and carried salt from Syracuse all over the world.

(Prints Division, New York Public Library; Astor, Lenox and Tilden Foundations)

5. In 1885, when this picture was taken for a stereoptican slide, the packet basin for Erie Canal boats in the center of Syracuse looked like this. Today, paved·over, it is called Clinton Square. *(Buffalo and Erie County Historical Society)*

6. One of the marvels of the Erie Canal was the Weighlock Building. The canalboats were weighed as they rode through the watery porte-cochere of this pretentious structure, a kind of tariff temple.

(International Museum of Photography, George Eastman House)

7. The tranquil canal scene, from a drawing in Basil Hall, *Forty Etchings Made with the Camera Lucida in North America*, Edinburgh, 1829.

(*New York Public Library Picture Collection*)

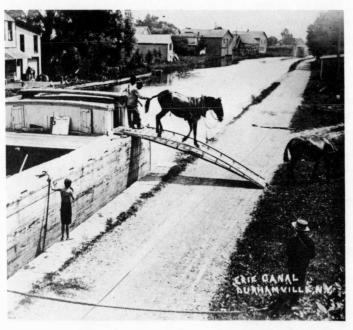

8. Canal buffs argue over the reasons, but it was customary for a canaler to hold on to the tail of a mule or a horse, like a sailor at the tiller, when the animals were debarking.
(*Buffalo and Erie County Historical Society*)

genealogy was usually apparent in their names. It is possible to trace the Erie Canal across much of New York State simply by looking for the towns whose names begin or end with "port" or "basin." Enthusiasm for the new canal and eagerness to be plainly identified with it probably accounted for the plethora of ports—Lockport, Brockport, Middleport, Fairport, Weedsport, Gasport, Wayneport, Spencerport, Port Byron, and Port Gibson. The same kind of inspiration went into places like Bushnell Basin, Shelby Basin, and Adams Basin. They were simple, no-nonsense, functional names, and they meant something, usually honoring pioneer settlers and achievers.

The tide of humanity that surged through Clinton's Ditch in its first ten years of use was, in the main, the pent-up population of New England, the old-line Yankee families who had been so long frustrated by their own rocky soil and who had had speculative eyes on the untilled but plainly fertile West beyond the Mohawk Gap and even further, in the Great Lakes country.

Something of the spirit that caused thousands of New England families to pull up stakes and take leave of their rock-strewn fields for the lush land opened up by the canal is to be detected in the songs of the day:

Then there's old Varmount, well, what d'ye think of that?
To be sure the gals are handsome and the cattle very fat,
But who among the mountains 'mid cloud and snow would stay
When he can buy a prairie in Michigamia?
Yes, yea, yea, in Michigamia.

Then there's the State of New York where some are very rich
Themselves and a few others have dug a mighty ditch,
To render it more easy for us to find the way
And sail upon the waters to Michigamia.
Yes, yea, yea, to Michigamia!

Among the popular songs of the westward movement, about the time of the 1849 Gold Rush, was one that later came to be identified more closely with the South. It was Stephen Foster's "Oh! Susanna!" and its message was:

Oh! Susanna! Oh don't you cry for me;
I'm a-going out to Oregon,
With my banjo on my knee!

Alabama was an alternate destination, it would seem.

The migratory flood of Yankees from New England and eastern New York had lasting effects on future events and the shaping of the nation. These forerunners set the political, social, and moral tone that would

147

prevail in the new cities and the new states of the Northwest Territory for generations. In Michigan, for example, of the state's first fourteen governors, six were from New York and six were from New England.

A mere thirty-six years separated the opening of the Erie Canal and the beginning of the Civil War, but time enough for the newly opened territory to become part of the abolitionist alliance, part of the opposition to the South and its stand on slavery.

There is a lot of room for speculation over what might have been. Had Clinton failed in his drive for a canal or if the project had been further delayed, as Presidents Jefferson and Madison had wanted it to be, the Civil War likely would have had a different ending. Prior to the arrival of the New Englanders and the New Yorkers by canal in the western country, the pioneers who lived on the far side of the mountains—in the land that became Ohio, Michigan, Indiana, Illinois, and Wisconsin—had found their strongest relationships, political and commercial, with the people of the South. Their trade routes went southward, mainly, by way of the rivers—down the Illinois River and the Ohio River into the Mississippi River.

As late as 1841 the nation's leading shipping port still was New Orleans. The value of the exports shipped out of that gulf port then was $34,000,000, compared with $33,000,000 from New York City. The largest city of the North would not even have been a near-competitor if it had not been for the trade funneled eastward by the Grand Canal.

There had to be a time lag between the settlement of the Northwest Territory and the returning commercial reward. There had to be time for the clearing of the forests, the building of cabins and barns, and there had to be time for the planting and harvesting of the fields. Not surprisingly, it was the near-West—in New York State—that paid off first. The Yankee farmers who had contested the flinty, unyielding soil at home for the barest of returns for so long quickly discovered the land they found in the Genesee Country to be as bountiful as it was beautiful. Wheat production, formerly reserved to the Mohawk Valley, shortly became an important part of western New York's agricultural economy. Rochester became known as "the Flour City." As late as 1846 New York State still produced more wheat than any state west of the Appalachians, its production total that year being sixteen million bushels.

The movement of population from the East, and later from foreign lands, followed a skipping pattern. Many of the newcomers paused in western New York long enough to savor the air, break the land, and build rude homes before they succumbed to the seductive stories of what lay on the other side of the mountains and moved on. Directories of the time in cities like Rochester and Buffalo showed a fantastic turnover in population during those early years.

Once the mountain barrier was circumvented by the canal, the Northwest Territory received people at a rate that escalated beyond all expectations. The largest single contributor to the growth of inland cities such as Cleveland, Milwaukee, Detroit, Buffalo, Chicago, and Toledo was the Erie Canal. Michigan's percentage increase in population between 1820 and 1840 was higher than that of any other state. Detroit's population jumped by more than 1,000 per cent in that period; Cleveland's rose by more than 2,000 per cent. But percentages lose their meaning when Chicago's massive growth is measured. The town of only 250 souls in the 1830s could count 109,000 residents in 1860.

Indiana in 1832 had some 350,000 inhabitants, a total that nearly doubled in the next eight years. By 1850 it had come close to the million mark—988,000. Illinois, which had only 157,000 population in 1830, had 476,000 in 1840 and 851,000 in 1850.

The Great Lakes were alive with ships carrying passengers from Buffalo deep into the middle of the continent during those hectic decades that followed the opening of the canal. Detroit was a popular place of debarkation for many of the restless travelers. For some it was the end of the water journey that perhaps had begun on the other side of the Atlantic Ocean and the beginning of a land journey that would take them to the Rocky Mountains or even beyond. In 1830 some 15,000 determined pioneers passed through Detroit on their pursuit of happiness farther west. The Detroit *Free Press,* on May 19, 1831, took note of the fact that lake steamers the previous week had brought more than 2,000 newcomers to the city. The story added, thoughtfully, that the arrivals were "nearly all in the prime of life." That was rather important for people who aspired to be pioneers.

Restless Americans continued to make up the main body of migratory hordes moving westward until the century approached its halfway mark. Immigration to America was minimal in the decade of the 1820s, averaging about 14,000 annually. A representative number of those arrivals, however, found their way inland by the canal route.

During the 1830s, the United States received fewer than a half-million immigrants. The annual statistic was not impressive until 1837, when about 80,000 foreigners arrived. The totals continued to increase. The number of newcomers in the 1840s—1,597,501—was triple that of the previous decade. The floodgates were opening.

The rush to America from 1851 to 1860 added 2,452,660 people to the native population, followed by 2,065,270 in the decade from 1861 to 1870—the slight decline being attributable to the Civil War.

Up to the midway point of the century, about half of the immigrants were Irish and approximately one fourth were German. Most of the new arrivals landed at the Port of New York and the majority chose to end their journey there, giving the nation's largest city an unmistakably greenish glint. Although nearly all had been farmers in Erin, the Irish generally chose to follow an urban existence in the United States. They accepted New York City as destination enough for anyone and settled there in large numbers, making that city, as Robert Considine has written, "The Irishman's capital in this country, affording protection to exiles, a base for the Irish resistance movement, a center of Catholic Church activity, and symbolizing wealth and opportunity for the poverty-stricken. This 'bustling country town' known as New York and the Irish grew up together."

The Hudson Valley was the land of the Dutch, and Albany and Schenectady were their major cities. The Mohawk Valley was the land of the Germans, especially those who fled the Palatinate district of the Rhineland before the Revolution. But west of Utica and all the way to Buffalo, there were the Irish again, in the newly settled towns and young cities flanking the canal, as many of the Irish laborers had chosen to settle along the canal after the digging job was done. There was a continuing need in that new country for people who could contribute hard work in the building of the countryside and the new cities. In Syracuse, for example, where the great salt industry was developing to supply a world-wide demand, Irish labor was welcomed. As canal construction had inched its way westward, it left behind little colonies of Irish families. While they did not enjoy high social favor in the beginning, they were gradually absorbed by the communities and in time they came to be a powerful force. In Buffalo they were especially numerous simply because that was where the canal terminated.

But the Irish and the Germans were only the vanguard groups. The vast expanse of North America had been a tantalizing lure to Europeans for a long time, and even as the spurs to action were digging deeper in the crowded, troubled nations of the Old World, the way to the interior of the New World at last had been opened by the Erie Canal. Migration to the United States offered advantages to both sides. In America people could find the promise of a new, better, egalitarian society and unbounded opportunity for economic betterment. In return, they had themselves to offer. America needed people to fulfill its destiny.

The advance groups of immigrants generally were well received in the United States. Glowing letters soon were on their way back to the old country—usually with money enclosed and their effect was to spread considerable restlessness and discontent in the family circles and the native towns of the adventurers. Like most travel writers, the ones who had migrated to America had a weakness for exaggeration, and some of their letters were fantastic in their descriptions of the lush life to be found in America. In a comparative sense, of course, the streets of the United States did seem to be paved with gold, and by mid-century the young nation's way of life and promise of plenty were finding a lot of takers from abroad.

Helping to tip the tide were the recruiting agents for shipping interests and American interests in need of manpower. One recruiting firm in New York, Rawson and McMurray, advertised in English newspapers in 1837 that anybody who chose to migrate to the United States could get ten pounds sterling per month, plus his food, as wages. The come-on stressed that everyone in America was on a perfect level of equality with everybody else, that the common laboring man received high wages and sat at the same table with his master, and that an independent fortune could be made by a man with ease.

The ocean voyage to America should have been enough of an experience in itself to subdue the most adventurous spirits, but the immigrants were not of a mind to criticize the accommodations offered by the sailing schooners. Most were aware that, while the trip was something less than deluxe travel, they were getting a real bargain. The price of the passage was right, even by the low standards of the day, thanks in large part to an imbalance in trade between Europe and America. Shipowners had a special reason for wanting to attract the immigrant trade. Most of the sailing ships that went heavy-laden to European ports, carrying the riches of America—the grains, lumber, salt, and furs—too often faced the prospect of returning home almost empty. That was not a desirable condition, either from an economic standpoint or from the viewpoint of the sailing master. Empty holds meant that the ships would be riding dangerously high in the water.

Immigrants were sought as a form of ballast, if nothing else, and shipowners and captains shrewdly kept the passage price low enough so that it usually was within reach of even the most impoverished Europeans. By the 1830s an immigrant could gain passage on a ship to America for as little as twenty dollars. It meant four weeks or more in steerage, a heaving, yawing, dipping nightmare of a journey usually, but it also meant escape from the oppressions of an old system weighed down with autocracy, religious intolerance, and the restrictions of a caste system. The uncomfortable ocean journey was nothing against the chance for a new life in a new land.

Not surprisingly, many immigrants were willing to settle for New York City as the rewarding abode at the end of their personal rainbow. It was, by comparison with most European cities, an enchantingly informal, gay, interesting place to live. But the people who craved land and the wonder of the unspoiled inland paradise, with its untapped riches, pressed on. Their route was usually the Erie Canal, and, fortunately, the cost of transportation on the canal was as much of a bargain as that of the ocean crossing. Large fleets of steamboats plied the Hudson, carrying canal passengers between Manhattan and Albany, and their competition grew progressively more spirited, much to the advantage of travelers.

The cost of the river voyage at first had been fairly substantial, but reasonable enough. A person would pay seven dollars, on the average, for a steamship ticket to Albany. By 1840, however, with about a hundred boats making the Hudson River run, the one-way fare had dropped to two dollars, and a few years later passage was down to as little as fifty cents a person!

As a matter of fact, the immigrants probably received their first introduction to high-pressure, fast-talking American salesmanship at the hands of steamship agents whose job it was to drum up business for their individual lines or for specific boats. As the bewildered newcomers debarked at the South Street docks in New York, they were met by scores of steamship representatives furiously intent on winning customers for the trip to Albany, as well as aggressive agents of lines seeking to recruit passengers for the canal trip itself.

It may be that 1849 offered the most remarkable bargains in transportation for the immigrants. Some of them, in that fortuitous year, would have crossed the ocean for fifteen dollars, taken the steamship from New York City to Albany for fifty cents, and then boarded a canalboat for the trip to Buffalo at a cost of somewhere between $4.50 and $6.50—a price that included board. At the going prices of the time, it's hard to see how any European could have afforded to stay home.

At the middle point of the century there was hardly a sailing ship on the ocean's westward lanes that did not sit solidly on the water, its bottom snugly immersed in the briny and its hold filled with hundreds of bright-eyed human beings on the first leg of their journey towards Utopia.

CHAPTER XVII

THE WAY IT WAS

Travel by canalboat was such an outstanding experience that hardly anybody who rode the Erie Canal during the years when horses and mules were the source of towpath power was able to resist the impulse to write about the sensations felt, the discomforts endured, and the characters encountered. Our literature is heavy with emotional passages from the diaries of canal passengers who, by the light of a smoking lamp, rushed their impressions onto paper before the vivid details had faded from mind.

What it comes down to is that the most romantic, most attractive mode of transportation ever devised by man left something to be desired, according to the journals of many of the canal passengers. The something that most of them agreed was to be desired was the kind of comfort that comes only with adequate elbow room.

Airline passengers who can remember transoceanic flights in crowded, propeller-driven aircraft will know why the canal customers drifted into morose, lugubrious passages as they tried to describe the long, slow trip in a crowded packet from, say, Albany to Buffalo.

The ordinary packet, although the aristocrat of canalboats, was not large. If it conformed to the usual dimensions, it was about eighty feet long and about fourteen feet wide. That was maximum measurement because of the size of the locks—ninety feet in length and fifteen feet in width. The clearance on either side of the boat was a matter of inches.

Less ambitious packets ranged from sixty to seventy feet in length and other canalboats averaged a modest forty feet long. The width varied. Some of the long, eighty-foot packets were only eleven feet wide.

A packet would have a snub nose or one that was pointed, depending on its age, and it usually featured a high railing around a box-shaped cabin, a lot of curtained windows, and brightly colored blinds. Limited deck space could be found on top of the cabin, and a small stairway provided access to the higher vantage point at the stern.

Showmanship was an important part of the packet business, no doubt because of the fierce competition for patronage that built up quickly in the game. It manifested itself, among other ways, in the dizzying use of paints in such combinations as to blind the farmers in the fields and dazzle the wild life.

"When the packets were in their glory," noted one observer solemnly, "[they] inevitably exhibited not only the seven colors in the spectrum, but symphonies in crimson, maroon, brown, pink, lilac, magenta, yellowish-green, and any other mongrel shade that an experimental mixer of paints might chance to hit upon."

Even the tow horses and mules had to exhibit some elegance in their roles as pullers of the classiest craft on the canal. Their harnesses commonly featured bangles and beads, bright brass, nickel, or silver mountings, and often a bright plume of feathers.

The people who whiled away their time on the bridges over the canal where it passed through a town or who sat in the sunny verandas that looked out on the canal loved most to see the packets come gliding along. It was a gay sight, especially from a distance, and it made up for all the squat, gray freighters, the nondescript line boats, and the interminable, uninteresting log rafts.

Everybody recognized the packet as the quality boat. It not only had passing rights when it overtook another craft of lesser rank, but officials sometimes looked the other way when a packet exceeded the speed limit of four miles per hour. As a matter of fact, packet racing was a common sport on the Erie. It was part of the general competition between packet lines and individual boats of the different companies. Captains boasted about the speed of their boats and challenged each other to races. It was possible, by lashing a double team of horses and by changing horses every ten or fifteen miles, to get the packets up to speeds as high as ten miles an hour in short bursts. It was illegal, of course, but the captain would hop off the packet at a lock and pay the automatic ten-dollar fine for speeding without being asked. The passengers usually got caught up in the excitement of a race even to the point of jeering the competition and hopping off the packet to grab hold of the towlines and try to add their strength to that of the horses.

The big attraction of an occasional race with another packet was that it relieved the terrible tedium of the long ride. It took an exciting day, indeed, to offset the uncomfortable, monotonous nights aboard the boats. The packets may have been the quality craft of the canal, but the element of quality was somewhat strained when it came to living in its cramped quarters for a week and a half or whatever time the trip took. That was a point on which there was almost unanimous agreement among passengers at the end of any journey. The interior cabin of the packet was the same kind of economical masterpiece as the latter-day Pullman berth in the crafty way it extracted maximum usage out of minimum space. As a matter of fact, George M. Pullman, who lived near the canal in the town of Albion, got his chief inspiration for the cramped railroad sleeping arrangement from the ingeniously designed passenger boats.

A guidebook in 1828 gave the following description of a packet's interior:

"The length is 60 or 70 feet, a large part of which is devoted to the dining room, where two rows of tables are set. At night, mattresses are spread on the seats on each side, and another row above them on cots suspended from the roof. The ladies are accommodated with births [sic!] in the cabin, which is usually carpeted, hung with curtains, and in other respects more handsomely furnished. The kitchen and bar are conveniently situated; and the tables are spread with an abundance, and often a delicacy, which may well surprise those not accustomed to the cheapness of travelling in this part of the country. A small library, a number of newspapers, &c., will serve to make the time pass agreeably, even if the traveller be a stranger, or the weather not inviting. In many places, the view from the deck is highly interesting . . ."

Ah, yes! The view from the deck! There certainly was much to see— fertile farm fields bordering the canal; still, deep, shady forest glens; flowered meadows and the charming vistas of misty hills in the distance; not to mention all the quaint little towns through which the canal passed. The big problem was a passenger's point of vantage. There was a definite limitation to how much sightseeing a person could do from the deck of a canalboat. Because the canal had cut through hundreds of farms and had bisected innumerable roads, it had been necessary for the Canal Commission to have built a sensational number of bridges over the canal so as to allow farmers to move their cattle and produce from one part of their divided fields to another and to permit road traffic to pass overhead without interruption. The construction cost of bridges was one of the expensive items in the original Erie plans, and to keep the expense down as low as possible, the bridges themselves were built as low as possible. There is a profound economic syllogism involved in this formula, it may be, but the result of the minimum-height policy is what really mattered to the people who rode the canalboats, passengers and crews alike.

Almost every time a canalboat rounded a bend, it seemed, it was greeted by a bridge with such minimum clearance that it was capable of sweeping all life off the observation deck, and sometimes did. The boats lost a lot of passengers that way, even a smattering of deckhands. The casualty toll undoubtedly would have been much worse if the boat operators had not taken the precaution to station a member of the crew as lookout to sound a warning whenever he sighted a bridge ahead.

"Low bridge ahead!" he'd holler, and sensible people would duck or flatten themselves on the upper deck.

David Harum, that wonderfully wise student of the human scene who was created out of the mainstream of canal life by Edward Westcott just before the turn of the century, touched on the universality of the familiar canal warning cry. Referring to a group of society gentlemen whose Blue Book credentials had failed utterly to impress him, he said:

"Wa'al, I was thinkin' 't I'd like to bet you two dollars to a last year's bird's nest that if all them fellers we seen this afternoon, that air over fifty, c'd be got together, an' some one was suddinly to holler 'Low Bridge!' that nineteen out o' twenty 'd duck their heads."

The familiar warning yell inevitably found its way into music, as well as literature. The refrain of one popular ballad, had as its opening lines:

> Low bridge!—everybody down!
> Low bridge, for we're going through a town!*

On some of the canal stretches there were so many bridges that it kept a crewman busy full time hollering the advance warning and there were times he'd get off the boat at the end of a trip so hoarse he could hardly speak. At the same time, the passengers who had managed to keep their heads—thanks to the shouted warnings—frequently debarked in a shuffling, semi-crouch which could have been attributable to the defensive posture they had been forced to maintain for so many miles and for so many days.

Bending to avoid the bridges was not the sole cause of the bent-over, twisted physique, however. The height of the boat from keel to roof was only little more than eight feet, imposing such a limitation on stand-up space as to force men of above-average height to move about the cabin in a stoop. As Charles Dickens wryly observed, a man of height could not walk erectly inside one of these boats "without making bald places on his head by scraping it on the roof."

Sleeping in the space set aside for him also demanded of the average passenger a real talent for adaptation, limber muscles, and fantastic flexibility. Almost every cubic foot of a boat had to serve double duty. How this was achieved is suggested in the following description by an anonymous packet passenger:

"Right in the bow, carefully cut off from the rest of the boat, was a tiny cuddy for the crew. Next back of this came the ladies' dressing room and cabin, sometimes a separate room, sometimes cut off from the main cabin only by a red curtain.

* Lines of lyrics from "The Erie Canal," collected, adapted, and arranged by John A. Lomax & Alan Lomax. TRO—© Copyright 1934 and renewed 1962 LUDLOW MUSIC, INC., New York, N.Y. Also reprinted by permission of Essex Music Group for South Africa, Essex Music of Australia Pty, Ltd.

"Next was the main cabin, 36 to 45 feet long, which was saloon and dining room by day and men's dormitory by night. Back of this was the bar, and finally, at the very stern, was the kitchen, almost always presided over by a Negro cook, who was usually the bartender also. He was kept busy 15 or 18 hours per day. The other members of the crew on the early Erie packets were the captain, two drivers and two steersmen, one each for the night and day trick.

"At nine o'clock in the evening, two or three members of the crew began carrying the adjustable berths, sheets, pillows, curtains, and so forth into the main cabin, and the passengers must go out on the upper deck or huddle themselves in the center of the room while the berths were made up. Each berth was a narrow wooden or metal frame with a strip of canvas fastened over it. It was held in position at one side by two projecting iron rods which fitted into two holes in the wall of the cabin; and on the other or front side by two ropes attached to the edge of the frame and suspended from hooks in the ceiling.

"There were at least three beds in a tier, one above another—sometimes four; and all fastened to the same rope. The tiers were set as closely together as possible all around the cabin, which thus furnished beds for from thirty-six to forty-two people. But the boats were frequently overcrowded, seventy-five and even a hundred or more people being jammed into a single cabin."

(At least one packet line boasted that it would accommodate as many as 150 persons within the tight confines of its small cabin.)

Even the considerable descriptive powers of Charles Dickens were put to the test by the sleeping arrangements of an Erie Canal packet. He wrote that when he went below to retire, he found "suspended on either side of the cabin three long tiers of hanging book shelves designed apparently for volumes of the small octavo size.

"Looking with greater attention at these contrivances (wondering to find such literary preparations in such a place) I descried on each shelf a sort of microscopic sheet and blanket; then I began dimly to comprehend that the passengers were the library, and that they were to be arranged edgewise on these shelves till morning."

Another literary great had to grope for words when it came to an account of his nighttime experiences aboard a packet. Nathaniel Hawthorne, who said he was "inclined to be poetical about the Grand Canal," found his packet journey to be one of "overpowering tedium." His attempt to sleep aboard the boat was especially frustrating, although there were only twenty other persons in the cabin. A curtain was lowered to separate the men and women, and the tiered shelves were dropped down to serve as berths at bedtime.

"For a long time," wrote Hawthorne, "our various incommodities kept us all awake except five or six, who were accustomed to sleep nightly amid the uproar of their own snoring, and had little to dread from any other species of disturbance.

"It is a curious fact that these snorers had been the most quiet people in the boat while awake, and became peacebreakers only when others ceased to be so, breathing tumult out of their repose. Would it were possible to affix a wind instrument to nose, and thus make a melody of a snore, so that a sleeping lover might serenade his mistress or a congregation snore a psalm tune!"

Some faintly erotic thoughts also bothered Hawthorne:

"Other, though fainter, sounds than these contributed to my restlessness. My head was close to the crimson curtain—the sexual division of the boat—behind which I continually hear whispers and stealthy footsteps; the noise of a comb laid on the table or a slipper dropped on the floor; the twang, like a broken harpstring, caused by loosening a tight belt; the rustling of a gown in its descent; and the unlacing of a pair of stays. My ear seemed to have the properties of an eye; a visible image pestered my fancy in the darkness; the curtain was withdrawn between me and the western lady, who yet disrobed herself without a blush.

"Finally all was hushed in that quarter. Still I was more broad awake than through the whole preceding day, and felt a feverish impulse to toss my limbs miles apart and appease the unquietness of my mind by that of matter. Forgetting that my berth was hardly so wide as a coffin, I turned suddenly over, and fell like an avalanche to the floor, to the disturbance of the whole community of sleepers. As there were no bones broken, I blessed the accident and went on the deck."

Hawthorne's experience was not nearly as unusual as that encountered by a German tourist named Friedrich Gerstaecker. In a dramatic account of a night spent aboard an Erie Canal packet in 1830, Gerstaecker recalled how he had awakened in his berth "with a dreadful feeling of suffocation.

"Cold perspiration stood on my forehead and I could hardly draw my breath; there was a weightlike lead on my stomach and chest. I attempted to cry out—in vain; I lay almost without consciousness. The weight remained immovable; above me was a noise like distant thunder; it was my companion of the upper story, who lay snoring over my head; and that the weight which pressed on my chest was caused by his body no longer remained a doubtful point.

"I endeavored to move the Colossus—impossible. I tried to push, to cry out—in vain. He lay like a rock on my chest and seemed to have no more feeling. I bethought me of my breastpin, which luckily I had not taken out of my cravat the night before; with great difficulty I succeeded in reaching the pin, which I pressed with a firm hand into the mass above me.

"There was a sudden movement, which procured me momentary relief; but the movement soon subsided, the weight growing more insupportable, and to prevent being utterly crushed, I was obliged to reapply the pin.

" 'What's that? Murder! Help!' cried a deep bass voice above me.

"Feeling myself free, I slipped like an eel from under the weight and saw by the dim light of the lamp a sight of no common occurrence. A stout, heavy man who slept in the upper frame without mattress was too much for the well-worn canvas; during his sleep it had given way under the weightiest part of his form, which descended till it found support on my chest.

"The thrust of my breastpin caused his body to jerk upward, allowing me to escape. As he returned to his former position with greater force, the support being gone, the canvas split still wider, and more than half asleep, he was sitting on my bed, while his head and feet remained in his own. He continued calling out, 'Help! Murder!'

"Everybody started up to see what was the matter and to laugh heartily at the extraordinary attitude of this stout gentleman."

A story, you see, with a happy ending.

Each packet line had its own system for assigning berths to the passengers. The most common methods were those based either on precedence of ticket purchase or by lot. Aboard the packet on which Dickens traveled, the latter method was employed, and it fascinated him to see the passengers "gathered around the master of the boat at one of the tables, drawing lots with all the anxieties and passions of gamesters depicted in their countenances; while others with small pieces of cardboard in their hands were groping among the shelves in search of numbers corresponding with those they had drawn.

"As soon as any gentleman found his number he took possession of it immediately by undressing himself and crawling into bed. The rapidity with which an agitated gambler subsided into a snoring slumberer was one of the most singular effects I have ever witnessed. As to the ladies, they were already abed behind the red curtain which was carefully drawn and pinned up the centre; though as every cough or sneeze or whisper behind the curtain was perfectly audible before it, we had still a lively consciousness of their presence."

Dickens and Hawthorne apparently shared not only a great literary talent, but a lively libido as well. Dickens also shared with Herr Gerstaecker the problem of the passenger hanging heavy over his head through the night, as he revealed in his account:

"The politeness of the person in authority had secured me a shelf in a nook near the red curtain, in some degree removed from the great body of sleepers," he wrote. "I found it, on after measurement, just the width of an ordinary sheet of Bath post letter-paper; and I was at first in some uncertainty as to the best means of getting into it. But the shelf being a bottom one, I finally determined on lying upon the floor, rolling gently in, stopping immediately I reached the mattress and remaining for the night with that side uppermost, whatever it might be. Luckily, I came upon my back at exactly the right moment.

"I was much alarmed on looking upward to see, by the shape of his half-yard of sacking (which his weight had bent into an exceedingly tight bag) that there was a very heavy gentleman above me, whom the slender cords seemed quite incapable of holding; and I could not help reflecting upon the grief of my wife and family in the event of his coming down in the night. But as I could not have got up again without a severe bodily struggle; and as I had nowhere else to go, even if I had; I shut my eyes upon the danger and remained there."

Mrs. Frances Trollope, the English novelist and mother of Anthony Trollope, found on her Erie Canal ride that the Americans aboard her crowded packet acted "upon a system of unshrinking egotism," and their rude Yankee speech exasperated her because it "got nowhere."

Things weren't much better on the larger American scene, for that matter, she noted. She was a bit crushed when the boat arrived at Port Byron and instead of a poetic port, as it surely should have been, she discovered it was nothing more than a whiskey store and a warehouse.

"From the canal," she concluded tartly, "nothing is seen to advantage, and very little is seen at all."

One of the most famous stage actors in early America, Tyrone Power, whose direct descendant carried on the family name and talent as a motion picture actor in modern times, wrote at length and in great detail about a trip he took on the Erie Canal in the summer of 1834. A heat wave hung over upstate New York at the time of his memorable ride.

"All this day, the air stood absolutely still," Power wrote the second night out from Buffalo. "At our places of halt we were joined by men who had left the stages in consequence of those vehicles not being able to travel. Our pace was reduced considerably; and the cattle, although in excellent condition, were terribly distressed.

"At Lockport we found business nearly at a standstill; the thermometer was at 110 degrees Fahrenheit. We passed several horses dead upon the banks of the canal, and were compelled to leave one or two of our own in a dying state. Here more persons joined than we could well accommodate, and I found positively that all movement by the stage route was at an end, forty horses having fallen on the line the day previous . . .

"This night I found it impossible to look in upon the cabin; I therefore made a request to the captain that I might be permitted to have a mattress on deck; but this, he told me, could not be; there was a regulation which positively forbade sleeping upon the deck of a canal packet; indeed, he assured me that this could be done only at the peril of life . . . I appeared to submit to his well-meant arguments, but inwardly resolved *coute qui coute*, not to sleep within the den below.

"I got my cloak up, filled my hat with cigars, and, planting myself

160

about the center of the deck, here resolved, malgre dews and musquitoes, to weather it through the night.

"'What is the name of the country we are now passing?' I inquired of one of the boatmen who joined me about the first hour of the morning.

"Why, sir, this is called the Cedar Swamp,' answered the man, to whom I handed a cigar, in order to retain his society and to create more smoke against the hungry swarms surrounding us on all sides.

"'We have not much more of this Cedar Swamp to get through, I hope,' inquired I, seeking for some consolatory information.

"'About fifty miles more, I guess,' was the reply of my companion, accompanying each word with a sharp slap on the back of his hand, or on his cheek or forehead.

"'Thank Heaven!' I involuntarily exclaimed, drawing my cloak closer about me, although the heat was killing. 'We shall after that escape in some sort, I hope, from these legions of musquitoes?'

"'I guess no quite,' replied the man; 'they are as thick, if not thicker, in the Long Swamp.'

"'The Long Swamp!' I repeated: 'What a horrible name for a country! Does the canal run far through it?'

"'No, not so far, only about eighty miles.'

"'We've then done with swamps, I hope, my friend?' I inquired, as he kept puffing and slapping with unwearied constancy.

"'Why, yes, there's not a heap more swamp, that is to say, not close to the line, till we come to within about forty miles of Utica.'

"'And is that one as much infested with these infernal insects as are the Long and Cedar Swamps?'

"'I guess *that* is *the* place above for musquitoes,' replied the man, grinning. 'Thim's the real gallinippers, emigrating north for the summer all the way from the Balize and the Red River. Let a man go to sleep with his head in a cast-iron kettle among thim chaps, and if their bills don't make a watering-pot of it before morning, I'm d——d. They're strong enough to lift the boat out of the canal, if they could only get underneath her . . .'"

While the canal ride unquestionably had its trying, uncomfortable, even painful, moments for sleepers who were not supple enough to adjust and for passengers who could not ignore the raspy background of snoring, it also was an experience that had many happy moments.

Among the testimonials that stress the positive aspect of canalling was one by Dickens, who was able to look past the trials he had encountered and say:

". . . There was much in this mode of traveling which I heartily enjoyed at the time and look back upon with great pleasure. Even the running up, bare-necked, at five o'clock in the morning, from the tainted cabin to the dirty deck, scooping up the icy water, plunging one's head into it and drawing it out, all fresh and glowing with the cold, was a good

161

thing. The fast, brisk walk upon the towing path, between that time and breakfast, when every vein and artery seemed to tingle with health; the exquisite beauty of the opening day, when light came glancing off from everything; the gliding on at night so noiselessly, past frowning hills sullen with dark trees and sometimes angry in one red, burning spot high up, where unseen men lay crouching round a fire; the shining out of the bright stars undisturbed by any noise of wheels or steam or any other sound than the limpid rippling of the water as the boat went on; all these were pure delights."

CHAPTER XVIII

THE FIERY SPIRITS

A line boat named the *Western Barge* slipped unobtrusively into the mainstream of westward traffic at Albany one day in early July 1832, on the beginning of a trip that would be remembered for a long time.

It was an ordinary craft in appearance, perhaps dirtier than most, but no dirtier than many others; which is to say that unsanitary boats were not uncommon on the Grand Canal. But immigrant passengers stood stolid and uncomplaining. They had learned not to complain about conditions in their homelands, and they were not about to begin protesting minor inconveniences in this New World which represented their best bet for happiness.

The midsummer heat bore down oppressively on the *Western Barge* as it moved through the still, shimmering Mohawk Valley at a pace of about two miles an hour, the usual average with that class of line boat. There was green scum on the surface of the water that the boat was able to break up into little clusters, but the coverlet quickly came together again as the modest wake quilted and the ripples rested. Some of the passengers walked along the towpath ahead of the mules, preferring exertion in the open to the stifling heat of the boat cabin. But beyond the general discomfort and a general listlessness, the first stage of the journey, as far as Little Falls, went without incident.

Eight miles east of Utica, the captain of the *Western Barge* died of cholera. Presumably he was taken ashore and buried. The boat moved on. At Perrinton, a woman passenger fell victim to the same disease. She also was taken ashore and buried. Now the canal grapevine sent word racing from boat to boat, from boat to locktenders, from locktenders to townspeople, and suddenly the countryside was tense in the dread knowledge that a plague ship was on the Erie waters.

Eastbound boats passing the *Western Barge* swung in as close to the towpath as they could get, and there was a conspicuous absence of the usual greetings or raucous exchanges between crew members. Meanwhile, the situation aboard the *Western Barge* was growing more critical. The cholera was picking up momentum, adding new victims. Another passenger died at Pittsford, only a few miles beyond Perrinton, and three new cases of illness were discovered on board.

Word was received, about that time, that the boat was not welcome in the towns on its route of travel and that nobody would be allowed to step ashore in any one of them. There was an exception. Rochester agreed to give the boat asylum, and while the sick were being taken ashore, the filthy vessel was given a thorough scrubbing. Other precautions were taken, but the plague continued to spread, now into the homes of the compassionate Rochester residents. In less than two months, during the remainder of July and through August, 118 persons died—an especially terrible toll in light of a total city population only little more than 10,000.

The hero of the crisis in Rochester was a man named Ashbel W. Riley, a real estate promoter, colonel in the state militia, and city Commissioner of Health. Colonel Riley steadied the panicky community with his matter-of-fact attention to his job, risking his life repeatedly without dramatics by going into plague-infested homes, nursing the sick, attending to the dying, and taking care of the remains of the dead. It was said that he hardly slept during the two-month epidemic, and that he personally placed eighty-six of the victims in their coffins, eleven of them in a single day.

As if that were not enough, Colonel Riley re-enacted his role of heroism a brief two years later, in 1834, when another cholera epidemic struck Rochester. The news reached him while he was on active duty with the militia, but he rushed back to Rochester and it was largely through his ministration and his calm, efficient supervision that the death toll was held down to fifty-eight. Colonel Riley again miraculously escaped infection himself, and, in fact, lived to the age of ninety-three.

(During his long adult lifetime in Rochester, spanning the years from 1816 to 1888, Riley saw the community grow from nothing to a major city. He lived long enough to see the city name a street after him, but he also lived to see the honor withdrawn. When the young University of Rochester moved to a new campus, the street that had been given Riley's name was rechristened University Avenue. "Riley Street," mused Arch Merrill, the distinguished Rochester columnist-historian, "was considered too plebeian a name for an avenue on which stood a university.")

But the cholera virus was not the only invisible passenger aboard the boats of the Erie; there were infectious agents of the mind and spirit that traveled the waterway, also, spreading new philosophies and reviving old ones, firing men's minds and lighting their hopes, often leading them down strange bypaths. Central New York became the scene of repeated religious and moral crusades, and wave after wave of evangelistic fervor, which left the people of the area spent and depleted by their own emotional binges. So marked were the phenomena that the countryside came to be described as "the burned-over district."

One who studied the many movements that had their beginnings in the area, Whitney R. Cross, held that the Erie Canal itself was the prime agent in making the twelve years between 1825 and 1837, especially, "years in which a series of startling events revolutionized life in the western half of the state."

The emotional eruptions did not occur only in the western area. There were, as Carl Carmer has observed, equally inexplicable doings in towns and farmlands bordering the canal in the eastern half of the state as well.

"Across the entire breadth of New York State," he noted, "undeviating, a hilly strip scarcely 25 miles wide invited the world's wonder . . . a broad psychic highway, a thoroughfare of the occult . . . In no other area of the Western Hemisphere have so many evidences of an existence transcending mortal living been manifest."

Religious and social reformers were everywhere and in large numbers. Abolitionists made the upstate area one of their strongholds, and the Underground Railroad followed there a network of routes in the transportation of escaped slaves to freedom in Canada. Hundreds of experimenters departed from the established, accepted conventions, to the horror of their neighbors, as they tested forms of communal living. Colonies of people ostensibly seeking a closer approach to perfection in human relationships sprang up and were short-lived sensations. Christian communism was given a whirl by the Shakers and the Oneida Perfectionists. Evangelism enjoyed one of its brightest hours, and revivalism became the order of the day. But it also was a time for new religions, including Mormonism and Seventh Day Adventism, that have survived to this day.

"For half a century before the outbreak of the War between the States," wrote an Albany newspaperman, Don C. Seitz, "Americans took their religion like their whiskey—straight. There were no fancy frills, no trifling with the temperatures in Hell. Satan was fought in the open. The fires of perdition were at white heat and Heaven was a paradise for those who accepted the faith . . ."

There isn't any question that a man named Charles Grandison Finney was among the most famous and the most outspoken of all the warriors on the side of the Lord during this period. He comes down through time with the most telling title of all: Finney the Great Evangelist.

None of the biographical outlines of Finney suggest in any way that he was a lovable individual. He was depicted as a stern, austere, irascible man, relentless in his determination to bring all mankind into the fold of his Calvinist persuasion. Toward this end he was not about to loiter in the company of diplomacy, reasoned debate, or honeyed persuasion. There were no Marquess of Queensberry rules, as he saw it, when you wrestled with Satan.

Finney, born in Warren, Connecticut, in 1792, lived his youth in Oneida County, New York, when it was part of the western wilderness. There was virtually no organized religion in the frontier settlement, and Finney, whose goal was to become a lawyer, didn't own a Bible until he was twenty-nine years old. He purchased one at that time because the law books he was studying contained repeated references to the Bible as the highest authority, arousing his curiosity. His studied attempt to satisfy that curiosity led him to take up the ministry as it has been taken up by few men—by the scruff, roughly, rather than in the usual dignified, genteel manner.

As Finney the Evangelist saw things, the reason people were having difficulty getting their prayers answered was their lack of strong faith, and he set out to remedy that condition. It had to be done in a violently personal way, though, because nothing could be more personal in a man's life than his religious beliefs and attitudes. From the time he was ordained a minister in 1824 at the age of thirty-two, the Reverend Mr. Finney stumped the canal country, denouncing the Devil and all his followers, thrusting the bony finger of guilt directly at the noses of startled churchgoers, and bringing about the most spectacular wave of revivalism in the history of the eastern United States.

The auditoriums in which he preached his steaming sermons must have looked like disaster areas when he was finished, if you can believe the eyewitness reports, which averred that bodies littered the floor and stunned sinners lay about raising anguished outcries in all quarters. One woman, overwhelmed by his fiery eloquence, lay in a trance for sixteen hours after he finished speaking—a record of a sort. It was not unusual for members of the audience to topple off their chairs onto the floor while he was approaching the apogee of his peroration.

When he was first ordained, Finney preached in Evans Mill, New York, two Sundays a month. Other denominations used the room on alternate Sundays. Finney, no man for idleness, arranged to conduct services on the odd Sundays in a Presbyterian church in Antwerp, some eighteen miles away. There, a biographer reported, Finney's preaching caused "an awful solemnity" to fall on the congregation, "which began to fall from their seats in every direction and cried for mercy."

Nearly all the members of the congregation were "prostrate" within two minutes after they first felt the psychic shock, and the preacher "was compelled to stop to await the fading out of the ecstasy."

Judging from his postservice commentary, even the Reverend Mr. Finney himself was pleased by the crowd reaction.

"If I had a sword in each hand," he said grimly, "I would not have cut them off their seats as fast as they fell!"

When the evangelist went to Rome to speak in the Congregational Church, his hearers were "magnetized as usual," although "they did not shriek but went out sobbing and sighing, and their sobs and sighs could be heard till they got out into the street."

It was Finney's technique, whenever he could, to single out individuals in an audience and, by exposing their sinful ways in a sort of stentorian roar, hold them up as horrible examples of what sin could do to a weak person. This practice led to a considerable disaffection among some of those so singularly honored. One of his bruised critics, indeed, had thoughts of nobody other than Finney when his doctor told him he was dying.

"Don't let Finney pray over my corpse!" cried out the distressed man.

There were frequent threats to tar and feather the preacher, and once an attempt to blow up his church was discovered before any damage was done. One man who attended a revival with the avowed intention of killing the evangelist made the mistake of listening to Finney before he carried out his dastardly plan. The longer he listened, the more contrite he got, until he finally fell from his seat, crying out: "I am sinking into Hell!"

The Hate Finney Club was not restricted to embarrassed sinners by any means. It also included numerous clergymen of the established Congregational Church who felt strong antipathy towards the unorthodox evangelist. Prominent in this ministerial circle of critics for a long time was the famous Dr. Lyman Beecher. He, however, conceded Finney's effectiveness, especially after Finney had conducted a revival in a most unpromising community, Rochester, which was not far behind Buffalo and Troy in any list of the Erie Canal's leading hellholes.

Even Finney had hesitated to tackle Rochester, despite some sensational successes in De Kalb, Rome, Utica, Auburn, and Troy. In Utica alone he had won some 500 conversions. But on to Rochester he went, his own doubts notwithstanding, and the result, in the words of Dr. Beecher, "was the greatest work of God and the greatest revival of religion that the world has ever seen in so short a time. One hundred thousand were reported as having connected themselves with churches as the result of that great revival. This is unparalleled in the history of the church and of the progress of religion. In no year during the Christian era have we any account of so great a revival of religion."

One awed reporter of the Rochester revival marveled over the fact that the conversions included even "a large number of lawyers"—just as though lawyers were beyond saving—as well as "judges, bankers, merchants and master mechanics and leading men and women in the city." During the great revival, interest ran so high that "grog shops were closed, the theater was converted into a livery stable, and the circus into a soap and candle factory."

The golden years of Finney's evangelizing in New York were the nine years from 1824 to 1832. In the latter year, he was named pastor of the Second Free Presbyterian Church in New York City. He collapsed of cholera during his installation—the same cholera epidemic that caused so many deaths in Rochester became a general plague throughout the East that year. While continuing with his New York pastorate for a long time, Finney in 1835 accepted a professorship of theology at the newly established Oberlin College near Cleveland, Ohio. He became president of the college in 1851 and stayed in that post to 1866.

Shortly after Finney arrived, Oberlin became the first college in America to admit women students (in 1837), discrimination because of color was disallowed, and the college became "the best organized center of abolitionism in the North"—so much so that it was not uncommon for protest-minded professors to be arrested from time to time, even as now. But any resemblance between the protesting faculty and students of modern Oberlin and Finney's Oberlin fades in light of the rigid religious discipline and, literally, the unsmiling piety that prevailed in the founding days.

The Reverend Mr. Finney did not approve of smiling. One of the iron rules at Oberlin was that students should cultivate "a grave outward aspect." One of the young women students, a natural, impulsive smiler, no doubt—perhaps even a compulsive smiler—was unable to hold herself in check. She walked about the campus smiling at other students, especially the men, with disturbing frequency, and, not surprisingly, an indignant coed went to President Finney and reported this breach of the rules.

"Leave her to me," said Finney, grimly.

A few days later he encountered the girl on the street and was presented with the opportunity, in the words of one biographer, "to crush the butterfly."

Sure enough, the coed smiled at the president; smiled right into his long, lean, ascetic face. But he met the smile "with a look of marble coldness."

"Good morning, daughter of the devil!" roared the evangelist-educator.

"Good morning, father," said the girl student, her smile widening, if anything.

It was a defeat for the great Finney, one of the few he ever suffered, and smiling came to be a common pastime at Oberlin thereafter—at least it did until recent times when a pall of seriousness settled heavily on the campus and the student body discovered there was nothing in the world left to smile at, or about.

The fact that Finney at Oberlin was among those responsible for opening the doors of higher education to women brings to the fore the curious intermingling of personalities and places in history and the fateful coincidences so often to be found in the evolution of events. In 1845, some thirteen years after this evangelistic proponent of women's rights—in a limited sense—had left the Genesee Country to pursue his ministry elsewhere, the family of Susan B. Anthony took up residence in a farmhouse on the outskirts of Rochester.

In those days the field of female employment was severely limited. Teaching was one of the approved areas of work, and it was the field Miss Anthony elected to enter. Her career as a teacher led her to a job at Canajoharie Academy in 1846 and it was there, in Canajoharie, New York, that she made the acquaintance of some strong-minded women who would quicken the developing concrescence of her thoughts on the sorry role of women in the world of men. The new friends were Elizabeth Cady Stanton and Lucretia Mott. It was Elizabeth Stanton and Lucretia Mott who were instrumental two years later, in 1848, in calling the first "women's rights" convention in history at Seneca Falls.

The history books are full of the year 1848. In Europe it is remembered as a year of revolutions, the time of attempted overthrows of ancient aristocracies, dynasties, and privileged classes. In a real sense, the same thing was happening when the indignant pioneer women came together in Seneca Falls. They were firing the first guns in a revolution that they knew would take a long time to win, but they were determined to upset the old caste system that had placed women in a position of inferiority in the human scale of things.

The advertisement announcing the convention appeared in the Seneca County *Courier* on July 14, which contained its own symbolism because that date, of course, is the anniversary of the fall of the French Bastille, another prominent symbol of man's tyranny at one time. The choice of Seneca Falls as the site for the historic meeting was an arbitrary one, but there was a background to the young town that made it a fairly logical place to begin a revolution.

Seneca Falls, without question, was an incredibly restless place, wide open to new ideas no matter how unorthodox they might be. It was the heart of the Burned-Over Region, scorched only a few years before by the fiery revivals of Preacher Finney. Still active there were abolitionist groups, temperance societies, Unitarians, vegetarian Grahamites, a Non-Resistance Society, proponents of homeopathic medicine, and even a newspaper whose goal was to bring about legal reform in the state. The agitators for women's rights blended in beautifully against this somewhat chaotic background.

Among those who attended the historic meeting, held in the Wesleyan Methodist Chapel, and one of the hundred signatories to the "Declaration of Sentiments" adopted, was a nineteen-year-old girl, Charlotte Woodward, an employee in a local glove factory. The remarkable thing about Miss Woodward was that she lived to see women in the United States win the right to vote with ratification of the Nineteenth Amendment to the Constitution in 1920, some seventy-two years later!

In his study of the woman suffrage movement, *The Better Half*, Andrew Sinclair quotes some telling passages from Charlotte Woodward's reminiscences in 1920 of the incredible inequities that existed between the sexes in her girlhood when the legal position of a woman was on a par, approximately, with that of a criminal, a lunatic, or a plantation slave.

"We women did more than keep house, cook, sew, wash, spin and weave, and garden," she wrote. "Many of us were under the necessity of earning money besides . . . We worked secretly, in the seclusion of our bed-chambers, because all society was built on the theory that men, not women, earned money, and that men alone supported the family . . .

"Most women accepted this condition of society as normal and God-ordained and therefore changeless. But I do not believe that there was any community anywhere in which the souls of some women were not beating their wings in rebellion. For my own obscure self I can say that every fiber of my being rebelled, although silently, all the hours that I sat and sewed gloves for a miserable pittance which, after it was earned, could never be mine. I wanted to work, but I wanted to choose my task and I wanted to collect my wages. That was my form of rebellion against the life into which I was born."

The highlight of that historic first convention on women's rights was the reading by Elizabeth Stanton of the Declaration of Sentiments which she had written. It was a paraphrase of the Declaration of Independence, and it struck home with considerable force. The meeting approved unhesitatingly a set of resolutions demanding opportunities for women in education, trade, commerce, and the professions; rights in property, free speech, and the guardianship of children. Then, climactically, the hundred women fearfully adopted a resolution calling on the nation to give women the right to vote. Even many of the delegates thought that was going too far, and that for them to embrace such an extreme goal perhaps would damage the over-all cause of women.

Elizabeth Stanton, for example, was more interested in a reformation of marriage that would give women a larger voice in curbing the lustful demands of their husbands than she was in any extension of their political rights.

"I disclaim all desire or intention to meddle with *vulgar* politics," she sniffed in 1852, ". . . to sit in council with vulgar, rum drinking, wine bibbing, tobacco chewing men, with thick lipped voluptuaries, gourmands and licentiates who disgrace our national councils with their grossness and profanity, their savage rudeness, and uncurbed ferocity; who, instead of sound reason and strong argument, resort to fist-cuffing, dirking and duelling, to settle nice questions of honour and statesmanship. No, until a new type of man shall be placed at the helm of the ship of state, rest assured we women shall decline all nominations for office."

Susan Anthony, while active in the temperance and abolitionist movements, did not join immediately in the campaign for equality of the sexes. She gave up teaching in 1849 and returned to Rochester in that year to take up work with temperance groups. In 1852 a convention of

9. When the canal workers arrived at the site of Rochester, it was hardly more than a clearing in the forest that closed in on the Genesee River and the famous waterfalls. The canal changed it into a city.

(Prints Division, New York Public Library; Astor, Lenox and Tilden Foundations)

10. Perhaps the most remarkable achievement of the men who built the Erie Canal was their construction of the famous locks at Lockport—two separate flights of five locks each that enabled boats to overcome the natural barrier of the Niagara Escarpment.　　　　　*(New York Public Library Picture Collection)*

11. Looking east from the top level of the Niagara Escarpment at Lockport to the Erie Canal below, showing the gate tenders at each of the five locks that raised and lowered the boats. The gates of the locks were opened and closed manually by the men pushing on the huge timbers.

(Buffalo and Erie County Historical Society)

12. The busy boat basin of the Erie Canal in Tonawanda, as it appeared in May 1905. The old Main and Delaware Street Bridge over the canal is seen in the background. *(Buffalo and Erie County Historical Society)*

13. A view, in 1900, of the Erie Canal locks south of Austin Street in Buffalo's Black Rock section. *(Buffalo and Erie County Historical Society)*

14. Canal watching was a popular sport in every city through which the Erie Canal passed, and town bridges offered the best vantage points. Interested onlookers here are shown on the Commercial Street Bridge in Buffalo sometime in the 1870s. *(Buffalo and Erie County Historical Society)*

15. Great Lakes sailing vessels and diminutive canalboats nudged each other at the docks in Buffalo during the heyday of Clinton's Ditch.

(*New York Public Library Picture Collection*)

the Sons of Temperance invited members of the Daughters of Temperance to be their guests. Miss Anthony, a card-carrying Daughter, made the mistake of rising and attempting to make a motion during one of the official sessions. At that point she ran athwart a champion male chauvinist, the chairman of the meeting. No question about this man—he was a thorough-going Son.

"Women," he roared, pounding his gavel as hard as he could, "are here to listen and learn!"

Not long after that Miss Anthony became a leading campaigner for women's rights, joining forces with the volatile Elizabeth Stanton to establish Rochester virtually as headquarters of the movement. Since the Fourteenth and Fifteenth amendments to the Constitution were to make (male) ex-slaves—no matter how poorly educated—the political superiors of women, the suffragettes grimly regrouped and dug in for a fight to the finish. She organized the National Woman Suffrage Association in 1869 with the specific goal of promoting a sixteenth amendment that would give women political equality and was made head of the association. She held that post for twenty-one years, braving ridicule and hatred with splendid dignity and courage.

Once, at a women's rights rally in Albany, the mayor, who was seated next to Miss Anthony on the platform, held a revolver in his hand to protect her against the hoodlums who had infiltrated the audience. He made his point. There was no trouble.

Convinced that the Fifteenth Amendment, which was ratified in 1870, enfranchised women as well as former slaves, Miss Anthony and some of her friends on Election Day in 1872 went to the polls in Rochester and tried to force the issue by voting. In only one of the wards would the officials allow the women, including Miss Anthony, to vote. But two weeks later she was arrested on a federal warrant, as were fourteen other women and three of the election inspectors. The women were indicted for illegal voting.

Miss Anthony stood trial in United States Circuit Court in Canandaigua on June 17, 1873. From all accounts, Justice Ward Hunt presided over the proceedings with approximately the same detachment and objectivity as the bartender at McSorley's Saloon in New York City displayed nearly a hundred years later when the first females came before his bar. At the conclusion of the testimony, Judge Hunt ordered the jury to bring in a verdict of guilty, but the jurors balked. The Court thereupon discharged the jury without asking for its verdict, directed the clerk to enter a verdict of guilty, denied a motion for a new trial, and fined the defendant $100. Even veteran court aides stepped back in admiration as the judge wrapped up the case like a prizefighter throwing a series of lightning left jabs and then crossing over with a roundhouse right for the coup de grace.

Miss Anthony weathered the jabs of jurisprudence rather well. Refusing to duck or even to clinch, she stayed on her feet and rejected the Court's decision.

"May it please Your Honor," she said, "I will never pay a dollar of your unjust penalty. All the stock in trade I possess is a debt of ten thousand dollars, incurred by publishing my paper—*The Revolution*—the sole object of which was to educate all women to do precisely as I have done —rebel against your man-made, unjust, unconstitutional forms of law, which tax, fine, imprison, and hang women, while denying them the right of representation in the government; and I will work on with might and main to pay every dollar of that honest debt, but not a penny shall go to this unjust claim. And I shall earnestly and persistently continue to urge all women to the practical recognition of the old Revolutionary maxim: 'Resistance to tyranny is obedience to God.'"

The decision went to the established male-dominated society as Miss Anthony and her friends failed in their attempt to vote, but it was an important skirmish, influential in the determination of the ultimate victorious outcome of the war for women's suffrage.

On February 20, 1906, a great banquet in honor of Miss Anthony was held in New York City, the occasion being her eighty-sixth birthday. But the guest of honor did not attend. She had taken ill while attending the National American Woman Suffrage Association Convention in Baltimore a short time before and was home, in her last illness, when the encomiums were being lifted in her honor. She died a few weeks later, in the early moments of March 13, 1906, and a public which, in turn, long had ridiculed her, held her up to scorn, vilified her, and laughed at her, at last saw Susan Anthony as something more than a crank-type crusader for what had been a hopeless cause.

Flags were lowered to half staff in her home city of Rochester and many business places closed as a mark of respect. Columns of tribute appeared in the same newspapers that earlier had mocked her and denounced her. Something of the change that had taken place in the nation's judgment of the pioneer suffragette was noted in the headline that appeared over Susan Anthony's obituary in the New York *World:*

HER NAME ONCE A JEST, NOW HONORED

CHAPTER XIX

SAGA OF SAM PATCH

"It is an enchanted city," mused Basil, aloud, as they wandered on, "and all strange cities are enchanted . . . Rochester is for us, who don't know it at all, a city of any time or country, moonlight, filled with lovers hovering over piano-fortes . . . a city of handsome streets wrapt in beautiful quiet and dreaming of the golden age. The only definite association with it in our minds is the tragically romantic thought that here Sam Patch met his fate."

—*Their Wedding Journey*,
by William Dean Howells,
1872.

Sam Patch came on the scene at precisely the right time. The canal country was searching about for a new kind of hero. The frontiersmen had slipped away, their moccasined feet not making a sound as they departed, and the sweaty, red-faced, gaunt-eyed canal diggers had shouldered their shovels and moved on to some new drudgery, not even knowing they were heroes.

But life in Rochester was not settling into a humdrum routine. To the contrary, the boom town that was springing up at the falls of the Genesee was a boisterous place, full of activity and excitement, with boats coming and going and the town basins choked with craft of all descriptions. It was a center of bustle and noise, of people and goods; a crossroads that brought something of the civilized world into the wilderness. There were fine gentlemen and elegant ladies from far-off Europe, drawn to the remote scene by curiosity, and they shared the boardwalks with grizzled men in fringed leather jackets, burly lumberjacks with high boots, strutting boat captains in shiny silk hats, and even some Indians who walked about, hunched under their blankets, still not comprehending what was going on. Most of all, there were the men from the canal-boats everywhere, and it was plain to see they were in search of entertainment, from their restless gait and the hard bold way they stared at the women.

There were the ordinary sources of amusement, of course—the saloons and the brothels, the cock fights and the bar brawls, occasionally a traveling theatrical company, a lecturer, or even an evangelist. But all of those divertisements paled in the light of the entertainment provided by the man named Sam Patch.

Patch came from a nondescript background. He had been a spinner in a cotton mill in Pawtucket, Rhode Island, but how that led to his becoming a daredevil, nobody seemed to know. Somehow he had discovered that he had a rare talent for jumping off high places and coming out alive. It was said that he began his professional career as a jumper in 1826 by dropping feet first from a building in Pawtucket into the Blackstone River. After that, presumably, spinning cotton lost a lot of its appeal and Patch began to look around for things to jump off—and, of course, things to jump into, because you can't very well have one without the other.

He found some bridges in Paterson, New Jersey, that lent themselves nicely to his talents, and he did so well in jumping from them that he became known for a while as "The Jersey Leaper." By progression, then, he came to the idea of jumping over Niagara Falls. A jumper cannot stand still. He has to move continuously, meeting new challenges and overcoming them, if he is to hold the public interest and satisfy his own inner appetite for achievement. Niagara Falls was a natural, inevitable target for Sam's talents. It was the biggest, most famous waterfall anywhere on the continent, a cataract made to order for the jumping man who stood at the peak of his profession.

On October 6, 1829, just as he had promised he would, Sam Patch jumped over Niagara Falls successfully—not once, but twice! He got up there on a wooden platform, some 125 feet above the thundering waterfall, did a little jig, it seemed to those below, and, after waving to the thousands of spectators who looked on from both sides of the international border, he leaped out high above the great abyss in the trim, confident style that almost always characterizes the man who knows where he is going. There was nothing flamboyant or gaudy about Sam's style. It was his professional wont, as exemplified in his Niagara jumps, to stand rigidly straight when he jumped, head tossed back, arms straight down with palms pressed against his thighs like a soldier at attention, and to hold that stiff posture as he fell feet first. He almost always cut the water cleanly when he hit.

Sam was in great form in his jumps over Niagara Falls, everybody agreed, and his leaps were publicized wherever there were newspapers to print the news. Reporters crowded around the new celebrity after each jump, just as they had back in Pawtucket and Paterson, pressing him for quotable remarks.

There aren't many intelligent questions that can be asked of a man who has just jumped from a mill roof, or a bridge, or even a waterfall.

What the reporters asked mainly was why Sam chose to risk his life by pursuing this mad specialty. Sam gave the same laconic answer to everything.

"Some things," he would drawl, looking thoughtful, "can be done as well as others."

The answer at first failed to impress. It has a very simple construction and a deceptively innocent ring to it. Yet it puzzled almost everybody who heard it or read it, and that raised the possibility that what he had said actually was rather profound. The reporters bobbed their heads knowingly as they scratched the same old answer in their note pads, but on their faces were the worried frowns that reporters always show when matters have slipped out of their hands.

The newspaper readers, however, grew to be very fond of that stock answer of Sam Patch's. They found that it covered for them, as it did for Sam, a multitude of questions. Husbands turned back their nagging wives by observing that some things can be done as well as others; schoolchildren chanted the aphorism in the streets, and editorial writers wrestled with the interpretation of the utterance in columns reserved for pure intellectual exercise. Some found it to contain a profound philosophy, just as there were those who judged it to be the neatest concoction of gibberish that ever had been put together to confound reporters. But the whole world, it seemed, rejoiced in the emptiness of the statement, tirelessly reciting the cryptical lines until everybody eventually wearied of the words.

As for Sam himself, his conquest of Niagara Falls had secured his place in history and made him one of the most famous men of his day, but in order to capitalize on his latest triumph, he had to keep jumping. Fame is a fleeting thing. So is autumn, especially in northwestern New York, and if Sam was to do any more jumping before the weather turned cold, it would have to be right away. Fortunately, less than a hundred miles away from Niagara Falls there was Rochester and its Genesee Falls. He accepted the invitation to jump over this secondary cataract and hustled to Rochester.

It was a great day when Sam arrived. Canalboats had brought in hundreds of spectators, as had stage coaches and family wagons. But even with the crowds on the streets, there was no mistaking the Great Leaper when he appeared in public because he always traveled with a trained bear on a chain and a pet fox on a rope. They tended, somehow, to set him apart on even a crowded street.

The headline in the Rochester *Daily Advertiser* of October 29, 1829, read:

ANOTHER LEAP!
SAM PATCH AGAINST THE WORLD

The story referred to the scheduled jump at the end of the first week in November as "Sam's Last Leap." As it turned out, it was not Sam's last leap at all. He got up on the platform, as promised, a dazzling sight in a pair of fancy white pantaloons, a close-fitting jacket, and a silk sash wrapped around his waist. The finery was part of a band uniform which he had borrowed from an innkeeper who doubled in brass as a horn player. Thus costumed, Sam made his jump in fine form, over the ninety-two-foot-high Genesee Falls and into the cold river below.

Artistically speaking, it was a highly successful jump, but commercially it left something to be desired. That is, the pay-off was smaller than expected. But people still were streaming into Rochester and the river still had not frozen, so Sam scheduled a repeat performance to be executed one week hence, on the afternoon of Friday the thirteenth! Street posters promised that this not only would be the last leap, positively, but that it would be one that would "astonish the world." A new platform was built twenty-five feet above the falls as the jumping-off place.

Thousands of spectators lined the bridges and riverbanks that historic afternoon when Sam climbed up to his platform. Some said he went up the ladder unsteadily, that he wavered as he spoke to the crowd, and some were willing later to testify that he had accepted too much liquid hospitality from his Rochester admirers on the day of the jump. It is possible. Sam was more garrulous that day than anybody could remember he ever had been before.

"Napoleon was a great man and a great general," the Leaper is said to have shouted in his pre-jump statement to the crowd. "He conquered armies and he conquered nations, but he couldn't jump the Genesee Falls. Wellington was a great man and a great soldier. He conquered armies and he conquered nations, but he couldn't jump Genesee Falls. That was left for me to do, and I can do it, and will."

With that, Sam Patch jumped. Somehow everyone seemed to know immediately that something was awry. It was not in any way the usual Patch form. Instead of leaving the platform like a ramrod, feet first, hands pressed against his thighs, he tumbled off the platform more like a pinwheel, arms and legs flailing, twisting and spinning as he fell. When he hit the water, it was at an awkward angle, and his body made a loud slapping sound. There was a terrible splash, followed by spreading concentric patterns in the water. And silence.

The crowd waited, tensely, but without confidence. Everybody was appallingly aware that this, indeed, had been Sam Patch's last jump. He never did bob back to the surface. After a long, stunned wait, the crowd in the amphitheater that looked into the gorge began to melt away, half in embarrassment, half in sorrow.

Henry Clune, long-time newspaperman and an authority on the Rochester scene, wrote about that last sorry jump that "as Patch's body hurtled toward the water, a sibyl in the crowd screamed shrilly, 'If there is anything in dreams, the man is dead!'" A prominent citizen in front-row position, he reported, was so carried away by the excitement of the moment that he bit off the tip of his thumb.

Sam did reappear on the Rochester scene four months later, when his body was found floating on the Genesee in a cake of ice. His bear, meanwhile, had been kept on display at the Rochester hotel where Sam had stayed. It was unquestionably the biggest single attraction in town as the story of the last great leap had been carried all over the nation and across the oceans and already was a firm part of America's folklore.

Sam himself had become a legend even before he was freed from his icy coffin, so much so that there were people who were skeptical of his having lived at all. In no time a melodrama based on his life was playing the boards under the title, *Sam Patch, or The Daring Yankee*. That, somehow, added to the unreality of the man. It was just as though Sam had been immediately admitted to the company of American mythology because he had never really existed. What he had done and what he had said in his lifetime became part of the national legend; entertaining, even amusing, but not to be taken seriously.

In her study of the national character, titled *American Humor*, Constance Rourke said of Sam Patch the Legend:

"He jumped over Niagara Falls, but was unable to leap the Falls of the Genesee, and plunged through to the other side of the world and bobbed up in China—pure Yankee again though still jumping, and promising to take the shine off the sea serpent when he got back to Boston. He bobbed up in Paris. Plays were written around him, stories told, poems composed. An epidemic of jumping developed. Clerks called themselves Patch as they jumped counters, country lads as they leapt over rail fences; men traveled through village streets, jumping. Sam Patch became a symbol of quickness and power.

"'Some things can be done as well as others,' said Sam Patch laconically.

"The character belonged to the backwoods, but the drawling tone and dry talk were Yankee."

Curiously, while Sam Patch's gravestone in Charlotte Cemetery has been given a bronze identification tablet in recent years, Rochester itself, to whom Sam Patch gave so much, has given him little in the way of memorialization. It is almost as if the city were still embarrassed by the tragic tomfoolery that took place at the falls. Sam, like Colonel Ashbel Riley, lives on only in his own deeds in Rochester.

Perhaps, as Nathaniel Hawthorne once observed, no further memorialization of Sam Patch was necessary, perhaps what he had done was enough in itself to keep his memory alive and green.

"How stern a moral may be drawn from the story of poor Sam Patch," mused Hawthorne after a visit to the Falls of the Genesee to join other tourists in looking at the scene of the Last Leap. "Why do we call him a madman or a fool when he has left his memory around the falls of the Genesee more permanent than if the letters of his name had been hewn into the forehead of the precipice?

"Was the leaper of cataracts more mad or foolish than other men who throw away life, or misspend it in pursuit of empty fame, and seldom do triumphantly as he?"

CHAPTER XX

CARTHAGE FALLS AGAIN

> Carthage is dead; and night-beasts dig
> their lairs where once her turrets pierced
> the evening glow . . .
> —*Carthage*, Miriam Allen De Ford.

Communities bearing the name of Carthage appear to share a built-in weakness for catastrophe.

The fall of Carthage, New York, was one that was glossed over by history, and while it did not bear comparison with the fall of ancient Carthage by any measurement, it was, in its own way, a happening of epical worth. In another day and another clime, it probably would have brought all the resident poets on the run, their robes flying and their lyres strumming. As it happened, though, it was an event of no more than passing interest to the growing society of the western frontier. It failed, even momentarily, to divert attention from the Erie Canal that just then was being built.

Rochesterville—as Rochester was known in its beginning years—was a newly incorporated village in 1817 when a group of promoters headed by Elisha B. Strong of Connecticut founded Carthage on a site just a few miles to the north of Colonel Nathaniel Rochester's settlement. He planned it as a rival for supremacy of the Genesee Valley.

The site of Carthage offered certain obvious advantages. It was on the east bank of the Genesee River at the Lower Falls, close to the river's mouth and the broad sweep of Lake Ontario's waters. A settlement called Hanford's Landing, half a mile downriver, had been the port serving the junction of lake and river, but it was a hard-luck place, one that had suffered severely from the recurrent attacks of "Genesee Valley fever."

Carthage, on higher ground, was not as vulnerable to the malady of the lowland and its promoters had high hopes of seizing the shipping trade from its troubled rival. Warehouses, docks, and homes sprang up on the new site and the population grew rapidly.

"The God of nature has fitted and destined our place to become . . . one of the principal establishments in the western country," the leaders of the new town boasted. But they were practical businessmen, and they were well aware that nature would have to be given a helping hand if Carthage were to succeed. They had hoped for a while that the builders of the Erie Canal would see fit to route the waterway through their town, but when Rochesterville was chosen, Strong and his associates went ahead with a daring, ambitious plan to bridge the Genesee gorge at the Lower Falls, connecting the famous Ridge Road at this important point and thereby making Carthage a vital center for land transportation as well as a shipping port.

The project, begun in 1818, was as courageous and as audacious in its own way as the Erie Canal itself, considering the limited technology of the day. What the builder was called on to construct in the middle of the snake-infested wilderness, was the greatest bridge of its kind in the world—a span 718 feet long with a center arch some 196 feet above the bottom of the river gorge. There had been, until its destruction about twenty years before, a longer bridge in Switzerland, but when the span over the Genesee was finished and ready for traffic in February 1819, it was unique in its outsized dimensions and truly one of the world's wonders.

It was a remarkably fast achievement, having been built in approximately a year's time. One reason for this was that the bridge was built entirely of wood, and the raw material was at hand on the construction site, a virgin forest thick with tall, sturdy trees. When the bridge was finished, it stood out as a magnificent example of man's creativity and determination—a graceful, soaring, thirty-foot wide span with a Gothic arch whose chord measured 352 feet, with a simplicity and beauty of design that suggested a great cathedral.

It may be that a lot of the people who used the new bridge at the Lower Falls also had the same compelling desire to pray that they would have felt in a cathedral. The builder had pronounced it to be capable of bearing loads of twelve to fifteen tons, and he had given the Carthage town officials a guarantee that the bridge would stand and serve for at least one year and a day—a modest guarantee, to be sure, but better than no guarantee at all. Nevertheless, the users of the bridge could not help but notice that it was a terribly shaky sort of structure with a definite and inescapable tendency to tremble and shake and sway whenever it was used. The uniform reaction when they got to the other side safely was one of relief.

It was agreed by one and all that the scary sensation that was an inevitable part of every crossing was most unfortunate, but, still, there was that heart-warming guarantee from the builder that the bridge would hold up safely for at least a year and a day. That gave courage and heart to all but a few cravens in the bosky neighborhood.

As a matter of fact, the great bridge at Carthage stood for close to a year and four months before it finally gave way with a great roaring sound that could be heard for a long distance. As it fell, it sent up a mighty cloud of dust and scattered birds and animals of the forest for miles around. The collapse occurred on May 22, 1820. The magnificent, graceful arch, which presumably had not been braced sufficiently to sustain its own tremendous weight, buckled in the middle.

With the fall of the remarkable bridge went also the high hopes of Elisha Strong and his associates who were instrumental in the founding of the town. Carthage flourished as a port for a while, but gradually lost both its function as a shipping transfer point and its identity as a separate community, in time becoming an indistinguishable part of the metropolitan sprawl of Rochester.

People who have a tendency to become sentimental over such tragic happenings will be cheered, perhaps, to learn that the name of Carthage still lives on in another part of New York State. There is a small town with that legendary name on the Black River in the north country above Rome, some twenty miles to the east of Lake Ontario, and some fourteen miles—one hesitates to mention the fact—from Lake Bonaparte. The town directly to the west, however, is Watertown, not Waterloo.

Anyway, the Carthage to the north seems to be hanging on nicely.

CHAPTER XXI

ROYALTY AND ROMANCE IN ROCHESTER

Winter comes on fast where New York State nudges the north. The harvest explosion is always a hot, flamboyant show, blotched with scarlets and crimsons, but it is the nighttime scene that tells the inside story with its pale moon and the icy glitter of hoarfrost.

The slow pace of the canalboats brought about a close association between nature and the people who made their living on the waterway. The relationship, of course, went deeper than that. Men did more than make a living out of the canal; they made their life on it, and that fact spelled an important difference. The canal was part of them, just as they were part of it.

The trailing vegetation along the soft banks, the bending trees, the familiar old farmhouses, the wide-eyed youngsters looking down from the country bridges, the sudden splash of a fish in the water—every detail of the twin panoramas that unrolled before their eyes at three or four miles per hour was as familiar to the canallers as the flowers on the wallpaper of somebody else's living room. They were as sensitive to any changes in the scene as the housewife would be to the sudden appearance of a grease spot on the wall. Like the Indians who so recently had stood in this remote country and breathed its rich air without challenge, the canallers, most of them, developed a keen sensitivity to the scents and the sounds of their habitat. They had no need of the calendar to tell the time of year. A yellow leaf floating on the water sometimes was enough to tell them all they needed to know.

When the freeze unmistakably and irretrievably was on the land and the boats were docked for the winter, most of the canal was drained and the maintenance crews would begin their walk of the uncovered bottom, cleaning it of its accumulated debris. This was the least glamorous time

183

of all for the canal. The draining-off invariably revealed a terribly sordid sight—a squalid ditch whose muddy quagmire was imbedded with the soggy, rusting, decaying refuse that had been cast into the canal during the season by thousands of passengers and boatmen and by the thousands who lived along its banks. It was, from all accounts and description, an astonishing assortment of litter that not infrequently included human remains; whatever the specific mixture, it was always a combination that sent up an overpowering stench of decay to make townspeople retch.

Autumn's draining time was not a happy time for anybody within smelling range. Glamorous though the canal is in retrospect, and glamorous though it undoubtedly was under ideal conditions at the time it was in its prime estate, the people who lived near the Ditch often regarded it with the repugnance that is born of too close association. It was when the Ditch had been freshly emptied for winter and its mucky underside lay bare that the feeling ran highest.

Here and there, though, some enterprising townsmen found ways to beat the sordid side of the canal in the off-season—as they did in Rochester. There the imposing aqueduct was put to splendid wintertime use by all the gay blades of the community. As soon as the weather turned from bad to worse, the bucks of the town braced for action. Once the time had been set for canal draining, these young volunteers would rush to the scene and pile sandbags in the channel at either end of the aqueduct, thus damming and holding the water against the approaching day when the temperature would drop and turn the aqueduct into an ice rink.

Rochester can recall no civic institution more romantic than the ice rink aqueduct, especially when the little refinements like the warming shed were added. Band music also was an occasional part of the scene, reserved, no doubt, for the milder days when the tuba player could perform without the risk of his metal mouthpiece sticking permanently to his lips. The high side walls of the aqueduct protected the skaters from the sharp winds that blew off the Genesee River in wintertime. The rink itself was large enough to accommodate the whole population of Rochester. Even the price was right: five cents a person in the afternoon hours, ten cents each in the evening.

The aqueduct meant a lot more to Rochester than merely providing the inhabitants a place to skate, of course. By carrying the Grand Canal across the river and serving the industry of the town—mainly the flour industry—the aqueduct was directly instrumental in the city's commercial development and its growth as the first big boom town of the newly opened West.

"There was not a house where Rochester now stands," wrote De Witt Clinton in 1828, shortly before his death, as he recalled the inspection trip over the proposed canal route in 1810.

It wasn't until 1812 that the first permanent white settler, Hamlet

Scrantom, moved to the site, even though the presence of the rushing Genesee River and its waterfalls with their tremendous promise of mill power had drawn many visitors to the scene through the years. Some went there to admire the beauty of the falls and some to ponder their practical application.

One of those who struggled through the wilderness to see the Genesee Falls in 1797 was a tourist whom Rochester has never forgotten. He was the young French nobleman-in-exile Louis Philippe, who later staged a comeback and became the King of the French. It is probably true enough, as some cynics have pointed out, that the woods were full of out-of-work kings in the old days, but Rochesterians always hasten to reply, correctly, that Louis Philippe was the only king in *their* woods. It's an important point.

The frontier people treated Louis in a style that was nothing less than royal, even if he was between engagements at the time. Their hospitality is especially noteworthy in light of the fact that the distinguished visitor arrived at the falls in a terribly testy mood. He came in the company of Thomas Morris, son of the Robert Morris who had vast land holdings in western New York. Young Morris did his best to point out all the interesting features of the falls—how high the spray rose, how much water flowed over the brink every calendar year, and such stuff that waterfall watchers ordinarily like to hear—but the future king was not in the mood for appreciating the cataract. He was hungry. The royal gut rumbled with want.

Fortunately, the tavern of Orringh Stone was not far away, and it was no ordinary tavern, but one which had a great reputation among the frontiersmen for good food. Morris, observing that Louis Philippe was getting more fretful by the minute, sent a runner ahead to advise Mrs. Stone, who did all the cooking, that a party of famished, famous Frenchmen was on the way. It was a shrewd thing to do. When the royal party, which included Louis's brothers, the Duke of Montpensier and Count de Beaujolais, arrived at the tavern, Mrs. Stone greeted them with a hastily thrown together snack that included roast pig, wild pigeon, roast turkey, corn bread, apple and pumpkin pies, plus generous noggins of Orringh Stone's applejack and pegs of native whiskey. Not a bad repast, really, if it is remembered that it still was very early in the frontier game, with Indians still darting from tree to tree, doubtless having gotten a whiff of the food. It was hardly a setting for gourmets and epicures, but the menu wasn't bad.

Notwithstanding all the facts in the situation, the hospitality of Orringh Stone's lodge failed to make the favorable impression that the American hosts had hoped it would. Some fifty years later, when Louis Philippe was securely seated on the throne of France, he happened to notice one day in Paris a large shipment of glass which was addressed for shipment to Rochester, New York.

"Ah!" exclaimed His Ungrateful Majesty. "What can they do with that in *that* awful mudhole?"

King Louis was speaking from memory, mind you, and in all fairness to him it should be acknowledged that Rochester's site, like that of Syracuse, got a bad press from all sides. The same city that one day would call itself the "Flower City," was anything but a garden spot in the beginning. For that matter, its first white settler, Ebenezer "Indian" Allan, was no sweet-smelling rose.

". . . neither Indians nor settlers thought much of the land in the territory in which the Allan land was located," wrote Henry Clune in his book *The Genesee,* describing the Rochester site as a "sunken, miasmic area, notorious for its numerous colonies of rattlesnakes and for a fever, supposed to be induced by the swamps, which at a later date swept through the small colony at Genesee Falls like the Black Plague."

As for Indian Allan, most Rochesterians would just as soon erase history's slate and forget his name. His dark reputation matched the melancholy setting. While he was an extraordinary man in many ways, too many of his ways were questioned by his contemporaries. The truth that emerges is that Allan was not the kind of man a city, given a choice, ordinarily would select as its First Citizen.

Indian Allan carried his sobriquet with good reason. While a white man by birth, he had taken to Seneca dress and Seneca speech early in life and, indeed, had lived with the Indians. His skin was burned a bronze tone that made him a natural at any tribal campfire. The Iroquois liked him and had accepted him as an adopted son.

Allan had been granted the hundred-acre tract that is now downtown Rochester by a pair of English land speculators, Oliver Phelps and Nathaniel Gorham, in 1790. In return, he agreed to construct at Genesee Falls, the principal asset of the site, a gristmill and a sawmill. Through this agreement, Phelps and Gorham would fulfill one of the terms in their acquisition of some 2,600,000 acres of land from the Seneca Nation—a promise made to the Indians that the mills would be built at the falls and would serve their needs as well as those of the white settlers.

The mills were built, as promised, on the west side of the river, but they were not successful operations. The Indians didn't use the facilities except on a small scale, and there weren't enough white settlers in the vicinity to keep the mills in business. On top of all that, Indian Allan was not the businessman type, not at all the kind of ambitious entrepreneur needed to launch a mill in the wilderness. He had other things on his mind, and usually they had to do with women.

Indian Allan, it was said, came from New Jersey. He had been a close friend of the Senecas before the Revolutionary War and had placed his services at the disposal of the British during the War for Independence. It was said that he had served with the notorious Butler's Rangers. In short, his background was the sort least likely to win him popularity in the American frontier.

But Allan did have some friends. One was the woman named Mary Jemison, famed as "The White Woman of the Genesee"—a truly remarkable person. She was a white woman who had been kidnaped and adopted by a roving band of Indians when she was a child. She had grown up among the Senecas, spoke their tongue, accepted their customs, and preferred their company to the very end of her very long life. She married twice, both times to Seneca warriors. The first disappeared on a hunting trip. Several years later, when she was still in her early twenties, she married a chief named Hiokatoo, about thirty years her elder.

Chief Hiokatoo and Mary must have made quite a couple. She was said to be four feet, six inches tall; he, six feet, four inches. They never allowed a mere two feet to come between them, however. They were married close to fifty years, old Hiokatoo being one hundred and four years old when he was cut down—probably by one of those white man's illnesses that didn't give a red man a fighting chance.

When the Seneca Nation foolishly yielded to pressure and sold off most of its land empire in western New York to the English land speculators, the Indians insisted that proper provision be made for Mary. Phelps and Gorham were not about to jeopardize the big land deal over the niggardly issue of a few acres, but as it turned out, Mary emerged from the transaction with some 18,000 choice acres in the Genesee Valley some forty miles south of Rochester, in the area of today's Letchworth State Park.

It was in that vicinity, at a bend in the river known as Gardeau Flats, that Mary Jemison made her home. It was here, also, that she entertained her long-time friend, Indian Allan. It was hard to beat her version of frontier hospitality. Allan was the guest who came to stay during the full winter of 1782–83, and presumably the two whites-turned-Indians whiled away the snowy months playing Seneca games and swapping old tribal legends.

Allan was not so preoccupied with his hostess that he didn't have time for the amenities with another couple living on the Jemison land, a white man and his Indian bride. It is said that when the husband took his several cows to a grazing pasture each day, Indian Allan would drop in on the lonely squaw and do a bit of grazing on his own. She was properly grateful, as most women appeared to be whenever the dashing frontiersman paid attention to them, and in a burst of sentimentality, she knit Allan a red woolen stocking cap—a style that was the rage in the woods at the time. But they were not pulling the wool over the husband's eyes. He became very angry in the role of cuckold and began to thrash his wife on a regular, around-the-clock basis until his hand was stayed by Chief Hiokatoo on one of his infrequent visits home. The affair between Allan and the woman continued through the winter. Not until spring did she take leave of Allan and return to her husband.

187

Allan then moved to the east bank of the Genesee, to a place which is now part of the village of Mount Morris. There he built a cabin and set up light housekeeping with an Indian girl named Sally. In time, two children were born to the couple, girls whom they named Mary and Chloe. But this was not to be the beginning of a quiet domestic existence for Allan. The British at the time still held Fort Niagara and other strong points along Lake Ontario, despite the fact that the United States had won the Revolutionary War. England still harbored hopes of reopening hostilities and downing the colonial upstarts. Toward this end they tried to incite the Senecas to hostile action in western New York, but Indian Allan, now partial to the idea of peace, foiled the British move. In reprisal, the Redcoats chased Allan back to his old hiding place—Mary Jemison's cabin—and made him a prisoner there for nearly a year.

When he was released, Allan made his way back to Mount Morris, but only briefly. In 1786 he moved to a 422-acre farm near Scottsville, built a log cabin, and there resumed his romantic career with a vengeance.

Historian Clune, in analyzing Allan, noted:

"There was . . . one distinct difference between him and the Indians with whom he lived on terms of free association. They were not as much given to the lusts of the flesh; Allan was as concupiscent as a Turkish Sultan. He seemed to feel, as a wit of a later day put it, that the way to get rid of temptation was to yield to it."

One day a New Englander named Nathan Chapman interrupted his westward journey with his family to pause at Allan's cabin. Any sign of human habitation was a welcome sight in the wilderness. But Chapman must have rued the decision to stop and visit because his daughter, Lucy, a handsome, strapping girl, quickly fell under the spell of Indian Allan. Before the father could protest, or perhaps in spite of his protests, Lucy became Mrs. Allan. The fact that there already *was* a "Mrs. Allan" and two small children in the household apparently was shrugged off as one of those awkward things. Perhaps the fact that the first Mrs. Allan (assuming she was the first) was an Indian girl made it less of a real marriage in Lucy's eyes. Another mitigating fact to be taken into account was that the man who performed the ceremony uniting Allan and Lucy Chapman was a cattle drover named Slocum, no clergyman in any way. A technicality, to be sure, but one that had to be given some weight.

It really didn't matter what people thought of the situation in the crowded Allan cabin as long as Sally and Lucy were content to share Ebenezer's bed and board—which they were. A child was born to Lucy in 1789, and while the children born to the Indian wife had been given white names, the son born to Lucy was given the name of Seneca.

Domesticity, it is interesting to note, didn't change Allan. He still liked to ride over to Gardeau Flats to visit his old friend Mary Jemison. There, on one of his visits, he met a pretty young woman and her elderly husband who were resting after their long journey from the east. Allan, an impressionable man, reacted positively to the attractive young wife. He invited the husband to view the mighty Genesee River in his company, and, as the man looked on the rushing waters admiringly, Allan pushed him into the river. It was November, and the water was icy cold. The husband splashed his way ashore safely, but he caught pneumonia and died a few days later in Mary's cabin. His grieving widow quickly accepted Allan's invitation to join his harem back in Scottsville, where she remained a member in good standing of the household for about a year and a half before withdrawing her membership in the unusual commune.

At one time or another, the Allan cabin held Wife Sally and her two children, Wife Lucy and her son, Lucy's parents, and Lucy's married sister; Indian Allan's own sister and her husband, Christopher Dugan; Wife No. 3; and, of course, Indian Allan himself. It was a busy place; lots of coming and going.

One story about Indian Allan alleges that he once numbered among his wives a girl named Millie McGregory, who eventually came into his disfavor. And Indian Allan had a powerful temper. The Indians, who knew him well, called him "Genushio," which also was the name they reserved for a part of the Genesee River that was an unmanageable, unnavigable torrent. When Millie McGregory somehow stirred Allan's torrential temper, it was said that he impetuously hired two men to take her out to the deep water of the Genesee in a canoe and upset the boat, leaving her to flounder and die.

The plan didn't work. Millie fought her way back to shore and outlived her husband. If she didn't dance on his grave, at least she had the satisfaction of inheriting some of his worldly goods.

Allan moved to the hundred-acre tract at Genesee Falls in 1790, after having spent most of the previous year preparing the site. A crude sort of raceway was scooped out and about a half acre in the center of the present heart of Rochester was cleared of trees. A rough sawmill was built and from it came the lumber to construct the gristmill. Fourteen able-bodied men were recruited to assist in the mill raising. The big timbers were heavy, but the job had its bright side. An extravagant supply of rum was put at their disposal, and dispose of it they did.

There were reasons why the mills failed to draw the patronage that the land company had hoped for. The site was not easily accessible to the few settlers and Indians in the area. Furthermore, it was neither a pleasant place to live nor a nice place to visit, judging by the dispirited accounts of those on the scene at the time. It was a bleak countryside, swampy and smelling of rotting vegetation, overrun by rattlesnakes, and cursed with the fever that made the valley a dread place.

After a year or so, Allan turned the mills over to Dugan, his brother-in-law, moved the family back to Mount Morris briefly, and finally, about 1792, he sold the hundred-acre tract at Genesee Falls back to an agent of

189

the land speculator, Robert Morris. Then Allan and his entourage crossed the border and took up residence in Canada.

Morris had grand plans for a city at Allan's millsite. He even had a grand name for it—Athens. Carthage, after all, would be just to the north. But the mills were abandoned, the plans for a town dropped, and the wilderness growth was allowed to take over again in 1794 as the western country tensed under the threat of new Indian uprisings and the possibility of renewed warfare by the British.

Not until those threats were erased did the millsite come to life again. It was purchased in 1803 by three Maryland speculators—William Fitzhugh, Charles Carroll, and Nathaniel Rochester. The latter, in 1811, laid out town lots on the property, and in the spring of 1812 the first permanent settler, Hamlet Scrantom, arrived on the scene in a covered wagon. In it were his wife, six children, and all his possessions.

It was May 1 when he arrived, a date calculated to fill a traveler with a fair amount of optimism. No doubt in distant lands the sun was shining, the buttercups were turning the meadows a golden delight, and the children were dancing around the Maypole. But in Rochester—or what soon would be Rochester—there was a blinding snowstorm!

The Scrantoms may have been mildly upset by the phenomenal weather, but they weren't worried. When they had purchased their lot in the new town the year before, they also had contracted to have a cabin built. Warmed by the knowledge of their own foresight, they crossed the choppy Genesee in the blizzard, using a scow as a ferry to carry their horses and wagon. On the other side, they glimpsed their cabin for the first time. It was quite a sight. The builder hadn't gotten around to putting a roof on it—one of those oversights that is hard for a builder to explain to this day.

Before the night was over, the snow had piled up a foot high, and the Scrantoms had to take shelter in the cabin of a frontier family on the east side of the river.

It was a dramatic entrance that Hamlet & Cast made into what, one day, would be Rochester. But Ebenezer Allan got there first with the curtain-raiser.

CHAPTER XXII

VENICE WITH SALT VATS

Time and change have done an overwhelming job of covering up the original Erie Canal, and yet there are bold traces of it still to be found, meandering sections that are almost covered over by the backwoods brush, pieces that look no more impressive than any ordinary, everyday gully, round-shouldered ravines running anonymously through distant grassy fields. Most easily identifiable among the remains of the once-grand Grand Canal are the jumbled stones that tell of an early lock.

But the old canal was buried more by progress than by nature. It was swallowed up by its successors, the rebuilt canal of the middle nineteenth century and the modern New York State Barge Canal that followed in the present century. Some parts that were lopped off the rebuilt canal, like the sections that ran through the cities, were quickly filled in and utilized as rights of way for streets and freeways and even—as in the case of Rochester—a short-lived subway.

The motorists who speed over the New York Thruway as it passes through downtown Buffalo and along the Niagara section on the west side are driving over the buried bed of the Erie Canal. It was almost like an archaeological dig when the preparatory work on those sections of the new Thruway was being done in 1957. The old canal had been covered over a long time before, in 1935, to serve as the base of the Commodore Perry Boulevard—but not without protest from sentimental Buffalo citizens. Some called the work a sacrifice to progress; others called it a sacrilege committed in the name of expediency. But when the Thruway workers sank their tools deep into the ground, they frequently hit historical pay dirt, as on March 8, 1957, when a bit of the old Erie Canal was uncovered at the foot of Austin Street—"for the second time in a couple of decades," wryly noted the reporter of the Buffalo *Evening News*.

"Excavation to reinforce a sewer at that point has revealed the old, gray stone walls of what may have been an original lock of the Erie Canal built in 1825," wrote Fred Turner. "Slightly to the north is a 150-foot stretch of 'Clinton's Ditch,' as its pre-construction opponents derisively called it. Along this trench is a wall of rough stone which rests on ancient cribbing.

"The cribbing consists of wooden piles driven to bedrock and surmounted by long heavy timbers and planks. The effect is to form a subterranean tunnel along the side of the old canal.

"Dr. Marvin A. Rapp of State Teachers College, a canal buff and an authority on the old waterway, believes it is an old sluiceway for dewatering the canal, since the land at that point seems to slope toward the Niagara River.

"'I believe the lock and the cribbing may date either from 1825 or from 1840 when a modernizing took place,' said Dr. Rapp. 'The wood seems to have been excellently preserved.'"

There were a few footnotes to the story that underscored the ignominy of what was happening, barbed words to tear at the flesh of canal partisans. One mentioned that "in the bed of the old canal a concrete sewer was laid in 1937." Another specified that "on the old Towpath a score of homes have been or will be razed between the canal and the New York Central tracks. Nearly everybody has vacated."

Nevertheless, a lot of Buffalonians felt a warm glow when the Thruway diggers brought up proof that the old canal that had done so much for their town was still down there somewhere, even if part of it was serving the mean function of a sewer pipe bed.

Not all of the original canal stays buried, by any means. Every now and then an old, forgotten piece comes to light, sometimes accidentally, but more usually through the diligent searching efforts of canal buffs. Some of these students of the old Erie call themselves "canawllers," which also is what they used to call the people who once lived and worked on the ditch. Today's canawllers frequently sponsor organized field trips in which they search for new-old traces of the canal. When they make a strike and uncover some hidden artifact or ruin that belonged to the canal's glorious early days, there is widespread jubilation.

For less sophisticated sightseers in the canal field, there are many gratifying remainders of the Erie still to be viewed. In Lockport, for example, the flight of five locks that date back to 1840 constitute perhaps the most impressive remains of the canal anywhere. But the aqueduct that crosses the Genesee River in Rochester commands attention, too, as does the Weighlock Building in Syracuse, near the heart of the city, close to the halfway point of the canal.

As its name suggests, the Weighlock Building was the building in which canalboats were weighed. It was in reality an enclosed lock. Built in 1849–50, it is the last of all the buildings that New York State erected in the nineteenth century for the administration of the canal, and today, most appropriately, it houses the Erie Canal Museum, which is operated by Onondaga County.

The best description of the Weighlock Building was provided by a writer who called it "a simple two-story red brick structure fashioned after the style of a Greek Temple." Not every simple red brick building is given to such grandeur. A lot of ingenuity went into the design of the building, inside and out, however—especially in the facilities that made it possible for the canal toll collectors to determine the charge to be levied against each boat.

The freighters rode the canal right into the building, wherein each in turn was admitted into the lock. When the lock gates were closed, the water was drained out and the boat settled onto a massive cradle that was suspended from a balance beam overhead. The gross weight of the boat was recorded in the scale room, where there also was a record that showed the registered (empty) weight of the boat alone. The empty weight was subtracted from the gross weight and the remainder was the net weight of the cargo on which the charge would be levied.

Syracuse, incidentally, is a city that holds strong attraction for fans of the Erie Canal. Apart from the presence there of the Weighlock Building and the canal museum, there is the city itself. Once it was known as the "American Venice" because the canal ran through the heart of the city. Here also the Oswego Canal, which connected the Erie with Lake Ontario to the north, made its presence felt. The Erie bisected the city into North Side and South Side, while the North Side in turn was bisected by the Oswego Canal. There were bridges everywhere, and at night when the gas lamps and the torches were reflected in the widespread canal waters, Syracuse was a romantic, glamorous place.

It has been said that Syracuse was "the first and most important of Mother Erie's own children." If that is true, then the village of Salina was one of the first of the canal's stepchildren. Salina, only a couple of miles to the north, on Lake Onondaga, already was an important center, with more than a hundred dwellings and several hundred salt works. By contrast, the site of Syracuse was a dismal lowland area with mudholes and cedar swamps. There was general agreement that it was both an unlovely and unlikely site for a city. Nevertheless, it was decided to build the canal through this area and Syracuse sprang into position as the important waterside community and shortly swallowed the older settlement of Salina.

"It has been said," wrote a Syracuse *Journal* reporter, "that probably no city in the United States was founded in such a dismal, uninteresting and impracticable spot as this."

When a traveler named Colonel William L. Stone visited the site of the future city in 1820—the year that the first canalboat reached the area—he looked out at the quagmire scene, at the "few scattered and indifferent wooden houses" and wrote, with lugubrious pen, that "it was so desolate it would make an owl weep to fly over it!"

In that year, Syracuse's population was about 250 persons, and it turned an unlovely, ungroomed face toward the passing boats as well as to the owls flying overhead. Stumps of oak and pine trees only recently toppled still marred Clinton Square in the heart of town. The main thoroughfares, Salina and Genesee streets, which intersected, were cleared of trees only to the extent of allowing wagons to make their way through. North and east of Fayette Park was a cedar swamp, and there was always in the air the musky, damp smell that most visitors found unpleasant.

There were then four frame structures in the town, and two of those were taverns, which would suggest something or other. About these central buildings were log dwellings and slab cabins, apparently placed in random layout, but no one was far from the closest tavern. Pioneering, after all, was very good in its own way, but it could be overdone. Anyway, Syracuse prospered as a port which funneled the salt of the Onondaga mines into the holds of Erie Canal freighters and on to distant markets. By the time the full canal was opened to traffic in 1825, Syracuse had tripled its population, which then hovered close to the 800 total. Five years later, the count reached 2,565; ten years later, in 1840, there were more than 10,000. By 1850 Syracuse was a city of more than 22,000 population.

The canal helped Syracuse and Syracuse helped the canal. The salt that poured into the holds of the freighters (even on rainy days), also seasoned the canal treasury, thanks to the tax of 12½ cent on each bushel. It was a high tax, but the salt interests paid it gladly because the waterway meant so much to the prosperity of their industry.

When De Witt Clinton was struggling to sell the idea of the Erie Canal in the beginning years, one of his outstanding supporters was Judge Joshua Forman, who lived in the Onondaga valley near Salina. He wisely recognized the value of the waterway as the instrument that could open up the state. More specifically, he saw the canal as the key to the large-scale development of the area's salt industry. Once low-cost bulk transportation to New York City were made possible by the canal, a world-wide market would be waiting for New York State salt.

A canalboat rider in 1829 marveled over the sight of the booming salt center:

"It is a very agreeable novel sight to me to behold at this place upwards of 200 acres actually covered with vats filled with salt water in the act of evaporation," he wrote. "The process is very simple. The quantity of salt sent to market from this shop is immense. As we passed the lake we had a fine view of it, which was very beautiful from our elevation of 50 feet above it . . ."

194

Those 200 acres were but the beginning. By the time the salt industry hit its peak, during Civil War days, some 6,000 acres of land were dedicated to the saltmaking process, which, as the traveler had noted, really was a simple one.

The Indians had known of the bubbling salt springs near Onondaga Lake and they had found the brine distasteful. A French priest, Father Simon Le Moyne, had visited the strange springs and written in his diary:

"We arrived at the inlet of a little lake lying in a large basin. The water was very low. We tasted a spring which the Indians dared not drink. They say it is inhabited by a demon who makes it fetid. I found it was a salt spring. In fact, we made salt as good as sea salt and carried a quantity of it to Quebec."

An ancient salt lake covered the area in prehistoric times and left a giant blanket of salt fifty to a hundred feet deep. An underground stratum between Tully Valley and Onondaga Lake acts as a great sponge, storing the natural seepage from the salt beds. It was from this "sponge" that the salt springs bubbled.

As the value of the salt deposits became evident, the state negotiated a treaty with the Onondaga Indians in 1788 which called for establishment of a 10,000-acre salt springs reservation under joint ownership. But somebody in Albany must have had second thoughts about the deal and negotiations were resumed with the Indians, culminating in 1795 in a new agreement in which the Onondagas gave up their rights to the reservation for a down payment of $700 and an annuity of $700 and 100 bushels of salt. It was an outstanding example of the white man rubbing salt in the red man's wounds.

Proving, perhaps, what a hard bargain they had driven back in the eighteenth century, the Onondagas are still collecting their salt bounty. New York State every June dutifully makes direct payment to the tribe, now numbering fewer than 800 members. In that month the state delivers four tons of salt to the Onondaga Reservation, south of Syracuse, and distributes it. Each member of the tribe receives about twenty-five pounds of salt. In addition, the state pays the tribe $2,000, or about $2.80 per Indian. There are no strings. The Onondagas can use the salt anyway they want to, and if they wish to spend the full $2.80 at one time on something foolish, they are free to follow their reckless impulses.

The salt industry in Salina began in 1790, when some 600 bushels were produced and sold at a dollar a bushel. The business picked up swiftly thereafter. By 1800, 50,000 bushels were produced, and that output was doubled within the following four years. With the canal facilitating the movement of the product to market, efforts were redoubled. The production of salt reached 1,000,000 bushels in 1828, 2,000,000 bushels in 1836. Peak production was reached during the Civil War, when Syracuse was the principal salt supplier in the nation—in 1862, when 3,000 men

195

were employed in the salt works, the production reached 9,053,874 bushels.

Toward the end of the century, competition from other areas caused a change-over in Syracuse. Salt was then used in a process for the manufacture of soda ash, caustic soda, bicarbonate of soda, and other chemicals—a prosperous new industry. But before turning to this field, Syracuse had shipped some 400,000,000 bushels of its "white gold" all over the world. The result was not only splendid financial returns to the city, but benefits to the entire state. The tax on salt helped to pay for the Erie Canal and the network of connecting canals whose construction followed the initial success of Clinton's Ditch.

Salt is still a strong part of Syracuse life. Everything about the city, including the speech, is flavored with the industry that dominated civic and industrial life in the area for so long a time. The nickname "Salt City" still obtains, and the main thoroughfare is still Salina Street. The badges on the police uniforms display a salt block and a canalboat, a pretty arrangment but only a condensed version of the city seal, which may be one of the busiest in all sealdom. The Syracuse municipal imprint carries a scene of acres of salt vats, salt block chimneys, smoking salt blocks, a moving canalboat, and a railroad train.

"An anonymous humorist offered a recipe for Syracuse," noted a writer in the Syracuse *Post-Standard:* "Take salt, drain off the swamp water, replace with canal water, add a quantity of limestone and a tincture of iron—both railroad and iron wills—stir in all sorts of experimental materials and a strong mental and artistic culture, a large dose of good will and plenty of pepper, and you have SYRACUSE . . ."

No doubt it was nothing more than a fortuitous coincidence that the bulwark of the salt-making labor force from the very beginning was provided by the Irish. They, of course, have a hereditary fondness for boiled potatoes, and there is nothing more essential to the enjoyment of boiled potatoes than a liberal sprinkling of salt. Irish potatoes and Syracuse salt formed a highly congruous combination. Not surprisingly, one of the best-known saloon keepers in Syracuse at one time was known to one and all as "Salt Potato Keefe" because the specialty of his place was corn and potatoes boiled in brine and washed down with a mug of beer. Sometimes two mugs of beer. His saloon on Wolf Street was one in which Irish connoisseurs congregated in happy throng.

When salt production was at its peak in the 1860s, there were some 400 wells along the shores of Onondaga Lake. The natural brine from subterranean pools was pumped to reservoirs and then carried by wooden pipes to the vats, which were shallow wooden cisterns about twelve feet square, raised on piles several feet above the ground. (Iron pipes and iron containers would have been chewed apart quickly by the salty water.)

Each vat had a wooden cover that was easily movable. When the sun was shining, the cover was slid aside so that nature could go about the job of evaporating the water in the vats. What was left was a thick residue of salt crystals which then could be ground and refined into the commercial product. This was the solar system of salt extraction, and it was both cheap and efficient.

The big flaw in the solar system was that there were days when the sun not only refused to co-operate by shining, but when the saltmakers had to cope with their worst enemy, rain. At the time when there were tens of thousands of vats spread over 6,000 acres of land in the Syracuse precincts, a sudden shower could be calamitous.

To guard against the disaster, there were "lofty watch towers which rose like lighthouses above the sea of vats," and in each tower was a vigilant sky-watcher who had at his disposal an alarm bell to alert all below. The sight of a dark cloud on the distant horizon was enough to put all the men in the towers in a tense state of readiness.

The clangor of the alarm bells was the signal for hundreds of workmen and their families to drop everything else they were doing and rush out to push the covers over the vats. The predominantly Irish work crews lived in little villages on the periphery of the vat yards, close enough so that they could get to the vats in a hurry.

An observant Syracusan, John S. Shanahan, left a personal account of the way it was when the rains came:

"One tap of the yard bell, rung by the watchful foreman seeing a storm stealing up, would be answered by a stream of people rushing from the houses like bees from an assaulted hive. Out would pour men, women and children to 'run the covers' over the vats lest the brine be spoiled. Each had their row and there was great rivalry to be the first to start a cover and finish a row, for which the winner got an extra shilling or two."

Another who remembered Syracuse when the saltmakers ran foot races with Mother Nature was E. Alexander Powell.

"When the watchers descried an ominous cloud on the horizon," he wrote, "a brazen warning was clanged out by the alarm bells. Thereupon hundreds of workmen, aided by their womenfolk and children, would drop all else to push the rollered roofs over the vats in frantic haste.

"The lowering clouds, the sudden tocsin, the hordes of scurrying workers, the mile-long rows of vat covers rolling forward in gray-brown billows, formed a singular and stirring spectacle . . ."

The vats were saltmakers to adults, but they added another dimension to the play world of children who grew up in the city at that time, as Powell recalls:

"The dim, dank space beneath the vats was a wonderful place for small boys to go adventuring, for the wooden piles stretched endlessly, like trees in a gloomy forest; overhead the seeping brine coagulated into stalactites—white, yellow, brown, henna red—which often assumed the most fantastic shapes. Some of the salt blocks covered many acres, and crawling beneath them on hands and knees was as fascinating as exploring a pirates' cave—though hard on the pants. One had the eerie feeling that almost anything might happen in those stalactite-hung, bat-infested reaches . . ."

As new nationality groups arrived to take their place beside the Irish, Syracuse became sectored according to ethnic identity. The First Ward was Irish, the Italians lived beyond the West Shore tracks, while the Poles, comparatively small in number, lived in the western area of the city. The Germans took over the northern district, which was still referred to as Salina.

There was a definite social stratification among the nationality groups. The Germans, who were brewery workers, took a disapproving view of the Irish saltworkers and the Italian railroad workers. They also did their best to keep alive the spirit of the "Deutschland" in their new home by a fair scattering of beer gardens and *Turnvereins*. They not only made beer, they believed in drinking it.

It ought to be said, with emphasis, that the German brewery workers in Syracuse were not ordinary, run-of-the-rathskeller beer drinkers. One of their contemporaries, in awed tones, once said of them: "They were Gargantuan, balloon-bellied fellows; human beer casks."

That this was a fair description is suggested by the fact that they once threatened to strike the brewery "unless their free allowance of beer was raised from 40 to 60 glasses a day"!

Even a casual study of Syracuse history makes it clear that no matter how many weeping owls were overhead, life in the great salt capital seldom was dull. It hardly could be that, with two large, busy canals criss-crossing the downtown, the Irish battling up and down the length of the First Ward, the Germans drinking beer, and all the other interesting elements of the city coming together to enliven the civic scene. There was, for instance, that struggling Methodist institution of learning, later known as Syracuse University, which was growing up on a hill about a mile east of the business district.

Among the eventual benefactors of the university were Lyman C. Smith—the L. C. Smith who built a typewriter factory in Syracuse in 1890. The writing machine, at the time, had caught world attention. Smith donated a chemistry building. John D. Archbold of Standard Oil contributed the money for an athletic stadium and John Crouse, a wealthy wholesale grocer, made possible the Crouse College of Fine Arts building.

A highlight in the Syracuse past was the time that the Crown Prince of Siam visited Syracuse for a first-hand look at L. C. Smith's plant. Smith, as host, naturally went to the railroad depot to greet the royal person, taking with him a delegation of leading citizens and civic officials, a loud brass band, and a coach of elaborate style drawn by four gaily caparisoned horses.

As Alexander Powell recalls in his amusing recollections of Syracuse, *Gone Are the Days*, the civic reception at the railroad station went

198

smoothly until the time came for the band to salute the crown prince with a rendition of the Siamese national anthem. The musicians, unfortunately, didn't have that particular piece of music—but, like most good musicians, they refused to allow a technicality to interfere with their performance. They immediately substituted for the national anthem a number that seemed to them the next most appropriate selection. Something Siamesy. Their choice was a popular rinky-tink tune whose lyrics, in part, sang:

> Oh, the elephant he goes 'round,
> And the band begins to play,
> And the boys around the monkey's cage
> Had better keep away!

Whether the little prince kept blinking his eyes and wiping his glasses throughout the performance because he was sentimentally overcome or merely surprised was never decided. But he undoubtedly had many things to think about as his tally-ho coach rolled off toward the factory, because he was seated on the box between Tycoon Smith, a portly man, and a celebrated driver from Cronin's Livery Stable—a man who had a reputation for being a fantastic tobacco-juice spitter. Sometimes in the life of a prince, protocol isn't nearly as important as being seated to the windward of a show-off coach driver.

The two sons of John Crouse, the philanthropist grocery magnate, stand out among the unforgettable Syracusans of the canal century. The truth is, they would have stood out anywhere, at any time. They were big men—John J. Crouse weighed nearly four hundred pounds, his big brother, D. Edgar Crouse, was even heavier, by how much nobody was sure. Each brother had his own following, but for different reasons: John J. because he was the mayor, D. Edgar because he was something of a showy fellow and certainly one of the fanciest horse fanciers ever.

One event they haven't forgotten in Syracuse is the time that Colonel William F. (Buffalo Bill) Cody visited town, back in the 1880s. The great Western hero apparently hadn't met many fat mayors while he was chasing around the Great Plains. Mayor Crouse impressed him greatly when the two met. When the mayor expressed a wish to see the Wild West Circus close up, Buffalo Bill accommodated him with a tour of the lot following the first performance, during which the mayor had sat in a first-row box as the guest of the management.

As they were walking around the lot, which was surrounded by a high board fence, there was a sudden, shrill warning cry: "Run for your lives! The buffalo are loose!"

Before anybody could move, a herd of snorting, pawing, frothing bison came galloping around a corner, headed straight for Colonel Cody and Mayor Crouse. The exact text of the conversation between the two men has been lost, but it was said by onlookers that Mayor Crouse, all four hundred pounds of him, broke for the ten-foot-high fence and hurled his huge bulk over it with an Immelmann roll that caused the canvas top to billow outward. But the leap carried him to safety. He presumably reduced to matchwood all the wooden seats on the other side of the fence, but that failed to detract from his achievement.

Powell, who described the incident in his book with unconcealed amusement, alleged that the entire incident was an elaborate practical joke by Buffalo Bill. He was curious to know how a man as fat as Mayor Crouse would react to the sight of a charging bison, according to Powell, and he found out.

D. Edgar's hobby was pampering his blooded trotters. He and his horses lived together in kingly style in the most splendid stables anywhere. Crouse lived upstairs and the horses lived downstairs. It was a nice arrangement, but the horses probably had the better of the deal. The cost of the stables was estimated to have been more than $1,000,000. The box stalls were of rosewood and mahogany, topped with bronze grilles and decorated with hand-painted tiles made in Holland especially for Crouse's horses. The mangers were of white marble and the fixtures were gold-plated. The large carriage room was paneled with rare woods, and glass cases in the tack room contained dozens of sets of gold-mounted harnesses.

Every afternoon precisely at four o'clock, provided the weather was good, D. Edgar would take a drive, and it was easily one of the finest sights in town—the equivalent in Syracuse, as one writer noted, of "the guard mount at Buckingham Palace." There was always a crowd around the Crouse stables on State Street at the appointed hour because it was an event that never got tiresome. First, there was the inspection of the horses and the red-wheeled buggy, built with special reinforced springs to carry its owner. Crouse, dressed in a driving coat of fawn melton, would move ponderously around the carriage with a white silk handkerchief in his hand, rubbing all parts of the vehicle with it and then examining the handkerchief for a speck of dirt. If there was a sign of dirt, he fired on the spot whoever was responsible.

The next part of the ceremony was one the townspeople seemed to enjoy the most. The stable manager, the head coachman, and a valet would join to boost the beefy sportsman into the narrow seat, no small accomplishment. Then somebody would tuck a fawn-colored rug embroidered with his monogram around the grocery heir's knees, while he, shrugging off the hostlers, picked up the reins, clucked once or twice, and rode grandly off, his ears ringing with the small cheers of the onlookers. He always rode alone, but it could hardly have been otherwise. He took up the whole seat.

The anticlimax of the D. Edgar Crouse story came after his death—as anticlimaxes so often do. A mysterious woman, allegedly an Austrian baroness, appeared on the scene and laid claim in court to a share of the wealthy sportsman's estate on the basis that she was his widow. Syracuse was thrilled to have nobility appear in its midst, but its welcome was reserved. Crouse's native city knew him only as a single man—in fact, the city's outstanding bachelor. But the baroness tossed her pretty head and explained that she and D. Edgar had been wed secretly in Europe and that their union even had produced a daughter, whom she had named Dorothea Edgarita Crouse. The jury, visibly touched, thereupon awarded the baroness half of the great estate. However, Syracuse, for the most part, remained skeptical of her claim.

As the nineteenth century moved into its final phase, it was evident that the two mighty factors which had turned Syracuse from a quagmire into a great, prosperous city were in irreversible decline.

The saltmaking industry, unable to compete with new, rival sources of salt, got caught in the economic rain and melted away, but a new chemical industry, taking advantage of the great deposits of salt and limestone, took its place on the Syracuse scene at the same time, in the late 1880s. Unfortunately, the new industry, in producing soda ash, caustic soda, bicarbonate of soda, and other chemicals, brought with it more than jobs and prosperity. Its waste effluence poured into beautiful Onondaga Lake and corrupted it beyond belief. Water pollution is not a modern problem by any means—as Syracuse knows better than most American cities.

The salt industry itself petered out, until, at the end of a long decline, it disappeared in 1926. The venerable old sheds, vats, and covers were removed in the 1930s, at the time that Onondaga Lake was rehabilitated to a degree and parkland created. Appropriately enough, a salt museum was built in Onondaga Lake Park, and in it the story of the industry's rise and fall is dramatically presented. But, less formally, there are reminders in the old iron salt-boiling kettles that still stand in so many yards, used now as flower pots or for nothing at all, except to collect rainwater.

The other declining giant, the Erie Canal, lost out to the railroads and its own inherent weaknesses, slipping in custom and favor until it was a subject of scorn in some quarters. There were Syracusans who forsook even the small grace of sentimentality as they took a harsh view of the once grand canal—as this editorial that appeared in the Syracuse Standard on July 30, 1892, clearly indicates:

"Were the canals of this state to begin to pay for their maintenance, they would still lack friends in this day and generation. The commercial importance they would have if part of a marine system might possibly save them from falling into utter disfavor. It is a stern fact, however, that the passage of the canals, through cities like Syracuse, is now a disadvantage of which the cities would be glad to be rid.

"In the spring of the year, when the water is drawn off, the empty trenches are a menace to public health. When navigation is open they are an impediment to travel and traffic as well as a peril to life. The return

201

the canals are now able to give as common carriers is inconsequential in comparison to the disadvantages they impose.

"Their abandonment in this city would be a blessing beyond valuation. The railroad problem would be instantly solved, inasmuch as the channels occupied by the Erie and Oswego Canals offer obstructions to a different rail route into the city, which engineering skill has confessed itself unable to overcome. Other cities on the line of the canals are in nearly as serious a plight. They would hail with joy the day when the water would finally disappear from the canal bottoms."

Where it passed through Syracuse, the old Erie was officially closed on May 15, 1918. In 1923 the city purchased the old canal lands for $800,000 and covered over Clinton's Ditch, building on top of it the modern Erie Boulevard.

Clinton Square, all paved over now, is a handsome city center, still with the power to stir sleeping memories, but it is lacking some striking elements of old. No longer does it have the sound of lapping water, nor the shimmer and sparkle it had in the moonlight on those nights when the canals made people believe that Syracuse, like Venice, was one of the blessed sights. The black macadam that covers all shines on rainy nights, but it isn't quite the same.

CHAPTER XXIII

TALE OF TWO CITIES

Archaeological digs are not at all uncommon in Rome, Italy. So much history, so many remains of the past, are buried in the ground beneath the Land of the Caesars that even the backyard turnip gardeners have to go gingerly with the hoe for fear they will destroy a priceless relic sunk in their soil.

The situation in Rome, New York, is not quite that delicately balanced, but there is a surprising concentration of history in the city, and there is archaeological excavation on a small scale.

Where most American cities are digging up their downtowns in preparation for the construction of new, glittering, glass-walled motels or office buildings, Rome is digging for buried treasure—the remains of Fort Stanwix that once stood alone on the site. The Big Dig was undertaken in an open field, formerly a residential block, on North Spring Street, near East Dominick Street. There used to be antique cannons marking the four bastions of the old fort, but some of the city officials got carried away by the fervor of a scrap drive during World War II and tossed the twelve-pound Parrott guns of Civil War vintage into the patriotic pot to be melted down.

When the National Park Service's archaeological crew has fully explored the site for historic remains and determined beyond doubt its authenticity as the place where the old fort stood, the federal agency will reconstruct Fort Stanwix in an eighteen-acre park, donated by the city, which will be dedicated as a National Monument. Fort Stanwix will rise again, a victory for people who have an appreciation of the past and an awareness of the importance of its preservation for the future.

Rome stands athwart what was the only practicable water route through the early West between the Hudson River and Lake Ontario.

Fort Stanwix helped to secure the most critical link in that route, the short portage place connecting the Mohawk River and Wood Creek. At the western end of the carry, close to Wood Creek, was another redoubt, Fort Bull. Where it stood, off Route 49 in West Rome, is now just an empty meadow. The fort itself was destroyed during the French and Indian War by a French raiding party that killed about thirty of the sixty to seventy men defending it. That was in 1756, but an old moat, choked with buttercups and brush, is still plainly visible. After the fort was leveled, the land was farmed for many years before being acquired by the Rome Historical Society. From 1890 to 1903, when the Frederick Teuscher family lived on the site, the children used to collect arrowheads, tomahawks, cannon balls, and other relics of the eventful past that were turned up by the plow. They sold the memorabilia for ten cents a pail or a basketful!

Rome wasn't always Rome. It started out under the name of Lynchville when it was first laid out in 1796 on 2,400 acres owned by a New York merchant named Dominick Lynch. Lynchville probably seemed like a terribly appropriate name, under the circumstances, but cooler heads must have pointed out the unsavory connotation in the name at a time in American history when lynching, while illegal, was close to being the national pastime.

At any rate, Lynchville became Rome, thereby joining the large body of communities in upstate New York sporting classical names. The popularity of names borrowed from ancient civilizations of the Mediterranean, while not confined to this part of the country, certainly was most widespread here. It was wholly appropriate to have a town named Rome among such communities as Romulus, Hannibal, Verona, Brutus, Pompey, Cato, Cicero, Virgil, Fabius, Junius, Sempronius, Ovid, Marcellus, and Italy itself.

The most appealing explanation for the eruption of such fancy names in the backwoods country was offered in a speech delivered by Dr. Willis J. Beecher of Auburn Theological Seminary before the Oneida Historical Society in Utica on January 8, 1889.

"The familiar story," said Dr. Beecher, "is that they kept a classical dictionary at the land office and went to it for names whenever there was a new settlement to be named.

"I suppose, however, that this classical dictionary is legendary. It exemplifies one of the natural processes of the human imagination, a process which is sure to emerge when favorable conditions offer. Probably somebody invented this land office classical dictionary originally as a jest, though it has been very generally accepted as a fact."

The use of the historic place names was a clear outcropping of the prevailing reverence for the classical cultures as America strove to move out of the backwoods type of civilization. It is a fact, for example, that Ilion was given its name in 1843 by a local postmaster who was a fan of Homer.

Hitherto the settlement had borne the prosaic names of Steele's Creek, Morgan's Corners, and, finally, Remington's Corners (after Eliphalet Remington, founder of the famous Remington Arms Company). Likewise the town called Palmyra after the famous trade route city in ancient Syria was known originally as Swift's Landing, Swift Town, and Tolland.

Even though Lynchville lost out to Rome, the Lynch family was not left without memorial in the town they founded. Dominick and his two sons, James and Jasper, have streets named after them.

While Rome is most intimately associated with the Erie Canal, there is another canal there that deserves mention—the Black River Canal, which ran northward from Rome, through the scenic Rome-Boonville Gorge, to the Black River. It was begun in 1836 and by 1851 had reached Port Leyden. When the railroads finally extended their service into the north country, the Black River Canal's importance as a feeder into the Erie near Rome diminished drastically. It was closed at last in the early 1900s. Its old right of way through Rome now is occupied by the Black River Boulevard.

The Erie did more than keep Rome on the main highway of waterway travel to the west and embellish its history. It also made a great contribution to the town and surrounding countryside by converting the Great Rome Swamp, immediately to the south and southwest, into rich agricultural mucklands. The original Erie Canal ran through the swamp, far enough to the south of Rome for it to be necessary to build a crude turnpike connection to the town through the quagmire in 1819-20, following the route of what is now lower South James Street. The toll road was of primitive construction—a foundation of tree trunks across which tree branches, planks, and loads of fill and cinders were deposited. Travelers paid five cents if they were riding a horse, ten cents if driving a team, at the toll house, which was about a quarter of a mile north of the present Rome State School. To facilitate the hauling of goods from the Erie, merchants of Rome had a better plank road laid on the route about 1830.

When the Erie was rebuilt and given a major realignment in route in mid-century, the engineers decided to cut through the summit of the divide between the Hudson and Oswego water system, where Rome stands, in order to obtain a single canal level from New London to Carey's Corners. The change placed the relocated canal through the north edge of the swamp some ten feet lower than the original Erie Canal and several feet below the water level of the swamp. The resulting drainage effect created the mucklands which today are so important in the economy of Oneida County.

Among the distinctive—and distinguished—institutions of Rome is its daily newspaper, the *Sentinel*, which traces its lineage back to the time, approximately, when the canal was changing the face of the countryside. It was founded in February 1821 by Lorin Dewey and given the name of the *Republican*. Six years later, a rival paper with the unoriginal name of the *Oneida Republican* was started in the town. The two *Republicans* were merged into one large *Republican* in 1830 and held that name until April 1845, when the paper was renamed the *Sentinel*.

Journalists in Rome during the nineteenth century, like their counterparts in editorial rooms elsewhere, favored political stories by a wide margin, but they also showed an unmistakable leaning towards such medical news as they could glean. A newspaper named the *Citizen*, for instance, related the unusual case of a resident female who died of dropsy in 1864. In his statistical wrap-up, the thoroughgoing reporter noted that the poor woman, in the six years she had suffered from the ailment, had been "tapped by her physician . . . 77 times, and over 2,600 pounds of water had been taken from her." Talk about the Rome Swamp being drained!

The *Sentinel*, not to be outdone, scooped both the opposition and all the medical journals, with the following story which appeared in its October 22, 1872, issue:

"A very difficult surgical operation was performed on the 11th inst., by Dr. G. L. Menzie, of Verona, upon the person of Joseph Sadler, a farmer residing in Westmoreland, near the Rome line. The doctor successfully removed a stone weighing nearly four ounces from the bladder of the gentleman named. The stone had to be crushed in the bladder before it could be taken out. The stone was very rough, and had caused the patient a great deal of pain. Mr. Sadler is doing well. Dr. Menzie was assisted in the operation by Drs. Reid and Evans, of Rome, Hutchinson, of Utica, and Mason, of Canastota."

W. J. P. Kingsley, M.D., who was one of the leading medical men in Rome at that time, somehow failed to get in on the big kidney stone crushing caper, but he may have been too busy in his laboratory, putting together the medicine that he promoted in the following newspaper advertisement:

"ASTHMA—Dr. Kingsley's Asthma Specific is the great discovery of the age, and warranted to relieve any case or money refunded. Cancers cured without the use of the knife—Doctors and Ministers cured of cancer free. Send for a circular."

Another medical man of the area, a Dr. Hunt of Utica, became a controversial figure in the Rome community through the way he rendered his professional services at the hanging of a twenty-eight-year-old convicted murderer, William Henry Carswell, on January 8, 1869. Carswell, convicted of violating and murdering a nine-year-old girl the previous April, was publicly executed in Rome. Sheriff George F. Weaver presided over the formalities, which drew some four hundred enthusiasts to the scene. Among the spectators were children as young as thirteen, all of whom had been provided with cards identifying them as deputy sheriffs.

Prior to the hanging, Dr. Hunt busied himself on the gallows platform in his best professional manner, even to the extent of asking the condemned man about his health.

Carswell thought over the question and allowed that he felt "a little pressure" on his head. Dr. Hunt, concerned, felt obliged to relieve the pressure by bleeding the doomed man. That didn't go over too well with the restive crowd, but Dr. Hunt went ahead with his ministration. He must have been very good at bleeding people or maybe his mind wandered while he was at it; anyway, he took sixteen ounces of blood altogether. But Carswell's pulse kept moving along at what was described as "a nice, regular 134."

"Well, Henry," said Dr. Hunt, pleased as Punch, "you keep up splendidly!"

The crowd rumbled in discontent over all the solicitude shown a criminal about to be executed, especially when Dr. Hunt then gave Carswell a treatment of chloroform, perhaps as an encore. Some of the onlookers, including city and county officials, complained that the sentence "was executed upon a lifeless, or almost lifeless, corpse." Apparently that took some of the fun out of the hanging.

The fact that Dr. Hunt came from Utica probably was a big mark against him in Rome anyway. The relationship between Rome and Utica from frontier days has been strained; competitive, to say the least. The two cities are but a few miles apart, but each has stood on strategic ground. While Rome held the summit divide of the east–west waterways, Utica, on the Mohawk River, originally was the "crossroads" of the Indian world, the place called the "Iroquois Busy Corner." At this site, called Unundadages by the Indians, was the only ford over which men could cross the upper reach of the great river.

If Rome had its Fort Stanwix, Utica had its Fort Schuyler. The first white settlers in 1773 built homes on the north side of the Mohawk and their town, called Deerfield, became part of the larger city, with the more distinguished name of Utica, that grew up on the banks of the river.

Utica dates its beginning year as 1789, when a small colony of families settled around the fording place, near Bagg's Square. Nine years later, the president of Yale College, the Reverend Timothy Dwight, journeyed through the village and was impressed by what he saw. He described Utica as "a pretty village containing fifty houses . . . almost all on a single street parallel to the river . . ."

The Grand Canal had great and lasting effect on the "pretty village," flowing through the center of the city along the route of today's Oriskany Street. Basins, where the boats could be moored and docked for loading and unloading operations, were vitally important. Miller's Basin, also known as the Public Basin and the Big Basin, was built between Third and Mohawk Street, where Ballou's Creek flowed into the canal, and extended southward close to Rutger Street.

On the southern bank of the canal where it passed John Street, a weighlock building in the popular Greek Revival style of the period was built in 1829.

"Bridges across the canal were constructed at every major street and grew in number as the city expanded," wrote Virginia B. Kelly, Oneida County historian, quoting *The Utica Directory* of 1828, which informed its readers that the bridge over the canal at Genesee Street had been "rebuilt in May 1828, and has liberal sidewalks with iron railings."

The wrought iron railings were more than a decorative touch. People had a distressing way of falling off Utica bridges into the water, occasionally landing on a surprised canaller dozing on a boat deck.

The land adjoining the Mohawk River was not suitable for permanent building because of the threat of flooding, but the banks of the canal, a controlled waterway, were quickly developed by builders of stores, warehouses, hotels, and other commercial enterprises. Among the few canalside structures still standing is a warehouse building of Brown & Griffith at the northeast corner of John Street and Oriskany Street, and the Devereux Block at the intersection of Genesee and Oriskany.

Utica, like every other town on the canal, reflected the influence of the Erie in its population figures. The village that had counted only 20 families in 1794 and 2,861 people in 1816 and thereafter went into a period of furious population growth: 5,041 in 1825; 8,330 in 1830; 10,183 in 1835; 12,782 in 1840; and 17,556 in 1850.

An Englishman, J. Mellish, visiting Utica in 1812, took time to count business places, perhaps to while away the time. He came up with a total of fifteen stores, two breweries, seven smiths and nailers, and six taverns. The contemplative student of statistics will marvel over the fact that it required two breweries and six taverns to slake the thirst of about 2,000 Uticans—a population estimate that included a lot of non-drinking infants and temperance women. The transient trade was a consuming factor, indubitably, but not nearly what it was after the canal began to carry thirsty travelers through the town.

Seven years after the canal went into full operation, Utica could count forty-four dry goods stores, sixty-three groceries, twenty blacksmith shops, forty-three attorneys at law, thirty-two physicians, twenty-eight inns, and five banks. The population of the town at that time was approximately 9,000, which meant that there was one attorney at law for every 209.3 Uticans—again a figure that included a lot of non-drinking infants and temperance women.

Like Rome, Utica was a two-canal town. The Chenango Canal, a major feeder waterway, was built from Utica south to Binghamton, close to the Pennsylvania border. The ninety-seven-mile-long canal, constructed between 1833 and 1836, was instrumental in making a textile mill center out of Utica by transporting wool from the farms of southern New York, as well as coal from the mines of Pennsylvania.

The printing and publishing field also was one in which Utica took a commanding lead over most other communities in the state. In 1828 the town had six printing firms and ten newspapers were being published there.

Utica was a major port on the Erie Canal, of course, and its growth was given tremendous impetus by the waterway. Rome, on the other hand, felt it had been given short shrift by the canal planners when the original Erie was routed to the south of the city instead of going through the central area. The inevitable urge to compare canal advantages did not make the Romans happy, nor did Utica's growth, far outstripping that of Rome, please the rival town.

The politicians and newspaper editors in the two cities were forever taking pot shots at each other. No item was too derogatory to shunt aside as indelicate or impolitic, although the opposing sides generally managed to hold on to their sense of humor. Still, it wasn't unusual to see in print an item such as the following, which appeared in the Rome *Sentinel* on August 1, 1865:

"In Utica they have been filtering their water through dead muskrats. One was taken from a pipe of the water works."

But modern population growth and expansion are beginning to do what 200 years of history could not. The once-sharp separation between Rome and Utica has gotten blurred and a metropolitan merger seems to be well underway. Once again, a means of transportation is a major factor in the growth of the two communities—Griffiss Air Force Base. It is a multimission base, the largest in the northeastern United States, and it has become an integral part of the economy of the Rome-Utica area since it was constructed in 1941–42, in the early years of World War II.

Griffiss stands on 7,392 acres of land and has more than 800 buildings. Its peak personnel year was 1961, when 11,587 persons were on the payroll—a payroll, incidentally, that averages about $70,000,000 a year. The Romans feel it was only appropriate that the federal government should have chosen to invest their city with a major defense base. The past history of Rome and the area around it demanded some such distinction and reward. The stubborn resistance of Fort Stanwix on the city site during the Revolutionary War led to an important American victory, thanks in large measure to the heroic performance of the troops of the Mohawk Valley Militia under General Nicholas Herkimer in stopping the British columns at great cost at the Battle of Oriskany, only six miles away. They haven't forgotten the historic happenings of the past in modern Rome, and they're not at all embarrassed if somebody accuses the city of flag-waving.

The point is, the American flag has a special meaning in Rome. The city long has claimed that here, on August 3, 1777, during the British siege of Fort Stanwix (sometimes known as Fort Schuyler), the new national banner was raised before a foe for the first time in American history. (A similar claim that the Stars and Stripes was first flown in battle at Bennington on August 16, 1777, has put the honor in an area of dispute.)

By way of coincidence, the Pledge of Allegiance to the Flag was written by a former resident of Rome, Francis Bellamy. He composed the famous pledge for *The Youth's Companion* magazine as part of the celebration of the four-hundredth anniversary of the discovery of America. Millions of school children throughout the nation recited the patriotic pledge on Columbus Day, 1892, and their descendants have been chanting it in classrooms and patriotic affairs ever since.

Transcending even the military glory that was Rome's, however, was the town's role in the peacetime victory represented in the successful construction of the Erie Canal. There was, of course, the fact that Rome's strategic placement gave the canal such a fast running start that it thereafter could not be headed off by its opponents. But more important, probably, was Rome's contribution of two brilliant men whose practical engineering genius proved to be so essential to the mighty task at hand.

Benjamin Wright and John B. Jervis were extraordinary men who, while lacking engineering training, helped to write the engineering textbooks through their innovative performances in guiding the canal to completion.

Wright, a lawyer-surveyor by training, served as chief engineer of the Erie Canal from 1817 to 1823 and chief engineer of *all* New York canals from 1817 to 1826. John Jervis, who was without formal education and whose first job on the Erie was that of an axman, was both a protégé of Wright and his successor. He performed brilliantly in all the responsible assignments given to him in a long career, during which he went on to become chief engineer of the Chenango Canal, engineer in charge of the Croton Water System of New York City, and chief engineer for several railroads. Port Jervis, New York, is named after him. When Jervis died in Rome in 1885 at the age of ninety, his home became the city's public library.

The first boat to ride the Erie Canal was built in Rome and named the *Chief Engineer of Rome* in honor of Benjamin Wright. It was designed by Pliny Darrow of Rome, after a model of an English canalboat brought back to the United States by Canvass White.

Rome remembers its past with almost the same avidity and fierce pride as the city for which it is named, even though urban renewal in the past few years has given downtown a new, modern look. The Rome Historical Society has brought together in its Fort Stanwix Museum a rather remarkable collection of artifacts, relics, and exhibits related to the area's lively past. Although the museum was evicted from its former home by the archaeological digging, it still stood in 1972 on the site of Fort Stanwix in its temporary quarters across the street, in an old grocery store at 112 Spring Street.

The grandeur that was Rome's continues, now with more real, honest-to-goodness Romans than ever before. Whether or not the classical city name was responsible, it is a fact that the Italian strain runs strong through the modern community. The old families are still entrenched, of course, and there are many typically American names to mull over—like the name of the man who for fifty-two years was city editor of the *Sentinel*, Wooster Ohio Jenks—but today's visitor will encounter such Romans as the Destito family, the Campanaro family, and the Coccia family. He will meet such as Luigi J. Bottini, Joe Adolfi, the Brunos, Fred P. Sestito, John Mercurio, the Muscarella family, Sam Barone, the Fontana family, Joseph Carollo & Sons, Augie Mariani, Frank and Louis DiBerardino, Anthony Barone, the DeAngelis family, the Pettinelli family, the Stumpo family, the Russo family; the Gigliottis and the La Gattas; Salvatore Mandronico and Joseph Grillone and Frank Mazzaferro.

What would Rome be like without such a musical sprinkling of Romans?

CHAPTER XXIV

HERO IN ABSENTIA

The highlight of the commencement ceremony of the University of Rochester in June 1941 was the conferral of the degree of doctor of laws upon Winston Churchill and the short but typically Churchillian response that the honor drew from the century's most famous Englishman.

It was all done in absentia, of course, because Churchill, as Prime Minister of Great Britian, was fully preoccupied at the time with World War II. The empire over which he presided was passing through its darkest hours. That he should have taken the time to acknowledge the honor bestowed on him by a distant American university was a sign of his coolness in a time of extreme duress.

It should be allowed, though, that Churchill probably was acting out of his awareness that the American college commencement platform also was a good propaganda platform—especially valuable at a time when Britain was trying to rally all the support it could arouse in the United States. Perhaps, also, Churchill was responding as well to the ancient call of family obligation in his choice of the University of Rochester as the place for the important speech that was quickly relayed to the country and the world.

Rochester had its rightful place in the Churchill story, as President Alan Valentine of the university suggested rather broadly in his address that day.

"Rochester," said Dr. Valentine, "is an English name, and the birthplace of your mother. From England we of Rochester learned the democracy of truth . . ."

Unfortunately, the truth, in this instance, was that Dr. Valentine was in error. Churchill's mother was *not* born in Rochester. She made her first appearance in an even less likely place—Brooklyn.

It is true, however, that Rochester was home for a long time to Churchill's maternal grandparents—in fact, to a large and interesting assortment of Jeromes. Among them were Leonard and Clarissa Jerome. It was their daughter Jennie, born several years after the Jeromes had moved East, who would become Lady Randolph Churchill.

Winston Churchill, ever the skilled politician and the master of tactful phraseology, was not the man to contradict the statement of a distinguished host, even one who had played loosely with some important Churchill family geography. His response to President Valentine that day in 1941 was a model of diplomatic circumlocution.

"As I speak from Downing Street to Rochester University and through you to the people of the United States, I almost feel I have the right to do so because my mother, as *you* have stated, was born in your city and there my grandfather, Leonard Jerome, lived for so many years conducting as a prominent and rising citizen, a newspaper with the excellent eighteenth-century title of the *Plain Dealer* . . ."

The Prime Minister moved gracefully from that opening into the mainstream of his speech—an appeal for American understanding, friendship, and aid—just as if he had not compounded, in a manner of speaking, a felony. If President Valentine had been wrong in his assertion that Churchill's mother was born in Rochester, Churchill had been equally wrong in his folksy recollection that Grandfather Jerome conducted in Rochester a newspaper named the *Plain Dealer*. He had not. Leonard Jerome and his brother Lawrence at one time owned an important interest in a newspaper called the Rochester *Daily American*. It was an interesting error, attributable perhaps to the fact that Churchill in earlier years had declared his fondness for the name of the *Plain Dealer* in Cleveland.

The Erie Canal country was the setting for the opening chapters in the American side of the Churchill story—specifically, in the little port town of Palmyra, about twenty-five miles to the east of Rochester. It was a town, curiously, where destiny chose to cross many paths leading on to history.

Palmyra has not been altered greatly by time. It is still small and unprepossessing, undisturbed—outwardly, at least—by the fact that important names once briefly called it home. Illustrating best the permanence of the setting is a steel tower that stands on Main Street. Being 150 feet high, it is a conspicuous part of the street scene and has been since it was erected in 1892 as part of the pre-election frenzy that marked the presidential contest that year between Grover Cleveland and Benjamin Harrison. The steel tower was put up by the Republicans in front of the old Palmyra Hotel (also known at various times in its 138-year history as the Eagle Tavern, the Nottingham, and the Powers Hotel). The townspeople presumably were so gratified by the structure's appearance, that they decided to let it stand—and stand it does, to this day. An equally tall wooden pole raised by the Democrats in the same campaign was hauled down shortly afterward.

Palmyra's picturesque, serene appearance, and the graceful way it has carried itself, once led Arch Merrill, the Rochester columnist, to dub the town "The Grand Dame of the Towpath." It was the setting for the popular Samuel Hopkins Adams novel *Canal Town*, a story later converted into a motion picture under the unlikely title *The Farmer Takes a Wife*. Palmyra once even crashed Robert Ripley's "Believe It or Not" newspaper cartoon series because at the intersection of Main, Church, and Canandaigua streets there are four churches, one at each corner, and this is said to be unmatched in any American community.

Whatever the attraction, Palmyra was the town chosen to be his new home by a Rhode Islander named David Wilcox in 1791. The Wilcoxes had a daughter, Clarissa, who came, in time, to be wed to a traveler named Ambrose Hall. The romantic story is that Hall, a resident of Massachusetts, was on a hunting trip through New York and stopped at the Wilcox cabin to ask for a drink of water. Clarissa was very pretty and Ambrose was very thirsty and pretty soon they got married. That's the way things sometimes go.

Ambrose and Clarissa made their home in Palmyra, of course, right in the center of town, where the bandstand is today. The issue of their union was a family of six daughters, all said to be most pleasing to the eye. Among the eyes comforted and charmed by the bevy were the Jerome brothers, Leonard and Lawrence, who lived in Palmyra with their lawyer uncle, Hiram K. Jerome. The youths were the sons of Isaac and Aurora Jerome, whose farmhouse on Pompey Hill, south of Syracuse, apparently was taxed by the family of eleven children. Uncle Hiram was a successful lawyer, later a judge of Wayne County, and Leonard studied law in his uncle's office. When Uncle Hiram struck out for the larger opportunities promised by boom-town Rochester, the two nephews accompanied him there in 1842.

But the beauteous Hall girls were not forgotten. Lawrence Jerome fetched Catherine Hall to Rochester as his bride in 1844. She presumably brought with her enough of a dowry to permit the Jerome brothers in 1845 to purchase an interest in the Rochester *Daily American*. Considering the nature of that newspaper, perhaps their distinguished British descendant Winston Churchill intentionally chose to give it a different identity.

The *Daily American* was an early voice of bigotry in upper New York; the organ in the Rochester area of the Know-Nothing party, which was a formal arm of the nativist movement. The nativists were one of the early America-for-Americans uprisings whose subscribers took a decidedly unfriendly position toward Catholics and "foreigners" who were flooding into the United States, especially by way of the Erie Canal. Assuming that Englishmen are to be considered foreigners, the Jerome newspaper, had it survived, one day would have had to look askance at a man named Winston Churchill had he had the effrontery to try to make America his home. No such problem ever arose, of course.

The Jerome colony in Rochester grew quickly. Leonard and Lawrence rented quarters at 74 South Fitzhugh Street (formerly no. 63), across the street from the house rented by Uncle Hiram. When Lawrence and Catherine Hall got married and moved to 65 South Sophia Street (then 219 Plymouth Street), Leonard moved in with them as a boarder.

In April of the following year, 1849, Leonard married Clarissa Hall, sister of his brother's wife, and the newlyweds made their home with Lawrence and Catherine, who had moved back to 63 South Fitzhugh Street. Still another tenant of the big house was a younger brother of the Jeromes, Isaac, Jr.

The association of Lawrence and Leonard Jerome in the newspaper venture in Rochester lasted less than five years—from 1845 to late 1849 or early 1850—but it had significant after-effects. The political rise of Millard Fillmore of Buffalo paralleled the Jeromes' newspaper career, and they enjoyed friendly relations with Fillmore because he, like the *Daily American*, was a nativist. When the Whig party, which had nativist support, nominated a victorious presidential ticket of Zachary Taylor and Millard Fillmore in 1848, the *Daily American* gave them active support. The Jeromes took a busy role in the Whig campaign.

It was about a year later that the two brothers divested themselves of their newspaper holdings in Rochester and, presumably, let the word trickle through to the White House that they had tuxedos and were willing to travel. The Taylor administration responded by naming Leonard Jerome the United States consul in Ravenna, Italy, on March 25, 1850.

Leonard chose not to accept that appointment, electing instead to take an executive post with the Merchants State Telegraphic Company in Brooklyn in 1850. The company was a short-lived venture, however, and in February 1852 Leonard again turned to his old friend, Fillmore—now President of the United States—and this time received an appointment as United States consul in Trieste, Italy.

He was stationed in Trieste about sixteen months when a new national Administration came into power and he was relieved of his diplomatic post. The Leonard Jeromes returned home to Brooklyn in mid-November 1853, beating the stork by a matter of weeks. Their second daughter, Jennie, was born in Brooklyn on January 9, 1854.

A scholarly researcher of the Jerome-Churchill legend, Blake McKelvey, author and city historian of Rochester, says it is likely that Jennie Jerome was born at 8 Amity Street in Brooklyn. It is where the family lived before moving on to New York City.

It was shortly after Jennie met and married Lord Randolph Churchill, in 1873, becoming one of the world's most glamorous women, that Rochester began to dispute Brooklyn's claim to Jennie. The confusion increased as Jennie's unorthodox behavior and great beauty made her more and more famous. The emergence of Winston Churchill as one of the great men of modern times further encouraged the long-standing story in Rochester that his mother was a native daughter of the city.

It was a tradition, McKelvey explains, "which gradually gained strength as elderly ladies began to tell each other and their daughters of their associations with the Jerome girls at school in Rochester!

"The tradition had not quite gained assurance by the time Winston Churchill first came to Rochester as a Boer War correspondent in 1900, however, for he was welcomed simply as a Rochester grandson. But, as his fame continued to mount, local recollections grew until they gained sufficient currency to win the credence of a recent biographer of Winston Churchill, René Kraus." (In a later book, *Young Lady Randolph,* Kraus gave Brooklyn credit as Jennie's birthplace.)

The Jennie Jerome tradition persists in Rochester, but the city's official stand on the matter was restrained and accurate. It was represented in a bronze tablet which, under the co-operative sponsorship of the Rochester Historical Society and the Rochester Museum Association, was attached to the old Jerome House at 74 South Fitzhugh Street. It reads:

LEONARD JEROME
Publisher, & Grandfather of
Britain's Winston Churchill
Resided Here 1844–50
He married Clarissa Hall
of Palmyra, April 5, 1849

Poor Jennie! For all her glamour, she didn't even get a mention in the credits.

217

CHAPTER XXV

FROM FLOUR TO FLOWERS TO FOTOS

Destiny usually plays its role dimly, from a position of obscurity, but it was brazenly open and shamelessly transparent in the way it approached Colonel Rochester's settlement by the side of the Genesee, at the place where the big river gathered itself for its descent on the steep stairway that would take it into the basin of Lake Ontario.

In that brief, final plunge, the Genesee sets up a climactic clamor before its waters spill into the great lake and lose themselves. It drops a total of 260 feet in a furious eight-mile finale that includes three cataracts —one ninety-two feet high—and a series of swift-flowing rapids. It is such a turbulent stretch, indeed, that plans to build a navigable canal between Rochester and the lake at one time were abandoned when it was determined that no fewer than twenty-two locks would be needed in that short run.

(The earliest visitors to the Rochester site could count four waterfalls, but one, a fourteen-foot cataract that had been harnessed briefly by Ebenezer Allan, was destroyed when the first canal aqueduct was built over the river.)

What the waterfalls spelled out, naturally, was the promise of water-power, and that message made clearly manifest the destiny of the otherwise foreboding site. It was strictly a bonus that the Genesee River also offered a commercial artery leading to the fertile country south and to the broad lake on the north.

With the building of the Erie Canal, Rochester was at a travel crossroads that gave promise to every direction, every horizon. There was no lingering doubt, even as the early settlers were still rounding up the last of the rattlesnakes, that Rochester would become a very important community once the canal became a reality.

Even before the first boat splashed into the canal, the town had begun to establish itself as a milling center. Wheat production in the valley mounted so rapidly that by 1818 three or four mills were in operation in Colonel Rochester's town. Most of the flour was hauled to the mouth of the river for shipment to Montreal. The Canadian market was the only one accessible to a community in the wild, forested land of western New York in those frontier days. Montreal, however, was not the ideal market. The flour shipments often accumulated there because of poor distribution facilities or because the frozen St. Lawrence River prevented transshipment to Europe. The result often was a lowering of the price paid to the Rochester millers, among whom there grew high anticipation of the canal-to-be. One Rochesterian of the time noted:

"Nothing but the high price of transportation to Albany has induced the millers of Rochester to send their flour to Canada. When the canal shall unite the Genesee with the Hudson, their flour will be transported to New York at much less expense than to Montreal, and it will meet a ready sale at every season of the year."

It was the end of 1822 before the canal link with the East was completed. By that time Rochester had a half-dozen flour mills in operation, and the forest surrounding the cataracts of the Genesee had been pushed back to make room for 3,100 residents. The first boat eastward, to Albany, carried barrels of flour—a tiny forerunner of what was to be. By the time the 1823 shipping season opened there was such a demand for the product in the East that the first ten shipping days saw 10,450 barrels of flour begin their journey to Albany and New York City aboard fifty-eight canalboats. The first stage of Rochester's destiny was underway.

(Historian McKelvey, probing into the old records, came up with some interesting information on what the boats were bringing to Rochester in exchange for the flour. The first forty-five, he reported, brought more than 4,000 gallons of beer, 2,300 gallons of whiskey, and "other miscellaneous supplies." Substantial evidence, altogether, that man did not live by bread alone in pioneer days.)

Two major products had to be completed before the full canal could be put to use. One was completion of the aqueduct to carry the canal over the Genesee River at Rochester. The other was to cut through the stone mountain that was the Niagara Escarpment between Rochester and Buffalo.

The Genesee River was both friend and foe of the canal builders. It was helpful as a source of water for the canal, but it posed many problems. It was notorious as a "flash" river—one that flooded suddenly at the time of spring thaw or heavy storms. Determining the route of the canal so as to avoid the river's flood plain required close study.

The Village of Rochesterville was incorporated in the same year in which the canal project was begun—1817. Among the few residents the following year was Colonel Rochester himself. No doubt his decision to put his person where previously he had put only his money boosted the morale of the other settlers. The colonel then was an impressive figure of a man, for all his sixty-seven years. He certainly was the opposite number to Indian Allan; a conservative, orthodox, Virginia-born gentleman with a distinguished blood line—just about the perfect front man for a new town on the edge of the wilderness where people of culture were scarce.

Construction of the great canal aqueduct was begun in November 1821, and an unhappier beginning could not be imagined. The foundations of the west pier of the aqueduct which were laid that autumn were swept away by the ice-choked river later that winter, and the work had to be started anew. In all, it took nearly two years and $83,000 to build the structure, but when it was completed, in September 1823—about eleven months behind schedule—it stood out as one of the finest features of the great canal.

The aqueduct was an engineering wonder in its day and it impresses even in retrospect. It was the longest stone-arch bridge structure in America—804 feet in length. The supports were nine 50-foot Roman arches and two smaller arches at the ends that lent an air of classic beauty as well as strength. The walls were of red Medina sandstone that, ironically enough, had been obtained from the river gorge near Carthage. The coping of the aqueduct was of gray limestone from Cayuga. Its piers were sunk into the bedrock of the river to a depth of a half foot or more, and iron clamps were fitted into holes drilled in the large stone slabs that made up the piers and arches, with bolts holding the masonry together.

It was a mighty impressive structure that the canal engineers threw across the Genesee, but, as time proved, it wasn't good enough. It had some serious flaws. The first was that the design called for boats on the west side of the river to make a right-angle turn onto the aqueduct. Another was that the span was only seventeen feet wide, restricting its use to one canalboat at a time. The result was that canalboat crews fought each other over accidents at the right-angle approach and they fought over who had prior passage over the river.

The narrowness of the aqueduct also severely restricted the flow of Genesee River water needed to replenish the canal to the east of the aqueduct. The water level was a critical canal factor and the narrow aqueduct undeniably was a bottleneck that interfered with the water supply. But the most distressing weakness of the monumental structure was its tendency to leak. During the winter months icicles of fearsome size hung from the under part of the span, causing almost as much embarrassment as the fact that the sandstone blocks that made up its foundation had begun to crumble almost as soon as they were put in place.

In the light of all its inadequacies and flaws, it isn't surprising that the aqueduct was a subject of high controversy from the moment it was finished until it was replaced only twenty years later. Construction of the new aqueduct was begun in 1838, but it wasn't completed until 1842. It was a more pretentious, more utilitarian structure by far. Its cost was a whopping $444,000—a sum of such size as to cause widespread indignation at the time. The project, nevertheless, was something of a godsend to Rochester at the time because it provided so many men of the town with work during the depression that followed the Panic of 1837. Perhaps even more important was the sense of pride that the new aqueduct stirred among the townspeople, not to mention the awe with which it was regarded by canal travelers. It was a most imposing sight: 848 feet in length and 45 feet wide, made mainly of limestone quarried near Syracuse and admirably watertight. There is no better testimony to its quality than the fact that it still stands.

There is always a note of irony running through history, and in the case of Rochester it is apparent in all the accounts that tell how the canal made the city the nation's greatest milling center in the middle nineteenth century. That same canal also was opening the lands deep in the interior that shortly would end western New York's role as the breadbasket of the nation. It spilled thousands of families onto the empty, fertile plains and unturned meadows of the vast inland country, and just as fast as their plows could break the rich soil they began to harvest fantastically large yields. Wheat production shifted westward, as did the flour milling industry.

So it was that even in the beginning, when Rochester's flour mills still were many in number and prosperous, it was apparent that the industry was only in temporary residence, merely marking time against the day of departure West. Two years after the canal went into operation, Rochester had seven flour mills in production. By the 1870s, almost a half century later, there were thirty-one mills producing about a million barrels of flour every year. That was like the last bright flare of a dying match, though, because the city already had lost its pre-eminence as the Flour City.

It was a happy coincidence that enabled Rochester the *Flour* City to become Rochester the *Flower* City. There had been a steady growth in the nursery business, which, added to a farsighted development of city parks with elaborate floral displays, led naturally to the new city nickname that required no more than a minor change in spelling.

Modern Rochester continues to be an important producer of nursery stock and seeds, but the old title of "Flower City" is no longer descriptive or representative of today's complicated industrial city. It has yielded generally to a more significant name, "the Kodak City."

Rochester has been many cities in its century and a half of existence. It has been the miller, the sawyer, the tanner, the boatbuilder, the shoemaker, and the tailor. It took and processed the wheat and the skins from the farmers and the trappers and the hunters. It took and processed the harvest of the forests, the tall trees that came to it from all directions, from the river, the canal, and the lake. Some of the logs went on to the East, but a lot of the floating forest never got past Rochester, where, by 1827, nine sawmills were doggedly trying to reconcile the supply of logs with the demand for lumber.

It was estimated at that time that approximately five million feet of sawed lumber was being carried down the Genesee annually to Rochester, and just as much lumber was coming out of the town's sawmills. Boatyards sprang into being naturally and spontaneously in this town where lumber was in such plentiful supply. Most of the boats were built for sale, but a large number were built to be operated by their makers. There were enough of the latter for Rochester to become a boat-owning center, a headquarters for fleets of canalboats. As early as 1827 there were six companies operating about 160 boats out of the port. There were just as many companies operating boatyards and building packets and freighters to give Rochester rank with Syracuse. By mid-century, the Rochester boatyards still were doing an important volume of business with fourteen companies producing about 130 boats a year (average selling price: $1,300 each).

The larger, more pressing demand made on the Rochester sawmills, however, was for lumber to house the incoming tide of people that surged into the boom town every day in the week.

"These were years of rapid building," recalled Edwin Scrantom, son of the first settler. "The sawmills ran constantly, getting out lumber, and every night I could hear Ezra Mason, who ran Brown's sawmill, filing his saw, after which he would sleep two hours, leaving the mill in the care of a man named Bill Bloomer, after which he would resume his labors. Although the contractors worked day and night they could not keep up with the demand for houses, and frequently families would bivouac for several weeks in their covered wagons."

A trickle of Jewish immigration in those beginning decades was responsible for the creation of the men's clothing industry that in time made the whole nation attach special weight to the words "Rochester Tailored." A peddler named Meyer Greentree, who had ridden the canal as far as Rochester, decided it was the place for him to settle down. He was hired as a clerk in a dry goods store run by Sigmund Rosenberg, but that was only the first foot on the ladder. Not far removed from the dry goods store was a children's clothing manufacturing business operated by an attractive woman named Elizabeth Baker. Miss Baker was a Gentile, but love on the frontier had a way of leaping over barriers that would have been insurmountable elsewhere, and before long Miss Baker was Mrs. Greentree. With her husband at the helm, the little business quickly expanded and, under the name of Greentree & Wile, became the nucleus of a great industry.

Immigration in the 1840s and 1850s reinforced the Jewish colony in Rochester, strengthening the clothing companies with their Old World talent for tailoring and heightening the reputation of the Rochester product. By 1856 there were more than 2,000 persons employed in the garment industry, but the Civil War shortly thereafter brought the shops in Rochester into their fullest production with its demand for Union Army uniforms. With this momentum, the industry continued to grow through the remainder of the nineteenth century and through the early decades of the present century.

There was, to be sure, a dark side to the clothing industry in Rochester, as there was in New York City and every other city where manufacturers operated their shops. The conditions under which clothing workers labored were among the most scandalously inhumane that existed in the American scheme of things during the early days of the Industrial Revolution and the years of development that followed.

Rochester became one of the sweat shop centers of the nation, thanks to the callousness of the employers of the day and the incredible indifference of a society that was willing to accept outrageous exploitation of women and children by employers. The clothing industry in Rochester was concentrated, appropriately enough, on Mill Street by the middle of the nineteenth century, but most of the workers—about 75 per cent of them—were women and young girls who worked in their own homes or in loft shops where sweat was a way of life. The females in the hire of the companies usually picked up cloth at the cutting rooms and took it to their homes or to a workshop to tailor it as specified. The average wage of the workers was $300 a year.

Out of this tawdry state of affairs emerged in time an industry in which hours, wages, and working conditions were held up as models to be copied—but only after decades of bitter struggle and costly strikes. To this day, the strongest union in Rochester is the Amalgamated Clothing Workers of America, whose membership includes even employees in industries far removed from tailoring.

There also was a time when Rochester was one of the leading centers for the production of shoes, with some seventy-five plants helping to shoe the nation at the turn of the century. There were at that time 4,600 employees on the industry's payroll, and they carried home about $2,000,000 a year—more than in any other industry. Labor unrest which led to a crippling strike in 1921 was a leading factor in the shrinking of the industry to minor size in the years that followed.

While Rochester has entertained many important industries in its civic lifetime, the giant that has stood high over all and cast its shadow on every phase of community life has been the Eastman Kodak Company.

Ever since George Eastman developed dry-plate picture taking and went into the photographic supply business in 1880, Rochester has been the photography capital of the world. The company that Eastman built has had a history of steady growth and near monopoly during its ninety-year history. At the end of 1970 it reported sales of nearly $3,000,000,000 and a net profit of $404,000,000.

George Eastman would have admired that financial statement. He was a very good businessman, as well as a very tenacious, determined inventor. It is as important for an inventor to be tenacious and determined as to be clever. A talent for doing business in the public market place could be the most valuable talent of all.

Before Eastman simplified the photographic process and put the picture-taking box in the hands of ordinary people, photography was one of the most esoteric of arts—an exasperatingly slow, extremely limited, most highly complicated technique—one, furthermore, that required an artist with a strong back to lug around the heavy, cumbersome equipment. All in all, the role of photographer called for a dedicated, patient, artistic, muscular man. Eastman took photography monopoly away from the technicians and made it every man's hobby. By the time his refinements had taken hold picture taking had become child's play.

The turning point, likely, was Eastman's development in 1884 of a practical paper film to replace glass plates. Then, with the help of an assistant, William H. Walker, he developed a roll-holder on which a continuous roll of film could be fastened to spools. A clock key revolved the roll of film when turned from the outside.

Optimistic about his company's chances for success in marketing this easy kind of photography, Eastman wrote to his brother-in-law in Cleveland, George W. Andrus:

"If the thing is a partial success, it will be a good thing while if it is a complete success it will dazzle the eyes of the gentle beholder. Still we expect to be given strength to gather in the divvys whatever proportions they reach . . ." ("Divvys" was slang for dividends.)

Although Thomas A. Edison and George Eastman had never met, they had had an early history of business relations, and it is clear that Edison benefited tremendously from Eastman's film discoveries when he set out to develop the Kinetoscope, the basis of the motion picture. Edison made the camera and Eastman made the first reel of film.

One of Eastman's greatest contributions to the marketing of his own camera was the name he gave it. "Kodak" was the kind of name that stuck in the public mind. It was easily remembered and, being absolutely unique, stirred a lot of curiosity. People wanted to know where the name came from and what it meant. The answer was that it came from Eastman's mind, and, outside of being the name of his photography products, it had no other meaning. Eastman invented the name "Kodak" just as he invented the product. His mother's name was Maria Kilbourn, a fact which apparently made the inventor partial toward the letter "K." It was, he contended, an outstanding sort of letter in an alphabet choked with flabby, commonplace letters; in his own words, it was "firm and unyielding." Proceeding then on the theory that two Ks would have to be twice

225

as good as one K, Eastman came up with the trade name of "Kodak" for his new camera in late summer of 1888. It turned out to be one of his best inventions.

Another sign of Eastman's marketing genius was visible in the slogan his company used to woo a public that had come to view photography as an occult science, one of the dark arts. "Kodak cameras," announced the Eastman advertisements: "You press the button, we do the rest."

The history of the Eastman Kodak Company is one of the great success stories of American business, but the life of George Eastman himself was strangely barren and bleak. He never married and, lacking the kind of warm personality that allows the formation of close friendships, he walked a lonely path through most of his adult life. To most Rochesterians, even his own associates, he was a distant, humorless, enigmatic individual. Most people dealt with him out of fear. He could be very petty. Yet George Eastman was no ordinary wealthy industrialist, but one of those extraordinary men of the late nineteenth century who built fortunes of such size as to be almost beyond the power of others to comprehend. He was THE man of the photographic industry world-wide just as John D. Rockefeller was the personification of the oil industry, Andrew Carnegie was the symbol of the steel industry, and Henry Ford the representative of the automobile industry. They were the supermen, the supercapitalists of their time.

Eastman probably was the least publicized and the least known of that exclusive Croesus Club. He was reminiscent of Rockefeller, silent and almost ascetic in manner and demeanor, but wilful—determined that the game would be played under the rules that he had laid down. He was a tough businessman in a time when there were no restraints on men locked in the fight for power and profits. He doted on detail, as so many successful men do, apparently detecting dollars in the little loopholes that crop up in the daily routine.

Rockefeller was another tycoon noted for his close attention to matters that seemed minor to their subordinates. One of the classic illustrations refers to a letter the world's richest man wrote to one of his refinery officials: "Last month you reported on hand 1,119 bungs. Ten thousand were sent you at the beginning of this month. You have used 9,527 this month. You report 1,012 on hand. What has happened to the other 580?"

Similarly, the close reckoning talents of Eastman were brought home forcefully one day to an architect he had hired to design the great six-thousand-seat Eastman Theater in Rochester. Eastman summoned the architect to his office to tell him that he had figured out a way to add two seats to the orchestra section.

The architect, whose head was swimming with larger problems, was somewhat nettled by such a picayune modification. He made it clear to the tycoon that he didn't think the addition of two seats in a theater planned to accommodate six thousand persons merited the redesigning work which would be required. Eastman held his ground in the face of this expert opposition.

"Each of those extra seats would net thirty cents a show," he said, measuring his words, "and if there are six shows a week, that's $3.60 for the two of them. At the end of a fiscal year that means $187.20—which, incidentally, is exactly 6% interest on $3,120 for the year. Do you care to explore this further?"

The architect, dazzled by the fancy financial footwork, shook his head in defeat.

"I'll take your word for it, sir," he said.

Eastman expressed part of his philosophy in some advice given to a friend. "To get on in this world," he said, "you have to be hard, hard, hard—but always reserve a small corner in your heart for tenderness."

Yet, according to Henry W. Clune, who knew Eastman well, "During those early years when he pursued the golden gods with the ferocious tenacity of a pit bull terrier, tenderness seemed almost excluded from his nature. Labor he exploited to the hilt. Competitors were his enemies and he fought them as such, pressing out the life of some, absorbing, rather than destroying in a finish fight, others whose properties and inventions promised to enhance the growth and productiveness of his own organization.

"With wealth that would have permitted indulgence in sybaritic luxury and license, Eastman was a bachelor whose life was neither softened by romance nor sullied by personal scandal."

Eastman's indifference to women, outwardly at least, was one of the things about him that cancelled a part of his humanity. His ambition and his acquisitiveness were traits that people could understand. They are known human weaknesses—or strengths, as the case may be—but still human. Eastman probably would have been forgiven by the community if he had detoured occasionally from his determined path to dally with some *femme fatale*, but he did not. Through his long lifetime he strode purposefully and straightfaced past any number of beautiful, seductive, willing, available women who had deliberately maneuvered themselves into his path or within his proximity. It made Rochesterians shake their heads to see the great man ignore such temptations.

There was at least one known occasion on which Eastman seemed to appreciate such charms, though. They came in the person of Mary Garden. She was at the time the glamorous diva of the Metropolitan Opera Company, a woman not only talented in voice, but of great personal beauty and intelligence.

Eastman was introduced to the famous singer by the music critic of a Rochester newspaper. She must have made an impression because he later persuaded her to return to Rochester to sing the leading role of an opera with a supporting cast of singers from the Eastman School of Music, which he had endowed. After the performance he gave a supper party

227

in his home. Miss Garden, the guest of honor, of course sat next to the host. She was the center of attraction, not only because she was an international celebrity, but also because of her magnificent bosom. Her gown was strapless and cut very, very low.

"During the course of the meal," wrote Henry Clune, "Eastman's cold eyes, now warmed by the delightful vision next to him, swooped caressingly over the softly-curved shoulders of the singer and stopped abruptly at the low-cut line of her decolletage.

"'I can't understand, Miss Garden,' he said, perplexedly, 'what it is that holds up that dress.'

"The diva turned upon him one of her most devastating smiles.

"'Only your age, Mr. Eastman,' she answered, tapping her host lightly on the hand. 'Only your age.'

"Eastman failed to blush. But his comment was stammered and incomprehensible. He picked up a fish fork and was instantly and deeply engrossed in the business of separating the bones from the finny carcass on his plate."

According to Clune, Eastman was "fiercely intense and at times cruelly exacting and so completely in sympathy with the doctrine of the survival of the fittest that more than once he privately advocated the use of the lethal chamber for the disposal of persons hopelessly ill, crippled, or insane.

"When his own life shambled down the last narrowing stretch to earthly oblivion, and senility threatened to devitalize both his physical and mental faculties, it was probably this doctrine that prompted him to end it with a self-inflicted bullet, leaving, together with a $20 million residue of his fortune, the motto, 'My work is done. Why wait?'"

Eastman was seventy-eight when he committed suicide in 1932, but, like John D. Rockefeller, he had presided over the liquidation of the bulk of his enormous fortune before his death. Some eight years previous, he had divided most of his millions among the University of Rochester, the Massachusetts Institute of Technology, and Hampton and Tuskegee institutes.

Rochester still bears the marks of Eastman's philanthropy in the Eastman Theater, the Eastman School of Music, the university, and scores of smaller institutions that benefited greatly from his gifts. He had reserved, it seems, a large corner of his heart for tenderness.

More impressive than anything to arise from his philanthropy, however, is the huge Eastman Kodak Company itself and the distant chorus of millions of cameras clicking all over the world.

Eastman has been dead a long time, but his picture is still sharp and clear in the memory of Rochester. The image is permanent. It is etched into the city itself.

CHAPTER XXVI

CARLSON MADE THE COPY COUNT

Inventiveness is a glowing part of the tradition of Upper New York State, but at times it cropped out in rather gaudy style, even with a byzantine flourish, as it did in the case of the Rochester inventor who tried to make canalboats independent of the towpath through the use of electrical power.

The basic idea of the innovation was the application of the trolley car principle to the canalboat. That may seem rather far out, but the state officials in charge of the canal were men with open minds. They authorized a test of the invention.

A section of canal running through the village of Brighton was chosen for the demonstration. A trolley power line was rigged up over the canal waters for a generous stretch and a canalboat was fitted out with a trolley and the mysterious mixture of innards that made streetcars such notably restless vehicles. The big experiment was then staged on an autumn day in 1893 before a distinguished audience that included the governor of New York State, Roswell P. Flower. Flower was a Jefferson County native who had become a millionaire and who had political aspirations beyond Albany. He brought with him a large party of state officials to view the historic demonstration.

All went as well as had been hoped. The odd-looking boat moved sedately past the reviewing stand with its trolley proudly upright, clinging to the wire overhead, and Roswell P. Flower was pleased. In the happy afterglow of the demonstration, it was freely predicted that before long the canal would be electrified along its entire length.

That did not come about. The trolley-boat, as a matter of fact, was hardly ever heard of again, except as an eye-catching footnote in the canal's book of lore and legend. There were numerous reasons, all compelling, why the idea was not adopted. There was, first, the cost of building power stations, the cost of electrifying the boats, and the cost of stringing a trolley wire overhead from Albany to Buffalo. Secondly, there was the fear that the combination of trolleys, electrical wires, and water would lead to mass electrocutions on the old canal.

More promising than the electric boat was the one that would use steam as its propulsive force. From the day the first section of canal was opened, men played with the idea of substituting steam for mule-and-horse power. The magazine *Ariel*, in an 1828 issue, noted that "a small steam canal boat, an experiment, passed Weedsport on the Erie Canal recently. She proceeded with great velocity and threw very little water upon the banks."

It was the same old story, though. The steamboat simply was too powerful for the fragile canal. The earthen banks could not withstand the damaging effect of the waves created by boats speeding through the channel at speeds in excess of four miles per hour. The average speed of the horse-drawn freighter was not quite two miles per hour.

Steamboats eventually became a fairly common sight on the Erie, by the close of the nineteenth century, but the towpath remained in heavy use until the end, when it finally was eliminated by the building of the modern State Barge Canal just before World War I. The argument against steam that persisted until the turn of the century was not based entirely on the excessive speed that it generated. Steam was regarded fearfully by the traveling public because of the tendency of boilers to blow up every now and then.

Seeking a way out of the power dilemma and determined to find a towing substitute which would be safer than steam and faster than towpath animals, the state of New York was moved to offer a reward of $100,000 to anyone discovering a new, better, safe means of propulsion. The predictable result was a flurry of dazzling inventions and far-out schemes that stunned state officials and jammed the canal with curious craft.

Among the most interesting of all the ideas was an underwater cable-tow system which had been developed in Belgium. A group of Watertown businessmen in the early 1870s sponsored an experiment with the cable system between Buffalo and Lockport. The basic idea was to propel a vessel through the canal in roughly the same way that the cable cars go up and down the San Francisco hills. A boat was equipped with a low-powered steam engine that turned a drive wheel over which the underwater cable was passed. The boat, in effect, "crawled" along the cable.

The first length of cable was laid in the canal bed from Buffalo to Lockport, approximately thirty-one miles, and the cable boat was fitted out with special equipment imported from Belgium. When it was ready for the trial, a reporter for the Lockport *Daily Journal* found it a sight well deserving his scientific attention. Describing the boat, he wrote that the "steam tug, itself, is a rara avis, having three ponderous wheels on the side of the tug, roughly and deeply grooved. The cable passed under one of these, over the center wheel and under another, and thus the cable is used as a means of resistance.

"The steam tug [he continued] is moved with great ease on the water by means of this cable, and, it is claimed, will be moved at the rate of 2 miles per hour, but more economically than they are now moved. This plan for towing, we presume, is not designed to compete for the $100,000 offered by a state law as it does not profess to comprise the conditions therein prescribed."

A notable shortcoming of the cable boat was that whenever it arrived at a curve in the canal, it insisted on following a physical law instead of the cable and tried to go straight ahead, invariably climbing the bank. Another drawback was that the cable itself had insufficient play to allow boats using it to pass other boats or lumber rafts. In spite of those drawbacks, cable towing still was used briefly in the ninety-four-mile distance from Buffalo to Rochester. It could not oust the animals from the towpath, however, nor could it compete with the newer steam tugs with their improved boilers. The experiment died out in the early 1880s.

Ironically enough, even as men wrestled with cable boats, steamboats, and other ideas, a Rochester patent attorney named George B. Selden had in hand an entirely new concept of power that was destined to revolutionize all forms of transportation. Selden, perhaps inspired by the efforts of his inventor-clients, had come up with an invention himself. It was a compression gasoline engine, the basic forerunner of the automobile engine. He filed a patent application in 1879, but did not receive it until 1895. Had he been able to retain his claim, he would have enjoyed a monopolistic control over the automobile, but Henry Ford contested Selden's patent and won in a landmark case.

Not for nothing is Rochester known as a city where invention has flourished. Its history is rich with instances of inventive genius rampant. Hardly anybody remembers, but it was here that Frederick A. Jockey invented the marshmallow before he died in 1902. America without marshmallows, after all, would not be quite the same.

Perhaps of more significance was the triumphant discovery of a Rochester dentist named J. B. Beers. In 1843 Dr. Beers came running out of his laboratory with the first gold tooth—"a hollow crown secured by cement to a screw inserted in the roots of the broken tooth." He featured the gold tooth thereafter in all the newspaper advertisements promoting his line of "incorruptible teeth."

Dr. Beers' contribution was hailed as a big step forward in remedial dentistry, especially as people in need of replacement teeth had very poor pickings in those days. Until that time the most elegant false tooth had to be carved from an ivory tusk—a time-consuming task whose results, while not always the most artistic, were always expensive. Low-budget false teeth usually came out of a jar filled with calves' teeth. The dentist had to rummage around in the jar until he found a tooth that seemed to fit, or one that could be "dressed to proportion."

By far the most resourceful of all the dentists in Rochester, however, had to be the one who advertised that he would "put in pivot teeth, selected from a bottle of human teeth procured in a Florida war." Sun-kissed teeth from Florida! But they couldn't compete with Dr. Beers's golden grinders.

Rochester was where James G. Cutler in 1880 invented the mail chute still used in tall buildings. It was where the first voting machine was devised in 1889 by Jacob H. Myers and where J. Harry Stedman came up with the idea of the streetcar transfer and took it to its greatest heights. The trouble with the ordinary transfer, as some former streetcar riders will recall happily, was that it lent itself to a great deal of cheating by wily riders. Conductors often were too busy to study a transfer to see if its time limit had expired. Stedman went to impressive lengths to correct the situation. Transfers to be used only in the morning hours were printed on white paper; those for the P.M. hours featured white printing on black paper. When cheating persisted, Stedman had the outline of two heads representing a man and a woman printed on the transfer. When a conductor issued a transfer, he punched a hole in one of the two heads. Then he had to punch out his selection of descriptive physical features printed on the transfer. They included: "clean shave," "full beard," "with mustache," "with side-burns," "with chin whiskers," "with bonnet," "with hat," "thin," and "plump." If the customer presenting the transfer to the conductor did not approximately fit the description on the transfer, he was in trouble. Women, especially, were suspect if their transfer had "with chin whiskers" punched out.

Inventions gushed out of Rochester in the last half of the nineteenth century. The first fountain pens were manufactured by Bishop & Codding in 1849, and Oscar W. Allison in 1880 invented a machine that would manufacture 150 cigarettes a minute. Perhaps his machine was intended to push a medicated cigarette invented in 1877 by a man named D. Wark. The wonder is, really, that Wark's product, supposed to alleviate the pain of asthma sufferers, didn't nip the cigarette habit before it grew into a national problem. Wark's "contribution to medical science" was a cigarette rolled in paper and saturated in a solution of nitrate of potash, juniper, tar, and oil of turpentine. Asthma must have become strictly a secondary complaint after one deep inhalation of Wark's cigarette.

An inventor who was not from Rochester but whose brain child found foster parents there who helped it to grow into one of the commercial and industrial giants of modern times was a man named Chester F. Carlson.

Carlson had to wait more than twenty years for success following his discovery in 1938 of an inexpensive process for instant, dry copying of documents and drawings. His office copying machine came out of a theoretical process that he had developed and which he had called "electrophotography." The process later was renamed "xerography" and the copying machine was called the Xerox machine.

Carlson, the son of a barber, had graduated in physics from the California Institute of Technology, but was in the employ of the patent department of an electronics manufacturer in New York when he evolved his far-out theory of electrophotography. He offered the basic idea to scores of large companies—including the Eastman Kodak Company—without winning any takers. Not until he demonstrated the process in 1944 to officials of the Battelle Memorial Institute in Columbus, Ohio, was he able to find an appreciative audience. The institute, a research organization, was interested enough in the idea to enter into a development agreement with the inventor.

News of the project caught the eye of Dr. John H. Dessauer, director of research for the Haloid Company of Rochester. His company, a manufacturer of photocopy paper and machines and photographic papers since 1906, was searching about at the time for a new "growth" product to add to its old sales line. Xerography sounded promising to Dr. Dessauer and the soon-to-be president of Haloid, Joseph C. Wilson, grandson of a former mayor of Rochester. After long discussions with Battelle scientists, the Haloid management took the plunge and joined the research institute in a development agreement.

It was a risky decision, calling for heavy investments that pushed the old company's capital resources to the outer limits as the years went by. Between 1947 and 1960 Haloid had to chip in about $75,000,000 to help finance the research project—an amount twice as much as the company earned from regular operations during the period!

During this trying period of the 1950s the trade name of "Xerox" was chosen for the copier. It was a name that grew naturally out of xerography (from the Greek *xeros,* for dry, and *graphein,* meaning to write), but there was a Rochester influence visible in the name of Xerox, too, specifically, the influence of Kodak. Haloid long had lived in the Kodak shadow and, like everybody else in the business world, long had admired the Kodak name. When they chose their new product's trade name, it, like Kodak, was a coined word, new to the language. It, like Kodak, had only five letters. And it, like Kodak, began and ended with the same letter. If Kodak was an inspired name, so was Xerox.

In 1958 the company name was changed to Haloid Xerox Corporation. In 1960 the company brought out its fabulous 914 Xerox copier, a machine that fulfilled all the promise that Carlson first and then scores of research scientists had seen in the unorthodox theory. What ensued has been described as "the American success story of the decade." Before the introduction of its new machine, the company was doing annual sales in the vicinity of $33,000,000—not at all a bad vicinity, but not to be compared with the heights, say, in which the company reveled in 1971, when it reported total revenue of $1,960,000,000!

A classic illustration of the Xerox success story is to be found in the experience of the Rochester taxicab driver who, against a background of jeering friends and associates, purchased 100 shares of Haloid Xerox stock at the time it was selling for less than $10 a share. After the company's stock had split 180 times, though, the cabbie found himself in possession of 18,000 shares of stock with a cash value of more than $1,500,000!

The University of Rochester, which had benefited so greatly from the generosity of George Eastman and the Eastman Kodak Company, elected to invest $200,000 of its endowment funds in Haloid Xerox Corporation stock about 1961. It was, at the time, a controversial decision, and there were critics who thought the university had gambled a lot of money out of a sense of hometown chauvinism. In the final judgment, though, H. W. Tripp, the university's vice-president for finance, came out of the situation *summa cum laude*. Any time a $200,000 stock purchase increases to the tune of $120,000,000, as the university's did in this case, there is not much room left for criticism.

It's worth noting that Chester Carlson, the brilliant man who invented the xerography copying process, did not go unrewarded, as so many inventors do when their creations achieve success. Carlson, like most of the principal officers of Haloid, had invested all his money in the effort to prove his theory a practical, profitable instrument. And, like the others, he had borrowed money from friends and relatives to keep the xerography development project going. His faith and ingenuity paid rich dividends in the end. His share of royalties in 1964 alone amounted to more than $3,000,000! In 1967 it was more than $6,000,000. Chester Carlson became a very wealthy man—one of the sixty-six wealthiest men in the nation, according to *Fortune* magazine—but not nearly as wealthy a man (in dollars, anyway) as he might have been if he had chosen to let his royalties accumulate. Instead he chose to distribute a large part of his mounting fortune in philanthropies, in the style of George Eastman. Carlson lavished money on the California Institute of Technology, the promulgation of Zen Buddhism, studies in extrasensory perception, psychical research, and other causes that interested him.

"If he had kept everything he earned," Mrs. Carlson said of her husband in 1969, "he would have had well over one hundred fifty million dollars. But of course he gave away what is now worth about one hundred million dollars."

Carlson did not long enjoy the luxury of great wealth or the pleasure that comes from giving it away. In September 1968, only eight years after xerography became a commercial success and began duplicating dollar bills at a furious rate for all those who had believed in it, Carlson, its creator, died in the seat of a motion picture theater in New York City. The next morning in Rochester they raised an American flag to the top of a pole next to the new thirty-story Xerox Tower, the central structure in the beautiful Xerox Square development in the center of the city. And then they lowered the flag to half-staff in honor of Chester Carlson—"without whom," later wrote his associate John H. Dessauer, "there would have been no Xerox Square."

Eastman and Carlson. Two inventors who changed the face of Rochester more than any other force in the city's history—outside of the Erie Canal, that is.

CHAPTER XXVII

LOCKPORT LORE

The canal ride from Rochester to Lockport was something of a lark. There wasn't a single lock to interrupt the trip in its sixty-three-mile length, known as the Long Level, and it was not uncommon for a boat captain, sensing home port ahead like a sailor at sea, to coax the animals on the flat towpath into a trot that hurried the miles along.

The approach to Lockport, after all, marked the next-to-last stage of a long, weary, cross-state trip. Only one great challenge stood between a boat and the western terminus of the canal at Buffalo, that being the great set of locks at Lockport. And while some captains quickened the steps of their mules or horses to gain a margin of time in the schedule, lest there be a traffic jam ahead at the locks, another reason was that the ascent to the top of the mountain, a ride up more than sixty feet in the air in five giant aquatic steps, constituted one of the authentic, lasting thrills of any journey on the Erie Canal. Not even the captains or crewmen could get blasé about that experience, as exalting as it was uplifting.

Lockport itself was an interesting town for travelers. It was a place for strolling or relaxing, for watching the busy locks in operation as a way of marking time whenever there was a delay or admiring the fine shops of the enterprising town which enjoyed an individual reputation both for its stores and hotel accommodations.

How far-reaching its reputation as a shopping place was can be measured by the story that appeared in a Lockport newspaper in 1861:

A suspicious looking box was received at the White House the other day addressed to Mrs. Lincoln.

The President thought he smelled a mouse and ordered it out of doors.

237

It was found to contain several elegant dress patterns from Tyler's Great Cheap Dry Goods Store, 72 Main Street, Lockport, N.Y.

A great explosion of laughter followed at the expense of the President who said he could stand it for he could easily fancy Mrs. Lincoln a bride again robed in those elegant dresses.

What pleased travelers the most about Lockport was that it had the frontier look that so many had been looking for upon arrival in the legendary West. Even the sawdust on the floors of so many of the business places had a fresher fragrance, as if it had come from trees toppled only yesterday to make way for the town.

At the time the canal was opened in 1825, Lockport and Buffalo were the same size, each counting a population of 2,500. From that time on, though, it was not much of a contest as Buffalo quickly grew into a large city. After its first spurt or two, Lockport made progress slowly, but if its population stayed small, its people were unusually endowed in individual brilliance and character, it seemed. It was a town that seemed to specialize in spawning interesting characters the way an Alaskan river spawns salmon.

Shortly after the canal opened, the picturesque settlement won favor as a good stopover point among discriminating travelers—especially those who couldn't stand another sleepless night sandwiched in the wall bunks of a packet. About that time a Lewiston tavern operator, George W. Rector, decided to switch his efforts to Lockport. It was a courageous move because he already had established a fine reputation for the excellance of the cuisine he offered at his Lewiston restaurant, the Frontier House, over whose entrance hung his special trademark, the Sign of the Griffon.

Rector prospered in Lockport, becoming in time proprietor of the National Hotel on the banks of the canal, close to the famous locks. Later, in 1862, he took over the management of the Judson House, in that part of Lockport known as Lowertown. It took its name from the fact that it was an area of the city below the mountain ridge. Rector died in 1884, the same year that his son, Charles Rector, opened his first restaurant in a basement at the southeast corner of Clark and Monroe streets in Chicago.

Young Rector's Chicago operation was an immediate success—especially its French cuisine and the specialty of the house, the oyster stew, which was forced on every visitor to Chicago whether he liked oysters or not. With this success behind him, Rector opened a restaurant in New York City in 1899, and while its meaning probably escaped the understanding of Manhattanites, the Sign of the Griffon hung prominently in place over the entrance, just as it had in front of his father's inn in Lewiston almost eighty years before.

Rector's was the leading restaurant in New York City for several

238

decades, until the proprietor lost his fortune in an ill-advised hotel venture. Later, in 1932, another George Rector, the grandson of the man who had been an innkeeper in Lockport for so many years, visited the lock city and commented wryly: "Dad started with an oyster stew and ran it into a million dollars—then ran it back into a oyster stew again!"

Another famous man who had his start in Lockport was Mark Hopkins, a resident from 1830 to 1846. In 1840 he served as elected clerk of Lockport. Six years later, he moved to New York City and ventured into the grocery business, with considerable success. He then opened a commission house in the food market and seemed set in his career until word of the California gold strike came through in 1848. Hopkins joined a group of twenty-six men who put $500 each into a fund to equip an expedition to the gold fields and went with the expedition as far as San Francisco. There he struck gold in his own way by opening a wholesale grocery store and later a wholesale hardware business. He parleyed his profits into a multimillion dollar fortune by investing in the construction of the Central Pacific Railroad, completed in 1869, and other lines.

One of the most interesting of all the notables who called Lockport home was a man named Charley Case. He deserves to be remembered for several things, but especially for the trick he played on the world, an inside joke, so to speak, which drew warm chuckles from all of Charley's old friends and admirers back home.

Charley Case was a blackface comedian who was one of the stars of American vaudeville for about a quarter century, during the closing decades of the nineteenth century, through the Gay Nineties, and into the beginning years of the new century. He was known in particular for the many jokes he told about his father and for one classic story about the time he had appeared in court and defended a client who was charged with stealing a cow.

Here was one of the oddities: Charley Case was, in fact, a lawyer. And the story he told about his first (and probably last) client, the cow thief, was true. Charley, in the manner of the day, had pursued his law studies in the office of a local attorney. When he at last was admitted to the bar, he was assigned by the court to be defense counsel for the accused cow thief.

Case, after listening with growing dismay to his client's side of the story, advised the accused to plead insanity. It was the only possible defense he could think of, under the damning circumstances. To bolster the plea and give strength to the defense, he called on the prisoner to act in as eccentric a manner as possible.

His client agreed and promptly did a very crazy thing. He confided to a prisoner in the next cell the brilliant strategy his lawyer had hit upon, boasting loudly of his acting ability and vowing that the performance he planned to put on for the court would set new standards of insanity in the juridical world.

But the fellow prisoner, it turned out, was a stool pigeon who promptly passed along news of the defense strategy to the district attorney. The DA in turn warned Attorney Charley Case that he was on to the planned fakery and that he had better come up with a different defense.

Charley was equal to the challenge. When the court convened he stood up and told a heart-wrenching story of the circumstances that had led his client, a misjudged man, into the web of justice.

"My client," he told the gaping court, "was merely walkin' along a road, alongside the pasture, not harmin' a soul in this world, when he suddenly spied a piece of rope in the road.

"'Well, now,' he says to himself, surprised, 'this sure is a pretty nice piece of rope to be just layin' in the road. I wonder how it got there? Somebody was very wasteful to throw it away. It is a sin to be so wasteful. Maybe I had ought to pick up the rope and take it home with me. It ain't that I need a rope right now, but some day I might.'

"So, y'r honor, my client innocently picked up the piece of rope, thinkin' to save it. He threw it over his shoulder and made his way home, not givin' it a second thought until he got to where he was going and turned around. You can imagine his surprise, y'r honor, when he discovered that there was a cow attached to the other end of the rope!

"It could have happened to anybody, y'r honor. My client is an innocent man."

The court clearly was fascinated by the explanation, but remained steadfastly incredulous throughout. The accused man was judged to be a bad actor, which he unquestionably was in more ways than one, and he was found guilty and sentenced to jail.

Even though Charley Case had lost his first legal outing, he had done such a superb job of entertaining the court that he was privately congratulated for his performance and urged to consider a career in show business. He took the advice and launched a career that won him national fame as a comedian and a considerable fortune. One of his stock stories was the story of the cow thief and the trial, but hardly anybody believed the tale. Even the newspaper reporters grinned skeptically when, during interviews, Charley would tell them that it had been an actual case and that he really had been the man's lawyer. Finally, to prove the point when a San Francisco newsman openly challenged the story, Case, in December 1905, wired Police Chief Molyneau back in Lockport and asked for verification of the story. The chief wired back: "Charley Case, the monologist, was Nick Buckley's lawyer. Defense was Buckley stole the rope, not knowing cow was tied to rope. Buckley convicted of stealing cow and rope and sentenced to Auburn State Prison for three years."

When Charley Case died in 1916 in New York City, Jack Lait of the New York *Daily Mirror* wrote a eulogizing story in which he described the Lockport comedian as "the funniest man that ever blackened up."

That was a great compliment in a day when vaudeville was crowded with blackface comedians. Charley Case would have enjoyed the compliment more than Lait could have realized because he had been enjoying his own private joke all the years he had been performing in the spotlight. Only the folks back home in Lockport could appreciate the humor of the situation now that Charley was dead. The truth that tickled them was that Charley Case, the blackface artist, was in reality a Negro. His father had been black and his mother white. Charley's skin was so light that he really needed the cork to play the role!

Show business had other reasons to be grateful to little Lockport. It was astonishing how much talent came out of the lock town. There was, for instance, that great performer, Signor Guillermo Antonio Farine, one of the leading daredevils of his day. The signor, better known to his Lockport neighbors as plain William Hunt, took the fancy moniker as a young man when he first went tripping across a cable strung over the gorge of Niagara Falls and dazzled the onlooking thousands with fantastic demonstrations of equilibrium. His outstanding performances came at a time in the middle nineteenth century when, led by a Monsieur Blondin, the air over the high gorge was thick with daredevils competing for honors. It was a time of exhibitionistic madness, sometimes called Niagaramania, with artists running back and forth on cables, dancing, riding bicycles, pushing wheelbarrows, leaping and pirouetting, hanging by their toenails and standing on their heads. Despite the keen competition for honors, Signor Farine was a standout. He was the pride of Lockport for a long time, this death-defying artist, who, in fact, staved off death until he was in his nineties!

Not as lively a performer but outstanding in his own quiet way was a Lockport show-biz personality named Jonathan Bass. He was a headliner for about twenty years, beginning in 1872, under the billing of "The Ossified Man."

Poor Jonathan, a normal young man with a strapping physique until he reached eighteen, was at work as a boatman on the Erie Canal in July of 1848 when his feet began to pain him. He was treated for rheumatism by a Dr. Chase of Lockport, but his condition grew steadily worse and he had difficulty walking. He used a cane for a while, then exchanged it for crutches, meanwhile continuing to work in Buffalo, where he operated a barn for canal horses and mules and did clerical work for a canal shipper.

It became apparent, in time, that Jonathan was undergoing gradual ossification. His body was turning to bone. By 1852 his condition was such that he had to quit work. By 1857 he was unable to leave his bed. His mother had to take care of him. Even though he was helpless, the disease did not affect his vital organs. His mind was clear and he retained his powers of speech. A Lockport cabinetmaker named Philip Murphy built a special bed for Bass, one which he did not leave for thirty-two years, even though he became a busy traveler. After his mother died

241

in 1872 he lived briefly with his brother in Niagara Falls. When his brother died, Jonathan took the only means of support open to him. He went on tour as a freak—"The Ossified Man"—all over the country, appearing in circuses, carnivals, and museums.

It was a sad, dessicated, pitiful remains of a man that the customers crowded in to gape at. For thirty-two years Bass's jaws had been virtually locked, and some of his teeth had to be extracted so he could be fed. Sometime after 1869 he went blind. But still he lingered on, being trundled from one town to another, lying stoically in public exhibition. Not until September 13, 1892, did Jonathan Bass's suffering end. Ironically enough, he was on exhibition in a museum in New York City when he breathed his last sad breath at the age of sixty-two.

Chauncey Olcott was more famous than The Ossified Man, but Lockport doesn't own clear title to the romantic Irish tenor, who also was talented as a songwriter and a wit. Olcott actually was born in Buffalo, on July 21, 1860, but because he spent his early summers with his grandparents in Lockport, there arose a conflict of claims to Olcott between the two cities.

The people in Lockport like to point out that Olcott's singing career began with his appearances on stages in their city and in such nearby canal towns as Medina and Albion, which is a fact. The Lockporters are quick, also, to remind the world that Olcott's mother, a native of Ireland, lived in their community during the 1840s and married one of their own, Mellon W. Olcott. (When her first husband died, Mrs. Olcott married Patrick Brennan of Buffalo, which won the approval of the people back in Lockport, who included, incidentally, an astonishing number of Brennans.)

Chauncey Olcott rose through the minstrel ranks to become one of America's most popular actors and singers, but he never forgot Lockport. He always made it a sentimental point to appear annually on the stage of the old Hodge Opera House. Every night after the show was party time as all his old friends and relatives came around to celebrate with their genial idol.

Olcott is better remembered for the songs he left behind than for his pure Irish tenor. He was a talented man. His most famous composition was "My Wild Irish Rose"—inspired, he said, by a visit to Erin with his dear old mother: "A friend showed us a flower which, she said, was a wild Irish rose, and my mother remarked that it would make a good title for a song. I composed the first stanza on the spot."

When Ernest Roland Ball of Cleveland wrote another classic Irish standard, "Mother Machree," he insisted that it be introduced by the great Olcott, and it was. The two Irish songs, his own and Ball's, became permanent highlights of the Olcott repertoire to the day of the great entertainer's death at seventy-three in Monte Carlo in 1932.

Not all the leading citizens of Lockport were entertainers, of course, but most of them managed somehow to be entertaining. There were a lot of substantial men like Orange H. Dibble, the man who helped the canal construction effort with his crane idea, and Lyman A. Spalding, who one time tried to introduce the silk industry to the area, encouraging farmers to plant large stands of mulberry trees in the late 1830s. The Japanese silkworms, unfortunately, refused to co-operate and the farmers turned to the growing of fruit. The countryside around Lockport is still a standout in the production of fruit.

Birdsall Holly, whose lyrical name would have been much admired in vaudeville, made some significant contributions to society that should have won him more universal appreciation and fame. At a time when fire was the scourge of America, an enemy that kept everybody in fear, Holly came up with a plan in 1864 to make water immediately available for the quenching of fires. It called for the construction of a central water-pumping station and a system of underground pipes and hydrants that would leave no neighborhood unprotected. It was the same basic system that still is used in cities all over the world. The Holly Manufacturing Company of Lockport installed the system in some two thousand towns and cities of the United States.

As if that weren't enough of a contribution, the same Birdsall Holly invented a central steam-heating system which conveyed steam heat through a system of underground pipes to buildings willing to purchase the comfort-producing commodity. That idea also was a tremendous success, and the steam heating supply system became an indispensable part of urban America.

CHAPTER XXVIII

GARGLING OIL AND GIRLS

There was hardly ever a dull year in the long history of Lockport. Excitement was virtually guaranteed by the canal traffic. Even so, certain events made one year more memorable than the next.

People who kept track of the highlight years had a fondness for 1893, for example, simply because it was the year that a man named Charles K. Lawrence stole the city's street railway. Other cities have had street-cars stolen, but this is the only recorded case in which an entire railway system has been kidnapped.

When Charles K. Lawrence—a short, stout, jovial man—breezed into town early that year, almost concealed behind a cloud of smoke from his favorite Havana cigars, he won immediate favor. He was the type of man people took a liking to instinctively. He was genial and generous, cheerful and charming. The world has too few such men, and Lockport was pleased to count this one in their midst. The fact that he had been hired as construction manager of the Lock City Electrical Railroad Company and was about to bring into being the city's first electrical streetcar line was added reason to like the man.

In due time, a train of the New York Central Railroad chugged into town carrying all the essential parts of the new city system—the ties, the rails, the trolleys, the cars, even the stoves to heat the cars. Everything. Lockporters went down to the railroad siding and beamed. It wouldn't be long, they knew, before they would be rocketing back and forth over the city's streets in the swift new electrical vehicles of the railway that Charles K. Lawrence was about to put together for their use.

But Charles K. Lawrence had other thoughts, and they were colored with larcenous intent. One night, after he had pressed sufficient bribe money into the hands of several New York Central trainmen, a switch engine hooked onto the freight cars loaded with trolley equipment and puffed off into the night. The makeshift express also carried a solitary passenger: Lawrence of Lockport.

Just where this daring, foolish fellow planned to take Lockport's street railway or how he planned to dispose of it is not known. The questions are of academic interest only, anyway, because the authorities had no trouble whatsoever apprehending the trolley thief and all the loot. It is almost an axiom that one cannot pull this sort of heist involving a streetcar system and a railroad train without leaving tracks behind him everywhere he goes. They quickly caught up with Charles K. Lawrence and his prize, separated one from the other, charged the former with "stealing one street railway," and, in September 1894, the genial Mr. Lawrence was sentenced to two years and five months in Auburn State Prison. He was popular to the end, though. It's hard to dislike a man who thinks big and acts big.

Some important developments that occurred in Lockport in the first ten years of the Erie Canal's operation are worth recalling. For instance, when it dawned on some smart investors from Albany that surplus water from the upper level of the canal could be used for developing power below the escarpment at Lockport, there began, about 1829, the development of that part of the city still called Lowertown.

The lower area in the beginning was a wilderness, but it was soon cleared, streets laid out, lots surveyed, and new buildings begun. At the time, Uppertown already had a population of 2,100, but Lowertown quickly took over as the important part of the community. It was the center of industry and commerce for many years. Only in recent times did the upper part of town regain the upper hand.

Even as the city was taking shape in 1833, the town pharmacist, Dr. George W. Merchant, was putting on the market a product that would be a significant, influential factor in Lockport life for nearly a century. It bore the unusual name "Dr. Merchant's Gargling Oil." It is not clear why that name was chosen. If anybody had gargled with Merchant's compound, his innards probably would have dissolved in a matter of seconds.

Gargling Oil was a liniment and apparently a good one. One story had it that the formula was that of a retired physician who donated it to the druggist. Another version claimed the druggist got the formula—for a price—from a pioneer. No matter whose concoction it was originally, it was Dr. Merchant who bottled it and made it available to the public. His timing was outstanding because as many of the canalboats arrived at Lockport on their westward voyage, their horses and mules were pulling up lame as the result of their long, arduous hours on the towpath. Some of the canal hostlers tried Dr. Merchant's magic liniment with satisfactory results and the demand for the product began to grow.

Perhaps some of the canallers themselves had need of liniment relief and experimented successfully with the Gargling Oil, but as time passed

246

the use of the stuff became common among people as well as animals. It wasn't long before sales began to soar. Business was so good that Dr. Merchant, now in partnership with a pioneer storekeeper named Morris H. Tucker, built a two-story frame building at Cottage and Walnut streets to accommodate the enterprise. It was, however, a short-lived partnership. Ill health caused Dr. Merchant to sell his share of the business in 1854 to a three-man combine which included Tucker, B. L. Delano, and Henry Walbridge. They formed a stock company to market the liniment, naming as one of the directors the governor of New York State, Washington Hunt, a home-town boy, the only son of Niagara County ever to become the state's chief executive. Walbridge was Governor Hunt's father-in-law and the two made an outstanding money-making pair. Together, in the 1830s, they had purchased some 32,000 acres of land alongside the Erie Canal through the Albany Land Company. When the canal sent land values soaring, Walbridge and Hunt became very rich. Hunt also became Niagara County's first judge in 1836, overcoming the handicaps of extreme youth (twenty-four) and extreme wealth. Not everybody looked on his appointment with approval. The comment of the *Niagara Courier* was: "Washington Hunt is to be appointed first judge —Who will pretend hereafter that a whistle cannot be made from a pig's tail?"

Dr. Merchant's Gargling Oil Company, bolstered by new financial resources and with the imaginative, enterprising Tucker running things, moved into sensationally prosperous years. Tucker was a promoter with ideas and methods far ahead of his time. In 1850, for example, he sent to the sultan of Turkey, through the co-operative United States consul in Constantinople, a dozen bottles of Gargling Oil in a satin-lined oak box. The sultan, no doubt taken aback by such an unusual gift, failed to issue a formal statement of appreciation, but American newspapers publicized the hands-across-the-sea gesture and liniment sales shot upward.

It was Tucker who, in recognition of the fact that horses and mules were not the only users of Gargling Oil, adopted the advertising slogan: "Good for Man and Beast!" In time, with some modifications in the formula, the company marketed products calculated to meet the peculiar needs of both. Gargling Oil in a yellow wrapper was for beasts; the stuff for human use came in a white wrapper. The different-colored wrappers presumably eliminated confusion, but other clues also were provided. The Gargling Oil for animals had a label that pictured an Arabian stallion having his forelegs massaged by a turbaned groom while another groom held the bridle, a depiction probably inspired by the gift to the sultan of Turkey. The oil for human use carried a label showing a man and his wife "in an apparent state of felicity" in front of a table on which stood some bottles of the liniment.

Gargling Oil moved into its most prosperous era when a smart young man named John Hodge joined the company as a clerk in 1861. He became president in 1886, succeeding Tucker. Not only had he proved himself to be a whiz of a businessman in the intervening years, but he also had had the good sense to marry Tucker's daughter. Like his father-in-law, Hodge was a promotional genius. He had a keen appreciation of the value of advertising, and he saw to it that signs promoting Gargling Oil were painted on anything that would stand still along the entire length of the Grand Canal, but barns were the favorite billboard background. It was Hodge who saw to it that the name of his product was blatantly displayed on the side of the *Maid of the Mist* on a day in September 1883, when the famous boat braved the rapids and the treacherous whirlpool of the Niagara River as part of a celebration organized by Niagara Falls businessmen in search of publicity for their town. It made the civic officials plainly wistful when the *Maid of the Mist* bobbed into view sporting banners that promoted an industry in rival Lockport.

Hodge's most spectacular promotional feat, however, resulted in the painting of an advertisement for Dr. Merchant's Gargling Oil on the side of the Rock of Gibralter! He never topped that achievement. By the time of Hodge's death in 1895, the Lockport liniment had become world-famous and its manufacture was one of the city's principal industries. But Gargling Oil, like horses and mules and towpaths, had no future in the twentieth century. Sales of the famous liniment steadily declined, and the company finally went out of business in 1928.

Lockport, as we have noted, is a city that has contributed in astonishing measure to show business and commerce. Its ultimate achievement, some admirers believe, was one that benefited both of those diverse fields: the Seven Sutherland Sisters.

The memory of the Sutherland girls has faded with the years, even in Lockport, but at one time they were internationally famous, perhaps even better known than Dr. Merchant's Gargling Oil.

They came out of a commonplace background and there was nothing in their genealogy to hint that the seven sisters one day would command top billing in the theater. Their grandfather Andrew Sutherland was one of many refugees from the unproductive hills of Vermont who migrated to western New York in the early years of the nineteenth century. He built a log house on the mountain ridge, just to the west of Lockport, where the town called Cambria came into being. His son Fletcher elected to live on the same farm, but replaced the primitive homestead with a frame house.

Fletcher Sutherland was an interesting man with a number of specialties. He called himself "Reverend" and preached vigorously in the countryside as a kind of casual clergyman, but he never had his own church nor was he ever formally ordained as a minister by any denomination. When he was not serving in this free-lance role of reformer, he liked to plead cases in the justice of the peace courts. The fact that he was not a recognized attorney was just another one of those technicalities that Fletcher would not allow to hamper him in his work.

What it boiled down to was that Fletcher Sutherland was a farmer who seldom farmed, a preacher without portfolio, and an amateur attorney. In none of those fields was he successful, but he was not entirely without achievement. He and his wife had a fruitful marriage. Seven daughters were born to their busy union. The girls arrived in the Sutherland home, in the graphic words of a Lockport reporter, in "a steady stream during the 1860s." The writer may have been overstating the situation a trifle, but, still, seven girls is a lot of girls. They were named Sarah, Victoria, Isabella, Grace, Naomi, Dora, and Mary.

"Seven they were," mused the same reporter, plainly impressed. "Seven, the mystical number. From time immemorial seven had been considered a lucky number. But was it lucky for the Sutherlands?"

A considered reply, from a distance, would be "Yes." It was certainly a lucky number for Fletcher Sutherland because he was not much of a farmer and seven girls to help with the chores certainly was a lot better than, say, five girls or no girls. Even luckier was the fact that they were "sturdy, well-knit girls, most of them taller than average and able to do a man's work."

People apparently were so preoccupied with the way the girls were knit and the splendid development of their biceps that it was some time before it dawned on the town that the girls also were above average in the hair department.

Pigtails were common at the time, but the ones sported by the Sutherlands were more like steamship hawsers in their length and thickness. It was said that when they let down their braids for washing or brushing the hair literally trailed behind them "in rippling, shining trains." And still it continued to grow as the girls matured until it reached such incredible lengths that the fame of the girls spread all about the countryside—as did, for that matter, the hair itself.

"It was," wrote the Lockport reporter, "a breathtaking example of nature's lavishness, concentrated on a single family. Naomi could wrap herself in her hair like the most discreet Godiva. Victoria's hair, from brow to tip, was a full seven feet. The other sisters were also blessed with these 'crowning glories.' It was a sight which could hardly remain undiscovered."

The reporter was reveling in understatement. Victoria was the family champion with her seven-foot-long hair, but the other girls weren't far behind. Isabella's hair was six feet long, Naomi's measured five feet four inches, Grace's was an even five feet, Mary's reached six feet, Dora's measured four feet six inches, and Sarah brought up the rear with three-foot-long locks. Altogether, it was a lot of hair; perhaps more hair than ever has been concentrated in one family in American history. There is no way of knowing.

If the Sutherland girls had kept their big assets under their bonnets in a prim, modest way, the world probably never would have become aware of their fantastic superabundance of hair, but the seven girls also had another talent. They liked to sing together, and whatever the quality of their voices, they were a novelty at church socials, farm grange shows, school programs, and other community affairs.

An act like the one put on by the Seven Sutherland Sisters couldn't be concealed for long. As the word got around, theatrical agents from afar began pilgrimages to the farm house in Cambria to see and to listen for themselves. Several of them offered show business contracts. The girls finally accepted an offer, signing a contract that stipulated only that all seven of them would have to be hired by any promoter—which, naturally, was precisely the way the show sponsors wanted it. Besides agreeing to show off their locks, the girls put together a singing routine and even learned to play some musical instruments so that they could accompany themselves.

At last they were ready for the big time. The only question that remained was whether the big time was ready for them. After all, there never had been an act like this one before, and the sophisticated audiences of Broadway were about to be put to a stern test. When the seven Sutherlands walked out for the first time into the spotlight and made their way, Indian file, across the stage, the audience gasped. Even in profile they could tell there was a lot of hair coming. Then, as the girls swung into a program of ever popular songs while plunking their banjos and humming on their musical combs, they would occasionally swish their heads in such a way as to give the customers a provocative glimpse of their hair.

It was the grand finale, though, that made the act truly sensational. That was when all seven girls turned their backs on the audience, revealing such a wondrous sight as to send a murmur of appreciation through the theater: A solid bank of hair that ran virtually from one side of the proscenium to the other, wall-to-wall hair that concealed the sisters almost entirely and that in places trailed off into the orchestra pit, perhaps clogging the flugelhorns and smothering the cellist.

Broadway never had known anything like this act or these performers before or since. Not even in modern times, with the musical *Hair*, has there been anything that could compare with the Seven Sutherland Sisters. The world of show business buzzed with news of the unique act, arousing the interest of the Barnum and Bailey Circus.

The girls had been making a fair amount of money in theaters, but their earnings jumped when they were hired by the circus. They found their fortune with Barnum and Bailey, and one of the girls, Naomi, found something even more precious—romance. Joseph Henry (Harry) Bailey, a son of Barnum's partner, became enamored of Naomi and they were married.

250

Meanwhile, back home in Niagara County, old Fletcher Sutherland had been giving a lot of thought to the success of his seven daughters, and it had occurred to him that they were not capitalizing on their hair quite as fully as they could be. Show biz was all right, and the money coming in was more than the family ever had known, but Fletcher had a brilliant idea for extending the take. His own hair had been thinning as he got older, and he had concocted a tonic to feed the follicles and stave off baldness. Why not market the product for growing hair with the name and endorsement of his daughters? Some say the idea was his, others say it was the brainchild of Harry Bailey. It doesn't matter. It was a natural. Soon the commercial hair tonic was being manufactured in a small plant in New York City and finding its way onto store shelves. It won immediate acceptance. Women everywhere stood in envy of the Sutherland sisters and clamored for the magic liquid that would thicken their hair and make their tresses grow in runaway style.

The placards, advertisements, and bottle labels, incidentally, co-starred the Reverend Mr. Sutherland with his seven famous daughters. There were, in fact, two pictures of Fletcher Sutherland featured in the advertisements. One showed him entirely bald and the other depicted him with such a shock of hair as to give him a top-heavy look. It was very dramatic, very graphic—before-and-after illustrations to give people pause. It also was outrageously fraudulent. Sutherland, it is true, had lost some hair, but he never approached the state of baldness in which he was pictured; neither did he ever achieve the growth of bushy hair that the tonic was supposed to have induced.

The public was willing to believe, however, that the Sutherland family really had stumbled on to some basic secret about the growing of hair. One look at the sisters was the convincer. Sales of the hair tonic soared to high levels and the distribution kept spreading, even as the seven sisters and Harry Bailey hurriedly added to the list of products bearing the Sutherland name and endorsement. In addition to the stuff for growing hair, there soon were shampoos, hair dyes, scalp cleaners, combs, brushes, and toilet articles.

Behind the success of the business, unquestionably, was Naomi's husband, Harry, who served as president of the company. Grace Sutherland had the duties of secretary and Dora was put in charge of the Canadian end of the business. The other girls served simply as directors. They were much too busy spending money to do much else.

One of the most extravagant outlays of money went to build a great mansion for the family. It was constructed, no doubt for sentimental reasons, on the site of the old farm house in Cambria Township. But tragedy mixed with triumph the year it was built, 1893, because that also was the year in which Naomi Sutherland died. It was the beginning of the end for the sensational Sutherland sisters.

Naomi was buried, according to the records, "in an elegant shroud of

251

white satin with her luxuriant hair spilling over each side of the casket."
Even in death, the Sutherland hair had to be on display. It took three
buggies to carry the overwhelming display of expensive flowers to
Naomi's grave in Glenwood Cemetery in Lockport.

Harry Bailey stayed on as president of the Sutherland company after
Naomi's death. He was trusted by the remaining sisters, even loved by
them. Furthermore, they doted heavily on their sister's children, Naomi
and Fletcher Bailey.

One of the sisters, Isabella, had married the scion of a prominent
Canadian family, Frederick Castlemaine, and together they had managed
the Sutherland Company's Canadian business out of Toronto. But they
always made it a point to spend their summers with the rest of the
family at the Sutherland mansion. There are still vivid memories of
Frederick Castlemaine in Niagara County. He was no ordinary summer
visitor, but a dashing, charming fellow who seemed to specialize in unconventional behavior. Being an excellent marksman, for example, he
liked to demonstrate his accuracy at every opportunity; in so doing, he
kept the townspeople on their toes. It was said that his favorite sport was
shooting the spokes out of the wheels of passing buggies, a hobby that
some found less than amusing. The tolerant people in town were entertained by the practice, just as they were delighted when Castlemaine shot
the pipe out of the mouth of a passing farmer. It was generally agreed,
however, that his best display of marksmanship was performed the day
his bullets severed the strings of a laundry bag a man was toting on his
back as he walked down the street. They toasted Castlemaine that night
at his favorite bar, Dan Rodenbeck's place in the old Hodge Opera
House.

The death of the fun-loving Castlemaine in 1906 brought on another
expensive display of grief by the Sutherlands. They liked that light-
hearted man, and they saw to it that he went on his eternal way with the
proper trappings. They gave him a solid mahogany casket with hand
carvings, costly lining, and silver mountings, along with the now traditional mountain of flowers. His remains were not lowered into the ground,
but placed in a mausoleum that cost close to $10,000. It was widely re-
ported that valuable diamonds and other precious possessions went into
the mausoleum with the body, and the rumor no doubt was responsible
for an invasion of the crypt by would-be robbers in later years. Their
work was in vain, apparently.

Another rumor that circulated widely claimed that Frederick's widow,
Isabella, frequently spent the small hours of the night within the mausoleum. It was said that she was trying to communicate with her husband's
spirit. Strange lights within were visible and eerie sounds were reported
by frightened passersby. But Isabella didn't grieve too long. She married again, only two years after Frederick's death. It was a short marriage. She followed Frederick in death in 1914, when she was sixty-two.

Funerals apparently brought out the family spirit. The five remaining Sutherland sisters saw to it that Isabella, clad in a white robe, was embalmed and sealed in a copper-lined, glass-topped mahogany casket and placed on stately display in the mansion. As usual, the floral display that surrounded the casket was overwhelming. Even more overwhelming, though, was the fact that they kept Isabella on display for nearly a month. After that they relented and allowed her to be placed to rest in the mausoleum.

The next tragedy to strike the family was least expected. Young Fletcher Bailey, who had taken over the vice-presidency of the hair tonic company, was fatally injured in a motorcycle accident in Buffalo. The Sutherlands saw to it that he, too, had a proper wake. His body was placed in a glass-topped casket and every night for two weeks his aunts would sit around, "gaze tenderly on the face of their beloved nephew, gather at the piano, and sing the songs he had liked in life."

Now death had become a regular visitor to the Sutherland mansion. Victoria had preceded Isabella in death. Dora, who had kept the Canadian branch of the hair tonic business going until the hair bob craze ruined it, was killed in an auto accident in 1919. Sarah died the same year at the age of seventy-three.

Sarah, incidentally, had the reputation of being "the sensible one" in the family. It was only a minor eccentricity that led her to keep seventeen cats as her pets or that caused her to bury each one with honors, elaborately and expensively, in the family pet cemetery on the mansion grounds.

In 1931, the family fortune spent, the remaining sisters, Grace and Mary, had to leave the grand home. They were by then pitiful in their appearance and in their manner of living. There were bars on the windows of Mary's room. She had been very ill for a long time. She and Grace still had the long hair that had made them famous, but now it was gray and stringy, sometimes matted from lack of care, and the way it hung down to their waists no longer was a thing of beauty.

Mary died in the Niagara County Infirmary in 1939. Grace died in Buffalo in 1946. She was in her nineties at the time of her death, the last of the Seven Sutherland Sisters.

CHAPTER XXIX

OF MEN AND MINSTRELS

When the sound of the hoofs on the towpath had died away and the canalboat could go no farther, you were in Buffalo. To many it must have seemed like the end of the world. It was as if the world were flat—once a traveler passed over that last horizon on the westward trip and arrived at the waters of the inland seas, there was nothing ahead but the fearsome infinity of the unexplored continent.

For ten days, perhaps two weeks, a canalboat had been the world of the travelers. They had gotten to know the motion, the sounds, the smells, and the limits of that world. They had come to react almost automatically to the intermittent cry of "Low bridge ahead!" and the faces of the crew and the other passengers had become the faces of an intimately associated family. The journey itself had become a way of life, snug and secure, even if terribly uncomfortable at times.

Now came Buffalo and the end of the canal world, the end of the last physical tie to home, wherever it had been. One strand after another had snapped as the line of travel had lengthened, but here the connection ended.

Buffalo was the outpost of the West, as its look plainly revealed. It had the raw, unweathered face of newly sawed lumber, and there was the smell of still damp mortar chinking. Here and there were charred remains of buildings that had stood on the site only briefly, having been put to the torch by the British in the War of 1812—Buffalo shared the same fiery fate as Washington in that conflict. The streets were dusty or muddy, according to the weather, and the stores of the main streets gamely tried to convey the impression of size and elegance with their false second-story fronts.

Some unnamed observer in 1825, the year the canal finally linked Buffalo with the East, described the town as "a place of great resort with five lawyers and no church and water only from a hogshead supplied by a spring." It was not a fair tally of Buffalo's resources. There also were several hundred cabins, a courthouse, post office, several stores, and as many taverns. Most important, perhaps, was the new harbor with its fine breakwater made up of large stone blocks. Not noticeable to the eye was that the mouth of Buffalo Creek had been newly dredged and now was ready to receive large boats that previously could not have ventured into its waters.

It is from Buffalo Creek that Buffalo derives its name. There was an abortive attempt to call the settlement New Amsterdam, but it didn't take. Buffalo somehow had a better sound to the people who settled there, even though there were no buffaloes that anybody knew of in the vicinity. How Buffalo Creek got its name is a matter for speculation.

The name of the town nevertheless made a deep impression on people back East. It was a suitable name for the remote western town that had been reserved for fur trappers, soldiers, and Indians until the building of the canal and its land counterpart, the Genesee Road. The population of Buffalo in 1825 was 2,412, not counting the frontier transients and the Indian onlookers. The original business section was along that part of Main Street that today would be measured from Exchange Street to Court Street. In this area in which the city began, interestingly enough, is the center of the modern, new Buffalo as the downtown district moves through the painful stages of urban renewal.

Where the original Erie Canal began, between Main and Pearl streets downtown, today stands the city's Memorial Auditorium. The site is a modern-day hub where the Niagara section of the New York State Thruway turns, crosses under, and connects with the Buffalo Skyway. After 150 years of change, it is still a vital crossroads of transportation.

The writers of western fiction and the makers of western movies, in choosing to go with geography rather than history, have managed to overlook in Buffalo perhaps the most exciting western outpost of the early days of the country. It was a city that came into existence almost overnight, the result of a sudden convergence on the strategic lakeside site of thousands of restless, seeking, daring people—the first great wave of humanity to flood westward through the Mohawk Valley and to pour into the new jumping-off place for the interior.

The immediate effect not only was a frontier city pulsing with growth, but a town genuinely deserving the label of "wild and woolly." Social turbulence is always an inevitability under the conditions of boom-town explosion, but the free, unrestrained behavior of the people who streamed into and through Buffalo in the hectic years of the nineteenth century was something special.

The tip-off on what the town would be like came early. A good pari-mutuel expert, viewing the exciting evidence of the year 1825, would have laid overwhelming odds in favor of Buffalo developing into one of the world's most interesting cities. While the major happening of that year was the opening of the Erie Canal, there were other events of interest—including, certainly, the arrest of the Thayer boys.

The three Thayers—Nelson, Israel, and Isaac—were prime prospects for trouble on anyone's frontier. In a day when religion counted especially heavily in the lives of people, the Thayers were not only loudly irreverent, vulgar, and shockingly disrespectful, they were downright profane. When they rode into town from their farm, proper Christian women covered their children's heads with their aprons and ran for a soundproof shelter.

The Thayers, it seems, had a habit of calling loudly to their oxen as they drove down the street. This, in itself, was not an unreasonable or un-American thing to do. Oxen have to be spoken to. The trouble was that the Thayers had named their oxen "God Almighty" and "Jesus Christ." Their loud demands for renewed effort by the plodding oxen took on a highly unusual coloration when the names were woven into the blistering language.

Even so, when the Thayers were arrested, it wasn't for profanity. A farmer named John Love, a miserly neighbor of the Thayers, had disappeared from sight, and the brothers (their father, too) were suspected of having done in the neighbor. Circumstances led the authorities in a logical line to the Thayer door. It was a well-known fact that they had not gotten along with Farmer Love, to whom they owed money. It also was known that in recent weeks they had begun badgering others who were in the farmer's debt, claiming that Love had given them power of attorney to collect money owed him while he was away on a trip.

It was an unlikely story. It made the authorities even more uncomfortable when the impoverished Thayers began spending money with a free hand. The sheriff, Wray S. Littlefield, decided to bring one of the Thayers into custody for questioning. He chose to arrest the youngest of the brothers, the one named Isaac.

After the lengthy questioning of Isaac in the old stone jail on Washington Street by Sheriff Littlefield and District Attorney Heman B. Potter had failed to yield any new information, the authorities and the people in the village of Buffalo began to search the Love farm. They soon found the old man's corpse in a shallow grave covered by a pile of freshly cut brush.

The three Thayers were found guilty of murder in a trial that began in the old courthouse at Washington and Clinton streets on April 21 and lasted only three days. The court sentenced them to be hanged on June 17. Justice on the frontier did not dally.

The brothers took their conviction in stride. They seemed to understand that it was all part of the losing game of life, and instead of being resentful, their attitude was almost one of good-natured relief. Once all the formalities and uncertainties of the courtroom were behind them, they got positively garrulous about the crime and all its details. They spoke of the victim, Love, in words that verged on admiration. They especially marveled over what a tough old bird he had been, and they certainly had good reason to pay him that minimal compliment. They first had shot the elderly farmer in their murder attempt, and when the bullets failed to down him, they shot him again and again. In the end, they were forced to deliver the *coup de grâce* with an ax. Love's power to survive evil was never more forcefully demonstrated.

One historian has written that forty thousand spectators turned out for the triple hanging from a gallows erected in a vacant lot in the center of town. The figure has to be regarded skeptically, but there is no doubt that this must have been one of the most congenial mass executions ever to be staged on the frontier.

The day's program began with a parade that led from the little jail to the gallows several streets away. The leader of the procession was Sheriff Littlefield, who held high a symbolic sword of justice as he marched. Behind him were his deputies, militia companies, and, of course, the three Thayers. The doomed men were dressed in black shrouds and wore white caps, and behind them in the procession were three carts, each carrying a coffin. Bringing up the rear was a military band that manfully tootled over the entire route to the delight of the spectators and all the little boys and girls who kept running in and out of the parade ranks.

When the processional finally reached the scene of action, the Thayers moved around in the crowd, shaking hands and saying good-by to all their friends. They even exchanged handshakes with the sheriff and other representatives of the law. Two ministers, the Reverend Mr. Fillmore and the Reverend Mr. Story, prayed aloud for the souls of the convicted men. Then, at 2:15 that sunny afternoon, Sheriff Littlefield used his great sword to cut the rope that sprang the traps, sending the three Thayer brothers to their death. After a half hour of dangling in the afternoon sun, their bodies were cut down and the crowd silently dispersed. All the gaiety was gone.

Another strange occurrence in Buffalo that year had to do with the selection of Grand Island in the Niagara River as the site of a homeland refuge for Jews. It was a bizarre, utopian venture, a piece of idealism that was destined to die, still-born, even as it was being celebrated.

The leader of the movement to colonize Grand Island with Jewish refugees was a Major Mordecai Manuel Noah, who had induced a Gentile friend named Samuel Leggett to purchase two tracts of island land totaling 1,775 acres as the site of a Jewish city. Its name was to be Ararat, after the mountain peak in Turkey on which Noah's ark supposedly came to rest.

Major Noah arrived in Buffalo in August 1825. He brought with him a sandstone cornerstone from a Cleveland quarry into which had been chiseled the words ARARAT, A CITY OF REFUGE FOR THE JEWS. Plans to lay the cornerstone on the actual site on Grand Island were abandoned because the Buffalonians had shown such enthusiasm for participating in the formal ceremony that not enough boats were available to carry everyone across the river. Instead, the ceremony was transferred to St. Paul's Episcopal Church in Buffalo itself.

It was a grand ceremony in a year filled with grand ceremonies. Every notable in town was on hand, every organization was represented, as the Reverend Addison Searle, rector of the Episcopal church, gave the keynote address. The church choir sang "Before Jehovah's Awful Throne" to the tune of "Old Hundred," and after a few prayers and the reading of the Bible in English and Hebrew, Major Noah gave the inaugural address. In it he outlined the purpose of the American Ararat and told of his plans for the development of the island refuge. Afterward the guests were treated to a banquet in the Eagle Tavern.

That was the peak of the Ararat movement. From then on, it raced downhill and finally dwindled away. Major Noah's idealistic scheme somehow failed to elicit any support among Jewish leaders in the New World. He tried desperately to win the backing of Jews in New York City, but was criticized instead for presuming to follow in the footsteps of the earlier Noah, even for trying to play the role of Moses in leading his people through the wilderness and across the river to safety.

The Ararat cornerstone was propped against the foundation wall of St. Paul's Church for a long time, finally being removed to the lawn of General Peter Porter's home in Black Rock where it was exhibited for a long time as a curiosity piece. A prominent Buffalo civic leader, Lewis F. Allen, then thoughtfully set the traveling tablet in a kind of shrine at Whitehaven on Grand Island. It was moved again, later, to a farm on the island, and then to a site at Sheenwater on the West River where, presumably, Ararat was to have been built. Its travels ended when it finally was placed in the museum of the Buffalo Historical Society where it is today.

Buffalo logically became the exchange-and-transfer center for the movement of people and freight between the Great Lakes and the Atlantic seaboard. Lake ships unloaded their cargoes in Buffalo for eastward shipment via the Erie Canal, while freight and people from the canalboats were filling the ships of the lake fleet.

The meeting of the two antagonistic forces, the lake sailors and the canallers, made Buffalo something of a natural battleground, although open conflict was restricted generally to what was called the "Canal District." That was a relatively small area bordered by lower Main Street, the Terrace, Erie Street, and the harbor. Through the center of the area ran the canal itself. A few hundred feet from the canal, on the harbor side, was Canal Street, once described as "two tough and torrid miles of trouble." The heart of the Canal District was called "Five Points."

Running parallel to the canal from Commercial Street to Erie Street, the principal thoroughfare of the district was Canal Street. Frequent changes in the name of the street failed either to change its character or to conceal its history. In the beginning, when it first was laid out in 1829, it was called Rock Street. That was changed shortly to Cross Street. In 1854 it took the name of Canal Street and held to that identification until the present century when, caught up in a reform wave, it became known as Dante Place in 1919. It continued to be called that until it was wiped out entirely by the changing city.

It was Canal Street when it was at the zenith—or nadir—of riotous behavior that won for it the distinction of being "the wickedest street in the world"—in a world, mind you, that abounded in wicked streets. It is no surprise, really, that Buffalo's international reputation put it in the select company of seamen's recreational centers like the Barbary Coast and the ports of Calcutta and Shanghai.

Some conscientious onlooker thought to count the number of saloons on Canal Street alone during the heyday of the avenue, sometime during the 1860s, and came up with the rewarding total of ninety-three. The figure, admittedly impressive, still did not tell the full story. There also were fifteen dance halls, with hundreds of girls in their employ, and there were any number of "sporting houses" that operated openly—nobody thought to count them.

In all the establishments of the canal district, in fact, women were in plentiful supply. Their presence was one of the major attractions from the very beginning. An English observer, one Thomas S. Woodcock, who traveled to Buffalo by canal in 1835, gave special attention to Canal Street (then Cross Street) in his book of travel recollections. He described it as "a corrupt place, with its denizens in a melancholy state morally."

One of the leading denizens was a woman known to one and all as Mother Carey. She was characterized by one of her numerous admirers as "a thrifty, unprincipled woman." Such a summation was no small compliment in the Five Points neighborhood of the time. Mother Carey's establishment was a sort of triple-threat combination that included a saloon, a dance hall, and, to put it delicately, a boardinghouse. Mother Carey's chickens were very popular with canallers and sailors alike. One of her diverse services was providing an employment agency through which lonely captains of canal barges could hire "cooks."

It was nothing short of amazing what a man could hire in the way of female talent in the canal district. The area directories were choked with the names of women who were available for hire, as many as 500 of them, under such classifications as cooks, laundresses, seamstresses, fortune tellers, and maids.

"On Maiden Lane, and in all the bars," wrote a reporter, "a lonely seaman or canaller had no problem finding a companion. It was sometimes harder, in fact, to keep them away.

"Dusk in the district was a magic time. It was then that it began to come alive, and it would live a whole lifetime in the following hours till dawn.

"The women of the district, their hair high on their heads and covered with wide-brimmed, feathery hats, were among the first to saunter onto Canal Street after dark, the rich colors of the velvet and lace dresses mixing with the golden glow of the street lamps.

"Seamen from the Lakes added the strength of their numbers to the canalers in the saloons—and pitted the strength of their muscles against them in the dusty street.

"The laughing, shouting mass moved along Canal Street, a portion of them pouring off into Maiden Lane, or Erie Street, moving from one bar to another, from dance hall to dance hall, and back to the saloons again . . ."

It was, without question, an evil, dangerous neighborhood when measured by the standards of a polite, moral society, but it also was an exciting, interesting district—one in which characters abounded, as might have been expected. Mother Carey and her girls did not stand alone. There were picturesque contemporaries all around the district: Pug Nose Cora, Choppy Fix, Frosty Face Carrington, Fisty McCue, Gallow Mag Moore, Soapy Kate Mills, and Mickey the Clam Man. Mickey, by the way, came by his name honestly; he sold clams.

Some of the saloons that backed up to the canal had especially sinister reputations among the roistering regulars. It was said that their unscrupulous operators, as a regular practice, would drug a visitor's drinks, rob him of whatever money and valuables he carried, and then drop his unconscious body through a trap door into the murky waters of the canal. It was not uncommon for bodies to be found floating in the canal at daybreak, and more often than not they bore marks of violence.

The city went through the formality of assigning police constables called "watchmen" to the canal badlands, although that move was not entirely in the interests of strict law enforcement. Civic authorities in the wild West took the reasonable view that drinking, gambling, cockfighting, prostitution, and assorted depravities were bound to assert themselves somewhere in the port, human nature being the imperfect thing it is, and they preferred that all forms of vice be kept corralled within the boundaries of a specific area so as not to contaminate the polite and innocent society of the city. For many years, the constables assigned to the district stood mainly as a reminder of the larger authority that watched on the perimeter of the sinful circle.

Not all of the policemen, incidentally, were content to play the passive role entirely. The February 6, 1863, issue of the Buffalo *Commercial-Advertiser* carried the following story of a Saturday night caper involving two of Buffalo's finest:

"Two city constables became guilty of the most outrageous conduct toward several females they met in Washington Street.

"The valiant bacchanalians waited in the shadows opposite Bonney's Hotel, and when a particularly decorous, hoop-skirted young lady came along, they pounced on her and dragged her through the street by the heels as if she was a wheelbarrow. Two of the victims were married women and they caused the arrest of the roisterers, who paid heavy fines for their drollery."

The canal district also paid a price for its wide-open, anything-goes atmosphere. Every night the city's constabulary would select wrongdoers at random, not with ill nature, and take them into court to be fined. The best known of the police justices who heard the cases was Daniel D. Bidwell, who, it was reported, received a salary of $2,000 a year, or $400 more than the mayor. The courtroom in which he heard everything from murder cases to petty thievery and the staging of cockfights was in the stockaded jail, the present site of the Buffalo Public Library.

In a day when entertainment usually took the form of an evangelist's frothy prediction of doomsday, a lecturer's florid description of his trip to the Dardanelles, or the solo performance of a bosomy soprano, men were sometimes hard put for exciting, competitive spectacles. They frequently found an outlet for that craving and the gaming opportunities that always accompany physical sports in cockfights. It was a sport, or spectacle, that enjoyed enormous popularity in the frontier settlements of early America. Genteel members of society liked to refer to cockfights as "chicken disputes." The euphemism didn't make them any less illegal, though.

A reporter for the Buffalo *Express,* in a story on April 4, 1860, noted that: "A great international chicken-dispute has been in progress at Black Rock for two days, and the occasion has called together a large number of roughs of the vilest description: Gamblers, shoulder-hitters, and all grades of blacklegs have assembled to witness the show."

Other popular divertisements among sports fans in Buffalo included races between cockroaches, grasshoppers, bedbugs, frogs, caterpillars, and dogs—in fact, almost anything that moved. It didn't matter if the animals or insects were unwilling to stage an exhibition; men found a way to make them fight, or race, or whatever.

The cruelty of the day, and the practice thereof, is illustrated in an account that revealed that in order to get a pair of bulldogs fighting mad and angry enough to want to tear each other apart, promoters of a fight would sandpaper the haunches of the dogs until they were raw.

Fight exhibitions between men usually were brutal affairs too, and if personal feelings happened to run deep or if an old feud were involved, the fight sometimes would be to the finish. It was not without reason that boxing "exhibitions" fell into social disfavor and the sport came to be outlawed. Fighting was not confined entirely to men, either. Once in a while the women got into the act, as the following story from a Buffalo newspaper verifies:

Two young women from Canal Street were brought up for fighting. Officer Harris found them in the cellar of one of the vile dens of that street, engaged in fierce combat within a ring formed by a crowd of beastly, brutal spectators of both sexes who incited the rage of the poor degraded girls against each other by heartless cheers and jibes. It seems they had been taunted by their worst associates into testing their physical prowess against each other in a deliberately planned encounter, and were in the midst of it when the officer got wind of it and made a descent upon them. He brought the two combatants into court and they received immediate trial.

As its reputation as one of the world's wickedest places steadily expanded, it was inevitable that Buffalo would receive a large number of visitors drawn primarily by the prospect of being close to evil rampant. Sin is always the spicy lure.

It would be a mistake to believe that the fun and games were restricted entirely to Buffalo's canal district. They could be found elsewhere, but not in the concentration and openness of the Five Points. Not far away, in the river port of Tonawanda, there was a kind of suburban Gomorrah to Buffalo's Sodom. What it was like in Tonawanda, which became one of the world's leading lumber centers by the 1880s, is suggested by a random recollection written for the Historical Society of the Tonawandas by a canaller named Richard G. Garrity:

"On arriving at Tonawanda, if a boatman inquired for a cook, he was usually told to look up 'Old Black Nell.' Nell was not a Negro, but was very dark complexioned. She could usually be found keeping house for some of the painted ladies on Goose Island. Old she might have been, but was still not beyond bestowing her favors on any old gentleman who happened to seek her out while housekeeping. If the boatman was desperate, she was hired.

"I believe Nell was a good enough cook, and being of a generous nature, well past the age of innocence, she did not care who shared the cabin with her. As a rule, she lasted for only one round trip, for, on returning to Tonawanda, she would draw some of her wages and go ashore to visit. On returning from her visit, she would be drunk as Satan and having a bottle of whiskey with her, she would not bother about getting any meals. A big argument would then ensue and she would get fired. Nell was quite a peppery and noisey old dame when full of whiskey.

"I once saw 'Old Black Nell' passing George Huber's store on North Niagara Street after being fired from her cook's job. She was hanging on to her hat, which was cocked to one side of her head, her long black sateen skirt dragging on the sidewalk, and her suitcase partly shut with some of her clothing dangling from it. She was looking back, mumbling and cursing about the unappreciative qualities of the boatman who had fired her. I don't know which disappeared from the local scene first, the Erie Canal boats or 'Old Black Nell.' . . ."

Perhaps Old Black Nell was the cook the canallers had in mind when they sang the following choruses of that favorite ballad "The Erie Canal":

> We were forty miles from Albany,
> Forget it I never shall,
> What a terrible storm we had one night
> On the Erie Canal.

(*chorus*)
> Oh, the E-ri-e was a-rising,
> And the gin was a-getting low,
> And I scarcely think we'll get a drink
> Till we get to Buffalo,
> Till we get to Buff-a-low.

> Well, the captain he comes up on deck
> With a spyglass in his hand
> And the fog it was so 'tarnal thick,
> That he could not spy the land.
> (Oh, the E-ri-e was a-rising, etc.)

> The cook she was a grand old gal,
> She wore a ragged dress,
> We hoisted her upon a pole,
> As a signal of distress.
> (Oh, the E-ri-e was a-rising, etc.)

> Well, the captain he got married,
> And the cook she went to jail.
> And I'm the only son-of-a-gun,
> That's left to tell the tale.
> (Oh, the E-ri-e was a-rising, etc.)

It seemed as though wickedness was in its most spectacular ascendancy during the years from 1825 through the 1850s, the years when the Erie Canal was the unchallenged lifeline between East and West. The railroads were in the process of emerging as the great new force in travel and transportation through much of that time, but the strength of the Erie was such that even the considerable growth of the rail service during those three decades did not diminish canal traffic. Whatever the Erie lost to the passenger trains, it more than made up in its increased freight tonnage. Even so, train passengers and crews found Buffalo to be a most interesting overnight stop before they proceeded farther West.

While sin indubitably was the principal product of Canal Street, there were by-products, too. For instance, the inhibition-free atmosphere of the district and the free spending tradition were ideal for the development of entertainment and the showcasing of talent, just as Las Vegas is today. Out of the gaiety of the Five Points emerged the new form of show business entertainment, the minstrel show—musical comedy in blackface, featuring singing and gags. It was a distinct departure from the stereotyped form of stage entertainment that prevailed in its time —the moralistic dramas, the reedy tenors, and the hambone school of elocution. It had a brightness, a looseness, and an unconventionality that were entirely at home in the canal district setting, where a lively today was of more concern than a grim tomorrow.

The minstrel show actually had its origin in many places and the South has a strong claim to it, but it does appear to have evolved into its final form in Buffalo. It was here that it took the shape and substance that made it an American institution until the end of the nineteenth century. Its prime mover and chief architect was a former Philadelphian named Edwin P. Christy, who moved to Buffalo to take his chances in the rough Canal Street district in 1839.

The world remembers this remarkable entertainer as Ned Christy. He was a musician of many talents—a singer, a banjo player, a dancer. He also was a sleight-of-hand artist, and in this area he was said to excel. But whatever talent he chose to employ in the theaters, saloons, or dance halls, he usually used the burnt cork for a blackface effect.

Competition among entertainers in the district was keen, and humiliation, if not physical injury, sometimes was the pay-off if the audience didn't approve of a particular performance—it was not a place that drew effete audiences. But there is an ego that buoys every entertainer, even in the face of physical retribution. It is a matter, more likely, of confidence than courage, but whatever it is, Ned Christy needed it when he volunteered to entertain, for a price, the customers in one of the better-known joints in the district—a place called Mrs. Harrington's Dance Hall. Perhaps the establishment had a more formal name, but that was what everybody called the place.

The impression has been passed along that this dance hall, which in fact was a sort of cabaret, was a formidable place, but it could not have been more formidable than Mrs. Harrington herself. She was from Palmyra, where apparently formidable individuals clogged the streets. When her husband died, she packed up her belongings, including her small son, George, and moved to the Buffalo waterfront to make a living. Eventually, through luck and pluck and a fine disregard for the niceties

so admired by the outside world, Mrs. Harrington came to be the proprietor of a leading dance hall. In this position, she came to be a keen judge
of entertainment, at least to the extent of knowing what her customers
liked. When Ned Christy came along and did his blackface song-and-
dance routine, interspersed with some reasonably competent sleight-of-
hand and a few banjo solos, Mrs. Harrington liked what she saw. Christy
became a regular performer in her dance hall.

The more Christy performed after that, the more Mrs. Harrington liked
what she saw, and it wasn't long at all until they were married. Young
George Harrington, who was then about twelve years old, heartily approved of the merger because he had become Ned Christy's most admiring fan. It was a mutual admiration society of a sort because Christy, for
his part, thought highly of the boy. He must have been tremendously
pleased when the lad voluntarily changed his name to George N.
Christy.

Christy, meanwhile, had been teaching his stepson how to dance jigs,
how to sing, how to play the banjo, and how to do all the little
stage tricks that he had acquired the hard way. The two became a team
and the dance hall patrons loved them. In time they added another jig
dancer, Lansing Durand, and another banjoist, Tom Vaughn, and the show
was better than ever. It wasn't long before a versatile performer named
William Porter was added to the cast and then an Irish fiddler named
Richard M. Hooley.

That was the nucleus out of which grew the famous Christy Minstrels,
whose product was a combination of comedy and music in blackface that
won feet-stomping, whistling approval from the tough Canal Street
crowds. It was rollicking, bouncing music, perfectly in accord with the
tempo of the times, and the broad jokes caught the homespun spirit of
the frontier people.

Perhaps the most popular of the songs sung by the Christy Minstrels
was "Buffalo Gals," given here in one of its several versions. It became a
standard favorite in the early years and is still performed and enjoyed
today:

> As I was lum'ring down de street,
>   Down de street,
>   Down de street,
> A handsome gal I chanc'd to meet;
>   Oh! She was fair to view.

(*chorus*) Buffalo gals, can't you come out tonight?
>   Can't you come out tonight?
>   Can't you come out tonight?
> Buffalo gals, can't you come out tonight?
>   And dance by de light ob de moon?

266

I ax'd her would she hab some talk,
   Hab some talk,
   Hab some talk,
Her feet covered up de whole sidewalk
   As she stood close to me.
     (Buffalo gals, can't you come out tonight? etc.)

I ax'd her would she hab a dance,
   Hab a dance,
   Hab a dance,
I taught dat I might get a chance
   To shake a foot wid her.
     (Buffalo gals, can't you come out tonight? etc.)

I'd like to make that gal my wife,
   Gal my wife,
   Gal my wife,
I'd be happy all my life,
   If I had her by me.
     (Buffalo gals, can't you come out tonight? etc.)

The Christy Minstrels offered far too much entertainment to remain corked up in the canal district. Word of the company's talent and its novel combination of entertainment brought them numerous offers from theaters in more respectable parts of town. In time, Christy took the group to some theaters in the Niagara Frontier country from which he would not have far to retreat to safety if the outside public did not approve of his brand of show business. They were tentative steps, but successful ones. Each performance seemed to add something to the company's routine. One technique after another was adopted, innovation after innovation was tested and tried, some to be accepted and others to be rejected. It was a time of improvisation and experimentation as Christy gradually worked out the full formula for his unique form of entertainment. What evolved, finally, was the form of minstrel show that caught the country's fancy, complete with interlocutor, bones, and men, and specialty acts, all borrowed heavily and unabashedly from the Negro culture.

The troupe's first formal appearance in Buffalo was in the Eagle Street Theater, and the reaction of the usually restrained audience was nothing less than sensational. The patrons plainly were aware that they were seeing something novel and good on the stage and they made their approval heard.

Word of the exciting innovation was quick to reach New York City, and the minstrel show soon was on its way to Broadway, where it opened in Palmo's Opera House on April 27, 1846. The reception there was just as hearty as it had been at Mrs. Harrington's Dance Hall and at the Eagle Theater back home. No doubt the public had become weary of the stuffiness, the formality, and the gloom of the theater, and here was a troupe that came dancing out of the glamorous West, directly from the country's leading sin city, rattling its tambourines and singing, laughing, clogging and joking, just as if the world truly were a merry place to live in.

New York audiences were carried away by the sheer fun and exuberance of the Christy minstrel show. They loved the way its jokes poked fun at staid, stiff institutions and pompous politicians. They loved the insouciance that ruled the minstrel stage. And here, also, was a new kind of music—a forerunner of the jazz music that was to win America—with its own infectious rhythm and memorable melodies. One of the songs that the Buffalo minstrels helped to launch and promote to national popularity was Stephen Foster's "Oh! Susanna!" Even though the song was not copyrighted until 1848, the Christy troupe somehow obtained a copy of it from Foster about 1844, during their second year of existence. It won instant favor on the Canal Street waterfront as it did later in New York City and elsewhere. Through the years it has retained its identification with the minstrel-type of entertainment. Its self-contained gaiety somehow seemed to typify the new mode of entertainment that emerged in the midway years of the nineteenth century.

After a long run in the opera house, the Christy Minstrels moved to Mechanics' Hall for another long run. Altogether, during the next six years, the troupe played some 2,500 performances in New York City. In that time, it probably became the most famous, most admired group of entertainers in America. Their fame spread to Europe as well, and they traveled to England for a triumphant, sell-out season in a London music hall.

Songwriters from everywhere naturally sought out Ned Christy and pleaded with him to play their tunes. If the Christy Minstrels sang a song, its success was virtually assured. Christy, never one to overlook a possibility, listened to a lot of music brought in to him by amateurs and professionals. Once in a while he heard something that he liked, as he did when a song called "The Old Folks at Home" was played for him. The young composer, Stephen Foster, gave Christy all rights to use and publish the song, including the claim of authorship, in return for payment of fifty dollars. It wasn't until years later, after Christy had realized a small fortune from the song, that the public finally learned that Foster, not Christy, was the composer.

Christy, without question, was a sharp businessman. He made a lot of money out of the minstrel show he had created. It was a happy formula, and for a long time a happy troupe. Sometime late in the brilliant run in New York City, however, Ned's stepson George Christy deserted the show and, with Henry Wood, organized a competing minstrel company under the name of Christy & Wood. It, too, was a most successful enterprise, although it brought about a confusion of Christys in the public mind. The demand for good minstrelsy was so strong, though, that there was more than enough business to go around.

Ned Christy retired from show business in 1854, a wealthy man. Sadly enough, the former song-and-dance man became a sort of recluse after he left the theater. It was said that he became obsessed with the fear of poverty, even though he owned a substantial fortune. One day in 1862, finally, the man who had made so many people happy with his contribution to show business fell to his death from an upper window of his New York residence. Nobody ever knew for sure whether he had fallen accidentally or had leaped. Only six years later, in 1868, George Christy also died.

Through them, Canal Street in Buffalo had given the world something bright and gay, even if it was spawned in a sinful atmosphere.

CHAPTER XXX

BUFFALO'S PRESIDENT

Three American Presidents became part of Buffalo's history. To one the city brought fulfillment. To another, deep disappointment. To the third, death.

The first of these men of destiny was Millard Fillmore, a far more interesting man than the history books have made him out to be. He was twenty-two years old in 1822 when his father moved the Fillmore family from Cayuga County to the township of East Aurora in western New York.

The Fillmores, father and son, had one thing in common at the time of the move: Each was a failure. The father had failed as a farmer; Millard had failed in his initial attempt to become a lawyer—although he had managed to become a teacher.

Buffalo, already booming in anticipation of the Erie Canal, which had inched its way westward across the state until it then was a mere eighteen miles away, was a town made to order for an ambitious young man in search of employment. Young Millard had no difficulty landing a teaching job.

Four years had passed since Fillmore had last seen Buffalo, in May 1818, and great changes had taken place in the interim, both in the town and in the man. As a youth of seventeen, he had walked 140 miles from the Finger Lakes region to see what the westernmost part of the state looked like. Buffalo at that time had not begun to feel the uplifting effect of the canal project, nor had it yet recovered from the punishment it had received in the War of 1812. The town presented to Fillmore "a straggling appearance."

"It was just rising from the ashes," he wrote, "and there were many cellars and chimneys without houses, showing that its destruction by the British had been complete."

After his long walk, mostly through undeveloped frontier country, Fillmore understandably was in no mood to be elated over the dreary ruins that greeted his eyes.

"My feet had become blistered, and I was sore in every joint and muscle; and I suffered intensely," he wrote. "I crossed the . . . Indian reservation to Aurora, and recollect a long rotten causeway of logs extending across the low ground from Seneca Street nearly to the creek over which I paddled myself in a canoe. I staid [sic] all night at a kind of Indian Tavern about six miles from Buffalo . . . A number of drunken Indians and white men kept up a row during most of the night. Next day I went through the woods alone to . . . Wales."

The Buffalo of four years later was a much more pleasing sight. The marks of military defeat had been all but erased and now the town was bustling with activity. Even a stranger could see that something big was in the making on the shore of Lake Erie. Houses and stores and warehouses were under construction on streets that hadn't existed the year before. The sound of the hammer and the rasp of the saw were everywhere to be heard. And out on the water was a flotilla of barges carrying large stones, freshly quarried, to add to the breakwater that was being built to protect the harbor. There were boatyards coming into being that soon would be manufacturing packets and freighters for the canal abuilding, and close by there were crews excavating the basins to accommodate the canalboats when they finally reached Erie's water.

That was Buffalo in 1822, and the sight smote Millard Fillmore with great force. "All his life," wrote a biographer, Robert J. Rayback, "he had rubbed shoulders with farmers and farmers' sons, and the sight of merchants, stage owners, hotel keepers, lake captains, and canal workers gave him a new outlook on life. Unlike sophisticated travelers from abroad who visited the growing West and complained about its uncouth, boisterous, mad scramble for wealth, Fillmore avidly absorbed the town's atmosphere and tried to become a part of it."

Fillmore enjoyed the role of teacher, but he still hung on to the ambition to become a lawyer. In the summer of 1822, he was hired as a clerk in the law firm of Asa Rice and Joseph Clary and began his studies under the tutelage of the partners. They were said to have been impressed by the serious, physically attractive young man. In this they were not alone. Fillmore made a lasting impression on most of the people that he met in Buffalo. Nobody there was really surprised when he was admitted to the practice of law in 1823, record time for the legal track.

After opening a law office in East Aurora, he quickly became the town's leading citizen. By 1826, already beginning to distinguish himself at the bar, he was preparing for admission to higher court practice when the advance winds growing out of the "Morgan affair" blew westward from Canandaigua, upsetting the political balance of western New York as it traveled from one county to the next.

William Morgan's kidnaping and disappearance after he had threatened to reveal the inner secrets of Freemasonry involved so many law officers and civic officials between Canandaigua and Niagara that there was political chaos. The immediate effect of the scandal was to arouse an anti-Masonic movement that became politically strong, especially in western New York, the setting of the sensational affair.

Public officials who belonged to the secret society were automatically suspect and were marked for political purging by aroused reformers. It was in this turbulent setting in 1827 that young Fillmore, sensing opportunity, took his place in the ranks of Freemasonry's foes. His timing was good as he managed to ride the crest of the short-lived movement into the State Assembly where he distinguished himself by sponsoring the law that abolished the jail penalty for persons who defaulted on their debts. That singularly enlightened and humane piece of legislation made Fillmore a state celebrity and virtually assured his nomination and election to the United States Congress shortly thereafter, in 1832.

Two years before that important development, in 1830, Millard Fillmore had moved his young family to Buffalo, to a six-room frame house just two blocks from Main Street, at 114 Franklin Street (now 180 Franklin Street). Less than a mile south of his home was the place called "the Dock," on the right bank of Buffalo Creek. The Dock was a wharfed and platformed area, a center of shipping activity, extending a thousand yards inland from the mouth of the creek which itself had been dredged to a depth of eight feet and widened to a hundred feet. The Erie Canal entered this artificial harbor at right angles and drew from it the waters of Lake Erie.

The Fillmore house was on land that looked down at this harbor junction of canal and river. Beyond it were visible tall masts of the lake ships at anchor in the outer harbor, beyond the screen of forest that still stood between Buffalo and the lake. Whatever the Fillmores could not see of the great activity at the western terminal of the Erie Canal, they must have been able to hear. It was business around the clock at the docks as the canalboats surrendered their passengers and freight and prepared to take on different passengers and new cargoes for the eastward journey.

Buffalo was a town in tumult, accepting new population faster than it could absorb it, outracing itself in every department of growth, and still falling far short of its needs.

When Buffalo became an incorporated city in 1832, it was Millard Fillmore who was instrumental in drawing up the city charter. When Buffalo sought enlargement of the canal's terminal facilities by the state, it was Fillmore who pressured the canal commission into acting on the requests. When Buffalo went after improvement and enlargement of the

273

lake harbor by the federal government, it was Representative Fillmore
who led the fight.

There was no question about the growing stature of the young con-
gressman in his adopted city, but as the anti-Masonic movement that he
had ridden so successfully began to lose its momentum, it appeared that
he was in danger of becoming a politician without a party—a very awkward condition for a man with ambitions. But Fillmore was equal to the
emergency. Like other members of the moribund movement, he adroitly
disengaged himself and cast his lot with the rising Whig party. Under
their label, he ran for governor of New York in 1843 but suffered the first
defeat of his career. He took it hard, agonizing loud enough for others to
hear: "All is gone—but honor!"

When the sun rose the next day, he must have changed his mind about
the hopelessness of life because he soon was back in the thick of things
political, even winning an important state post, that of comptroller. It
was a job so powerful that the man who filled it automatically was called
a "one-man government." In this position Fillmore proved a friend of the
Erie Canal by supporting expansion measures then current. He also saw
to it that Buffalo benefited from state projects, one of which called for
the enlargement of the canal basin in Buffalo.

It was while he was in the relative obscurity of this state post that
Fillmore—thanks to the influence of Governor Hamilton Fish of New
York—was singled out by the Whig Convention of 1848 to become the
running mate of Zachary Taylor on the national party ticket. It turned
out to be the winning ticket, of course, and Fillmore, the one-time farm
boy from the Finger Lakes district of New York, suddenly found himself
the Vice-President of the United States. Even more suddenly, sixteen
months later, on July 9, 1850, Fillmore assumed the presidency as
President Taylor succumbed to a violent stomach disorder following an
attack of heat prostration.

Buffalo and all of western New York State rejoiced and called life
good. The wilderness had been subdued, the Erie Canal was in its most
glorious hour, and now a son of the upstate area was the first citizen of
the land.

Fillmore's accession to the presidency came at a critical hour in the
nation's history. The festering issue of slavery was coming to a head.
Loud, angry talk of war and secession already could be heard. Fillmore
took a conciliatory approach. As a professional politician, he knew the
need for give and take and threw his support behind the Compromise of
1850, using the presidential powers and patronage to bring Northern
Whigs into line.

The compromise staved off the war for the moment, but Fillmore's
endorsement of the measure so embittered influential members of his
own party that the Whig Convention of 1852 rejected the incumbent

President and chose General Winfield Scott as its nominee. (Scott lost to the Democratic nominee, Franklin Pierce.)

When President Fillmore left the White House, a rejected man, he at least took with him the affection of the American business community. Seldom has the highest office in the land been filled by a man so completely sympathetic to business. He was, in particular, a friend of the American railroads. He also was the great and good friend of the Erie Canal, but he probably did more to spur the railroad growth that eventually detracted from the canal's importance than any other President.

During that era of his political peak, railroads were just assuming an important role in the nation's economy. It was under President Fillmore that the policy of granting federal lands to subsidize railroad building was adopted, a most powerful stimulus to growth.

Fillmore tried a presidential comeback in 1856 as the candidate of the nativist, anti-foreign-born, anti-Catholic American, or Know-Nothing, party, running against James Buchanan and John C. Frémont, the nominees of the Democratic and Republican parties, respectively. The spectacle of the former President embracing such a tawdry program and struggling against such opposition for the nation's highest honor was nothing short of pathetic. Buchanan won an easy victory, polling twice as many votes as Fillmore, who won only one state—Maryland. Fillmore, while not surprised by his loss, admitted he was a "little mortified" at "being so unanimously rejected."

The awkward thing, really, was that even at that time, although he already was four years out of the White House, Fillmore still was only fifty-six years old. It is not easy for a former President of the United States to find a job that is consonant with his past background. Fillmore felt deeply about the situation. He thought the nation ought to provide its former Presidents with pensions that would allow them to live out their years with some dignity and comfort—say, $12,000 a year.

"It is a national disgrace," he wrote, "that our Presidents . . . should be cast adrift, and perhaps be compelled to keep a corner grocery for subsistence . . .

"We elect a man to the Presidency, expect him to be honest, to give up a lucrative profession, perhaps, and after we have done with him we let him go into seclusion and perhaps poverty."

In March 1853, at the inauguration of Fillmore's successor, President Franklin Pierce, a ceremony held on a chill, damp day in front of the Capitol, Mrs. Fillmore caught a cold that quickly turned into pneumonia. Three weeks after leaving the White House she was dead.

Five years later, in 1858, the former President married a fifty-two-year-old widow, Mrs. Caroline C. McIntosh. She was well-to-do, and the alliance brought Fillmore companionship and the means he so badly needed to live in the style befitting a former Chief Executive. His new

275

home in Buffalo, a great mansion on Niagara Square, became the center of Buffalo's social life.

When the Civil War began, Fillmore organized a company in the home guard. It was called the Union Continentals, and it was made up of retired officers of the militia, all over forty-five. The uniforms were colorful to the point, almost, of being comical. The commander of the company was none other than "Major" Fillmore, and when the Continentals marched, he was at the head of the column, "stately and erect . . . wearing a sword and plume and looking like an emperor."

The sight of the former Commander in Chief of the United States Armed Forces leading a pathetic handful of over-aged patriots through the downtown streets of Buffalo apparently did not impress anybody with its incongruity. Or it may be that those who were struck by the sad sight were too polite to say anything.

One of the things that bothered Fillmore in the crucial days of the war was the possible threat to the Erie Canal, which was playing a tremendous supply role between East and West. He feared especially that sabotage of the dam at Lockport would dry up the canal and render it useless. He tried repeatedly to get the federal government to enlarge the canal locks so that larger, more capacious barges and boats could use the waterway.

Fillmore, incidentally, had not done his reputation any good just before the war, in 1859, when he lent his name and sponsorship to the idea of a Buffalo inventor named Rollin Germain. It was Germain's plan to build an iron-hulled ship 1,000 feet long that would be capable of carrying 3,000 tons of freight and 3,000 passengers across the ocean at speeds up to fifty miles an hour!

The proposal dazzled Fillmore and many of his fellow Buffalonians—as indeed it should have. The idea would have been worthy of Jules Verne. Fillmore became chairman of a group organized to build the ship, and there was a great splurge of publicity linking him with the project and giving it considerable credibility. When the wild scheme collapsed three months later, Buffalo winced and the former President sputtered. It was embarrassing.

No doubt Buffalo forgave Fillmore his follies, just as it forgave him a controversial wartime speech in which he criticized the Lincoln administration and spoke of forgiving the South at war's end. Some called the speech treasonous and vandals smeared the Fillmore house with black ink. But Buffalo always knew that President Fillmore was the city's biggest booster and most loyal friend. Once, in a speech delivered to the Board of Trade, he predicted that Buffalo was "destined" by its position "to be what Alexandria and Venice were" to the world of their time.

"It is now more than fifty years since I first became an inhabitant of Buffalo," he noted. "I remember well that about 1825, when the Erie Canal was completed, the commercial advantages which Buffalo possessed gave a great impulse to our growth and prosperity, and it seemed . . . as though Buffalo was to be chiefly a commercial city. Buffalo had little available water power and Rochester had it in abundance, and she turned it to a very good account . . ."

But, added the former President, the introduction of cheap coal, an abundant mineral, as a source of power had restored the bright outlook for Buffalo.

"The busy hum of industry is heard on all sides, and the worshippers in this temple have laid upon its altars their choicest offerings for the admiration of the world . . . I see no reason why Buffalo should not become a great manufacturing city."

It would have pleased Fillmore to have seen this prediction come true—not so much through cheap coal, but through the harnessing of Niagara Falls.

Twenty-four years after he had succeeded to the presidency of the United States, Millard Fillmore died in his beloved Buffalo, a forgotten man in the national scheme of things long before he succumbed at the age of seventy-four. He was buried in Forest Lawn Cemetery under a simple obelisk. His grave marker carries the basic facts—his name, date of birth, and date of death. It does not go beyond those essentials, not even to hint at the mighty world role once filled by the man.

CHAPTER XXXI

BIG STEVE

October days in Buffalo usually are mellow and mild, but the nights can be very mean—as mean as they are sudden. As soon as the sun goes down, melting in its own red wake on Lake Erie, there is a chill that spreads across the land. Often it carries with it a light mist, sometimes a fog, but always an unfriendly dampness. On such a dank night, the air has the power to penetrate layers of clothing with ease.

The night of Saturday, October 11, 1881, was just such a night in all its bleak, cheerless aspects, and the five men who turned their steps from Commercial Street onto Pearl Street had the turned-up collars and the hurried walk of men with a warm, comfortable refuge clearly in mind. In this instance, their destination was already in sight, given away by the golden patch of light that slanted onto the flagstone sidewalk from the mullioned windows of Bill Drainger's Saloon at the corner of Eagle and Pearl streets. They turned into it with relief, reveling in the warm, yeasty air as they threw off their wraps and sat down at an oak table darkened by time and use. They called out their orders to the waiter even as they settled themselves.

Drainger's was one of many fine taverns in the Buffalo of that era, a congenial establishment known mainly for its excellent German cuisine and its hearty tankards of beer. Those are strong recommendations at any time, but they are virtually irresistible on a chill, damp night.

Counted among the steady patrons of Drainger's was an inordinate number of politicians and lawyers, the two being very closely related, as everybody knows. And the five men who settled themselves at the table on that fateful night in 1881 were leading representatives of both breeds; they were lawyers and politicians both. One thing about them, though, was especially notable. They were uncommonly quiet—you might even say dispirited and come closer to the mark. Partly their mood was due to the weather, but mostly it resulted from the arduous, fruitless day they had spent together.

The five men constituted a committee that had been duly authorized by the Democratic party in Buffalo to seek out a suitable candidate to run for mayor of the city on the party ticket in the forthcoming municipal election. All day long, under the leadership of Peter C. Doyle, county Democratic chairman, the committee had trudged from one prospect to another, holding out high before each the glittering prospect of the civic honor, but to no avail. The men who shaped up as mayoral possibilities were too bright to be deluded by optimistic talk. Buffalo was firmly in the grip of a bipartisan ring of thieves that was not about to allow its sticky fingers to be pried loose of City Hall—not easily, anyway. The Buffalo Ring, as it was called, was made up preponderantly of Republicans, but there was a nice realism in the set-up that allowed a number of Democrat aldermen—and most prominently John C. Sheehan, Democratic leader of the First Ward—to share in the spoils. In the face of this powerful political partnership, it would be folly, plainly, for any Democratic candidate for mayor to entertain hopes of success. That, in substance, was what each of the men interviewed that day had informed Doyle and his committee.

It was against such a background of failure, a sure setting for melancholy thoughts, that the committee had lapsed into moody silence. And it was just then that the outer door opened and the hulking figure of "Big Steve" Cleveland filled the entranceway. The sight of him was a tonic to the committee, which immediately revived and began thumping tankards on the table to draw the newcomer's attention.

Everybody in Buffalo knew Big Steve. Eleven years before, when he was but thirty-three years old, he had been elected sheriff of Erie County. His one term had not been without incident. He had uncovered graft and cheating inside the sheriff's department—for that matter, inside the jail itself—and even though he had chosen not to run for re-election, he had left the county office with the rare reputation of being an honest politician and a most unconventional individual—if that is not being tautological.

The committee at Drainger's Saloon welcomed Cleveland into their midst. He was a popular man. While he was notably lacking in personal political ambition, he was an industrious party worker. He attended party meetings regularly, accepted the meanest assignments handed down to him by the ward leader, and on election days he could always be found outside the precinct booth, handing out sample ballots to arriving voters. He was, in short, the type of party man that only a professional politician could appreciate fully.

Once Cleveland had been settled at their table and had been supplied with a tall stein of lager, Doyle told him in mournful tones of the unsuccessful day that the committee had spent in search of a mayoral candidate. He told of the polite refusals from the leading citizens who had been approached—men like Stephen C. Clarke, the banker, and Delevan T. Clarke; Stephen O. Barnum, the merchant, and Charles A. Sweet, another banker, and Charles G. Curtiss, the president of the Board of Trade.

As Doyle ticked off the failures of the dismal day, Cleveland leaned back in his chair and made little effort to conceal his smile. He found amusement in the picture of a political party pounding up and down the avenue in pursuit of a candidate.

Even as Cleveland listened, and occasionally chuckled, the members of the committee gradually were coming to look at him with a new interest. A common thought had struck home.

"I tell you," one of them said, "I think we've found our man."

The dialogue that ensued was described as spirited, but the committee was determined and was not about to be put off by any protestations of the popular ex-sheriff. After first refusing outright to allow his name to be entered in the mayoralty campaign, Cleveland, perhaps out of party loyalty, began to hedge. He listed conditions that would have to be met. He said he'd have to have the final say on his running mates on the party ticket. He said he would not follow the conventional campaigning system of speechmaking. The party committeemen looked at him blandly and agreed to the terms. They were not about to let their candidate off the hook.

It occurred to Cleveland then that he had been maneuvered into a position from which there was no retreat. He hastily summoned a number of new reasons why he would not be a desirable candidate, but the rebuttal was overwhelmingly in favor of his candidacy and at last he had no choice but to surrender.

"Waiter!" roared the delighted Doyle. "Another round! We're having a celebration!"

Three days later, on October 25, Stephen Grover Cleveland was officially nominated as the Democratic candidate for mayor by a city convention of the party. The platform, accepted without argument, was reform in the city government, and Cleveland for the first time publicly enunciated the principle that was to be the major theme of his campaign and his entire political career—that any man who is elected to public office must consider himself the beneficiary of a precious gift called "public trust." The public, he said, had a right to demand honesty in government.

What followed was one of the most interesting, most unconventional political campaigns in Buffalo history. Grover Cleveland, as he preferred to be known on the formal level, shrugged off invitations to speak in the politer circles of society and chose to attack the enemy in his own stronghold, the notorious First Ward in the waterfront area. It was John C. Sheehan's ward, and as far as Cleveland was concerned, Sheehan, while nominally a Democrat, was the real enemy because he not only had condoned dishonesty in City Hall, he had participated in the machinations of government that worked toward dishonest ends by consorting with the opposition party in power.

Cleveland did not like campaign speechmaking. His only concession in that direction was to try to visit as many of the hundreds of saloons in the waterfront area before the election as he could. In most of the taverns he took a prominent table, ordered a stein to wet his political pipes, and told the other drinking customers what was wrong at City Hall and how he proposed to right the wrongs. Sometimes, spurred by the clamor of customers at distant tables, he would climb to the top of his table, his beer clutched tightly in hand, and deliver his remarks from that more prominent platform.

There was nothing subtle about Cleveland's political speaking style. He hit out hard at graft and corruption with sincere distaste, naming names and providing specific instances of dishonesty. He cited, for instance, a strange state of financial management under which the county treasurer was entitled to the interest on public money in his keeping. He broke most of the rules of campaigning, even speaking critically of Civil War veterans who were forever seeking special privileges from the city administration, and said he was tired of "the old soldier business." Professional politicians shuddered at such heresy, even though they privately agreed.

The Buffalo political establishment and newspapers viewed Cleveland's campaign as incredibly inept, even for a man who had no chance to win. The voters, on the other hand, found his performance refreshingly honest, and they admired what they considered to be a rare display of political courage by a campaigner who eschewed all the tiresome phraseology to which they had become accustomed.

The result was one of the biggest political upsets in Buffalo's young history. Big Steve Cleveland, beer drinker extraordinary, one of the town's most picturesque and most controversial characters, was elected mayor. He took the oath of office in January 1882, at the age of forty-four.

If Cleveland's victory was surprising, what followed was stunning. Nine months after his election as mayor, Cleveland was chosen by the Democratic state convention as the party's candidate for governor. He won that election handily and was sworn in as Governor of New York in January 1883—one year after he had become mayor of Buffalo.

The following year, 1884, Governor Cleveland became the presidential nominee of the Democratic party and went on to whip the Republican James G. Blaine in the election. He took the oath of office as President of the United States in March 1885.

Just slightly more than three years after he had walked into Billy Drainger's tavern in Buffalo, nothing more, politically, than a ward worker, and had taunted the party committee over its inability to find a man to stand for mayor, Stephen Grover Cleveland became the twenty-second President.

Considering the distance covered and the brief time that elapsed from the hopeless start to the triumphant finish, the suddenness of the Cleveland career makes it one without parallel in American history. Just as remarkable was that in order to achieve the ultimate political honor, Cleveland had to overcome ostracism and prejudices that no other candidate for the Presidency ever found in his path, before or since.

Cleveland's birthplace was Caldwell, New Jersey, where his father, the Reverend Richard Cleveland, was pastor of the Caldwell Presbyterian Church. In 1841 the family moved to Fayetteville, New York, just east of Syracuse. Little Stephen was four years old at the time, old enough, probably, to appreciate that his parents had chosen one of the world's most interesting settings for a boy to grow up in—a land of lakes and rivers, drumlins and valleys, fields and forests, and, perhaps most interesting of all, the Erie Canal at his doorstep.

Rexford G. Tugwell, who achieved international fame as a member of President Franklin D. Roosevelt's "brain trust," once wrote a biography of Grover Cleveland in which he emphasized the influence of the canal on the boy.

One of the industries in Fayetteville was a limestone quarry whose product sometimes piled up along the canal basin, awaiting a freighter that might have space to carry it. The quarry shrewdly hired village boys willing to stand on the canal bank and call out to the captains of passing boats, seeking to intercept one or more that would be willing to take on some of the limestone shipment. For each successful interception, a boy would be paid ten cents by the quarry. According to Tugwell, young Stephen would get up before dawn and hustle business on the canal while his friends were still asleep. It is the sort of story, apocryphal or not, which presidential biographers appreciate more than anybody else because it sets a future President apart from the crowd very early in the game.

Cleveland's first trip of any length on the canal came in 1850, when he was fourteen years old, a year after the family had moved to Clinton, New York, not far from Utica. That summer he rode a boat to Black Rock, near Buffalo, to spend the vacation months with his uncle Lewis F. Allen. Allen, a well-to-do, influential man, lived in the large house that at one time had been the residence of the legendary General Peter Porter. It faced on Niagara Street, but its backyard looked toward the Niagara River. As famous as Grover Cleveland came to be, it is possible that his Uncle Lewis was the greater man so far as comparative contributions to Buffalo's greatness and growth are concerned. Allen was a pillar of the expanding community, a civic leader with widespread interests and deep concern for the good of the city.

Besides Allen's large house overlooking the Niagara River, he also owned a 600-acre ranch on Grand Island farther downriver, toward the falls. The image of Buffalo as a Western outpost becomes more convincing if it includes the fact that Lewis Allen's Grand Island ranch was the home of America's first shorthorn cattle herds. Allen imported the basic stock from England with the intention of establishing the shorthorn breed as an integral part of the developing American agricultural scene. He was successful in his attempt. Playing and working on his uncle's ranch was part of the wonderful, carefree summer that young Cleveland spent in Black Rock.

In 1855, five years later, his father dead and the family home now in Holland Patent, a few miles north of Utica, young Cleveland decided to go West with a friend. They got as far as Buffalo. There Cleveland insisted on paying a courtesy call on Uncle Lewis while they were waiting for the boat that would carry them from Buffalo to Cleveland. (It was in Cleveland that young Stephen had decided to settle. The town had been founded by a distant ancestor, Moses Cleaveland, and the novelty of living in a city that bore his family name captured the youth's fancy.)

Uncle Lewis, however, was opposed to the idea. He saw no reason why his nephew should not settle in Buffalo and he advanced some persuasive arguments to support that stand. Cleveland said that he planned to study law when he arrived at his Ohio destination and Uncle Lewis immediately promised to place him with a Buffalo law firm in which he could work and study for the bar. He offered his nephew a place to live in his luxurious home and even offered him a paying job taking care of the shorthorn herd book.

The logic and inducements were too powerful for Cleveland to resist. He said good-by to his traveling companion and made Buffalo his home.

The year was 1855, an exciting time to become part of the city at the westernmost end of the great canal. Buffalo was still in the throes of furious growth, having reached close to 50,000 population. It was a city of eye-bugging activity to a young man from placid Holland Patent. Through his uncle's influence, Cleveland was taken on as an office boy-law student by the most important law office in the city, the firm of Rogers, Bowen, and Rogers, the original law firm of President Fillmore. The employment by the firm of Grover Cleveland gave it the distinction, later, of being the only firm in the nation that could boast of having had two American Presidents on its payroll.

Cleveland was an apt student and gained admission to the New York State bar after four years, when he was twenty-two. Despite his intelligence, his diligence as a student, and his competence as an employee, Cleveland and his Uncle Lewis drifted apart. An important reason was Cleveland's disinclination to mingle with the social friends of his blue-blood aunt and uncle. Even more disconcerting to the Allens, no doubt, was Cleveland's growing fondness for the fleshpots of the canal district.

Somewhere the young man had discovered that it was a lot more fun to drink beer than to read Blackstone. After he had been admitted to the bar and hired as chief clerk by Rogers, Bowen, and Rogers, at the splendid salary of $600 a year, Cleveland hit on equitable division of his time—daytime was for office duties and serious business, nighttime was for drinking beer and having fun. It was a nice, balanced arrangement and he grew fond of it.

One of the developments that stretched the taut family ties to the breaking point was Cleveland's decision to ally himself with the Democrats. Uncle Lewis not only was a staunch Republican, he was one of the leaders of the party in the Niagara Frontier country. The gap between uncle and nephew widened to the point of such an uncomfortable relationship that the two finally parted company. It was not a bitter separation. In the American Herd Book for 1861 which he published, Allen gave a generous credit line to his young nephew—"my young friend and kinsman, Grover Cleveland, Esq., of Buffalo, a gentleman of the legal profession who has kindly assisted my labors in correcting and arranging the pedigrees for publication, and to him is a portion of the credit due for the very creditable display which our American short horns make before the agriculture public."

Cleveland took up residence in a rooming house, deep in the city, close to the sound of clinking glasses and hearty laughter. At last he was his own man, free to live as he chose—and the way he chose to live showed on him quickly. Beer and *Bratwurst* had an unmistakable influence. His face filled out and jowls formed, his neck swelled and his collars shrank. Most noticeable of all, though, was his stomach, which grew to Falstaffian profile. Before long his friends began to call him "Big Steve." His nieces and nephews, when he visited them, were more to the point. They called him "Uncle Jumbo."

Identification had been a lifelong problem for Cleveland.

"My name is Grover," he said once, back in Holland Patent, "but the kids all call me Clover."

Shortly after his arrival in Buffalo, the city directory of 1856 listed him as "Cleveland, S. Grover, law student . . ." By the time of his twenty-first birthday, he had dropped the use of his first name and even the initial. He preferred to identify himself as Grover Cleveland. But friends, and especially drinking friends, have a perverse way of ignoring personal preference in the matter of names. "Big Steve," or "Cleve" sometimes, to their minds fitted the rotund roisterer better than a sober name like "Grover," and so they continued to ignore his preference in the matter.

Even though Cleveland spent many of his evenings in public bars, it should be noted that he displayed good taste and discretion in his choice of drinking establishments. The Buffalo of his day may have been the saloon capital of the New World and certainly offered a problem of selection to the man intent on tippling. One count of saloons in the city, although entirely unofficial, came up with a total of 799. A large number of dives were included in what deserves to be called that staggering result, but Cleveland preferred the places that were less sensational in their attempt to satisfy—that were, in fact, downright respectable.

In his study of the Cleveland career, Rex Tugwell, who was a leading force in the New Deal Administration that scrubbed bathtub gin and restored alcohol of the drinking kind to a legal place in the American scheme of things in 1933, noted that Buffalo saloons in Grover Cleveland's time sold "Monongahela rot gut, a famous spirit distilled, often, by moonshiners in the Pennsylvania mountains and delivered to the saloons in barrels. It sold for a few cents a drink; whiskey, it was said, was the cheapest thing in town."

Generations of American frontiersmen who held Old Monongahela in high esteem would not have taken kindly to Tugwell's derogatory words. In the case of Grover Cleveland, any argument over the merits of Old Monongahela would have been strictly academic. He seldom drank hard liquor and he seldom frequented the canal dives that lived off cheap whiskey. The places in the canal district were in business strictly to attract the hard-drinking transient trade: the sailors, canallers, railroaders, and the traveling men in search of excitement on the waterfront. Cleveland gave his patronage mainly to the German-style beer halls where men of moderate taste held out, where a schooner of the foamy amber cost a nickel and the food catered to the hearty taste.

Among his favorite emporiums were Louis Goetz's Restaurant (often called "The Dutchman's"), John Schaller's Saloon, Bass's, Gillick's, Schenkelberger's, Drainger's, and a tavern known cryptically as "The Shades." All of these were places where he could meet good friends, eat, drink, play pinochle or sixty-six, talk man-talk, or join in an occasional song fest.

The most unusual of the drinking places he frequented was unquestionably The Shades. It was owned and operated by a man whose first name has been lost in the flurry of events and the confusion of time, but whose surname was plain and simple: Smith.

Smith deserves to be remembered for two reasons at least. One was his original concept of what a no-nonsense saloon should be like. Another was his sublime faith in his fellow man, especially his drinking fellow man. The Shades was an establishment that had neither a bar nor a bartender. It was a saloon without tables, chairs, or booths to accommodate the drinking patrons—only standing room. Its walls were lined with barrels and kegs that contained beers, whiskeys, brandies, wines, and whatever other alcoholic beverages the customers craved. In the center of the tavern were two tables. On one table stood many clean glasses. On another table was loose money, paper and silver, of all denominations.

The system at The Shades was simplicity itself. A customer took a glass from the table, filled it from the keg or barrel of his choice, and then deposited the price of the drink on the money table, picking out his own change if he had any coming.

It may be that Smith's place of business was the world's first self-service saloon (probably the last, as well). Where Smith kept himself while his cutomers were busily drawing drinks and balancing the books is not known, but he never worried about the system because he was convinced that man, by his personal definition, was "an honest animal." As a piece of proof, he used to boast that no customer ever had violated the honor system by cheating him. Smith and The Shades exercised a strong attraction for Cleveland, a man who admired honesty so passionately.

Cleveland apparently was as much intoxicated by the hearty, happy atmosphere that he found in the several beer gardens he patronized as he was by the brew they sold. What his friends found in marriage and the cozy home circle, he found in the saloons. An anecdote that suggests how completely they were part of his pattern of living is related by one of his biographers, Dennis Tilden Lynch:

"One of the beer gardens sold a cigar that Cleveland liked above all others. So he had some of these made up and sent to his room. He lighted one. But it did not taste the same. He smoked another. But that one also seemed to lack something. At last he hit upon what was lacking—it was the sanded floor of the beer garden. He missed the crunching of the sand underfoot and all that went with it—the gas lights, the gay laughter, the foaming steins, the joyous songs, the pretty women."

In a later year, Cleveland looked back and admitted that he had "lost a great deal by absence from home and family," but the record really made him look much worse than he really was. Cleveland, in truth, was a moderate man in his drinking habits. Being single and being gregarious by nature, he sought companionship where he could find it in its most congenial, most natural setting. That the setting invariably was a beer garden, a rathskeller, or an ordinary saloon merely added a touch of piquancy.

On the more conventional side, Cleveland enjoyed a fine reputation as a lawyer, and his practice was better than ordinary. His personal preference was for civil cases rather than criminal. He repeatedly and consistently turned down would-be clients charged with criminal offenses, and once he was heard to declare that he would never defend a known crook. He especially favored the role of legal counsel to businessmen, but not exclusively. He once refused a lucrative offer to become general counsel of the New York Central Railroad for western New York.

Cleveland built an impressive income from his law practice, but he conscientiously sent a large part of his earnings to support his mother and three sisters living in Holland Patent. Occasionally he spent money on his own clients as well—for example, the time he paid off the mortgage of a woman who was about to be evicted from her home.

It was a routine political plum that began Cleveland's formal political career. In January 1863 he was appointed assistant district attorney for Erie County. His first bid for elective office followed by two years, when he ran for district attorney. He lost by 600 votes to his own roommate, Lyman K. Bass. After that, he determinedly turned to the task of building up his law practice and his own financial position.

It was during this period that Cleveland chose one night to go pub-crawling with a group of good friends that included a brawny man named Mike Falvey. Falvey was one of the few men in Cleveland's circle who could look him eye-to-eye, or, putting it another way, stomach-to-stomach.

As they cruised along, reporting in to their favorite taverns as they progressed, their talk turned to political matters. The discussion, stimulated by the frequent refueling, turned into an argument, and when Falvey called Cleveland a liar, the argument turned into a fistfight.

Admiring onlookers reported that the two heavyweights fought their way in a steady movement from the corner of Seneca and Washington streets northward through several city blocks until at last, winded, both men paused for breath. They noticed, while resting, that they were conveniently near Gillick's Saloon, whereupon they "put on their bowlers again and, with their seconds, retired to the saloon and everybody drank everybody else's health." The contest apparently had ended in a tie, and, being sensible men, the two combatants presumably decided to tie one on in celebration.

No doubt the news of the brawl, which quickly circulated in Buffalo, shocked Cleveland's aunt and uncle and his proper business associates, but there is the likelihood that it also raised his stock with people who placed a premium on virility—especially those who believed public servants should be two-fisted men. Not long after he and Falvey had had their set-to, Cleveland was nominated for sheriff of Erie County and won a narrow victory over a popular opponent named John B. Weber.

There is nothing in the record to indicate that Cleveland had any fierce, burning desire to be the sheriff, but the office had a certain financial appeal that induced him to run. It was the most remunerative public office in the county, and Cleveland, thirty-three years old, needed the financial boost it was sure to give him.

His most notable achievement in his one term as sheriff of the roaring western community had nothing at all to do with the glamorous, adventurous side of law enforcement. Cleveland was no swaggering gunman in search of shoot-outs; he was a lawyer and he did know a lot about crooks and their modes of operation. He hadn't been in office long before he discovered there was crookedness being practiced brazenly in the sheriff's department itself. Suppliers were shorting the county in their deliveries to the county jail of flour, oatmeal, firewood, and other commodities. There was clear evidence of collusion between the suppliers and certain Democratic politicians and jail personnel who were getting kickbacks in return for their influence in awarding the lucrative supply contracts. Three of Cleveland's predecessors in office, all Democrats, had awarded profitable contracts to other party faithful who were not above cheating the county.

Sheriff Cleveland quickly exposed the dishonesty that was rampant in the jail, fired the crooked suppliers, and ruled that henceforth all purchases would have to be based on public bids. After that his life as sheriff settled down for a while into an easy, uneventful routine that allowed him a lot of time for the things he enjoyed most—hunting, fishing, and drinking beer. But that placid, happy round was interrupted when Cleveland was made suddenly and chillingly aware that as sheriff it was his official duty to hang personally a pair of prisoners who had been handed the death penalty by Buffalo juries.

The act was so repugnant to Cleveland that he seriously considered turning in his resignation rather than go through with the hangings. One of his deputies, Richard Harris, sensing Cleveland's anguish, offered to execute the men, but the sheriff, while tempted, insisted on going through with the distasteful duty himself, asserting that it was his responsibility.

On September 6, 1872, Cleveland sprang the trap of the gallows on a prisoner named Patrick Morrissey, who had killed his mother in a drunken rage. Then, on St. Valentine's Day in 1873, he again performed as hangman in the execution of John Gaffney, who had murdered a man in a poker game dispute.

Not surprisingly, Cleveland refused to run for re-election. The office had served its purpose. It had helped to shore up his personal finances, as he had hoped it would, but Big Steve wanted no more of the job. He gladly prepared to relinquish the badge and return to the practice of law.

It was during this lame-duck period in 1873 that Cleveland was introduced to a tall, attractive widow named Maria Crofts Halpin, who was at the time employed as a clerk in a department store. Mrs. Halpin, thirty-five, one year older than Cleveland, had moved from New Rochelle to Buffalo with her husband and two children four years before. Mr. Halpin had died the following year.

The relationship between Cleveland and the widow moved rapidly from the friendship stage into the romantic. Mrs. Halpin lived at 39 Swan Street, only a block and a half from Cleveland's apartment above his law office at Swan and Main streets, and the two met frequently.

Some Buffalonians said later that the widow, a cultured woman who spoke and read French fluently and who attended St. John's Episcopal Church regularly, did not restrict her dates to the burly sheriff. There were those, indeed, who were willing to testify that she scattered her favors among several admirers. Nevertheless, it was Grover Cleveland—the only single man in her circle of intimate acquantances—at whom Mrs.

Halpin pointed the finger of accusation when she found herself pregnant in 1874.

Cleveland undoubtedly was embarrassed, but he raised no protestation. If he was aware that there were other men in Mrs. Halpin's life, it made him no less gallant. He accepted the responsibility of paternity without complaint, footed the bills, and saw to it that the widow had the best medical attention.

The child, a boy, was born on September 14, 1874. Cleveland named the child, Oscar Folsom Halpin, after his former law partner, Oscar Folsom, a questionable gesture that led some people to believe that Folsom was involved in the situation, but the suspicion was never proven —not publicly, at least.

Cleveland, meanwhile, saw to it that Mrs. Halpin and her children were settled in a house at 11 East Genesee Street, some five blocks north of his apartment-office. He was generous in his support, it was said, but adamant in his refusal to marry the widow. Whether it was because he had doubts about the paternity of the child or because he did not want to give up his life as a bachelor, Cleveland refused to yield to Mrs. Halpin's entreaties. As she realized that there was no hope of getting him to agree to marriage, she turned to drink.

Acutely and painfully aware of the deteriorating domestic situation, Cleveland, who was deeply concerned over the welfare of the two-year-old child, decided in the spring of 1876 to place the youngster in a better home environment. He had some close friends who were anxious to adopt the child and he knew they would provide good care. He himself was providing money for the child's support and education.

As the first step in getting the boy adopted, Cleveland prevailed on an old crony, John C. Level, Overseer of the Poor, to issue orders to the police to seize the child by drawing Level's attention to an obscure paragraph in the state law that gave him the power to do this. Two police detectives managed to wrest the child from his mother, but not before she had given them a fierce tug of war that left them disheveled and panting. The boy then was given into the custody, temporarily, of the Protestant orphan asylum.

The second part of Cleveland's master plan called for the police to take Mrs. Halpin to the Providence Asylum on Main Street, where she could be treated for her alcoholism. She was not placed under arrest nor was she compelled to stay in the institution, but she elected voluntarily to remain at the asylum for five days of treatment. When she returned to her home, she seemed to be resigned to the state's plans to put up her child for adoption. Cleveland offered her money to begin a small business in Niagara Falls, not far away, and she accepted.

About six weeks later, Mrs. Halpin, who had visited little Oscar at the orphanage several times, abducted the child and fled. A police search was begun immediately, but she was elusive. It was not until three months later that the authorities were successful in apprehending mother and child. The boy was returned to the orphanage, but only briefly; the adoption moving through briskly, giving the child a new name and a new start. The happy ending to his story was that he grew up to become a very successful man in the community, and, according to Dennis Lynch, added to the "luster" of his new name "by countless deeds calling for self-sacrifice and great knowledge. The world is richer for his birth."

Mrs. Halpin, after threatening to sue Cleveland for damages and upon being informed that he was prepared to resist her claims in open court, dropped her suit and gave up all claims to the child. She left Buffalo shortly thereafter and returned to her former home, New Rochelle, where she later remarried.

Strangely, there was little publicity in Buffalo about the paternity case or the kidnapping and successful chase of mother and child that followed. Neither was there any open criticism of the former sheriff. The community, if anything, apparently had been impressed by Cleveland's forthright acceptance of responsibility and his obvious concern for the child, even though there was reasonable doubt about its paternity.

The matter, curiously, failed to be an important element either in Cleveland's mayoral campaign of late 1881 or in his bid for the governorship in autumn of 1882. For that matter, in neither campaign was Cleveland's well-known appetite for beer and his fondness for the company of tavern types held against him by the electorate. The candidate's personal candor and his proven ability to rout dishonesty out of government unquestionably tipped the scales in his favor.

As if to emphasize his own dislike for hypocrisy, Mayor Cleveland continued to patronize his favorite German saloons as much as his busy schedule would allow. His favorite stopping place was Schwabl's Tavern, but official duties and the pressure of party politics actually left him little time for the nightly relaxation he loved so well.

Events moved swiftly from the day he took office as mayor. Before he even had time to become comfortably adjusted to the routine he found himself in the thick of the contest for governor. Appropriately enough, when the news of his nomination for governor by the Democratic State Convention in Albany came through, it found the mayor in Bill Drainger's saloon in the company of his old friends. The tavern was jammed with his supporters, with hundreds more out in the street. When it was announced that the convention had nominated Cleveland, he was forced to make an appearance on the balcony of the saloon building to acknowledge the cheers of his followers. The few words he spoke to the crowd in the street constituted his only speech as a candidate in his winning campaign to gain the state's highest office.

Just how unconventional a politician Cleveland was is suggested in the recollections of a political reporter named William C. Hudson, who wrote:

"A few days before the inauguration of Grover Cleveland as governor, Lieutenant Governor William Dorsheimer said to me: 'Cleveland does not want to occupy the executive mansion.'

"He [Cleveland] thought he could establish himself at one of the hotels [in Albany] and live the same bachelor life as in Buffalo.

"It would have been a tremendous error. A number of us—strong friends of his—got at him in protest. We told him that he would offend the sense of the people of the state, who had provided for their chief executive an official residence and who desired to see the man they honored hedged about with the dignity which is part of his great office. And also on the ground of expediency we showed him that it would be a mistake, for he would be overwhelmed in the easy approach hotel life would afford.

"He has yielded and will occupy the mansion, but I think the argument of expediency rather than the other swayed him."

His first six months as governor left Cleveland no time for relaxation of any kind. It was a lonely, demanding job, which kept him at his desk in the capitol from early morning to midnight and even later. His only company at the Executive Mansion, a mile from the capitol, was one of his sisters, who served as his housekeeper. He was a stranger in a strange job in a strange city, and some pining for the old, relaxed life among good friends in Buffalo was inevitable.

As the legislative session drew near to adjournment for the summer of 1883, the governor gleefully wrote to some of his hometown friends to expect him soon and, in effect, to brace themselves for a good time.

His trip home turned out to be quite a visit, one in the best Cleveland tradition of tavern touring. Accounts passed along do not agree in every detail—they never do—but no room is left for doubting that the governor had a roaring good time on his brief vacation outing with his friends in Buffalo.

The most graphic account of all came from the pen of Dennis Tilden Lynch:

"There are many tales of Cleveland's few visits to Buffalo when he was governor," wrote Lynch, ". . . but two lively nights at the Dutchman's, as related by one who played a part, are here set down:

"On one of these evenings, after Cleveland and his companions had finished the first keg of beer and another had been set up on a table in the Dutchman's back room, the singing began, Cleveland leading in his favorite melody, 'There's a Hole in the Bottom of the Sea.'

"One by one, man after man went home until there remained but four, Cleveland, Charles Miller, Tim Mahoney, and Shan Bissell—and Louis Goetz, of course.

"Then Shan Bissell, hiccupping, 'I've had enough,' waddled out of the saloon. Down Pear Street he staggered, shouting, 'I don't want one!' as Miller ran after him and exclaimed, 'Wait, I'll get a cab!'

"And before long Cleveland had no one to join him in 'There's a Hole in the Bottom of the Sea' save the faithful old Louis Goetz, who continued the role of Ganymede after Mahoney had departed.

"On another evening the governor decided to leave the Dutchman's at a reasonable hour. All rose to leave together. Cleveland went first, banging the door behind him. Tim Mahoney and Shan Bissell stayed behind long enough to say good-night to Louis.

"When they opened the door they saw two men rolling on the sidewalk, one choking the other. The man being choked was an editor of a local paper. Cleveland was doing the choking.

"As they pried Cleveland's hands loose and helped him to his feet, Bissell and Mahoney asked: 'What's up, Grover?'

"Cleveland, as he dusted off his clothes, while his journalistic foe stalked off, replied: 'I was just having it out with the ——— of a ———!' "

Perhaps Cleveland, having passed unharmed by scandal through the mayoral and gubernatorial campaigns, had convinced himself that the Halpin affair was a forgotten incident, a regrettable part of the past but no longer of significance. He soon learned otherwise. Immediately upon his nomination for the presidency by the Democrats in summer of 1884, the Republicans began to dig deeply for material to hurt the Cleveland candidacy. They came up with the Halpin story and in no time at all the mud was flying.

Churchmen denounced Governor Cleveland from their pulpits. Editors, suddenly aware of his depravity, condemned him in their editorials and in their news columns. Influential national organizations passed resolutions censuring him, and private citizens in the streets chanted an assortment of jingles, some amusing and others vicious, about Cleveland and Mrs. Halpin. The case seemed to awaken all the latent creativity of every political mudslinger in the country, and their product was nothing less than astonishing.

One of the most popular of the chants promoted by the Republicans was:

> Ma, ma, where's my pa?
> Gone to the White House! Ha! Ha! Ha!

The Democrats were not about to stand by and listen to such scurrility without proper retort. They replied with the following chant in honor of the Republican candidate, James G. Blaine:

> Blaine! Blaine! Blaine!
> The Biggest Thief in Maine!

That chant didn't take in enough territory to please most of the Democrats and it was quickly revised to read:

Blaine! Blaine! Jay Gould Blaine!
The continental liar from the State of Maine!

Feminist organizations especially took a dim view of Cleveland, as could have been expected. One such group, the Moral Education Society, headed by Caroline B. Winslow, M.D., adopted several resolutions condemning Cleveland in its convention in Washington, D.C. One of the resolutions read:

"Resolved, that through the victims of Grover Cleveland the purity of womanhood has received a deadly blow. Therefore we call upon women in every station in life, high and low, rich and poor, the cherished wife and the betrayer's victim, to do all in their power to prevent Grover Cleveland from being made the chief executive of the nation."

The unkindest cuts of all, though, were being dealt Big Steve back home in Buffalo, where the Republican partisans in journalism and in the church went all out to besmirch their old friend and mayor.

The Buffalo *Telegraph* waited only ten days after the nominating convention to publish a full account of the Halpin affair; a story described by Lynch in his biography as "exaggerated and distorted, leading readers to think Cleveland had seduced an innocent child under promise of marriage, and after the birth of their child had deserted her, and thereafter treated her brutally."

When friends in Buffalo called on Cleveland to sign a statement repudiating paternity of the child, he refused, saying, "No, it isn't true." When other friends frantically wired him for advice on what to say in reply to the bad publicity, Cleveland wired back: "Whatever you say, tell the truth."

But the *Telegraph's* sensational treatment of Cleveland's affair with Mrs. Halpin was only its opening gun. It followed five days later with a lead editorial that said, in part:

"The libertine is a foe of the home, and is therefore, in a certain sense, a traitor to the Republic.

"Take it to yourselves, brothers! How would you feel about it if Maria Halpin were your sister?

"Take it to yourselves, fathers! What would you do about it if Maria Halpin were your daughter?"

Similar sentiments of manly indignation and horror over the thought of Cleveland's election were expressed in other newspapers in the nation.

"We do not believe," intoned the Boston *Journal*, "that the American people would elevate to the Presidency of the United States a betrayer of women, a man of shameless and profligate life. The failure to meet and disprove these charges will be a confession of guilt."

The New York *Sun* was right up there on the firing line with other Republican journals. Its editorial sharpshooter, Charles A. Dana, presumably choosing his words carefully, wrote:

". . . We do not believe the American people will knowingly elect to the Presidency a coarse debauchee who would bring his harlots with him to Washington and hire lodgings for them convenient to the White House."

Cleveland endured the slander and denunciation dealt him in that campaign with a calm and equanimity that are rare even in a good politician, but he couldn't conceal the hurt that he felt in the brutal going-over he got from the people in Buffalo whom he considered his friends. The pain went deep, so very deep, indeed, that it led to a permanent estrangement with the city that he had loved so much.

At the peak of his presidential campaign, Cleveland, no doubt aware that he had been nicknamed by a Republican pamphlet as "the Beast of Buffalo," went home to speak. He was welcomed by the largest, most enthusiastic rally he had encountered anywhere in the nation. A torchlight parade three miles long wound through Main Street in the pouring rain, all the way to the Genesee House where the bareheaded Cleveland stood on a balcony overlooking the crowded street. There was more to this turnout than politics. The people were trying to say something to him, perhaps they were trying to atone for the lashes he had felt at the hands of Buffalonians. They stood in the open, under the falling rain, and they gave their former mayor cheer after cheer, assuring him with their shouts that he still had friends back home.

No man could have been untouched by such a tremendous expression of affection and loyalty.

"More than rain streamed down his face," wrote one reporter. "His voice sobbed as he responded . . . Here was his city—his home he had called it in a public address not so long before—at his feet. But not the whole city, for there were a few malignant ones, and these were driving him from Buffalo. Those who knew him intimately knew that he was bidding this town that had honored him a forced goodbye."

His speech had the ring of a reluctant, regretful farewell—which it was. Cleveland took special note of his tumultuous reception and interpreted it as saying "that my neighbors are still my friends."

"It assures me," he said, "that I have not been altogether unsuccessful in my efforts to deserve their confidence and attachment. In years to come I shall deem myself not far wrong if I still retain their good opinion; and if surrounding cares and perplexities bring but anxiety and vexation, I shall find solace and comfort in the memory of the days spent here, and in recalling the kindness of my Buffalo friends."

When the rally was ended, the torches doused, and the cheering throngs departed, a silent man looked out of the window of his hotel room and spoke a silent good-by to the city that had meant so much to him.

His stay in Buffalo was brief. There was a campaign to be waged, a presidency to be won; most of all, there was the vindication that he so desperately needed now and which he could find only in victory.

Victory and vindication came together on Election Day. Considering the handicap of the candidate, it was an astonishing result. Many Americans must have felt like joining the Democrats in the song that was heard everywhere:

> Hurrah for Maria! Hurrah for the kid!
> I voted for Cleveland, and I'm damned glad I did!

Big Steve went on to Washington and Buffalo never saw him again.

CHAPTER XXXII

MARK TWAIN IN BUFFALO

The immediate, overwhelming success of the Grand Canal not only spoiled the wilderness, it almost overwhelmed the little town that stood innocent and fearless even in the presence of evil at the end of the line.

There was nothing that could have conditioned Buffalo for what it was to undergo. Not even the most preposterously optimistic predictions of success could have been enough to prepare the westernmost outpost for the ascending consequences of the canal.

The open ditch across the top of the state poured goods and people into the primitive port in such volume and number as to sink it in utter confusion. It took a period of frantic floundering and thrashing about before the outline of order asserted itself. Clapboarding went over the log buildings, cobblestone pavement replaced the muddy lanes, and Buffalo gradually took on the appearance of a much older, more settled community than it really was.

But even though the rough-hewn look yielded to the more elegant flourishes that denote permanence and the conquest of civilization, the basic problems in Buffalo remained for a long time. Cargoes continued to pile up on the wharves and canalboats continued to fight for space in the basins. Lake boats often had to anchor offshore while awaiting entry to the crowded harbor. Warehouse space was a critical part of the general shortage of facilities as shipments multiplied with geometric vigor, exceeding all expectations.

Most pressing of the problems, by far, was that of accommodating the thousands of people who were being carried to Lake Erie's edge by the endless relay of canalboats. There was no way of staying the migratory rush. Buffalo's population figures reflected only part of the crisis, but they suggested something of what was happening. The town grew from 200 persons in 1812 to 2,100 in 1820, just before the canal came into use. The count by 1840 was 18,000; in 1850 it was 42,261. By the 1860s the 100,000 mark was in sight.

Despite such fantastic growth, the number of people who became part of the permanent settlement was as nothing compared with the number that merely paused in the town while awaiting transportation by lake boat to some point even farther west, to one of the new places like Cleveland, Toledo, Detroit, Chicago, Milwaukee, or Duluth. However brief that stopover in Buffalo might be, however, the travelers still needed food and shelter, and that posed a problem that grew critical at times.

The direct result of the housing emergency could have been predicted on the basis of human nature. Greedy, unprincipled men and women are always with us, ready to respond to every crisis with a self-serving solution. In Buffalo their answer was to create instant slums, hovels which were made to serve as hotels at most unreasonable rates and always with a lot of room disservice, including robbery and vermin, tossed in gratuitously.

Agents of the hotels and boardinghouses roamed the waterfront in quest of business, singling out the canal customers as fast as they disembarked—especially the poor souls who looked especially bewildered or especially in need of accommodations. The average traveler, subjected as he was to the solicitations and importunities of business agents representing steamship lines, canal lines, flop houses, and the lake vessels, must have been among the most harassed of individuals.

A short-lived alternative to lodgings in the canal district—and certainly a more imaginative one—was the community that was known, while it lasted, as Bealesville.

Bealesville was a most unusual housing project, the creation of an enterprising man named Jake Beales who had a talent for putting two and two together. Beales, after observing the housing shortage in busy Buffalo, also observed that there were many old abandoned canalboats rotting away on the waterfront at a place called Sandy Town. Appropriating the old boats and adding to them all the derelict boats he could find between Buffalo and Albany, the result was Bealesville—a fleet of floating flop houses, a colony-on-the-water reminiscent of the permanent sampan colonies in the Asiatic harbors of Hong Kong and Canton.

The result did not exactly beautify Buffalo's waterfront, but the civic authorities were not about to look too critically at anything that would help to relieve the town's distressing housing problem, and Bealesville was allowed to exist and serve travelers until nature took a hand. The bargetown was destroyed by a storm that lashed the Buffalo area on October 17, 1844.

Buffalo life in those early days had the same sense of impermanence that Bealesville had represented. There were many thousands who chose to halt their journeys at the end of the canal, but only while they rested and decided their future direction. Buffalo was a place to rest for a while, a place, perhaps, to gather courage before plunging on across the vast lake and toward the empty horizon. The basically restless nature of the adventurous people who paused in Buffalo was reflected in the town's population, which showed an astonishing turnover from one year to the next.

Among those who made Buffalo his home, if briefly, was the nation's greatest humorist, Mark Twain. When he took up residence there in 1869, he was a young man, only thirty-five, and his pen name was relatively new. He was better known by his right name, Samuel Langhorne Clemens, although the success of his book *The Innocents Abroad* already was changing that condition. From the proceeds of the book he was able, in August 1869, to invest $25,000 in purchasing a one-third interest in the Buffalo *Express*. A short while later he took his place at that newspaper as a part owner and a star writer.

Twain's stay in Buffalo was short and, from a professional standpoint, rather undistinguished. There were a few journalistic highlights to mark the period, but that stage of his career was taken up mainly by a hectic schedule of personal activities. The author, fresh from his travels that had taken him to the other side of the continent and all the way to Europe, had chosen Buffalo as the place to settle down, and the *Express* as his permanent platform for journalistic expression.

He introduced himself to the Buffalo audience in an opening editorial titled "Salutatory":

Being a stranger, it would be immodest and unbecoming in me to suddenly and violently assume the associate editorship of the Buffalo *Express* without a single explanatory word of comfort or encouragement to the unoffending patrons of the paper, who are about to be exposed to constant attacks of my wisdom and learning. I only wish to assure parties having a friendly interest in the prosperity of the journal, that I am not going to hurt the paper deliberately and intentionally at any time. I am not going to introduce any startling reforms, or in any way attempt to make trouble. I am simply going to do my plain, unpretending duty, when I cannot get out of it; I shall work diligently and honestly and faithfully at all times and upon all occasions, when privation and want shall compel me to do it; in writing, I shall always confine myself strictly to the truth, except when it is attended with inconvenience; I shall witheringly rebuke all forms of crime and misconduct, except when committed by the party inhabiting my own vest; I shall not make use of slang or vulgarity upon any occasion or under any circumstances, and shall never use profanity except in discussing house rent and taxes. Indeed, upon second thought, I will not even use it then, for it is un-christian, inelegant, and degrading—though to speak truly I do not see how house rent and taxes are going to be discussed worth a cent without it. I shall not often meddle with politics, because we have a political editor who is already excellent, and only needs to serve a term in the penitentiary in order to be perfect. I shall not write any poetry, unless I conceive a spite against the subscribers.

Such is my platform. I do not see any earthly use in it, but custom is law, and custom must be obeyed, no matter how much violence it may do to one's feelings. And this custom which I am slavishly following now is surely one of the least necessary that ever came into vogue. In private life a man does not go and trumpet his crime before he commits it, but your new editor is such an important personage that he feels called upon to write a 'salutatory' at once, and he puts into it all that he knows, and all that he don't know, and some things he thinks he knows but isn't certain of and he parades his list of wonders which he is going to perform; of reforms which he is going to introduce, and public evils which he is going to exterminate; and public blessings which he is going to create; and public nuisances which he is going to abate. He spreads this all out with the oppressive solemnity over a column and a half of large print, and feels that the country is saved. His satisfaction over it, something enormous. He then settles down to his miracles and inflicts profound platitudes and impenetrable wisdom upon a helpless public as long as they can stand it, and then they send him off consul to some savage island in the Pacific in the vague hope that the cannibals will like him well enough to eat him. And with an inhumanity which is but a fitting climax to his career of persecution, instead of packing his trunk at once he lingers to inflict upon his benefactors a 'valedictory.' If there is anything more uncalled for than a 'salutatory,' it is one of those tearful, blubbering, long-winded valedictories—wherein a man who has been annoying the public for ten years cannot take leave of them without sitting down to cry a column and a half. Still, it is the custom to write valedictories, and custom should be respected. In my secret heart I admire my predecessor for declining to print a valedictory, though in public I say and shall continue to say sternly, it is custom and he ought to have printed one. People never read them any more than they do the 'salutatories,' but nevertheless he ought to have honored the old fossil—he ought to have printed a valedictory. I said as much to him, and he replied:

"I have resigned my place—I have departed this life—I am journalistically dead, at present, ain't I?"

"Yes."

"Well, wouldn't you consider it disgraceful in a corpse to sit up and comment on the funeral?"

I record it here, and preserve it from oblivion, as the briefest and best 'valedictory' that has yet come under my notice.

Mark Twain

P.S.—I am grateful for the kindly way in which the press of the land have taken notice of my irruption into regular journalistic life, telegraphically or editorially, and am happy in this place to express the feeling.

From the tone of his salutatory, it was clear that Mark Twain was not ready to abandon himself to the life of editorial bombast or the ponderous pronouncements of an editorial writer—that was an uncomfortable role, one for which he simply was not fitted. Humor is a handicap in the makeup of an editorialist and generally is frowned on in that solemn section in which a newspaper judges the world of the day and all the people in it.

It was inevitable that Mark Twain's sense of humor should make itself felt in the pages of the *Express,* as it did the time he commented on the visit to Buffalo, in September 1869, of the glamorous Prince Arthur of Connaught in the company of the Governor General of Canada. The distinguished guests lunched at the Tifft House with a selected group of only five Buffalonians, including former President Millard Fillmore and excluding Mark Twain.

Twain, then a resident of Buffalo less than a month, pretended to be miffed by the failure to receive an invitation to the luncheon—although he really may have felt slighted. Anyway, he wrote the following commentary for the *Express* the day after the affair:

"He made no remarks to us; did not ask us to dinner; walked right by us; never inquired our opinion about any subject under the sun; and when his luncheon was over got into his carriage and drove off in the coolest way in the world without ever saying a word—and yet he could not have known but that was the last time he might ever see us. But if he can stand it, we can."

Six months after he had cast his lot with the *Express,* Clemens married Olivia Langdon. The ceremony was performed in Elmira, New York, on February 2, 1870. The couple returned to Buffalo by train the day after the wedding. They were met at the railroad station by a real estate agent named Slee whom Clemens had commissioned to find a suitable home for him and his bride.

Slee informed the writer that he had found just the right house. The couple got into the real estate man's carriage and started out for their love nest. It was an uncommonly long, tiresome ride through the city and Twain was in a testy mood by the time the carriage pulled up in front of the large, brightly lighted house at 472 Delaware Avenue.

"This is it," announced Slee. "You're home!"

Clemens, startled, looked at the house and shook his head. It not only was brightly lighted, but it was plainly crowded with people, some of whom were on the porch waiting to greet the newlyweds. Among them was Mr. Langdon, the father of the bride.

The look of puzzlement on Clemens's face was too much for his wife. "Don't you understand, youth?" she was quoted as saying to her husband, as she waved toward the house. "It is ours—all ours—the gift of father!"

During the evening's festivities, Mr. Langdon ceremoniously presented the deed of the house to his famous son-in-law. The humorist, by then recovered somewhat from his surprise, spoke an acknowledgment:

"Mr. Langdon, whenever you are in Buffalo, if it's twice a year, come right here. Bring your bag and stay over night if you want to. It shan't cost you a cent!"

Everything, on the surface, seemed to point to a contented life and a successful stay in Buffalo. Fame and fortune were crowding in on Mark Twain in those years, and the vista was unclouded. The way it turned out, though, Buffalo was not to be a buoyant environment for the humorist, nor was the gift house to be a happy home. Instead, it would be the setting for a series of tragic events.

Only about six months after the wedding, Mrs. Clemens's father died in the house that had been his gift. Six weeks later a woman house guest, a long-time school friend of Mrs. Clemens, died of typhoid. Four weeks later, Mrs. Clemens gave birth to her first child at home two months before it was due. Then she herself became critically ill for several weeks.

That series of unhappy incidents apparently proved to be too much for Mark Twain. Perhaps it was the culmination of a general discontent. At any rate, as soon as his wife had recovered her health in 1871, he sold his interest in the newspaper at a considerable loss—said to be for $10,000—and the couple left Buffalo.

It had been a short stay there for Mark Twain, less than fifteen months altogether.

Within weeks of the time that Mark Twain and his wife were to bid Buffalo good-by, Grover Cleveland won election as sheriff of Erie County. The paths of the two men, editor and politician, had crossed frequently, and, judging from a letter that Clemens wrote to Cleveland on the occasion of Cleveland's birthday in March 1906, there must have been a feeling of affection between them. It was a serious, emotional Mark Twain who wrote:

21 Fifth Avenue

Grover Cleveland, Es.
   Ex-President

Honored Sir:
   Your patriotic virtues have won for you the homage of half the

nation and the enmity of the other half. This places your character upon a summit as high as Washington's. The verdict is unanimous and unassailable. The votes of both sides are necessary in cases like these, and the votes of one side are quite as valuable as are the other. When the votes are all in a public man's favor the verdict is against him. It is sand, and history will wash it away. But the verdict for you is rock, and will stand.

With the profoundest respect,

S. L. Clemens

CHAPTER XXXIII

PARALLELS NEVER MEET

There were two separate, unrelated happenings in the beginning years of the nineteenth century that followed parallel patterns of growth and almost simultaneously exerted profound influence on the travel and movement of man in the New World.

It was in 1807 and 1808 that the Erie Canal had its genesis in the publication by the *Genesee Messenger* of a series of essays signed "Hercules," in which Jesse Hawley outlined his concept of a statewide waterway that would connect East and West.

And it was in 1808 that a man named Richard Trevithick, in London, England, displayed his high-pressure steam locomotive on a circular track to a marveling public.

Two historic beginnings—out of one grew the canal that was the major means of opening the North American continent and solidifying the Union; out of the other grew the railroad that superseded the canal and conquered the vast continent.

It was a close, interesting race for a while, one in which the canal took an early lead. The two forms of transportation followed parallel paths— as parallel, say, as the banks on either side of the canals or the tracks that the trains ran on. Where one went, the other usually followed. There was early competition and it aroused certain emotions—at first amusement, then wonderment, and eventually enmity. But the final outcome made itself apparent early in the contest. The race had to go to the swift in the end, and it did.

A curious part of the twin courses followed by the rival forms of transportation was that in 1825, when the Erie Canal opened to operations on its full length, George Stephenson in England already was at work building the first commercially practical locomotive engine. In fact, closer to home, a news story in the Buffalo *Emporium* casually noted that "a proposition has already been made in New-York for an experiment to ascertain the value of the invention of rail roads and steam carriages."

In 1828, the year of De Witt Clinton's death, construction was begun on the first section of the Baltimore and Ohio Railroad, a thirteen-mile line that was opened to traffic in 1830. It was a small beginning, but it had significance far beyond its size.

There was further treading on the heels of the newly opened Grand Canal in that year of 1830 as construction began on the Mohawk and Hudson Railroad. When that little line went into operation the following year, it was the beginning of direct competition between the railroad and the Erie Canal. The first locomotive of the Mohawk and Hudson was named—"impudently," in the eyes of one historian—the De Witt Clinton. Perhaps even more ironic was the fact that the railroad itself was built by John B. Jervis, one of the self-made engineers who had masterminded the building of the canal.

The first judgment of the railroad by astute onlookers was that it would serve as a system of transportation secondary to the canal system, a sort of subsidiary carrier, and the first rail lines were built with that harmonious, agreeable thought in mind. When the Mohawk and Hudson Railroad's locomotive made its exhibition run between Albany and Schenectady on August 9, 1831, it was believed—indeed, hoped!—by the canal interests that this novel machine would relieve the waterway of part, at least, of the onerous burden of carrying passengers. The new rail line more than met this expectation by banking a $9,000 profit in little more than four months of operation exclusively as a passenger carrier.

The immediate goal of the railroad investors was to build a line that would parallel the canal along the highly desirable water-level route between Buffalo and Albany. Construction at first was piecemeal. Where the Mohawk and Hudson line ended at Schenectady, the baton was picked up by the Utica and Schenectady Railroad, which carried it westward some seventy-eight miles to Utica. That new service was inaugurated on August 1, 1836. The Utica and Syracuse Railroad then took over and extended service to Syracuse. There the Auburn and Syracuse Railroad carried on to Auburn, yielding in turn to the Auburn and Rochester Railroad.

The junction of the Attica and Buffalo Railroad with the Tonawanda Railroad and six other rail lines completed the connection between Albany and Buffalo by 1842. The link between Albany and New York City was ready to operate by spring of 1851 as the Hudson River Railroad was completed.

Within only twenty-one years altogether, a rail network had been established from New York City to Buffalo as a rival to the prestigious canal. In those twenty-one years the trains had progressed from dinky novelties to powerful carriers. Locomotives, grown steadily larger, were able to pull tremendous loads of freight and large numbers of passenger cars more safely and more swiftly than anybody had dreamed in 1830.

While it had taken ten separate railroads altogether to cover the distance between New York City and Buffalo along the water-level route, one massive merger in 1853 turned the ten little railroads into one superline called the New York Central Railroad.

There wasn't the kind of civic celebration that had marked the opening of the Erie Canal, but now it was official—the railroad had arrived as a powerful force in the American scheme of things. Rail lines had grown in wild profusion from a mere 23 miles in 1830 to nearly 1,100 miles in 1835, 2,818 miles in 1840, 9,021 miles in 1850, and 30,626 miles in 1860. Through the 1850s the growth of railroads was at the average rate of 2,000 miles a year!

In the ten-year period following its grant of a charter to the Mohawk and Hudson Railroad, New York State granted a total of 106 railroad charters. Three trains were running between Albany and Buffalo by 1843, and by 1849 there were four trains leaving Albany for Buffalo each day.

By mid-point of the century the passenger packets had all but disappeared from the Erie Canal, sunk by the railroads. There simply was no comparison between canal and railroad when it came to passenger comfort or speed of travel. The railroads were more expensive, but not by an unreasonable margin. Average rail fare rate in 1843 was three cents a mile, or little more than $10 for the 363 miles from Albany to Buffalo. But where that trip would take ten days to two weeks on the canal, it took only about fifteen hours on the fastest train. Passenger fares on the packet lines dropped steadily in a futile effort to meet the competition, falling as low, by 1849, as $6.50, including board, for the trip from Schenectady to Buffalo. It was strictly no-contest, though. Only novelty-seekers and people who wanted to laze away some time chose to travel by canalboat.

The effect on the packet lines was calamitous, of course, but the owners of the passenger boats could stir little sympathy or help from their fellow canallers, there being a common dislike of the packets among the boatmen and the officials of the canal. The packets, those greyhounds of the canal with their four-mile-an-hour speeds, did the most damage to the waterway with their waves. And years of having to yield to the packets at the locks had made the freighter captains and the line boat officials terribly sensitive to the canal caste system. When the packet lines finally surrendered to the railroads and went out of business at midcentury, their capitulation was hailed by canallers and railroaders alike.

The really fierce fight was between the canal interests and the railroads over the larger prize—freight. Railroads chartered by the state in the beginning were not permitted to carry freight except during the winter months when the canals were frozen. Even then, they were compelled

307

to pay the equivalent of canal tolls to the state for the privilege. The tariff was intended to protect the state's own means of transportation, the canal system, and it served to hold back the railroads for a while.

The difficulty was that the Erie Canal was, in its own way, too successful. Such a flood of people and produce had been borne by the canal from the very beginning that it had incited a wild outburst of expansion. Lateral canals to tap into the Erie and connect the Big Ditch with remote regions of the state so that they could draw on its riches were promoted on all sides. The effect was to drain away the Erie's wealth and squander it on canal projects that were basically unsound for one reason or another. Meanwhile, the press of business had created problems for the Erie itself. It had to be redesigned and rebuilt to accommodate the demands being made.

The year 1851 was an important one in canal history because it was then that the state legislature tried to be all things to all men—more than usual, that is. On the one hand, the legislators approved appropriations to improve the Erie and other state canals so that they could better compete with the railroads. On the other hand, a bill was passed which abolished payment of tolls by the rail carriers. That important concession to the railroads was an admission of a growing fact of life—the strength and importance of trains in the transportation scheme of things.

The rail interests, in acquiring financial and political power in an astonishingly short time, had grown giddy with success. Where previously they had tipped their hats respectfully whenever anybody mentioned the Erie Canal, a sacred institution in the estimation of the people of the state, now they had lost their deference and began to make slurring remarks about the great waterway. They openly derided its slowness, dwelt on its inadequacies, and even raised an audacious demand that the Ditch be filled in and turned over to the railroads for use as a track bed! That last proposal was made directly to the state Assembly, which was not about to accede to any such request, even though the canal system was going through dark hours at the time.

The giant New York Central combine reached an early peak of arrogance. Put together by Erastus Corning and others in a financial syndicate in 1853, the railroad, only five years later, petitioned the New York State legislature to ask the voters to call a state convention for the purpose of revising the state's constitution along lines which it—the New York Central Railroad—thought more desirable!

The railroad's plan of revision called, first, for the abolition of the executive and legislative branches of the state government. It then proposed transferring the powers normally held by the two branches of government to the president, the vice-president, and the board of directors of the New York Central System!

It was a very businesslike proposition. Simply wrest the state out of the inept hands of the people and the politicians and put it in the skillful hands of the paternal railroaders who, when they were not preoccupied with the job of running the trains, would take care of the secondary problem of running the state and tending to the needs of its people.

As preposterous as the whole scheme was, the members of the state legislature were not about to offend the railroad men in any way. The New York Central's proposal was solemnly presented to the voters of New York at the next general election, and the bedazzled voters, just as impressed with the omniscience of railroaders as the politicians, almost turned the state over to the officers of the New York Central. The measure was defeated by a margin of only 6,360 votes.

In spite of the terrific competition of the railroads and the mismanagement of the state commission, the Erie Canal continued to grow. At the mid-century mark, there were approximately 25,000 persons in the canal's working population. The number of boats in use continued to increase, as did the revenue totals—up to 1847, anyway. The canal income that year was $3,635,380. Revenue remained above the $3,000,000 mark annually for the next four years, which was a remarkable level considering that the Canal Commission had lowered its toll rates, ostensibly to remain competitive with the railroads. Only a steady annual growth in tonnage totals kept the canal returns from skidding downward.

The sputtering, on-and-off program of canal improvement finally was completed, after twenty-five years of sporadic effort, in 1862. Its effect was to allow boats as big as 150 tons or more to use the entire length of the Erie for the first time. The reconstruction also reduced the canal's length from 364 miles to 350½ miles and cut the number of locks from eighty-three to seventy-two. The result was a more efficient, more effective means of transportation, better able to meet the still heavy demands of the growing nation.

Concurrent with the finishing touches to the rehabilitation of the canal was the readjustment of the toll schedule upward to more realistic levels in 1860. The higher tolls, far from discouraging business, put the Erie back on a self-sufficient basis as income jumped from the 1859 total of $1,723,944 to more than $3,000,000 in 1860.

The timing of the rebuilding program was most fortunate, for both the state and the Union, as the beginning of the Civil War in 1861 suddenly put a tremendous demand on the expanded waterway. The closing of the lower Mississippi River in the early days of the war diverted shipments eastward on the Great Lakes to the Erie Canal and to the new rail carriers as well. Traffic in 1862 on the New York canal system brought a peak revenue totaling $5,188,943. The Erie's contribution was the lion's share—more than $4,800,000. In that same year, more than 5,000 boats were busy hauling goods essential to the war effort on the waterway.

Income from the Erie continued high after the war. Through 1870 the average total of toll receipts was in excess of $4,000,000, and the number of craft using the canal rose to 6,870. Congestion was worse than ever, despite the larger dimensions of the canal, as tonnage and traffic continued to increase even in face of the railroad gains. Tonnage reached its peak in 1880—4,608,651 tons.

The Hudson River probably has never been busier than it was in the two decades following the Civil War, thanks mainly to the canal traffic. There was no towpath along the mighty Hudson, of course, and the canalboats had to be towed to New York City and back. The demand for vessels capable of towing the boats during this time of peak traffic became so pressing that even passenger liners were diverted to the towing role. One steamship could tow, at one time, a flotilla numbering anywhere from sixty to eighty canalboats. The record tow was set by the steamship *Connecticut,* which went up the river to Albany on one notable trip pulling 108 canalboats behind her!

It was a happy, prosperous time for the canal and all associated with it, but actually it was a case of too much prosperity. Suddenly the Erie Canal was overburdened again and the need for major reconstruction to meet the heavier traffic of the time was imperative. The railroads, while flourishing and prospering in a popularity that seemed to have no bounds, continued to regard the canal as an enemy and picked away deftly at the politically controlled waterways through its powerful legislative lobby.

Among the factors that had kept the Erie Canal a potent political institution was that it was not only self-sufficient, but actually a profit-making enterprise. Not many government agencies could make that claim. Rather than the canal being dependent on the state, it was almost the other way around. Being a breadwinner kept the Erie in a position of power and independence.

In 1882, however, canal toll rates, which had been trimmed back considerably, were abolished completely, and the state's canals became free waterways. It was, in a sense, the most remarkable admission of the Erie's total success. The canal no longer owed anything to the state that had built it. It had paid for itself many times over, and now, toll-free, it was truly what many had been calling it, "Everyman's Highway." Now anybody could use it without paying a fee for the privilege.

The trouble was that the Erie couldn't accommodate any more traffic in a toll-free condition than it could when tolls were demanded of its users. It was at its physical outer limits. Not even its deepening by the state in the 1890s helped more than superficially. It was generally acknowledged that the canal faced its most serious crisis, that the next step taken would have to be a giant one if the Erie were to survive as a useful part of the modern transportation network. The old Erie Canal, that quaint, twisting waterway that had turned New York State from a frontier land into a great commercial and industrial empire, would have to be completely rebuilt or be abandoned—perhaps to be filled in and used for railroad track right of way or highway, as many canal opponents were urging.

There were sharp differences even among canal supporters as to which course of improvement should be followed. One school held that a new canal capable of being used by ocean ships should be built as the logical successor to the old small-boat canal. Such a project, of course, would have drawn the traffic and commerce that now follows the St. Lawrence Seaway, but it lacked the needed support.

The canal's future became a burning political issue in the 1890s in New York State. The 1892 state legislature, recognizing the fact, stipulated that one of the duties of delegates to the 1894 state constitutional convention be "consideration of amendments relating to the care and improvement of the state canals." The affirmative stand of that constitutional convention led to the adoption by both political parties at their 1902 conventions of a plank pledging the construction of a barge canal to replace the venerable Erie.

A bond issue of $101,000,000 was approved by voters for construction of a barge canal system in a 1903 referendum. Later bond issues, passed in 1909, 1911, and 1915, brought the total construction appropriations to $154,800,000. That amount included money for the improvement of the Cayuga and Seneca Canal (to barge canal dimensions) and construction of freight terminals.

Construction of the new Barge Canal System, incorporating the Erie Canal, was begun in 1905. Unlike the original Erie Canal, it utilized, wherever possible, rivers and lake channels. The Mohawk River, for example, was canalized and made a usable part of the system.

The new canal system made widespread use of concrete and movable dams and replaced the old, small, manual locks with large, electrically operated locks. The towpath was no part of the new canal because, in its enlarged dimensions and modern construction, it was a waterway of self-propelled barges, tugs, and motorized craft of all descriptions. The horse and the mule were retired, no longer a part of the canal as it was reshaped for the future.

The Barge Canal System, which went into service in 1918, swallowed the old Erie Canal, but not wholly. The historic name remains to the extent that the present Erie Canal is one of four divisions in the over-all system, which also includes the Champlain Canal, the Oswego Canal, and the Cayuga and Seneca Canal.

The modern system altogether encompasses some 524 miles of waterway, of which 10 miles is made up of side connections to canal harbors in Utica, Syracuse, and Rochester. A total of 370 miles of the system is accounted for by canalized rivers, streams, and lakes, while the remaining 154 miles is in land-cut sections, as was the original Erie.

Only in a rough, approximate sense does today's Erie Canal follow the route of its distinguished pioneer predecessor. Its path westward is from

Waterford-Troy on the Hudson River, via the Mohawk River to Frankfort, where it continues as a land-cut channel to New London, just west
of Rome. It then uses Wood Creek, Oneida Lake, and the Oneida River
to Three Rivers Point north of Syracuse. The Seneca River is used from
Three Rivers to Mays Point; there the Clyde River takes the traffic to
Lyons. At that point, an artificial land-cut channel goes all the way to
Lockport, a section that constitutes perhaps the most interesting part of
the canal because the channel is as much as sixty feet higher than the
adjacent countryside. In its final section, from Lockport to Tonawanda,
the Erie follows a land-cut channel into the canalized Tonawanda Creek.

The modern Erie Canal is shorter than the old Erie by some 16 miles—
348 miles as compared with 363 miles. The channel width in the modern
canal varies, but it is, in all respects, wider than the original 40 feet of
Clinton's Ditch. Today's Erie averages 200 feet in width in river sections,
120 feet in rock-cut sections, and 160 feet in land-cut sections. It averages
104 feet in width at the bottom, retaining its original prism shape. The
average depth of the canal today is 14 feet.

A significant contrast is that where the Erie Canal of 1825 could accommodate boats of only about 30 tons capacity, restricted severely by
locks that were only 15 feet wide and 90 feet long, today's barge canal,
with its outsized locks, permits the use of craft as large as self-propelled
300-foot-long barges with a capacity of as much as 3,600 tons, or the
equivalent of more than two average train loads.

Perhaps the feature of today's canal that would please yesterday's
canallers most is the way the modern bridges have virtually eliminated
the threat of decapitation. The minimum vertical clearance above the
maximum navigable pool is 15½ feet, and the boats and barges using the
canal now slip under the 300 highway and railroad bridges with a generous margin of safety. No more ducking necessary. A certain sporting
element went out of canal travel when the cry of "Low bridge ahead!"
was eliminated, it is true, but such is progress.

CHAPTER XXXIV

VIOLENCE AND VICTORY

What came alive in 1900 was more than a new century. The sun rose on a new, nervous world and a different way of life in which there was no place for a primitive waterway, not even one that had been an awesome accomplishment a mere seventy-five years before.

The contrast between then and now stunned the senses of people who had lived for a while. It was painfully apparent that a tiny boat, pulled by mules plodding along a towpath, didn't fit into a scene which already had high-speed trains shuttling across the state, the first crude automobiles on the roads, and even experimental airplanes fighting to achieve flight through the sky.

The canal that had created Buffalo had become lost in the great city of its making, as had, to considerable extent, its historic meaning. The Erie was old-age in a world that was new. Even the canal district had lost most of its glamour and wicked allure. The temptress was gone and people saw a wrinkled, frumpish eyesore, a civic blight, whose continued presence in the maturing city bore down on the public conscience.

Reform campaigns repeatedly had tried to wipe out the evil concentration in the old area without success. But what public and private indignation had been unable to do was achieved by the chemistry of time. The canal district was undergoing transformation like the city, like the world. Much of the gaiety and laughter had disappeared from its streets and a sere look was setting in. The boisterous, uninhibited old waterfront whose very mention used to make sailors and canallers dreamy-eyed was a place that belonged to the past. Even by 1900 the district had been disciplined and gentled to a noticeable degree—to such an extent, indeed, it was said that "a lakeman could walk the length of Canal Street without being challenged to a fight by a canaller."

313

The district that had survived near-disaster, even the great fire that wiped out virtually every wooden structure on its streets in 1851 and that had learned to live with the toughest element of humanity for many generations could not withstand the invasion of simple, decent people. They were the Italian immigrants, too poor to go anywhere else when they arrived in Buffalo, who took up residence in the disreputable canal district in the 1890s. Their arrival was not a militant invasion as much as it was simple recognition that the old forbidden enclave was coming open to a more respectable kind of occupation.

Even before the arrival of the immigrants, there had arisen in the Five Points area a noticeable uncertainty that was not characteristic of the former neighborhood. There were signs, like the creaking of timbers in an old building, that told everybody that the sinful structure of the district was tottering. The city itself was having second thoughts about its policy of allowing vice to flourish unchecked within the ghetto, and police were beginning to lean hard on the saloons, dance halls, and houses of prostitution. Enforcement of a new liquor law enabled the city to close many places that were especially troublesome.

The remaining centers of sin, the bordellos and sordid pleasure palaces, were doomed when the immigrants moved in. They could not hope to exist side by side with the traditionally religious newcomers. A Catholic church, Our Lady of Mount Carmel, was built at the corner of Fly and Le Courtelux streets, and its pastor, Reverend John J. McMahon, began an effective drive to close the disreputable establishments of the district. His successor as pastor of the church, Reverend J. V. Hennessey, continued the crusade against the underworld people and extended it. He not only wanted the wrongdoers routed, but the very name of Canal Street itself expunged so that even the lingering connotations of evil could be destroyed. He finally got his way in 1919 when the city officially changed Canal Street's name to Dante Place.

Perhaps the most severe blow among the many that rained down on the old storied district in the early years of the new century was inflicted, ironically enough, by the railroad people. It came through the construction by the Delaware, Lackawanna, and Western Railroad of a station at the foot of Main Street and the laying of tracks all along the harbor front. The iron rails were driven into the very heart of the canal district.

The password of the dawning century was "progress." Such change was part of progress.

Perhaps it was most fitting that Buffalo should have been chosen as the site of the nation's most singular celebration of its advances, the Pan-American Exposition of 1901. It was, in a sense, the send-off party for the new century, and the people who had planned the big jubilation of 1825 that had marked the opening of the Erie Canal in Buffalo would have liked the way their successors went at this assignment.

The Pan-American Exposition was an expression of victory, a song to be sung by a victorious people. It was a melodic mixture of pride and wonderment, hope and awe, of miracles achieved and marvels anticipated. It was a substantive preview of some of the scientific wonders that would become commonplace in the years ahead, but mixed in with the marvels of tomorrow was a merriment of the moment represented by an irrepressible carnival atmosphere. It was a show set in the most dazzling framework that the world ever had seen, for the Pan-American Exposition featured electric light!

The show, spread out over 350 acres of city land, was fashioned in the Spanish Renaissance school of architecture, admittedly something of an anomaly in the setting of Victorian Buffalo, but it had the desired exotic look. There was great satisfaction over the curious new skyline it created with its stately domes, beetling turrets, and ornate minarets, all outlined in electric light bulbs. The night sky reflected the flow of the lights that lined the stuccoed midway, more than a mile long, but above all other sights, there was the Electric Tower—the remarkable structure that was the centerpiece of the entire exposition. It was a sight so spectacular that millions traveled to Buffalo to see it. The tower rose 375 feet above the Pan-American grounds, which was wondrous enough in itself but the tower's beauty left onlookers breathless. It was a delicately designed steel framework that was tinted with light from its fountained base to the jeweled glass balls at its very top.

"It was beauteous beyond description," wrote one of the exposition officials, Henry Marks Nicholls, as he went ahead and described it anyway. "The Tower, with its myriad of colored lights, was like a filagreed piece of jewelry, studded with diamonds, sapphires and rubies. It needed only the 'golden streets' to be a tiny touch of Heaven."

An outstanding feature of the tall tower was the fountain built into its base. "From the center of the basin, in a series of steps, rose a mound that terminated in an apex 55 to 60 feet above its base," wrote Nicholls. "The main flow of the fountain, when turned fully on, could throw a large stream of water 70 or 80 feet into the air. Falling back, the water cascaded down over the steps into the basin. It was here, and also in the basin, that the underwater lighting was installed."

Everybody agreed that the tower alone made the trip to the Pan-American Exposition worth while, but a lot of visitors who strayed knowingly outside the exposition grounds found a happy side attraction in what remained of the notorious canal district. It was the last gasp of many of the saloons and dance halls, not to mention a lot of the girls sometimes obliquely referred to as "soiled doves." The civic pressure had been such as to put them in a fluttery state and to make them look about for safer roosts, but they had stayed on in large numbers anyway in the expectation of patronage from the wandering exposition visitors. It was a fairly reasonable supposition on their part that a number of the out-oftowners would be interested in something other than gawking at electric light bulbs, splashing fountains, and old mission architecture.

That thought, not surprisingly, also had occurred to a number of enterprising girls who normally confined their activities to New York City. They had drifted into Buffalo in large numbers after the exposition opened on May 1, hoping to share in the fun and profits, but there was a big surprise awaiting them—namely, the aroused and beleaguered women of the canal district. The hometown girls attacked the invaders with a fury that made the Electric Tower a pale, secondary attraction. The hair-pulling, punching, scratching, wrestling, and kicking went on for more than eight hours and is listed officially in the police records as a riot. Which, indubitably, it was. Police patrol wagons made thirty-two trips altogether into the district during the memorable conflict and that night the jails were jammed with screaming, hysterical women. The courts dealt out summary justice. The invading hordes, if that isn't too strong a word, were scolded and given twenty-four hours to leave Buffalo in what one reporter rightly described as "a noteworthy victory for the protection of home industry."

Aside from a few minor distractions like that, the exposition was everything in Buffalo that year. It was a sight beyond compare, and the people of the city were desperately proud of it. Only one thing more was needed. Their satisfaction would not be complete until the first citizen of the land, the President of the United States, had seen with his own eyes what had been created and had added his official plaudits to those of the millions who had hailed the wonderful show. As far as Buffalonians were concerned, their city itself was part of the show, and they were just as anxious to have the Chief Executive see what they had wrought in the community they now were calling "The Queen City of the Lakes" and "The Electric City" as they were to show off the Electric Tower and the gaudy midway.

President's Day at the exposition was Thursday, September 5, 1901, a date made all the more notable by the fact that President William McKinley had been scheduled to visit earlier in the season, on June 13, but his trip had been postponed because of the illness of his wife. Mrs. McKinley had recovered, at least to the extent of accompanying her husband to Buffalo for the September date.

The President's special train arrived in Buffalo on Wednesday, September 4, but the arrival was not exactly routine in its nature. The plan was to bring the special train directly to the Amherst Station on the exposition grounds. (The engineer could hardly have missed the station. It had been painted a lurid violet as part of the exposition's rainbow color scheme.) On its way the train stopped briefly at the Exchange Street Depot to pick up William Buchanan, former United States ambassador to the Argentine, then resumed speed, heading toward the Niagara River and the exposition grounds.

316

As the train passed the Terrace Station, the President and all his distinguished fellow passengers received a big surprise—a twenty-one-gun salute from a Coast Artillery crew under Captain Leonard Wisser.

Such a salute was not in itself without precedent. It is a traditional way to welcome a President, under terribly formal conditions in fact, but usually it is known in advance by the dignitaries, and everybody has time to brace himself. Under the circumstances that obtained during the visit of President McKinley to Buffalo, all the members of the official party, with the possible exception of McKinley himself, were especially nervous. Anarchistic-inspired violence was rampant all over the world, and the President of the United States was among the prominent world leaders who had been publicly marked for assassination by the anarchists. There was mounting apprehension among the presidential aides as the train rolled toward the crowded exposition grounds, where an assassin would find conditions ideal for violence and escape.

It was at that nervous moment that the cannonading of the dutiful gun crew at the Terrace Station began.

Ordinarily twenty-one-gun salutes don't do much damage, but in this extraordinary instance the green cannoneers had made the mistake of placing their cannon too close to the railroad tracks. When the lanyard was snapped for the first round of fire, the result was a great billow of smoke and an explosion that caused the three-car train to shake "as if torpedoed." There was the shattering of glass windows breaking and the screeching of the train's wheels as the engineer brought it to an emergency stop, spilling people and luggage in the aisles.

There was pandemonium inside the train. Nobody knew what had happened, but everybody feared the worst. The interior of the train was the sorriest of sights. Besides the luggage strewn about, the fallen people, and spilled drinks, glass was everywhere. All eight windows in the front car had been broken by the concussion, as had dozens of windows in office buildings in the neighborhood of the station. The incident had all the marks of a dynamite explosion, and crowds of worried spectators who had been assembled on the station platform to watch the special train go by now pressed forward anxiously to see if the President were safe.

McKinley was a man of remarkable composure. Even as his faint wife was being given a restorative, he picked his way through the glass-littered aisle and went out on the platform of the observation car to reassure the crowd. He smiled, waved, and doffed his high silk hat in response to their cheers before the train got under way again for the remainder of the trip to the exposition grounds. Once there, the presidential party toured the grounds and then, to the relief of the security people, the cavalcade went on to the home of Mr. and Mrs. John G. Milburn on Delaware Avenue. Milburn was president of the exposition and the McKinleys were to be his house guests during their stay in Buffalo.

The next day's schedule was a busy one. In the early morning the President spoke from a flag-draped bandstand on the Esplanade, unaware as he talked that among the many thousands jamming the area was a man who had been stalking him for some time—an anarchist named Leon Czolgosz. Fortunately, the enormous crowd and his own uncertainty as to which one of the top-hatted, frock-coated dignitaries was the President foiled the would-be assassin's plan to shoot McKinley.

The rest of the day was taken up with a presidential tour of the grounds, a review of troops in the stadium, looking on as seven thousand carrier pigeons were released, viewing some of the exhibits, and, that night, admiring a fantastic fireworks display that was climaxed by the likeness of the President and the caption: WELCOME MCKINLEY—CHIEF OF OUR NATION AND OUR EMPIRE.

The next afternoon was the function that the presidential aides dreaded most of all, a public reception in the Temple of Music. The President had insisted on that part of the program. He was a friendly, fearless man and a good politician. He enjoyed meeting people, and this would give him an opportunity to do just that. It also gave Czolgosz the opportunity he needed to carry out his dark deed. He took his place in the long line of people waiting to shake McKinley's hand.

Everything seemed to conspire against the President and to work in the favor of the anarchist. There was a blazing sun in a cloudless sky that day, and the heat was oppressive. Czolgosz wrapped a white handkerchief around his right hand, concealing the gun in the palm of the hand, and occasionally patted his perspiring forehead with the handkerchief. It gave him a perfect cover for the weapon because it was a perfectly natural thing on such a hot day to hold a handkerchief in one's hand.

When the quick-moving line finally brought Czolgosz face to face with the President, and as McKinley extended his hand in greeting, the assassin fired twice. McKinley staggered back, clutched at his stomach and was pitching forward when a detective caught him and supported him while other policemen fell on Czolgosz. They were hammering him with their fists when the half-conscious President opened his eyes and said audibly, "Go easy on him, boys."

An electric ambulance quickly took McKinley to the small first-aid station on the northeast corner of the exposition grounds, a quarter of a mile from the Temple of Music. Examination revealed that one bullet had struck the sternum on the left side, between the second and third ribs. The second bullet had entered the abdomen, causing severe injury. The decision was made to operate on the scene rather than risk a jouncing trip to the hospital.

The shooting occurred at 4:07 in the afternoon. By 5:20 P.M., when the operation began, the low, slanting rays of the sun lighted only part of the operating theater. One of the doctors stood close to a window and held a mirror in such a way as to reflect the sunshine toward the operating table. The only other light was from an electric light bulb equipped with a reflector. The operation ended at 6:50 P.M., and at 7:30 the unconscious President was put into an ambulance and taken to the Milburn home.

The twenty-eight-year-old gunman, son of a Polish refugee couple, was held at the police station that night as lynch mobs milled through Buffalo's downtown streets. The largest crowds gathered around the Iroquois Hotel, at Main and Swan streets, and began to move down Swan Street toward police headquarters. A triple cordon of police blocked the mob at Pearl Street, but some heads were bloodied by billy clubs before the forward surge was stopped. Police Captain "Big Mike" Regan was the star of the evening. He called on two National Guard regiments to stand by while he directed his men in forays that halted an angry mob at Pearl and Church streets and then again at Franklin Street. It was a restless, fearful night in Buffalo.

One of the calmest men in the city that night, it seemed, was the assassin himself.

"Did you really intend to kill the President?" he was asked by District Attorney Penney.

"Yes, I did," he replied.

"What was your motive?"

"I am an anarchist, a disciple of Emma Goldman. Her words set me on fire."

(Emma Goldman, called "the high priestess of anarchism," had made an inflammatory speech in Cleveland in May of that year. Czolgosz, a resident of Cleveland, had heard the speech.)

The medical judgment after the operation was that the President, while wounded seriously, had a good chance of recovery. As the days passed, an even higher degree of optimism seemed justified. The President's strength seemed to be returning, and on Sunday, two days after the surgery, his condition was called "first rate." On Monday, he was so much better that two cabinet members, Lyman Gage and Philander Knox, returned to Washington, and United States Senator Mark Hanna described the President's health as "just glorious."

The turn for the better was reflected in a relieved atmosphere in the city and a return to laughter at the exposition, which had been in a state of shock since the shooting. At least one concessionaire, however, had done his best to turn the attempted assassination to advantage. He was Morris Gest, who ran a midway concession in which patrons, for a price, were allowed to throw balls at a nimble Negro target. The day after the President was shot, Gest hired a new target—a man who dressed as Czolgosz did on the day of the shooting. The new banner over the sideshow read: "Hit Czolgosz on the head and win a cigar!" Gest went on in later years to success on Broadway.

The upswing in the President's health continued until Thursday, September 12. Late that day he had a relapse and a bulletin said he was "not so good."

The next day was Friday the thirteenth, and the weather was as gloomy as the mood of the people in attendance on the suffering McKinley. Dark clouds rolled in over the lake from the west and thunder rumbled as a mixture of chill winds and rain splattered the city. At five that afternoon, the President suffered a heart attack and the correspondents in press tents outside were told that the White House spokesman, George Cortelyou, was unable to come out.

"Tell the boys that the President is dying," his message said. "They might as well know."

The President was still alive, though, when the Buffalo *Commercial* put on the streets just before midnight an extra whose headline read HE IS DEAD. Other newspapers followed suit in the hour that followed.

To add to the macabre mixup, the coroner of Erie County, a man named Wilson, presented himself at the door of the Milburn mansion sometime after midnight. Cortelyou met him there and asked him what he wanted.

"I am the coroner," Wilson was quoted as saying. "I have come to take charge of the body."

"Please leave the house," said Cortelyou. "We will send for you when we want you."

It was not until 2:10 Saturday morning that the President was pronounced dead. An autopsy conducted several hours later disclosed the official cause of death to be gangrene.

Theodore Roosevelt was sworn in as the new President of the United States at 3:30 Saturday afternoon. The ceremony took place in Buffalo in a mansion topping the sloping terrace at Delaware Avenue and North Street; the home of his old friend Ansley Wilcox. The new President wore a gray frock coat and a pair of gray pin-striped trousers which he had borrowed from Wilcox's wardrobe.

The body of President McKinley was taken down Delaware Avenue in the rain to lie in state in the concourse of the Buffalo City Hall all day Sunday. It was put aboard the funeral train for Washington the following morning.

The assassin, who earlier had been removed secretly from his cell at Police Headquarters to the Erie County Penitentiary on Trenton Avenue on the west side of the city, was immediately indicted for murder. He was taken to a cell on the third floor of the old city jail across from City Hall. His trial began on September 23, nine days after the death of the President. Selection of a jury took an hour and a half. The trial ended on September 24 with a verdict of guilty. On Thursday, September 26, Czolgosz was sentenced to be executed on October 28. He died in the electric chair in Auburn State Prison on that date, but there was some grumbling over the slowness of justice.

* * *

The Pan-American Exposition stayed open until November 2. By that time, more than eight million persons had passed through the turnstiles and admired the wonderful sights and sounds. The crowds continued to come in large numbers after the shooting of President McKinley, and the buildings that figured in the assassination, the Temple of Music and the small hospital, drew as many silent spectators as the Electric Tower.

The exposition was never quite the same after the death of the President. The show went on, but the glow of optimism and cheer that had pervaded the grounds and lighted the skies had been snuffed out by the tragedy. The shadow of the event never retreated.

For Buffalo and all of upstate New York it was a tragic, sobering climax to an era, to a century, to what seemed a lifetime of uninterrupted triumph that had all begun with the digging of a ditch through the wilderness and a sort of shotgun marriage between the waters of the Atlantic Ocean and of Lake Erie.

It was a romance that Americans have never grown weary of talking about, and almost all of the talk has been good, although once in a while somebody raises a new point about the old canal. For instance, science recently raised a question about whether the wedding of the waters was all that wonderful.

Two scientists, specifically, have come up with the theory that the construction of the Erie Canal, and later the Welland Canal in Canada, in opening the way for marine invaders from the Atlantic Ocean, can be held responsible for the destruction of the native fish population of the Great Lakes. Dr. William I. Aron of the National Oceanic and Atmospheric Administration, and Dr. Stanford H. Smith of the Great Lakes Fishery Laboratory, outlined that theory in an article in *Science*, official journal of the American Association for the Advancement of Science, and it was given general circulation by David Dietz, the distinguished science editor of the Scripps-Howard newspapers.

According to the scientists, the alewife, a member of the herring family common to the Atlantic Ocean, made an appearance in Lake Ontario in 1873, presumably swimming there by way of the Erie Canal. In 1880 another invader from the Atlantic, the sea lamprey, was noted in Lake Ontario. Both species did considerable damage, upsetting the ecology of the lake in such measure as to result in a decline in the abundance of all major game and commercial species of fish, according to the scientists. The sea lamprey was noted in Lake Erie in 1921 and in the upper lakes after that, becoming well established in Lake Huron by 1932. The

321

major victim of the sea lamprey was the lake trout, and as the trout declined the invaders turned their attack on other species.

It ought to be pointed out, however, that the foreign fish allowed into the Great Lakes by the Erie Canal or any of the subsidiary canals could not have done nearly as much damage to the fish population of the lakes as the pollution of the water by our great cities.

In any auditing of the books, the canal that De Witt Clinton and his contemporaries built was one of the most profitable ventures that this nation has known.

* * *

The Erie Canal was unique. It represented the achievement of the impossible. It was an example of man's ability to outdo himself even under the least favorable of conditions.

If it is possible to think of a ditch as having nobility, the Erie Canal could claim that distinction. It stood out against the gray background of human failures as a bright, glowing tapestry that had been woven from the silken threads of faith, intelligence, confidence, and the indomitable spirit that filled the frontier nation. And if there is nostalgia for the canal, it is as much for what the canal represents—the priceless qualities of human excellence—as anything else.

The nineteenth century was a time of revolution in many areas of life, not the least of which was in the field of transportation. In the United States, the Erie Canal represented the first major victory in that revolution. In its triumph, it pushed back the wilderness and moved the West back where it belonged, far beyond the Appalachian Mountains, therewith giving the Union a unity it never had before.

It was, as far as Americans were concerned, the most wonderful Ditch in the world. No wonder they called it the Grand Canal.

BIBLIOGRAPHY

Ackerman, Carl W. *George Eastman.* Boston: Houghton Mifflin, 1930.
Adams, Samuel Hopkins. *The Erie Canal.* New York: Random House, 1953.
Andrist, Ralph K. "The Erie Canal Passed This Way," *American Heritage Magazine,* October, 1968.
Beltz, R. A. *Charles Finney—A Great Evangelist.* Hall of Fame Series. Wheaton, Ill.: Van Kampen Press, 1944.
Best, Herbert. *Watergate.* New York: Land of the Free Series. New York: Winston, 1951.
Bobbé, Dorothie. *De Witt Clinton.* Empire State Historical Publication XI. Port Washington, N.Y.: I. J. Friedman, 1962.
Brooks, John. *Business Adventures.* New York: Weybright & Talley, 1959.
Campbell, Wallace Hamilton. "In The Erie Canal Days," Rochester *Democrat & Chronicle,* May 2, 1971.
Carmer, Carl. *Dark Trees to the Wind.* New York: William Sloane Associates, 1949.
——. *The Hudson.* Rivers of America Series. New York: Rinehart, 1939.
——. *Listen for a Lonesome Drum.* New York: David McKay, 1936.
Cerf, Bennett. *The Laugh's On Me.* Garden City, N.Y.: Doubleday, 1959.
Chalmers, Harvey, II. *How the Irish Built the Erie.* New York: Bookman Associates, 1964.
Clarke, T. Wood. *Utica for a Century and a Half.* Utica, N.Y.: Widtman Press.
Clune, Henry W. *The Genesee.* Rivers of America Series. Holt, Rinehart and Winston, 1963.
——. *Main Street Beat.* New York: Norton, 1947.
——. "Skating down Broad Street," Rochester *Democrat & Chronicle,* February 23, 1969.
Considine, Bob. *It's the Irish.* Garden City, N.Y.: Doubleday, 1961.
"Copy Machine Boom—and Xerox Zoom." *Newsweek,* November 8, 1965.
Dessauer, John H. *My Years with Xerox.* Garden City, N.Y.: Doubleday, 1971.

Draheim, Paul. "The Canal in the Mohawk Valley." Utica *Daily Press*, March 27, 1954.

Dyer, Louisa A. *The House of Peace*. New York: Longmans, Green, 1956.

Federal Writers Project. *New York Panorama*. American Guide Series. New York: Random House, 1938.

———. *Rochester and Monroe County*. American Guide Series. Rochester, N.Y.: Scrantom's, 1937.

Garrity, Richard G. *Recollections of the Erie Canal*. Tonawanda, N.Y.: Historical Society of the Tonawandas, 1971.

Graham, Lloyd. *Niagara Country*. New York: Duell, Sloan & Pearce, 1949.

Harlow, Alvin F. *Old Towpaths*. New York: Appleton, 1926.

Hepburn, A. Barton. *Artificial Waterways and Commercial Developments, with a History of the Erie Canal*. New York: Macmillan, 1909.

Hislop, Codman. *The Mohawk*. Rivers of America Series. Rinehart, 1948.

Hoyt, Edwin P. *Grover Cleveland*. Chicago: Reilly & Lee, 1962.

Kimball, Francis P. *New York: The Canal State*. Albany: Argus Press, 1937.

Lewis, Clarence O. *History of Lockport, N.Y.* Niagara County Publication, 1962.

———. *The Morgan Affair*. Niagara County Publication, 1966.

———. *History of Niagara County*. Niagara County Publication.

Lockport *Union-Sun Journal*. Centennial Edition, July 17, 1965.

———. Niagara County Sesquicentennial Edition, August 28, 1971.

Lynch, Dennis Tilden. *Grover Cleveland: A Man Four-Square*. New York: Horace Liveright, 1932.

McKay, Richard C. *South Street: A Maritime History of New York*. Putnam, 1934.

McKelvey, Blake. *Rochester: The Water Power City*. Cambridge: Harvard University Press, 1945.

———. *Rochester and the Erie Canal*. Rochester History. The Rochester Public Library. Vol. XI, Nos. 3 and 4, July, 1949.

———. *Winston Churchill's Grandparents in Rochester*. Genesee Country Scrapbook. The Rochester Historical Society. Vol. III, No. 1, 1952.

———. *From Stagecoach Taverns to Airline Motels*. Rochester History. The Rochester Public Library. Vol. XXXI, No. 4, October, 1969.

Merrill, Arch. *Down the Lore Lanes*. New York: American Book-Stratford Press, 1961.

———. "The Towpath." Rochester *Democrat & Chronicle*, 1945.

Payne, Robert. *The Canal Builders*. New York: Macmillan, 1959.

Powell, E. Alexander. *Gone Are the Days*. Boston: Little, Brown, 1938.

Rapp, Marvin A. *Canal Water and Whiskey*. New York: Twayne, 1965.

Rayback, Robert J. *Millard Fillmore: Biography of a President*. Buffalo Historical Society. Buffalo, N.Y.: Henry Stewart, 1959.

Rome *Daily Sentinel.* Special Centennial Edition, August 1, 1970.

Seitz, Don C. *Uncommon Americans.* Indianapolis: Bobbs-Merrill, 1925.

Shaw, Ronald E. *Erie Water West.* Lexington, Ky.: University of Kentucky Press, 1966.

Shriner, Charles A. *Wit, Wisdom and Foibles of the Great.* New York: Funk & Wagnalls, 1918. (Republished by Gale Research Company, Detroit, Mich., 1969.)

Sinclair, Andrew. *The Better Half.* New York: Harper & Row, 1965.

Syracuse *Post-Standard.* Special Edition, September 13, 1953.

Tebbel, John. *The Compact History of the Indian Wars.* New York: Hawthorn Books, 1966.

Tugwell, Rexford G. *Grover Cleveland.* Chicago: Reilly & Lee, 1962.

Twain, Mark. *Roughing It.* New York: Harper, 1890.

Ulmann, Albert. *New Yorkers: From Stuyvesant to Roosevelt.* New York: Chaucer Head, 1928.

Westcott, Edward Noyes. *David Harum.* New York: Appleton, 1898.

Wildman, Edwin. *The Builders of America.* Famous Leader Series. Boston: Page, 1925.

Williams, T. Harry, Richard N. Current, and Frank Freidel. *A History of the United States.* New York: Knopf, 1965.

Wyld, Lionel D. *Low Bridge! Folklore and the Erie Canal.* Syracuse, N.Y.: Syracuse University Press, 1962.

——(Ed.). *40′ x 28′ x 4′—The Erie Canal: 150 Years.* Rome, N.Y.: Oneida County Erie Canal Commemoration Commission, 1967.

Xerox *Annual Report.* 1970.

325

INDEX

Abolitionism, 148, 165, 169
Adams, John, 36
Adams, John Quincy, 121
Adams, Samuel Hopkins, 57, 66, 70, 215
Advertising, 206, 248, 251
Aged Pilot Man, The (Twain), 141–44
Albany, N.Y., 1, 2, 4, 13, 77, 78, 82, 307
  opening day celebration, 99
  population, 119, 146
Albany, boat, 94
Albany *Gazette*, 82
Albany Land Company, 247
Alewife, 321
Allan, Ebenezer ("Indian"), 186–90,
  219, 221
Allegheny River, 112
Allen, Lewis F., 259, 283–85
Alley, Saul, 38
Allison, Oscar W., 232
Amalgamated Clothing Workers of Amer-
  ica, 224
American Airlines, 95
American Association for the Advance-
  ment of Science, 321
American flag, 209–10
American Herd Book, 285
American Humor (Rourke), 177
American Notes (Dickens), 16
American Revolution. *See* Revolutionary
  War
American Society of Civil Engineers, 54
Anarchism, 317
Andrus, George W., 225
Animals, on board flotilla boats, 6, 96,
  105
Anthony, Susan B., 169, 170–72
Anti-Masonic movement, 273, 274
Aqueducts, 78–79, 99, 184
  at Rochester, 192, 220, 221–22
Ararat movement, 258–59
Archbold, John D., 198
Ariel, magazine, 230
Arks, canalboats, 15
Armstrong, John, 36
Arnold, Benedict, 33
Aron, William I., 321
Arthur of Connaught, Prince, 301

Astor, John Jacob, 122
Attica and Buffalo Railroad, 306
Atticus, Clinton's pen name, 49
Auburn and Rochester Railroad, 306
Auburn and Syracuse Railroad, 306
Auburn Theological Seminary, 204

Bailey, Fletcher, 252, 253
Bailey, Joseph Henry (Harry), 250, 251,
  252
Baker, Elizabeth, 223
Baldock, Lieutenant, 103
Ball, Ernest Roland, 242
Baltimore and Ohio Railroad, 306
Bank of the United States, 49
Barnum, Stephen O., 281
Barnum and Bailey Circus, 250
Barrows, Storrs, 55–56
Barstow, Joel, 17
Barto, Dr., 58
Basin, in place names, 147
Bass, Jonathan, 241–42
Bass, Lyman K., 288
Bates, David, 55
Battelle Memorial Institute, 233
Battle of Lake Erie, 94
Battle of Oriskany, 33, 209
Bayard, William, 47
Beales, Jake, 298
Bealesville, 298
Beaujolais, Count de, 185
Beecher, Lyman, 167
Beecher, Willis J., 204
Beers, J. B., 231–32
Believe It or Not (Ripley), 215
Bellamy, Francis, 210
Better Half, The (Sinclair), 169–70
Bidwell, Daniel D., 262
Big Buffalo Creek, 78
Birdsall, John, 95
Birdseye, Victory, 81
Bishop & Codding, 232
Bissell, Shan, 292, 293
Black River, 181, 205
Black River Canal, 205
Black Rock, N.Y., 41, 78, 80, 283
Blaine, James G., 282

326